CITIES, CITIZENS, CLASSROOMS AND BEYOND

Cities, Citizens, Classrooms and Beyond

Essays for Narayani Gupta

edited by
PARTHO DATTA
MUKUL KESAVAN
KUMKUM ROY

PRIMUS BOOKS

PRIMUS BOOKS

An Imprint of Ratna Sagar P. Ltd.
Virat Bhavan
Mukherjee Nagar Commercial Complex
Delhi 110 009

Offices at

CHENNAI LUCKNOW
AGRA AHMEDABAD BANGALORE COIMBATORE
DEHRADUN GUWAHATI HYDERABAD JAIPUR JALANDHAR
KANPUR KOCHI KOLKATA MADURAI MUMBAI
PATNA RANCHI VARANASI

First Published 2025

ISBN: 978-93-6627-004-3 (Hardback)
ISBN: 978-93-6627-929-9 (PoD)

Published by Primus Books

Typeset by Manmohan Kumar
manmohankumar2015@gmail.com

Printed and bound in India by Replika Press Pvt Ltd.

Contents

History Woman

MUKUL KESAVAN

THIS BOOK bears witness to Narayani Gupta's standing as a historian of Delhi, but my job is to produce a friend's account of a life lived in the institutions that make history possible. Narayani has taught history all her adult life. She has done this in two public universities, Delhi University and Jamia Millia Islamia. The arc of her career encompasses a time that might come to be seen as the high noon of history writing and history teaching in republican India, given the ongoing destruction of Delhi's public universities over the past decade. The shadows she cast during this long midday (and I use the plural deliberately) give us some sense of the importance of being Narayani.

I first knew Narayani as the wife of Partha Sarathi Gupta, who was professor of British and European history in Delhi University's Department of History, when I enrolled for an MA in 1977. PSG (he was known by the initials that represented him in the small squares of the department's timetable grid) was one of the main reasons for doing a degree in the department. He had a DPhil from Oxford, he had walked alongside Edward Thompson in the early Campaign for Nuclear Disarmament (CND) marches, his lectures on the Entente Cordiale suggested that he committed Europe's diplomatic archive to memory, and, endearingly, he thought that his class of time-serving idlers were as committed to Clio as he was. We didn't know then that he was one half of a history writing and teaching partnership that was the beau ideal of academic life.

Narayani was teaching undergraduates in Indraprastha College at the time. My friend and fellow classmate, Hari Sen and I, would visit the Guptas at their house in Masjid Moth for advice, academic references and conversation, the things for which graduate students depend on their professors. It was a house alive with two small children, several cats, shelves upon shelves of books and a limitless supply of unfussy hospitality. PSG was in his early forties and Narayani in her mid-thirties, but to our young, careless eyes, they were veteran teachers, settled in their scholarly ways, content with the longueurs of academic life. My attitude to history was instrumental. I saw the subject as a way of winning a scholarship and going abroad, not in the cause of scholarship but in the much greater cause of 'abroad'.

My first year in Cambridge coincided with PSG's fellowship at St. John's. His family moved to Cambridge for that year and my first step towards knowing Narayani as a friend rather than as a student hanger-on, was the evening I babysat Niharika and Himadri. PSG and Narayani were to dine at St. John's high table, and they needed someone to mind the children. This responsibility came with the promise of a hot chicken dinner, and since I was often hungry and unsettled in my first term in *vilayat,* I was happy to volunteer.

The evening went as badly as it possibly could. Niharika transitioned from cherubic infant to howling banshee the moment she realized that she had been left in the care of a stranger. Himadri, some years older, was composed but unhelpful. He cynically suggested that I feed her, and it sort of worked. She quietened for the time it took me to spoon chicken curry and rice into her, and then returned to unfinished business and began wailing again. When Narayani returned, she was concerned but not excessively so. It wasn't clear to me at the time, but in retrospect, it was from that day on, that Narayani and I became friends. Tending to someone else's raging child makes either for a breach or a bond; luckily for me, it was the latter.

But it was in 1987 when Narayani joined Jamia Millia Islamia's Department of History that we became friends in the wry, long-suffering, companionable way that is the special privilege of colleagues. Ironically, it was in that academic setting that I came to appreciate Narayani for the way in which her relationship with history transcended the practice and protocols of our discipline.

Narayani is an urban historian. Her book *Delhi Between Two Empires* is the classic account of the post-Mughal city. But that tells us very little about Narayani as an historian. Chris Bayly's first book, *Local Roots of Urban Politics* is a book of urban history centred on Allahabad. It was an excellent book that treated Allahabad as a case study to make a larger argument about the nature of Indian politics in the period just before and after the end of the nineteenth century. There was nothing, as there often isn't in professional history-writing, personal about it.

Narayani's scholarship, on the other hand, is rooted in an almost proprietorial love for Delhi. The term 'citizen' has been hijacked to describe a member of a nation-state, but a citizen in the earliest sense of that word was the inhabitant of a city. Narayani is a citizen-historian; her love for the living city drives her to reconstruct its past in ways that transcend the strictly academic.

The best example of this is *Delhi, the Built Heritage: A Listing*. It's a large format two-volume book published in 1999 that attempts a stocktaking of Delhi's historical buildings, to build a baseline that can be used by urban planners and conservationists to both assess and forestall the loss of heritage. Narayani co-authored this book with Ratish Nanda, a conservation architect, and O.P. Jain, then coordinator of the Indian National Trust for Art and Cultural Heritage's (INTACH) Delhi chapter. It's typical of Narayani that she should work in this collaborative way for a cause close to her heart—in this case the documentation essential for conserving Delhi.

The professional historian seldom concerns himself with the landscapes of the past that he writes about. Narayani is exceptional in that she contains within herself both an archival historian and a passionate conservationist, willing to work painstakingly through institutions and civil society organizations like the Urban Art Commission, INTACH and the Delhi Conservation Society, to preserve the brick and mortar of Delhi's past.

This is a rare combination. When added to her principal vocation, teaching, you have that unicorn who has written history's narratives, conserved its material legacy and conveyed to generations of students the excitement of understanding the ways in which the past informs the present. Most college and university teachers experience at some stage of their careers a form of lecture fatigue, a sense of diminishing returns as the years of chalk, talk and supervision pile up.

As someone who taught alongside her for more than twenty years, suffered with her the obtuseness of university bureaucracies and the tedium of department meetings, inherited some of the courses she designed and the research students she nurtured, I can testify that Narayani's enthusiasm for teaching young people never flagged. It was hard to be world weary and cynical when someone who began teaching fifteen years before you did, still met colleagues and students with affection and unfeigned patience, year after year.

I have a familial claim to Delhi's past. A maternal ancestor, Munshi Nathmal, was a clerk in the last Mughal's court before he turned his coat and joined the Company army that laid siege to Delhi and finally conquered it in 1857. Somewhere in Haider Quli is a modest house built around a single courtyard still occupied by my cousins, Munshi Nathmal's heirs. And yet, for the longest time, I felt not the slightest attachment to either Shahjahanabad or the New Delhi that succeeded it. It was fashionable in my cohort of *dilliwallahs,* to celebrate our escape from the narrow lanes of the old city to the suburban modernity of republican Delhi.

It was Narayani's love for Delhi, her sense that we lived in an extraordinary city that might lose the past that constituted it unless it was remembered, storied and conserved, that jolted us out of our easy indifference to the living history of this great metropolis. I used to joke that it took a carpetbagger from Kerala to pioneer a revival in writing, both academic and popular, about Delhi's past and the movement to conserve its built heritage. Narayani would have none of it; she was a *dilliwali,* born and bred. But claims to place are irrelevant; the lesson of her life as a writer and historian is that to truly own the past you need to love it enough to pay attention.

Introductory Note

PARTHO DATTA
KUMKUM ROY

J'espère avoir écrit ce livre sans préjugé mais je ne prétends pas l'avoir écrit sans passion.

I hope to have written this book without prejudice but I do not claim to have written without feeling.

– Alexis de Tocqueville

THIS QUOTE, which appears in the Preface to Narayani Gupta's *Delhi Between Two Empires,* is a credo that has sustained her scholarship and passions over many decades. A growing circle of admirers have been marvelling at her commitment to Delhi and everything urban, her concern with pedagogy and teaching and her quiet determination to get things done. This collection is a celebration and a tribute by scholars, colleagues, students and friends. The essays include memoirs as well as discussions on various facets of urban history, and issues of pedagogy.

Narayani Gupta is the *doyenne* of Delhi studies. Her pioneering scholarship and concern with the fate of Delhi and campaigns to make the city a habitable space continue to inspire. *Delhi Between Two Empires* was published in 1981. Subsequently, the study of Delhi has flourished and many monographs and popular histories have delved into the city's medieval and colonial pasts and the burgeoning behemoth that it has now become. *Delhi Between Two Empires* has however remained a benchmark, central to writing and thinking about the city, acknowledged for showing the way, for anticipating many themes. It contributed to Delhi's status in colonial urban historiography and rivalled the domination in scholarship of attention to metropolises such as Madras, Bombay and Calcutta.

Delhi Between Two Empires tackled a range of themes: the effects of the British conquest of Delhi in the early nineteenth century, the flourishing publics enabled by a vigorous print culture, 1857 and military pacification, and the early colonial institutions and the modernization of governance. Delhi's place as a site for durbars and imperial invention of traditions meant that despite its diminished status post-1857, it was never far from the grandiose imagination of the British. The transfer of capital and the creation of New Delhi put new imperatives at play as Delhi became connected to global trends in architecture and planning. However, the dynamics of the local remained important in Narayani Gupta's work even when the metropolitan loomed large.

For long, the standalone history or a small clutch of monographs set the trend for colonial urban histories in South Asia. Narayani Gupta's book came out contemporaneously with that of Anthony King and Robert Grant Irwing and formed a formidable trio of scholarly books on Delhi. For Calcutta, there was Pradip Sinha, on Lucknow, Veena Oldenburg, on Ahmedabad, Kenneth Gillion and Howard Spodek and a range of insightful essays by Jim Masselos on Bombay. Work on urban centres and urbanization in Punjab by J.S. Grewal and Indu Banga and on the political economy of Calcutta by Atiya Kidwai were also influential. What this trend indicated was the relatively marginal status of urban history in the larger historiography of modern India which was obsessed with the rural and the mobilizational possibilities for Indian nationalism in the countryside. All the more reason that Narayani Gupta's work and that of her peers and friends remained so influential. The work of urban historians in this phase was consolidated when the Urban History Association was set up and started holding its sessions concurrently with the annual Indian History Congress.

However, Narayani Gupta's concern with Delhi was not simply academic. Simultaneously, she has been a pioneer in the conservation movement. Her work started modestly with the Conservation Society Delhi, a voluntary organization set up with colleagues and friends. The inspirations were Syed Ahmed Khan, Garcin de Tassy, Zafar Hasan, Percy Brown and Percival Spear and the legacy of their writings. Winter walks by volunteers to Delhi's big and small monuments led to a growing interest among Delhi's citizens in relating meaningfully to their past, not just the pre-British but also to the colonial past. The planning of New Delhi had carefully incorporated existing structures into the diagonals and vistas of the capital. Yet post-Independence Delhi was quick to declare Shahjahanabad a slum, with the network of canals allowed to deteriorate into mere *nullahs.* These and other concerns, the heavy hand of the national, the disregard for the historic character of Lutyens' Central Vista, overenthusiasm to rename streets, casual vandalism and insensitivity to neighbourhood planning have given conservation an activist edge in Delhi. This has in no small measure been due to Narayani Gupta. For years now she has been championing the work of Patrick Geddes and his respect for the ecology of the local. An important contribution has been *Delhi, The Built Heritage: A Listing,* for the Indian National Trust for Art Culture and Heritage, a much-needed update on the condition of monuments, which she published with her student Ratish Nanda in 1999.

As a teacher in Indraprastha College, Jamia Millia Islamia and the erstwhile TVB School of Architecture she has inspired students to relate to spaces, empathize with the past. Her continuous endeavour has been to persuade through academic writing, talks and op-eds. An enormously important endeavour has been engagement with institutions, and the creation of textbooks. In 1987, *Our City, Delhi* was written for children in Delhi schools, probably the first of its kind. She has also written and contributed to the textbooks in Hindi for Delhi schools sponsored by the SCERT (State Council of Educational Research and Training, Delhi) in 2004 and was one of the editors and consultants for the revision of textbooks published by NCERT (National Council of Educational Research and Training) in 2006. In 2011 she published *Let's Explore Humayun's Tomb*, an illustrated guide for children with illustrations by Anitha Balachandran, part of a series of books sponsored jointly by the Archaeological Survey and the Aga Khan Trust.

The editors, authors and several friends who have made this volume possible, as well as the publishing team at Primus hope that these essays will resonate with some of Narayani Gupta's many concerns and enthusiasms. Many thanks to Niharika Gupta and Shruti Chakraborty for compiling the Bibliography.

PART I

THE IMPORTANCE OF BEING NARAYANI

1

A Shared Ownership

RAMU DAMODARAN

I FIRST met Narayani (then Menon) when she was 13 and a half years old and I an hour and a half. A remarkably well-preserved photograph from a few months later shows me reaching outward from her arms, almost as if, enthralled by the stories she shared of the city around us, I was anxious to leap free and discover them on my own.

It was a time I understandably know of from second-hand accounts. In the central secretariat offices, not far from where we lived, civil servants and scholars had begun to work on what was to emerge as the ponderously titled 'Ancient Monuments and Archaeological Sites and Remains Act' two years later. It included in its definition of 'ancient monuments' any 'article, object or thing illustrative of science, art, crafts, literature, religion, customs, morals or politics in bygone ages', an elaboration memorable not just for its unbureaucratic, unselfconscious use of the word 'bygone' but the sweep of history with which it invested the crowded geographies of their location, a history which allowed each monument to be a mirror as much as a marvel.

That they had stories to tell was never in dispute; a question often asked and repeated from year to year in the school examinations in the city and the time in which Narayani grew up was to 'imagine a conversation between Old and New Delhi', a challenge that assumed the animate nature of both, of their pasts, of their present. In their depths, in the canyons of our national and urban histories, nature's geology of their alluvial landscapes was enriched by the geologies of human craftsmanship that lent gentle double meaning to the expression 'storied cities'.

Take Delhi's Qutb Minar, for instance, whose creation and re-creation Narayani captured in a conversation between Manya and Krishna in the UNESCO World Heritage Sites of India children's book series—how its successive storeys were built as new sultans emerged and how destruction caused by earthquakes led to the assertion of identity over symmetry where Ferozeshahi white marble replaced the pink sandstone of an earlier era, only letting itself collapse and yield to a cupola wrought by a British major. Each story, present and past, its own tale, represents a point from where, in Narayani's phrase, the Qutb would 'talk to the eagles, smell the rain in the monsoon clouds and send a greeting through my carrier pigeon to my brother in Afghanistan, the Minar-e-Jam.'

It was not just the imagination of them as beings blessed by mind and tongue that made monuments animate, it was their realization of human potential, a term that has come to command its own vogue today, of which there could be no greater manifestation than the anonymity of effort and excellence with which each stone was laid, each façade chiseled. We know of the orderers—the monarchs and commanders whose words shaped the idea behind each—but not the ordered, the men and, yes, the women who brought the ideas into being. Perfection in collective endeavour can be far more difficult to achieve than in an individual work of art which is why, even in its anonymity, it deserves what Narayani describes as the 'respect or affection for the work created by gifted artisans', secure in the laboured splendour of their moment, that pride inhibiting foreboding of their environs succumbing 'to the bullying of the modern predator'.

But was it pride, or was it resignation, an echo of the Hemant Kumar refrain of '*isko hi jeena kahte hai to, yoonhi ji lenge*'? There is, clearly, no ready or immediate answer to it and it is here that the distinction and continuity between 'understanding towns' and 'teaching history' comes in, allowing the evidence before one's eyes to kindle an understanding—and its derived conclusions—wholly one's own, that echoes with the phrase of Dorothy Sayers, who graduated from Oxford's Somerville College many years before Narayani did—'The sole, true end of education is simply this, to teach men how to learn for themselves, and whatever instruction fails to do this is effort spent in vain.'

'Teaching to understand' could well sum up Narayani's formal and informal pedagogy; I was and still am a beneficiary of the latter, where lessons were not premised on a lecture that invited questions, but on questions to which answers were attempted, even if those answers needed to be thought through by the questioner. In many instances this brought the palpable and 'seen' urban topography of the present to the immediacy of history, a history made immediate because it was shaped by precisely the same force, skill and talent as are at work today, albeit in their remotest versions. The enormous aggregation of human imagination allows for the creation of an intelligence which, for all its artifice, extends the limitation of the humanly possible.

It was precisely that imagination that Narayani taught us to understand, to understand in a world where the more tedious attributes of the construction industry, such as bricklaying, have been outsourced to robots, to understand an earlier landscape quite literally peopled by constructions entirely human in their vision and creation.

When, a half century ago, Robert Hunter crafted the lyrics to the Grateful Dead's 'Ripple', he wrote, 'Let it be known there is a fountain that was not made by the hands of man.' Many interpretations of that phrase suggested it referred to the role of the divine in creating the resources for human sustenance, but its intent could well have been less ecclesiastical and more an affirmation that the 'hands' of man fashioned only what his head, and his heart, envisioned, a truth that animated the towns through whose metaphor Narayani taught history, a history blessed, in her phrase, by 'shared ownership', a phrase that connotes both possession and a commonality of possession, the surest source of pride as much as promise.

2

The Narayani I Know

SRIMANJARI

SOME FORTY years ago, way back in 1983, I knew very little about Prof. Partha Sarathi Gupta and Narayani. I had enrolled for M.Phil. at the Department of History, University of Delhi, and PSG, as he was widely known, was my supervisor and subsequently my guide during Ph.D. I met Narayani during the long hours that I spent in PSG's study when he would very patiently go through the tardy drafts of term papers and chapters of my M.Phil. dissertation. Narayani, passing by the study, would unfailingly say, 'Partho, do ask the poor thing for tea'. My feeble smile invariably broadened when Putul di placed samosas, *mishti*, and tea in front of me.

It is over the years, and through many interactions that I have come to know Narayani as Narayani. Working on a Class VIII textbook for Delhi Government schools in 2002–4 with Narayani and Visalakshi Menon was one such close interaction. The monotony of long dreary evenings spent at the printing press was broken by our conversations on all things under the sun, from the inane to the interesting. Once, a discussion on the bubbling sounds made in the process of smoking a hookah provided much merriment! A few months later I was pleasantly surprised to receive a gift from Narayani—a small brass hookah with a tiny note in memory of our evenings spent at the printing press! Narayani has always known the secret of making memories.

In 2006–7, I got an opportunity to read Narayani's work in a consistent manner when the university introduced a course on the history of Delhi. It was a pleasure for me, a Dilliwali, to teach that course in college that enabled me see Delhi with new eyes. Now, as I revisit her chapter on Delhi in R.E. Frykenberg's edited volume *Delhi Through the Ages*, I marvel afresh at the wealth of information Narayani's work provides on the role of the Ridge in preventing soil erosion, which was a significant factor in the choice of the site of Shahjahanabad.

As I read the names 'Jahan panah, Jahan–numa, Chandrawal, Roshanara', I think of the places I have visited or seen their names on the boards of the DTC buses. I feel I know the city a little better because of the painstaking work done by scholars like Narayani to dig out and put together information in a narrative which connects the old and the new, from the making of the Yamuna canal and the Gujar villages of Delhi to the sacking of Metcalfe House in 1857, the making of Civil Lines and the new capital of the Empire–New Delhi.[1]

Narayani's perseverance in research seamlessly transitioned into regular interactions with college students on aspects of urban history and heritage during Indian National Trust for Art and Cultural Heritage (INTACH) workshops that speak for the kind of person and intellectual Narayani is—always alive to the possibility of engagement. In 2015, a student of mine, Soumya Sahai, wrote a particularly good report on her field visit to the *baoli* near the Pir Ghaib, the eleventh century monument of the Tughlaq period behind the Bara Hindu Rao Hospital. Not only did Narayani appreciate the article, she also opened up a world of possibilities for the young undergraduate. In her email to the student Narayani wrote almost poetically:

When you wander on the Ridge go back in time:

- Forest and wilderness have a very special place in our culture, and the 'kan-phata' sadhus who have been in that area for years are an interesting part of Delhi.
- Then try to visualize how Feroze Shah made his way from his *kot* to Jahan-numa (the name of this area of the Ridge)—which road did his cavalcade take? What was the role of shikar in the image-building exercise of rulers?
- Was the mosque in a clearing or in the forest?
- The first Survey of India, Trigonometrical Survey, used Pir Ghaib for a triangulation point…
- Much later, why does Fraser choose to live here (the house he later sold to Hindu Rao)?
- Read Mutiny accounts of this area by British soldiers.
- In the 1960s, the line of the Yamuna was clearly visible from this point. Why not now?
- Is neglect of older buildings an inherent part of our culture? Can it be changed, and how?

There will be lots of other questions that will occur to you. Remember that in history asking questions is more challenging than locating answers!

I have reproduced a significant portion of the mail here only to indicate that for Narayani it was not just enough to appreciate the young scholar but also coax her into a further exploration of the fascinating landscape of the Ridge. It is not surprising that Soumya founded the first student led Heritage Walk society in Miranda House, called *Musafir.*

Narayani's suggestions emanated from a concern not only for monuments but for lived histories that surround monuments. It is remarkable how Narayani constantly endeavours to remind us about the real purpose of history. In an article written after the NCERT deleted significant sections from history textbooks in 2023, Narayani stated: 'Recall Charles Dickens making time to write A Child's History of England. Thoughtful histories do not simply glorify or denigrate rulers, they explain the intersection between the earth and human activity, between the forces of nature and technology. They help us understand the world.'

No wonder the enthusiasm of students to have 'Narayani Ma'am' in their midst remains unabated. In March 2022, she did a podcast for our students at a time when some online teaching was still going on even as we had started taking offline classes. The impact of Narayani's podcast was such that the students wanted to meet her in person. What one of the students cherished the most was the beautiful message she received from Narayani:

> I seem to be echoing a teacher we had in our 4th standard in school, a Miss Williams who seemed to have been born old, with wrinkles like lace on her face. She fiercely told us NEVER to use the phrase 'killing time' or to say we were 'bored'. Now that I have become a Miss Williams myself, I pass on her words of wisdom to you. Enjoy every day, and never be afraid to speak the truth.

Can there be anything more meaningful than this?

Notes

1. Narayani Gupta, 'Delhi and Its Hinterland. The Nineteenth and Early Twentieth Centuries', in *Delhi Through the Ages. Essays in Urban History, Culture and Society*, ed. R.E. Frykenberg, Delhi: Oxford University Press, 1986, pp. 250–69.

3

Worlds Within a World

GEETA WAHI DUA

DURING ONE of our conversations with Professor Mohammad Shaheer, landscape architect and academician in 2007–8, we were exploring potential subjects and themes and prospective authors from outside the formal professional domains of spatial design, who could contribute to the *Journal of Landscape Architecture* (known as the *LA Journal*). He promptly introduced us to Dr Narayani Gupta, an erudite and perceptive historian. In our first-ever close encounter with a historian, Narayani came across as a simple soul, eager to know and learn more about us while sharing what she had, a pool of immense knowledge and wide experience. It didn't take us long to understand that we share a common world, with many similar values, sources of joy, and areas of concern. Over the next two decades, our association with her has grown in myriad ways. She has been generous enough to contribute to our various creative endeavours—such as *LA Journal*—from time to time and review Studio's[1] studies and research work in the realm of history and culture. Various engaging conversations with her have been about diverse fields ranging from children's literature, history, culture, migration, art, and design to spatial planning and urban design. Delving into the dynamic landscape of India's historic cities has always been a cherished subject for her. Reflecting on these encounters serves as a heartfelt tribute to a nurturing teacher and mentor.

Blurring Boundaries

In the past few years, Narayani has reviewed some of the scholarly books on subjects like gardens, archaeology, and Indian heritage for the *LA Journal.* Erudite pieces of writing and learning, these reviews are not only about the subject in question, but they provide thoroughly researched knowledge bases about its context and the allied aspects. In the review of *Islamic Gardens* by D. Fairchild Ruggles,[2] Narayani's meticulous scholarship brings to the forefront other similar sources from the Indian context like detailed inventories of garden-plantation in Dr Shaukat Ullah Khan's *Ahmedabad 1411–1817: Environmental Facets of a Medieval Urban Centre* (2007). Her insightful observation extends to recognizing the significance of not just architects but also gardeners in shaping our environments. She highlights the transformative power of engineers, who, beyond traditional materials like steel and concrete, built and utilized water channels and collection systems. This approach fosters a sense of collective ownership among a broader community, offering a compelling perspective on creation and collaboration.

In her review of historian Ebba Koch's scholarly work,[3] *The Complete Taj Mahal,* she compares the meticulous documentation and detailing of the World Heritage Site with other examples, while referring to the works of mapping and documenting the sites of Vijayanagara (Karnataka), a medieval Hindu empire, by George Michell and John Fritz, and to the fort of Senji (Tamil Nadu) located near the eastern coast by Jean Deloche. While drawing a comparison between these cities with the present ones, she laments the soulless language of modern town planning while cherishing these historic places.

In an interview feature, she observes:[4]

> Nostalgia is something emotional, whereas memory can be a resource for historians. It can also be seen as a design tool for a designer, making his sense of a place three-dimensional. Today's modernity is tomorrow's tradition. The younger generation of the present is curious about the past, without wanting to accept all 'traditional values' unconditionally, which is very encouraging.

Always trying to negotiate the past and the present in her writings, she can re-contextualize historical facts in an appropriate and relevant way in which they inform the present while staying true to their spirit.

As Narayani puts it, it is very important to dream for the future. During her tenure at the Delhi Urban Art Commission (DUAC) in 2005, under the Chairmanship of Charles Correa, she, along with other members, was responsible for bringing the exciting possibilities of what public areas can be.[5] 'Imagining Delhi' was the outcome of the work generated by twelve Task Forces (Urban Villages, Master Plan, Planning Issues and Housing, Bye-Laws, Public Spaces, Safety and Design, Architecture, Heritage and Conservation, Traffic Transportation, North Delhi, Shahjahanabad, NDMC, East Delhi, South Delhi, and West Delhi) headed by professionals, grouped in a way as to involve the citizens of Delhi in dialogue and point to possible routes which the city could take to become more livable as per world-class standards. It brought these efforts together in a tripartite relationship to involve professionals, government bodies, and the citizens of Delhi to chalk out a sustainable future for the capital.

Nurturing Institutions

Regarding the general apathy of professionals and experts in spatial design and planning and conservation fields towards various government institutions and their working, Narayani's sympathetic approach towards these centres of governance opens new directions of discourse. While acknowledging their limitations, especially in the context of a multicultural country, she underlines their achievements. She credits the Delhi Development Authority (DDA) for greening the capital city, creating a hierarchy of greens with regional parks, district parks, and neighbourhood gardens, and hence, providing a great service to its citizens. She empathizes that a vast country with an enormous wealth of built and natural heritage has left the Archaeological Survey of India (ASI), one of the oldest bodies, with a low sense of self-esteem. In her view, it is unfair to expect the organization to be sensitive to and also knowledgeable about urban situations. Heritage areas in the country need a larger group of people with different expertise to conserve and manage them, where the ASI plays a prime role. At the same time, she contests the law under the Ancient Monuments and Archaeological Sites and Remains (AMASR) Act followed by the ASI which prohibits construction within 100 meters of Protected Monuments.[6] While citing the example of settlements around the temples in Kerala, which are an integral part of the spirit of the place, she suggests replicating the same in the old city of Shahjahanabad. In 'Invitation to a Jugalbandhi', published in the *Indian Express*, she insists that only a cooperative effort between the state and the community can protect India's heritage, a pragmatic as well as a visionary thought. The absence of a holistic way of thinking about our historic cities is another matter of concern when she has often advocated a full-time five-year undergraduate programme that introduces young students to the ways of understanding the present socio-cultural context of a monument or historic site, its relationship with the surrounding natural geography, and cultural linkages.

Reaching Out

A profound belief in the importance of exploring and integrating people's roles into every professional discourse has been a cornerstone of Narayani's philosophy. She has always promoted the idea of bridging the gap between scholarly discourse and understanding by the common masses, often quoting the names of William Dalrymple and Abraham Eraly who, in her view, have brought history closer to the sensibilities of the masses. In 2005, during her tenure at the National Council of Educational Research and Training (NCERT), to advise and compile textbooks on history for schools, she noted the difficulty of making University teachers speak in a language children would understand and enjoy. It is rare for an intellectual, expert, or professional to step out of her serious, complex, and often introverted world and ideate something for a completely different user base. She has been writing books for school children for decades. These have been part of the growing up for generations of Indians. These annals of Indian history paint a beautiful picture of a bygone era and at the same time relate it with present realities for easy comprehension by young minds. *Our City, Delhi,* written by her and beautifully illustrated by Meera Deshprabhu and more recently,[7] Mapin's children's books on World Heritage Sites across India, edited by her are testimony to her passion for the cause. These are works of pure joy and beauty, bringing the knowledge of the history of these places closer to the understanding of young minds, and inculcating a sense of love, care, pride, and belonging for local heritage.

A Dilliwali

Narayani's long association with the city of Delhi, for now more than five decades, has led her to develop a perspective and a vision, from the point of view of a growing individual, for a changing city. Her immense love and concern for the city comes across through her erudite work in the form of city-centric books, talks on local subjects, and eloquent writings about them in different forums including newspapers. The subjects have been varied—spatial design, planning, and cultural values associated with the city, then and now; imagination of the city beyond the physical; the value of contemporary heritage; the disconnect between the people and the State; aspirations and role of history in development; manifestation of the past as history and heritage and the city's cultural and environmental issues in contemporary times. In every discourse, she has made a strong case for a sensitive and contextual approach toward new developments in the capital where the past is equally respected and integrated while carving the future:[8]

> From the 1920s, the kandrat were mapped and identified by the Archaeological Survey of India. Interspersed were the areas broadly called Jungle Bahhar (the forests outside). The landscape of these was familiar to the city folk, for here lay the shrines they visited—Hindu, Sikh, Sufi. Between the trees and shrubs lay jheels, streams, rocky outcrops, and fields all the way south of Mehrauli. Nature and manmade habitats intersected in the Delhi Triangle (the area between the Yamuna and the arc of the Ridge from the south curving round from west to north, sloping into the river before Wazirabad). All the Delhis till the present one were within the triangle.

The imagery is shaped by an understanding of the city as a syncretic space, nestled peacefully in the bounties of nature. In response to the city authorities' plan to remove some of the fourteenth-century 'encroachments' and develop urban recreational facilities, she adopts a pragmatic approach while relying on the versatility of the historic city to inspire, imbibe, and change:[9]

Of course, the perceived needs and aspirations of town dwellers change. But our historic city has a richness that can reconcile modern activities with the spirit of the past. The monuments of centuries past communicate with the visitor who approaches them quietly. The issue is about control of land. This becomes easier to achieve if one is not distracted by sentimental arguments about heritage. History may be past but heritage is present. The patina of years changes it and makes it more appealing.

She laments the ignorance of authorities:[10] 'Our city's most impressive monuments include three towers housing decision-makers—the Vikas Minar looking down on the Jama Masjid, the Nagar Palika on Sansad Marg, and the Nagar Nigam looming over south Shahjahanabad. From that height, they draw a map of the city. How, from that height, will they hear our little voices?' She further notes that the discourse about historic architecture and landscapes is often 'fuzzy, listless and confrontational' and needs to be negotiated with much knowledge, pragmatism, and grace.

A few years ago, her dissent to the redevelopment of Central Vista, the grand project sponsored by the State, stemmed from the concern about the destruction of this stock of collective memory and the public-ness of the space with the proposed series of guarded and fenced government buildings around. She observes:[11] 'It is a space of power but also democracy. It is national and not simply a site of history, bringing togetherness between generations of people. The project to modify it will kill the oxygen of the mind as much as the oxygen of the trees.' In 2017, while condemning the demolition of the Hall of Nations, an important part of the city's contemporary heritage, she wrote in the *Indian Express*: 'When "heritage" is subsumed under "urban development", what is the likely outcome?' Being quite outspoken about her views, she has written many articles and aired her views in different forums, calling professionals to work out and explore ways for the conservation of contemporary heritage, which lies unprotected. Her various engagements with the city have kept her abreast with new thinking and knowledge about urbanism in developing countries, from where she often cites examples in her discussions and conversations.

Remembering a Friend

While remembering her colleague and friend, landscape architect Professor Mohammad Shaheer, whom she greatly admired, her observations are in sync with her line of thinking:[12] 'In a desert of spent ideas, Shaheer finds fresh meanings in familiar architectural forms, as a reaffirmation of continual perceptual curiosity and intellectual discipline. Above all, his sense of what is right in aesthetic terms went with a will to put himself out to enable others to achieve it.'

Again,

> He was full of questions—a lifelong student and the perfect communicator. His tribute to his teacher, Professor Jhabvala, can be applied to him as well ('where the love of explaining is supported by real knowledge, close observation, and experience, without mystification or cant'). It explains why he did not talk about himself or his work. One learned about these from others… He also drew students away from the obsession with easy success and the fear of failure.

Although belonging to different fields, both shared many common interests and concerns. The ability to look for the extraordinary in the mundane, appreciation of beauty and its origin, the importance of refining processes over solely achieving a finished product, strong belief in natural and cultural continuities, deciphering connections between art, environment, culture, and architecture, concern about the state of the city of Delhi and the attenuation of the capacity of authorities and the civic system to imagine and connect are some of the common themes. Both individuals garnered considerable popularity within their respective departments as teachers, thanks to their ability to inspire students to surpass conventional boundaries and strive for excellence with a touch of empathy, eschewing the clamor of competitiveness. Their brief stint together as members of the DUAC (2005–8) and collaboration for a set of books for Rashtrapati Bhavan in later years further nurtured the bond.

No One India

In the context of present-day discourse about nationalism, Narayani's ideas about India attain a special significance.[13] She states that there is no one India. Rather than geography, it is more of an idea. It is a mix of cultures, in which we can't have one derogating the other. The country, spread across geographies and cultures, makes us much more tolerant of other people's views, which is not the case in other regions. Her ineffable vision for the country makes her see the co-existence of worlds within a world as annals of diverse cultures, as connected, mingling, thriving civilizations with a united past that cannot be delinked from the present. Her unwavering commitment to the idea of 'India' as a concept of interconnectedness and inclusiveness are values that need to be cherished and celebrated, especially in the present times.

And the World

Narayani observes that a spirit of place is created cumulatively with nature, people, and buildings along with activities, bringing together different generations of birds, trees, and other life forms. Her idea for landscape architecture has been to create an island of serenity in government schools, dispensaries, government hospitals, and police stations—areas that generate apprehension, tension, and fear. She has always rooted for the idea of people first, encouraging vibrant, happy, and resourceful places like public parks, weekly bazaars, and public art rather than shopping malls and amusement parks.

As we reflect on the impact of our collaborations with her, it becomes evident that Narayani has played a pivotal role in shaping our sphere of the world and its intricate ways.

In 2017, we undertook a pilot study project—'Delhi, Hills, Forests, and a River', with the idea to explore the changing relationship of nature with culture as seen through the history of a city. She was gracious enough with her time to review it and offer many useful suggestions and later proudly released it at the Department of History, Jamia Millia Islamia. She followed the journey of the work during its presentation in INTACH, thoroughly enjoying the later edition of the maps by the studio for other Indian cities. Her introduction of the work to the Department of History at North Carolina State University, NCSU, in 2019, led to our first trip to the US, a country that we have always admired for its academic excellence, diversity, opportunities for personal and professional growth, and a commitment to holistic education. In later years, the association with the University opened many new avenues for us to connect with like-minded academicians and researchers working in similar fields.

Narayani can see meaning and perspective in different aspects of life—an interconnected web of situations, circumstances, opportunities, and encounters. In her companionship a new world of thought and consciousness unfurls, the study of the subject of history is now more exciting, thought-provoking, analytical, realistic, exploratory, and relevant, transcending from mere narratives of political empires, wars, and dates. The aspect of *what* has metamorphosed into *where, why,* and *how,* making historical narratives more meaningful and contextual in terms of present-day realities.

Narayani has introduced us to many strands, unknown, unexplored, and forgotten in formal formats, of the natural and cultural milieu of Indian cities, which has informed and enriched our understanding of their different sites, people, culture, and their inter-relationship of dependence and symbiosis. We have encountered some remarkable individuals throughout our journey with *LA Journal*, all thanks to Narayani's gracious introductions. As I write this article, I realize that her suggestion for a Children's Special Issue in *LA Journal* is unattended, food for thought for the future.

Preferring to remain discreet about her numerous accomplishments, she often refrains from showcasing them on public platforms, even hesitating to provide a photograph for interview features. At times, she expresses dismay at the prevalent trend among practitioners of being overly self-referential in conferences.

With Narayani's chatty, pleasant, patient, and amicable demeanor, her presence in our lives is a great source of sustenance and strength. We extend our heartfelt wishes for her continued good health and unwavering high spirits, characterized by an unstoppable enthusiasm and boundless curiosity that are inherent to her nature.

Notes

1. The work of the studio, while exploring the interrelationship of nature and culture in the realm of spatial design, is manifested in the form of studies and documentations of diverse related aspects, produced as books and nature culture maps of Indian historic cities.
2. 'Islamic Gardens and Landscapes', *LA, Journal of Landscape Architecture,* vol. 34, 2012, p. 945.
3. 'A Labour of Love', *LA, Journal of Landscape Architecture,* vol. 17, 2007, pp. 40–1.
4. 'Looking Back is to Look Forward', *LA, Journal of Landscape Architecture,* vol. 45, 2015, pp. 34–9.

5 'Imagining Delhi', *LA, Journal of Landscape Architecture,* vol. 45, 2006, pp. 21–37.

6. 'Looking Back is to Look Forward', pp. 34–5.
7. Malvika Bajaj, 'Look What We Have Found When We Planted Seeds of Curiosity', *LA, Journal of Landscape Architecture*, UNESCO World Heritage Site Series, vol. 58, 2019, pp. 110–13.
8. 'All that it Holds', *Indian Express*, 16 February 2024, p. 12.
9. Ibid.
10. Ibid.
11. 'Practitioners, Academicians, Thinkers—Discourse on Central Vista', *LA, Journal of Landscape Architecture*, vol. 62, 2022, pp. 70–3.
12. 'Every Day is the Start of Another', Notes, *LA, Journal of Landscape Architecture*, 2016, pp. 3–5.
13. 'Looking Back is to Look Forward', pp. 34–5.

4

The Historian and Two Architects

SNEHANSHU MUKHERJEE
ANISHA SHEKHAR MUKHERJI

> …[T]here are so many of us … who would feel better if they frequently did something small and immediate for Delhi's heritage, instead of leaving the custodians to soldier on alone, or the 'experts' to prepare plans which take years and crores to become a reality. Isn't it possible that this will be the way to create the sense of citizenship which our young mega-city still has not developed?
>
> — 'My pre-history for FrASI (to rhyme with Crazy)'[1]

THESE ARE the lines with which Professor Narayani Gupta rounded off a thoroughly engaging piece for Friends of ASI (FrASI), written some years ago. This is how she began:

> Thirty short years ago Kamaladevi Chattopadhyaya (whose stretch of imagination was as long as her name) conjured up an Environment Group at the India International Centre. Lots of people turned up, each with at least half-a-dozen grumbles in her pocket. And Kamaladevi looked around with her winning smile and said 'Right. Now *do* something about it!'

To us, these two quotes sum up Narayani's inspirations and aspirations, her objectives, and her methodologies—to create a sense of citizenship, and to awaken citizens to the heritage of what she titles 'The Indomitable City';[2] to protect the different historical layers that have shaped the evolution of the city we live in and added richness to it and to our lives; to remind everyone that 'Delhi was 1000 years old, and there was still so much to discover, so much to cherish!'[3] Above all, her vision to do something.

FrASI itself, which Narayani roped us into, was one such effort. It was, as she put it, her birthday present to commemorate the 150th year of Archaeological Survey of India (ASI). An initiative of civil society supported by ASI, the aim of FrASI was to identify potential friends who could facilitate positive interaction between themselves, ASI, and the larger public so that friends of ASI and of our heritage keep increasing.[4] Though FrASI as a group has now become dormant, yet in the brief period of its active existence, it did manage to demonstrate important lessons in what can be achieved if we come together to do something, however small, for Delhi's heritage.[5]

As we reflect upon this, we realize how much Narayani has enabled us, as well as other architects, to look at Delhi—and other cities—beyond the conventional abstractions of commercial, residential, or industrial functions. The different ideas and insights put forth in her books and articles, the many conversations we have had with her, her encouragement to us to write and publish, the projects initiated by her that we have been co-opted in, have also acted as catalysts to take forward varying and various pursuits.

Indeed, it is her writings through which our acquaintance with Narayani really began. Snehanshu encountered her book *Delhi Between Two Empires* as part of the research for his thesis on unauthorized housing in Delhi, while doing his Master of Science in Architecture Studies at the Massachusetts

Institute of Technology. Several years later when Anisha was researching on the Red Fort, while doing her Masters in Architectural Conservation at the De Montfort University, she was introduced to the same book, which helped understand how Shahjahanabad and the larger area of Delhi worked through important times of transition in their history.

On returning to Delhi from Boston after his post-graduation, Snehanshu started teaching at the School of Planning and Architecture along with running an architectural studio—Team for Engineering, Architecture and Management (TEAM) with his friends. A few years later, he joined the TVB School of Habitat Studies[6] in its initial years, which was experimenting with unconventional ways of teaching appropriate to the needs and developmental challenges of India. Luckily, for the students—and for both of us—Narayani was also teaching an elective there. When Anisha began to work on a book that extended her thesis on 'An Approach towards Spatial Conservation' with its focus on the Red Fort, it was Narayani who helped to hone it and get it to its publishable state.[7]

Almost at the same time, *Shahjahanabad/Old Delhi: Tradition and Colonial Change*, whose first edition contained essays by Narayani along with four other distinguished scholars, was republished. The publication of this second edition was coordinated by Narayani, on the request of the editors, Eckhart Ehlers and Thomas Krafft, and contained an additional essay written by Anisha focusing on the Red Fort.[8] Narayani is also instrumental, along with Partho Datta, for the publication of an important facet of Snehanshu's research in public housing and urban form. This book[9] was the outcome of a seminar in June 2015 themed 'Urban Spaces in Modern India' curated by Narayani and Partho at the Indian Institute of Advanced Study at Shimla. For the seminar, Narayani and Partho invited academics, researchers and professionals from disciplines that ranged from literature, film studies, art, urban studies, and architecture. When Narayani telephoned Snehanshu to ask him to participate in the seminar, she, in her characteristic manner told him to talk about what was wrong about the way our cities were being planned. This single simple instruction caused him to put down for the first time on paper, the culmination of several years of research and analysis into a consolidated essay. One can imagine how, through direct and clear instructions, Narayani has possibly helped nudge scholars, academicians, and professionals to find their paths to move forward and come closer to their quest.

So, our first forays into authoring writings on history and architecture owe their appearance to Narayani. She also helped to sustain our experiment with independent publishing. When a motley crew of us (which included three architects) resolved to start a niche publishing house based on the fragile foundation of a decided opinion on books, and some experience in writing, designing, and printing—Narayani was most encouraging. She was also brave enough to entrust to us the publication of her elder sister's writings on the temples of south India. This book, *Rhythms in Stone,* puts together and conveys the exhilaration of Indira Menon's journeys recorded in her diaries and photographs (earlier in black and white, and later in colour) to temples in south India, especially Karnataka and Tamil Nadu in the 1970s. Working on the book gave us the opportunity to interact with Indira briefly, and experience for ourselves her great interest in, and knowledge of, Carnatic music, history and architecture, which come together in her writings.[10]

At a personal and larger level, the connection forged at TVB between practitioners and professors of architecture and urban history was also carried to School of Planning and Architecture (SPA) when Snehanshu joined as a full-time faculty and invited Narayani to guide a batch of his students for the newly introduced 'Seminars on Architecture'. The SPA students did not put in the requisite effort on the topic of 'Delhi as an Onion' which was based on a short piece that

Anisha had written for a journalist friend, Isabelle Chaise, while in the UK. Though the students did not do justice to Narayani's guidance, she was very appreciative of even their somewhat meagre effort. At the seminar presentation, she did not say a word of discouragement as her feedback, and instead urged them to develop their ideas further. Much after Snehanshu moved away from full-time teaching at SPA, she readily continued to lend her scholarship to students of architecture—in the same way as she still does, to all manner of aspiring students even after retiring from full-time university teaching.

Many others, who may not be students or have not met her or known her personally, have also partaken of her wide-ranging and deep knowledge through her writings and talks in the public domain. These are tools that have been effective in shaping the discourse of how our cities need to grow—and an extension of her ability to engage with people, and her concern with not merely identifying an issue or problem, but looking for possible paths to solutions.

It was this concern that gave rise to initiatives such as the Conservation Society of Delhi (CSD). Registered almost exactly four decades ago—on 5 February 1984—the CSD, Narayani revealed, had its beginnings as a sub-group on monuments in an environmental organization set up in 1982 on a two-year grant from India International Centre (IIC), at the suggestion of Kamala Devi Chattopadhyay (1903–88). As Narayani recollects, it had an initial strength of only three members of which she was one! These were an architect, a photographer and a historian: Malay Chatterjee, Ram Dhamija, and Narayani Gupta. From this modest beginning, the CSD grew to 100 members. One of its members, Nalini Thakur (who later headed the Conservation Department at SPA) was invited by the Delhi Development Authority (DDA) to prepare a report on Mehrauli, which resulted in the delineation of the Mehrauli Archaeological Park.

Many of us probably do not realize the significant role the CSD has played in influencing tangible aspects of Delhi's history, including successfully halting the demolition of two unprotected monuments: a tomb in Mehrauli acquired by a builder in 1988, and the canopy that used to house the statue of King George V near India Gate.[11] The uncontrollable rise of commerce and real estate all over the country since then means that almost every day we are confronted with the news that significant parts of our cities and towns have been removed overnight. It was Narayani who informed us about the Public Notice issued on 24 December 2023 in the *Times of India* by the Chief Architect, New Delhi Municipal Council (NDMC). This announced the decision of the NDMC to apply to the Heritage Conservation Committee for the removal of the Sunehri Masjid, a Grade III Heritage building at Rafi Marg, on the grounds of traffic management and 'sustainable mobility'. The Notice invited objections and suggestions by the general public to be sent in by email till 1 January 2024, giving barely a week's time. According to a report published in *The Telegraph* on 3 January 2024, nearly 85,000 comments were sent in by citizens from all walks of life—including historians and architects—leading to a deferment of the decision, at least for the time being. But, in a chilling reminder of the need for eternal vigilance, we came across this news item shortly after, on 1 February 2024, tucked away in a corner of the main page of *The Hindu*: 'Mehrauli Mosque razed citing DDA's demolition drive.'[12]

Why are many of us, architects included, ineffectual when it comes to conserving even tangible aspects of our heritage such as architecture? An important reason, as Narayani stresses often, is that people have no idea of the history behind the architecture they see, inhabit, or pass by. Even the names of the architects of buildings are unknown to most, except to a few students of architecture or architects. Therefore, perhaps, one of the first things to do is to communicate something as simple as the name of the architect/s or makers of buildings in our city and bring alive their associations with history. The CSD did this effectively by engaging with school students, architects, ASI, and DDA officials through workshops, seminars, audio-visual presentations and heritage walks. In fact, it was one of the first in the country to conduct heritage walks, now an indispensable tool to popularize history and sensitize citizens and visitors to the many layers of urban forms.

In a recent online talk titled 'The Conservation Moment',[13] Narayani shared her memories of the momentous time in India's history that she was part of, when there was a deep sense of involvement and pride with all aspects of culture. As she reflected on difficult periods of Delhi's life and that of the country, the war of 1971 and the violence in 1984, she spoke of finding peace in walking in Siri and Bijay Mandal: 'The patina of time softens and blurs violence in the past but violence in the present is too raw for us to accept.' For those of us who are not familiar with those times through our direct experience, or have not interacted with many of the famous figures she speaks of, or have only known some of them later as senior teachers, the incidents she relates are like a peep into the pages of a history book and yet astonishingly descriptive of what we still see today. When she mentions how, so many years ago, Kamala Devi Chattopadhyay 'became increasingly concerned about the ugliness spreading in our cities' which included 'synthetic fabrics, garish shop-fronts, neglected gardens', it as if she is cueing into our present dilemmas and experiences.

Snehanshu maintains: 'Narayani is one person I know, who actually has in her house a set of the ground-breaking and now forgotten and out-of-print *Urbanisation Commission Report* led by Charles Correa and M.N. Buch which was written during Rajiv Gandhi's tenure as the Prime Minister of India.' Narayani told him that she actually found several hardbound copies of the report lying around in the corridors of the Urban Development Ministry, ready to be junked! She managed to retrieve a set and take it home for her library. The Commission's recommendations, if the government of that time had implemented them, would have ensured that we would not be in the unsustainable real estate-driven development agenda that we are saddled with today.

Her interest and knowledge of contemporary urban issues is remarkable even when compared to other academics from disciplines directly related to urban studies and architecture. Narayani's presence, along with Partho Datta, in a recent conference organized on Architectures of Transition in South Asia,[14] was doubly special in a gathering largely composed of architects. During the last session, Rahul Mehrotra, the prime mover behind the idea and organization of the conference, running out of time, decided to not take any further questions from the attendees, and instead requested Narayani to make the closing comments. This she did in her inimitable style. Pithy and thought-provoking, her words constituted both a challenge and a call to architects to take up their responsibilities and their role in shaping the future of our cities before it is too late. Indeed, the best gift to her—and our city—would be for all of us to heed that call.

Notes

1. See https://friendsofasi.wordpress.com/memoirs/my-pre-history-for-frasi-to-rhyme-with-crazy-narayani-gupta/.
2. Narayani Gupta, 'The Indomitable City', in *Shahjahanabad/Old Delhi: Tradition and Colonial Change,* ed. Elmers Eckart and Thomas Krafft, 1st edn., Stuttgart: Franz Steiner Verlag, 1993; repr., New Delhi: Manohar, 2003, pp. 29–44.
3. See https://friendsofasi.wordpress.com/memoirs/my-pre-history-for-frasi-to-rhyme-with-crazy-narayani-gupta/.
4. See https://friendsofasi.wordpress.com/about/.
5. See https://friendsofasi.wordpress.com/2017/06/25/whose-site-is-it-anyway-the-question-of-custodianship/.

6. Set up in 1990; now USAP GGSIPU (University School of Planning & Architecture, Guru Gobind Singh Indra Prastha University).
7. In an interesting coincidence, after twenty years, the second edition of *The Red Fort of Shahjahanabad*, has just been published by Westland.
8. Anisha Shekhar Mukherji, 'The Changing Perception of Space, History of the Red Fort of Shahjahanabad', in *Shahjahanabad/ Old Delhi: Tradition and Colonial Change*, ed. Elmers Eckart and Thomas Krafft, New Delhi: Manohar, 2003, pp. 45–70.
9. Narayani Gupta and Partho Datta, eds., *Urban Spaces in Modern India*, Shimla: Indian Institute of Advanced Study, 2018.
10. See https://ambiknowledgeresources.wordpress.com/2012/09/12/httpambiknowledgeresources-files-wordpress-com201209outside-cover1-jpg/.
11. See https://www.facebook.com/neighborhooddiaries/videos/343116691931450.
12. *The Hindu*, 1 February 2024.
13. Organized by Shapno Ekhon, 19 January 2024.
14. 14–16 December 2023, India International Centre.

PART II

THE MANY TEXTURES OF TOWNS

5

The City and Colonial Planning

A History and a Survey

PARTHO DATTA

WHEN WE think about modern planning we confront the figure of the planner. Planning as a profession is little over a hundred years old and is an amalgam of architects, engineers, doctors, social reformers, housing activists and their concern with urban spaces and cities. According to some historians the profession came into its own with the 1910 Town Planning Conference in London.[1] Pioneers like Raymond Unwin, Patrick Geddes and others with an interest in town planning were participants. The reified category of the planner emerged at this time. The conference spurred numerous activities. The profession consolidated itself through an association, numerous town planning journals began publication. Planners started lobbying for commissions. It is well worth remembering that the planners were all white men. A point that is missed in most Western histories of planning is the connection between colonialism and modern planning. The emergence of the profession of planning is closely tied to the great commissions for building cities in the colonies: Canberra, Singapore, New Delhi, Johannesburg, and all over Africa. The figure of the travelling planner is a significant one. These men traversed continents, spreading the word of progressive Western urbanism in the colonies, preaching a kind of modernism, creating a body of work that defined planning that set important norms.[2] A related point might be kept in mind. Till quite recently historians were convinced that modernity and models of governance from the metropolis were mimicked in the colonies. The approach usually was to look for planning models innovated in England and then trace the history of its transfer to India. The precedents in India show that innovations happened in tandem and often anticipated initiatives in the metropolis. This fits in well with what historians of colonial India have been arguing for some time—that techniques of governance were often first innovated in the colonies[3] (examples include the Archaeological Survey, surveillance techniques like finger printing, government funding for public education, 'English literature', etc.). This view helps to integrate Indian planning history into larger movements throughout the world instead of seeing it as a pale shadow of the metropolis. The reports of Patrick Geddes in India stand out because he not only qualified and critiqued mainstream planning but was instrumental in championing Indian urban traditions.[4]

Just because the figure of the planner emerged late does not mean that cities were not planned before. During the medieval and early modern era, emperors, women in the royal harem, merchants, religious institutions, universities, and from the early nineteenth century, i.e. the modern period, military adventurers, engineers, doctors, bureaucrats, and industrialists were actively engaged in planning towns and cities. Writers, poets, even painters took an interest in cities and planning, engaged with urban spaces and had ideas about them. When Ebenezer Howard published *Garden Cities of Tomorrow* (1898, 1902), one enthusiastic respondent was the American poet, Walt Whitman. T.J. Clark and Alain Corbin have shown how the French impressionist painters were envisioning new city spaces in their canvases, anticipating the momentous changes in Paris brought about by Haussmann.[5] The response to changes in urban spaces was widespread. It is therefore important to differentiate modern planning from pre-modern planning. According to Francoise Choay, modern planners were addressing the new reality of industrial capitalism—what she called *critical* planning.[6] Capitalism and the modern economy needed new buildings, infrastructure, transportation networks. Cities needed to be upgraded to meet this demand. Town planners offered plans to meet this challenge.

The state was at the forefront of planning—only the state could garner the resources, financial and administrative, to effect large-scale change in the cities. The agenda was reformist—transforming and upgrading cities meant changing people and changing people meant changing society.[7] For this reason, planning embodied the political will of the state. City planning was an instrument for control and modern and colonial states invested in urban spaces. Nation states too invested in planning since it demonstrated the will to transform and modernize society. States had been intervening critically in cities since the mid-nineteenth century. By the early twentieth century two broad trends or models of planning had emerged.

One model envisaged decisive intervention in the existing city to restructure it along principles of modern hygiene and commerce. This was the famous model devised by Haussmann for Paris. The other was to escape the chaos of the existing city altogether and begin anew on an empty plain, exemplified by Ebenezer Howard's model for the Garden City. Both these models were adapted to India and became spectacular examples of colonial planning. But this 'transfer' was not without its problems and had violent consequences. The unsuitability of a plan designed for elsewhere was rarely taken into account and risked being imposed on a people with totally different needs.[8]

Haussmann's plan quickly became a model that planners adopted all over the world. The success of the model owed a lot to its systematic implementation in Paris and became proof of how a city could be modernized. Haussmann saw the city as fragmented and dislocated and he wanted to bring unity through a new kind of spatial ordering. He connected economic nodes like docks and railway stations to facilitate circulation of goods and services.[9] Roads in his plan served as public spaces where the writ of the state ran without any opposition. The citizen on the street was a new person, someone who would have to imbibe new rules of self-regulation. The Grand Boulevards that emerged in Paris were outstanding examples of regulated public spaces which met the approval of the bourgeoisie. Clean and orderly, they were policed but pleasurable as well.[10] In the colonies however, planning was more instrumental. Demolitions and displacements for the sake of making the city clean were ruthlessly implemented in Bombay and Calcutta after the plague epidemic of 1896. Such precedents had existed since 1857 for Delhi (see below) and Lucknow. Haussmann had been anticipated in the colony. The work of the Calcutta Improvement Trust (1911) is a dramatic example of the success of Haussmannian planning. By 1927, the Calcutta Improvement Trust had displaced 50,000 people.[11] If this history is not well known and integrated into global planning histories, it is because the violence of modern planning in the colonies has not been accounted for.

Ebenezer Howard's Garden City Model envisaged beginning anew on empty land.[12] Howard's design was a response to the inherent problems of scale confronting the megalopolis and he offered a smaller sustainable urban community. For this reason, his new townships were integrated into the countryside and nature. His urban community would be situated in a sea of green. Howard wanted to build model townships for the industrial workers—the aim was to produce a politically quiescent and satisfied working class by containing class conflict and alleviating the harsh realities of industrial squalor. However, it was one of the ironies of planning history that a town planning model for the labouring population was soon appropriated to the suburban and bucolic longings of the bourgeoisie which wanted to escape the smoke and grime of the industrial city.[13] The greatest example of this in the colony is the planning of New Delhi where Lutyens combined the spatial outlay of a cantonment with the green spaces of the Garden City.[14] New Delhi is celebrated for its formal beauty but it throws open all the dilemmas of modern planning. New Delhi's spacious green model and neo-classical design perpetuated imperial grandeur. Segregation was confirmed and became the norm as Anthony King has argued.[15]

Public spaces and modern planning are closely connected. When we think of planning and public spaces we think of rationalized spaces. This is the space where the writ of the state runs, where law determines movement and the implementation of rules are impersonal. But public spaces can also be informal spaces: anything from the space of the neighbourhood to the local bazaar. The story of modern planning is a tussle between rationalized formal spaces and these informal spaces. Modern planners were champions of rationalized spaces and made little provision for the informal in their plans. The historical record shows that the imposition of rationalized spaces had disastrous results and the process was violent. Planning theories emerged that tried to negotiate a more benign fit between the rationalized space of planning and the informal space of community and society.

The bid by planners to rationalize was a response to the emerging nature of spaces in modern cities. In South Asia, the modern metropolis was generated in colonial India and is best known by the cities of Calcutta (now Kolkata), Bombay (now Mumbai), Madras (now Chennai) and New Delhi which represented a distinct kind of urban space. The nature of these cities was determined by various parameters: population, density, scale, class structure, built form, and the economy. The nature of colonial urban space determined the kind of challenges modern planners had to confront.

These parameters have best been studied by geographers and sociologists. Planning historians have drawn on the work done in these disciplines. A great deal of the early work on colonial cities was based on an important data base that had been generated by colonial rule. This was the decennial census which began tentatively from the 1870s and more systematically from the 1880s, which has been used critically and extensively by social scientists. If one looks at the work of say, geographer Atiya Habeeb Kidwai on Calcutta, one can see the connecting arc of concerns between her work and the early pioneering investigations of sociologist Nirmal Kumar Bose.[16] Kidwai showed that despite Calcutta's premier status, the nature of its economy was not industrial, most of the economic activity was related to trade and services. The implication of her argument was that British colonial rule had failed to industrialize and modernize the Indian economy and this had led to the skewed nature of urbanization in colonial India. Bose had used the census to map spaces and delineate the emerging morphology of Calcutta. This too was important since settlement patterns determined the shape and form of colonial cities and the nature of urbanity. Censuses remain vital to the study of colonial cities but urban and planning historians today are likely to approach the matter a little differently.

The relentless quest by the colonial government to gather data also produced a plethora of municipal reports, sanitary commissions, health reports, surveys, maps—an archive crucial to understanding colonial spaces. One influential reading of the material following Michel Foucault and Alain Corbin has pitched this discourse on urban spaces as a binary between the filthy and clean city, between disorder and order (where filth and disorder are inextricably linked).[17] The generation of this discourse was a response by the state to epidemics (notably cholera, malaria, plague) in the nineteenth century The colonial state in India was typically heavy-handed—it prised open neighbourhoods, ran diagonals, bulldozed densely built areas, created broad corridors and sanitary voids. The goal was circulation of air, sanitation, and better accessibility. Crisis management of epidemics by the colonial state in India enabled it to control and effect the nature of urban spaces decisively.

Mercantile activity and the needs of modern administration also reorganized spaces in the city which led to a gradual separation of places of work from places of residence. This signified a profound shift and a rearrangement of the spatial structure of the city. Historians drawing on the ideas of Max Weber have argued that the evolution of the modern city led to a division between spaces of production and spaces of consumption. Even if this feature did not unravel quite so clearly in colonial cities in India, a related feature which was more visible was a new concentration of property (private wealth) and sovereignty (political authority) signalling a new political reality.[18] In Calcutta, for instance, the centre of the city became known as the 'office para' where government and the offices of mercantile firms were concentrated. Planners responded to these developments constructing functional zones in the city that signified the rational use of space. Connectivity and the circulation of goods and services became a primary concern. In a related development in American planning practice, zoning became an important category in planning which was adopted by planners all over the world. Zone became all that its 'other' was not. Mixed spaces in cities which combined residence with retail were now condemned as unproductive, chaotic, and backward.

The overwhelming economic reality in the colonial city was however wage labour and it represented a new form of labouring. Examples included work in offices, factories, workshops, casual employment, domestic service, and in the new entertainment industry like theatre and cinema. Women, though a tiny minority of the formal labour force were significant in this sector, their entry into the modern economy profoundly disturbed the old patriarchal order, unsettled domesticity, questioning the nature of work. The unsettling of patriarchy was reflected in the contentious nature of the public sphere and print cultures in the colonial city.

Wage labour indicated a profound shift in the relationship between the propertied and the labouring poor in the colonial city. Previously this relationship had been mediated through ties of village and caste and through patronage of festivals by the elite, reflected in the spatial structure of urban settlements. Landlords settled the labouring poor around their mansions in the late eighteenth and early nineteenth centuries in Calcutta, drawing sharp comments about the mix of the high and the low from British observers.[19] By the end of the nineteenth century, slums proliferated where the relationship was much more impersonal and the landlords connected with the poor through the mechanism of rent. Slums in effect became a pool where casual labour could be recruited.[20] The escalating price of real estate often became a flash point for conflict between the working classes and landlords and was an underlying cause for communal tension as in the Talla Riots of 1898 in Calcutta studied by Dipesh Chakrabarty.[21] The rise of the homeless in the city was also a modern phenomenon which profoundly defined space in the city.[22] All these factors led the governing classes to call for order and a more comprehensive and connected city plan. The ruling elite, both colonial and indigenous, supported and approved the rationalizing impulse of the market and real estate to establish modern spaces. They threw their weight behind modern planning schemes and were complicit in using town planning as an instrument for the demolition of slums in cities.

However, the clearing of spaces in the city and the norms these were creating for planning were not just a functional response to the changing dynamic of the colonial city. The establishment of new spaces were impulsively symbolic as well. The *Maidan* (eighteenth century) in Calcutta, Marina (nineteenth century) in Madras, Marine Drive and Central Vista (twentieth century) in Bombay and New Delhi respectively aligned the city to new histories or gestured to new centres of power. In Calcutta, the *Maidan,* popularly known in Bengali as *Gorer Maath,* was a large area fronting Fort William (1781). This enormous space in the middle of the city defied all logic of an open space in the city. The need to create a straight line of fire should the 'natives' rise in revolt had quickly lost its function after the decisive defeat of the last Bengal Nawab Sirajudaullah in 1757. The *Maidan* instead became the 'lung' of the congested city besieged by miasmas, malarias, and epidemics. Importantly this vast sanitary void came to symbolize distance and the lofty power of the colonial state. Spaces in the city were acquiring new meanings. This is where planning and the modern plan came in. The plan promised to cohere the city anew. It would rationalize and make functional these emerging spaces in more efficient ways. Structures like monuments, avenues, parks, water bodies would generate a new symbolic order. Categories were invented to 'read' these spaces which determined state policy and the way urban dwellers related to the city.[23] Planning (and plans) were utopian, i.e. they projected the present into the future. We need to ask: what consequences did they have for cities?

In India, as the preceding paragraphs have indicated, it was the interventionist nature of the colonial state which determined decisively the way city spaces evolved over time. Pacification and cleanliness fused together driving urban policy. This history is depressing: land acquisition, demolitions, and displacement. Colonial planning was the legacy of three important events—the Revolt of 1857, the plague epidemic of 1896, and the transfer of the capital from Calcutta to Delhi in 1911. New Delhi was built adjacent to the old city of Shahjahanabad in accordance to a preconceived plan and for this reason it finds a place as 'planning' in urban histories. However, the move to reorganize spaces in the city had begun long before as the examples of 1857 and 1896 show. Significantly, the close association and predominant role of the colonial state in India indicated the deeply political nature of urban planning in colonial India.

All three events established the very modern nature of town planning in India not only because they happened in the second half of the nineteenth century but also because of the way in which modern technology played a vital role. The most dramatic example is the advent of the railway in the city. This not only established the significant impact of modern technology but also its instrumental role in determining spaces. The railway was hailed as the town planner extraordinaire in the nineteenth century—clearing spaces, demolishing slums, laying down new lines of development. Two principles of planning were adopted by city planners from the railways (the railways arrived before critical planning became the norm in the twentieth century). Railways laid bare that connectivity was vital to the economy of cities. Railway networks were built by colonizing land and this too set an important precedent for cities where acquisition, demolition and rebuilding were seen as key to refurbishing, repurposing, and modernizing cities. In Calcutta, in the early part of the twentieth century, there was serious talk about razing to the ground the oldest business locality, the congested Barrabazar, to make way for a central railway station.[24] John Kellett and Anthony Wohl have written and theorized about this for the Victorian city and have shown how public spaces and their regulation emerged as a crucial ingredient of town planning due to the strategic needs generated by railways.[25] The British in India invested ideologically in the railway[26] and some of the most grand and monumental buildings were colonial railway stations, an enduring legacy of the Raj.[27] Railway stations emerged as examples of structured and regulated public spaces. The British themselves saw railway stations as islands of rational rule in the sea of traditional and backward India.

The most extraordinary use of railways was political. Delhi was the most dramatic example explored in the pioneering essay by Narayani Gupta.[28] Delhi was the epicentre of revolt in 1857 and after a bloody battle the British recaptured the city. The colonial government was determined that the city should not be able to rise against the rulers again. One advantage of Delhi was that it was enclosed by a wall, which made it invincible to attacks from outside—the British knew this only too well, having to camp for months outside the city before it could be re-taken. Plans for post-1857 reconstruction of Delhi by the government decided to run the new railway line through the northern part of the walled city. This permanently broke the fused and closed character of Delhi, ensuring that the city would never be able to fortify again. Interestingly, having imposed a military peace on the city, the imperatives of restructuring the bruised town took on other agendas. Maps and photographs of re-building in post 1857 Delhi show that large areas around the Red Fort (the Mughal palace and symbolic centre of political power) had been demolished. Areas around the Jama Masjid, another important religious and cultural centre, were razed to the ground and replaced by formal rectangular parks dotted with gazebos. Clearly the circulation of air and sanitary needs had overtaken strategic needs of defence. The British themselves moved out of the city and built a spacious Civil Lines outside the old city. The separation of spaces took on a new meaning in colonial India. Daniel Headrick has commented that colonial administrations failed to separate the germs from the people; instead they ended up separating those with germs from those without.[29] Cantonments were no longer mere barracks for billeting troops. Detached from the old towns they were laid out generously along grids. Houses had enormous compounds and segregation of the ruling class was implemented through separation of living quarters. Institutions like the club, church, library, department store further enhanced this segregation. As a sanitized space the cantonment/civil lines stood in sharp contrast to the older Indian towns and cities.

Railways were visible. But the other forms of ubiquitous modern technology lay underground and were hidden: sanitation and water supply. Here the extraordinary network of tunnels below the ground showcased the latest in engineering where knowledge of topography, geology and hydraulics fused into a grand scaffolding beneath the city. Asa Briggs, the well-known British historian, has commented that unable to control the chaos of market society, the state retreated underground to achieve order.[30] Unencumbered by conflicting rights over property, the writ of the state was unchallenged underground where it was sovereign. The history of sewage and water supply was however not a confident story of progress in science and technology. There were retreats and mistakes and a trail of victims. In Calcutta uncertain science and local enthusiasm installed the water supply system without adequately providing for drainage, resulting in water-logging and rise in diseases.[31] Another extraordinary impact was the loss of livelihoods. Simm's *Report of the Establishment of Water Works to Supply the City of Calcutta* (1848) casually mentioned that a few thousand *bhisties* (water carriers) would lose their jobs when the city transited to the piped water system.[32] This is as good an example of deindustrialization as any.

Plague (1896) indicated the failure of the colonial state and the inability to determine and regulate spaces. That is why there was a renewed attempt at making its presence felt. Sanitation, road building, regulatory provisions for spaces, i.e. all the instruments of modern planning, were brought together in a range of institutions with new powers. The response of the state was to renew its control of spaces through the setting up of new institutions. The innocuous sounding Improvement Trusts which were set up first in Bombay (1898), then in Calcutta (1911) and then all over India were unique institutions with no precedents in planning history and which go unmentioned in general surveys of planning. They wielded extraordinary powers. Improvement Trusts were ostensibly inspired by parent institutions in Britain. Important precedents for the Bombay Improvement Trust were Glasgow and Edinburgh.[33] But instead of looking for precedents why not look at the histories? There is no doubt that the hard wedge of demolition and displacement in India made Improvement Trusts qualitatively different from the experience of the metropolis. Here there were no organized trade unions or enfranchised rate payers to oppose schemes floated by the state. Improvement Trusts in India had enormous powers and their natures were overtly determined by the presence of the white ruling establishment who were unhappy about concessions made to elected Indian representatives. Improvement Trusts were detached from any pressures and contacts with Indian representatives and all decision making was firmly in European hands. The plague provided just the kind of excuse that would nicely justify a reversal of the move towards inclusion and representation of Indians. The Improvement Trusts wanted to clear public spaces to control disease. But their reach ran to private spaces as well. In breaching the delicate line between the public and private, they ran foul of the complex rules that governed purity and pollution in Indian society.[34] When the authorities forcibly entered the Indian home in Bombay and Pune and ejected the sick and quarantined them, a new precedent was set for colonial intervention. This move elicited a violent reaction and led to the assassination of Plague Commissioner Rand

and military assistant Ayerst by the Chapekar brothers. Indians, especially the emerging bourgeoisie in cities and towns, too had been wary of such moves and a remarkable petition in 1889 by Calcutta citizens had already talked about the breach of privacy by the state and had warned of the consequences.[35] In 1911, the imperious reach of the Calcutta Improvement Trust provoked nationalists from Surendranath Banerjee to C.R. Das to take a stand against the arbitrary powers of the Trust.[36] As urban planning entrenched itself in the cities, the regulation of public spaces extended to the private and domestic as well. The justification was the larger public good. This view was widespread and even Indians found it convincing. True, the opposition to the Improvement Trusts took on nationalist hues but despite reservations, a larger consensus was emerging among the Indian middle classes about the benefits of modern sanitary standards and they started reforming their domestic habits like eating, dress, leisure hours, hygiene. The regulation of the body linked to the reform of urban spaces marked the distinctive modernity of urban planning.[37]

As the need for security from the rebellious population diminished, the model of the cantonment became even more attractive and found its spectacular fruition in Lutyens' plan for New Delhi. The layout and the growth of spaces like this had the effect of segregating European enclaves from the native city and this approach persisted. Much later the push to build suburbs showcased the same principles in planning. With the transfer of the capital to Delhi, the breach was complete. Lutyens' plan drew a *cordon sanitaire* around the old city in the form of a broad road. Across this his classical vision took shape through stunning vistas, radiating lines, monumental buildings. This township was for the governing classes; the lower bureaucracy was accommodated in the fringes in carefully calibrated housing blocks where class and status were clearly marked out.

Colonial planning set important precedents for modern planning. Planning was a way to order urban space. Planners began with restructuring and creating public spaces but their ambit soon reached the domain of the private and domestic. This breach, justified in the name of public health and the larger public good, became the norm. The consequences were violent and the brunt was felt by working class inhabitants in towns and cities who had few resources to resist. Historians of planning argue that to understand the nature of cities it is important to understand this dynamic—for cities get their character not only from the built form but also the way urban spaces are distributed and regulated. Indian cities in the north especially, experienced major change in the 1940s as war, famine, riots, Partition and Independence undid the settled principles of colonial planning. To address the spatial problems in post-colonial India, bureaucrats and planners had to think anew about spatial order.

Notes

1. *Town Planning Conference, London 10–15 October 1910, Transactions,* London: RIBA, 1911.
2. Norma Evenson, *Indian Metropolis: A View Toward the West,* Delhi: Oxford University Press, 1989; R.K. Home, 'Town Planning and Garden Cities in the British Colonial Empire 1910–1940', *Planning Perspectives,* vol. 5, no. 1, January 1990.
3. Barbara D. Metcalf and Thomas D. Metcalf, *Concise History of India,* Cambridge: Cambridge University Press, 2006, p. 91.
4. Jaqueline Tyrwhitt, ed., *Patrick Geddes in India,* London: Lund Humphries, 1947.
5. T.J. Clark, *The Painting of Modern Life: Manet and His Followers,* London: Thames and Hudson, 1985; Alain Corbin, *Time, Desire and Horror, Towards a History of Senses,* Cambridge: Polity Press, 1995.
6. Francoise Choay, *The Modern City: Planning in the Nineteenth Century,* London: Studio Vista, 1970, p. 23.

7. Christian Topalov, 'From the "Social Question" to "Urban Problems": Reformers and the Working Classes at the Turn of the Nineteenth Century', *International Social Science Journal*, vol. 125, August 1990, p. 321.
8. Anthony King, 'Exporting Planning, the Colonial and Neo-colonial Experience', in *Shaping an Urban World*, ed. Gordon Cherry, London: Mansell, 1980, p. 210.
9. Choay, *The Modern City*, p. 17.
10. The figure of the *flaneur* emerged as a new way to experience the city.
11. Partho Datta, *Planning the City, Urbanization and Reform in Calcutta c.1800–c.1940*, Delhi: Tulika Books, 2012, p. 269.
12. Robert Fishman, *Urban Utopias in the Twentieth Century: Ebenezer Howard, Frank Wright and Le Corbusier*, New York: Basic Books, 1977.
13. Hampstead in London, designed by Raymond Unwin, was a successful example of Garden City principles adopted to an upper-class residential suburb.
14. Robert Grant Irving, *Imperial Summer, Lutyens, Baker and Imperial Delhi*, Delhi: Oxford University Press, 1981; Evenson, *The Indian Metropolis.*
15. King, 'Exporting Planning', p. 210.
16. Atiya Habeeb Kidwai, 'Urban Atrophy in Colonial India, Some Demographic Indicators' in *The City in Indian History*, ed. Indu Banga, New Delhi: Manohar, 1991; Nirmal Kumar Bose, 'Calcutta, a Premature City', in *Cities*, Harmondsworth: Penguin, 1965 and *Calcutta 1964: A Social Survey*, Bombay: Lalvani Publishing House, 1968.
17. Michel Foucault, 'The Politics of Health in the Eighteenth Century', in *Power/Knowledge, Selected Interviews and Other Writings, 1972–1977*, Brighton: Harvester Press, 1977; Alain Corbin, *The Foul and the Fragrant, Odor and the French Social Imagination*, Cambridge, Mass: Harvard University Press, 1986.
18. Ira Katznelson, 'The Centrality of the City in Social Theory', in *The Divided Heritage, Themes and Problems in German Modernism* ed. Irit Rogoff, Cambridge: Cambridge University Press, 1991.

19. Mrs. Nathaniel Kindersley (1768) wrote: '...the appearance of the best houses is spoiled by the little straw huts, and such sort of encumbrances, which are built up by the servants for themselves to sleep in...' quoted in P. Thankappan Nair, *Calcutta Corporation At a Glance,* Calcutta: Calcutta Corporation, 1989, p. 164.
20. E.J. Hobsbawm quoted in H.J. Dyos, 'The Slums of Victorian London', *Victorian Studies,* vol. 11, no. 1, September 1967, p. 34.
21. Dipesh Chakrabarty, 'Communal Riots and Labour, Bengal Jute Mill-Hands in the 1890s', *Past and Present,* vol. 91, May 1981.
22. Datta, *Planning the City,* p. 130; Daniel Buchanan, *The Development of Capitalist Enterprise in India,* New York: Macmillan, 1934, pp. 244–5.
23. One such category was 'salubrity'. Michel Foucault has written, 'Salubrity referred to the state of the environment and those factors of it which made the improvement of health possible'. He adds that it was 'in connection with this that the concept of public health appeared, as a technique for controlling and modifying those elements of the environment which might promote that health, or on the contrary harm it'. Michel Foucault, 'The Birth of Social Medicine' in *Power, Essential Works of Foucault,* vol. 3, ed. James D. Faubion, London: Penguin Books, 2002, p. 149.
24. Datta, *Planning the City,* p. 193.
25. John R. Kellett, *The Impact of Railways on Victorian Cities,* London: Routledge and Kegan Paul, 1969; Anthony Wohl, *The Eternal Slum,* London: Edwin Arnold, 1977.
26. Michael Satow and Ray Desmond, *Railways of the Raj,* London: Scholar Press, 1980; Lajpat Jagga, 'Colonial Railwaymen and British Rule—Railway Labour Agitation in India, 1919–1922', in *Indian Left, Critical Appraisals,* ed. Bipan Chandra, Delhi: Vikas, 1983.
27. Vinoo N. Mathur, *Indian Railway Building, Heritage, History and Beyond,* Delhi: Niyogi Books, 2022.

28. Narayani Gupta, 'Military Security and Urban Development, A Case Study of Delhi 1857–1912', *Modern Asian Studies,* vol. 5, no. 1, 1971.
29. Daniel R. Headrick, *Tentacles of Progress, Technology Transfer in the Age of Imperialism 1850–1940,* New York: Oxford University Press, 1988, p. 147.
30. Asa Briggs, *Victorian Cities,* Harmondsworth: Penguin, 1968, pp. 16–17.
31. Datta, *Planning the City,* p. 154.
32. Ibid., p. 152.
33. Prashant Kidambi, *The Making of an Indian Metropolis, Colonial Governance and Public Culture in Bombay 1890–1920,* London: Routledge, 2007; Caroline Arnold, 'Bombay Improvement Trust, Bombay Millowners and the Debate over Housing Bombay's Millworkers 1896–1918', *Essays in Business and Economic History,* vol. XXX, 2012; P.J. Smith, 'Planning as Environmental Improvement: Slum Clearance in Victorian Edinburgh' in *The Rise of Modern Urban Planning 1800–1914,* ed. Anthony Sutcliffe, London: Mansell, 1980.
34. Dipesh Chakrabarty, 'Open Space/Public Space, Garbage, Modernity and India, *South Asia,* vol. XIV, no. 1, 1991; Sudipto Kaviraj, 'Filth and Public Sphere, Concepts and Practices about Space in Calcutta', *Public Culture,* vol. X, no. 1, 1997.
35. Datta, *Planning the City,* p. 183.
36. Ibid., pp. 221–2.
37. Timothy Mitchell, *Colonising Egypt,* Berkeley: University of California Press, 1991, p. xii; Datta, *Planning the City,* p. 111.

6

Patrick Geddes, Town Planner?

The Nature and Scope of His Work in India, 1914–1923

HELEN MELLER

PATRICK GEDDES did not think of himself primarily as a planner. A creative and original thinker, who had studied the natural sciences, especially the theory of evolution and the 'life forces' that produce it, he was also a pioneer of the sociology of cities, concerned with the social consequences of mass urbanization, the major transformation happening in his lifetime. He perceived how it was transforming the natural and built environment and with it, the culture and well-being of human society. He belonged to a generation of writers, academics, and philanthropists who were piecing together a critique of the Industrial Revolution (a term

*I am delighted to contribute to Professor Narayani Gupta's festschrift volume. We have been friends for more than half a century and encouraged each other with our work for which I am so grateful. I am in awe at what she has achieved in her many publications, her teaching and her conservation work for India's built heritage (INTACH) and most of all the inspiration she imparted to me, to her students, to anyone who cares about the built environment of the past, just how important it is to the present and future.

coined in the 1880s when Geddes was in his 30s) and some of its major negative social consequences for both people and cities. Geddes, in his evolutionary mode, invented the term 'Paleotechnic' for the Industrial Revolution stage; followed by the Neotechnic Age; and finally, what he hoped for in his own lifetime, an incipient Eutechnic age (Eu meaning 'good') when the social and cultural welfare of citizens and the cities they lived in would be paramount.[1]

He created a study centre with practical activities to work out his methods and to figure out ways to promote this objective. In 1892 he acquired the building that became his Outlook Tower Museum in Edinburgh: a study centre for his civic 'social gospel'. Geddes' 'social civic gospel' was how his work was understood by his followers. His mission was to awaken citizens of the world to the prospect that modern technology and knowledge could transform the process of world urbanization from a destructive force of people, place and the natural environment to the opposite: cities, citizens and the natural environment thriving into the future. He used practical methods in his planning work and a philosophy for pedagogical purposes, both outlined in lectures he gave from 1904 to 1906 titled 'Civics: As Applied Sociology'.[2] His version of sociological studies needed volunteers and students to have greater understanding of the evolutionary future. The 'social civic gospel' was his message to recruit citizens to this urgent cause.

He gained much support from Edinburgh students and one of them, Victor Branford, a rich businessman and sociologist himself, founded the British Sociological Society in London in 1903 as a vehicle to promote his ideas. The pioneering years of British sociology were crowded with many groups and societies seeking ways to improve the social welfare and cultural life of citizens. It was a period when there was an overarching philosophy of idealism also amongst British sociologists, for example, E.J. Urwick and

L.T. Hobhouse, both at the London School of Economics, sustaining citizen social workers and academics alike. Geddes gave major lectures at the Sociological Society each year from 1904 to 1907 on 'Civics: As Applied Sociology' in which he accepted he was idealistic but also argued persuasively that his ideas were practically achievable.[3]

His focus on the practical application of his ideas ruled him out of becoming a leading sociologist in Britain among academic social scientists. However, a group of architects, involved in the nascent town planning movement of the time, were much more responsive to the practical side of his work. They became not only interested, but desperate to recruit him to their cause as they were facing a challenge. The Liberal government had just passed the 1909 Housing and Town Planning Act, the first such act on the statute book. The architects had not been consulted: worse still, they did not know what role they might have in housing and town planning in the future. The Royal Institute of British Architects had to act urgently. The world's first ever International Conference on Town Planning was organized in London in 1910 with the hope to impress the government and hide the lack of interest they had previously shown in planning.[4]

There was, however, a major problem. Most international speakers were happy to come with exhibits of their work and the galleries of the Royal Academy were duly hired. But British architects had nothing to exhibit. The great modern idea of the British had been the Garden City. Already much touted around the world, it could not be the big idea this time. Raymond Unwin, the senior architect in charge of the exhibitions, had been to Edinburgh to see Geddes' work in his Outlook Tower and recognized that his work had a sociological tendency that would fit the Housing and Town Planning Act. He invited Geddes to bring his exhibition material to London where he was given a small gallery to himself at the Academy.[5] Geddes was delighted. During the conference, he sat daily in his gallery, his material all around him, talking about his civic 'social gospel' to anyone who would listen. The material from the Outlook Tower was piecemeal: maps, drawings, pencil sketches, scraps of paper making miscellaneous points.

What was crucial was Geddes' sustained discourse on his sociological viewpoint and the objectives of the civic 'social gospel' to achieve a better future. He suggested that for urban environments to evolve in a healthy and sustainable manner, their history and culture, economic base, local environments, geological and natural features needed to be understood and developed in a sustainable manner. He introduced his audience to the idea of the Region and the specific geographical context each region gave to the cities within it. He argued that, as cities grew in industrial regions, their suburbs could become connected with the suburbs of adjoining cities. He coined the term 'conurbation' for this phenomenon and insisted it should be planned in a way that sustained the quality of life of people and environment. A regional planning authority would be able to guide this process. Sometimes, he managed to confuse many international delegates with his synoptic view of planning. Patrick Abercrombie, then a young architect from Liverpool University, gave a gleeful account of the consequences:

> It is safe to say that the modern practice of town planning in this country would have been a much simpler thing if it had not been for Geddes. There was a time when it seemed only necessary to shake up in a bottle the German town-extension plan; the Parisian Boulevard and Vista; and the English Garden Village to produce a mechanical mixture which might be applied indiscriminately and beneficially to every town in the country, thus would it be town-planned in accord to the most up-to-date notions. Pleasing dream! First shattered by Geddes emerging from his Outlook Tower in the frozen North at the great Town Planning Exhibition of 1910.[5]

Abercrombie might have thought Geddes' ideas were 'shattering', indeed excellent, but few understood what he was talking about. Yet Geddes was already perfectly clear that to achieve his 'Eutechnic' age just making plans for single cities was not enough. The people, including rural dwellers in the hinterlands, had to be at the forefront of what was done and how it would be done. He did not deviate from how he saw this whether he was in London or later in India: *town planning* had to be the *regulator* of architecture, and his *sociological civics* to be the *regulator* and *educational influence* on any discussion of *town planning*.

This was not a congenial prospect for architects. Patrick Abercombie, then Editor of the *Town Planning Review*, tried to overcome resistance. He had picked up Geddes' facility for composing simple 'mantras', to help architects understand how all the elements could be brought together. How to start planning, for example, was summed up as 'Survey, Diagnosis, Plan'. Abercrombie published an article in the *Town Planning Review*, offering his readers what was meant by these terms for the planning process which proved a lifeline to many architects that lasted through both world wars. After the Second World War, architects were still muttering 'survey, diagnosis, plan', though by then they were under the tutorship of Jacqueline Tyrwhitt, acting director of a spin-off organization of London's Architectural Association: Association for Planning and Regional Reconstruction. She used many of Geddes' mantras: '*conservative surgery*', '*a sociological approach*' '*planning for health*'—all of which she illustrated with short extracts from the Indian Reports that she actually rewrote to update his writing style, in her influential little book, *Patrick Geddes in India.*[6]

The path that took Geddes to India was almost as serendipitous as his invitation to the 1910 Conference. The two architects involved with Geddes at that conference continued to help him with his civic 'social gospel' campaign. Raymond Unwin enrolled Geddes in his newly established Town Planning Institute in London in 1913, but crucially, as a sociologist (the only one!), not a planner. H.V. Lanchester, as an old 'India' hand, had an architectural office in Lucknow and would give much practical help to Geddes during his decade in India. Both men supported Geddes' next big idea, that is, to make his 1910 Cities and Town Planning Exhibition peripatetic in the UK, taking it to any city that invited him. This was an important step in promoting his ideas. Over the next four years, he was invited to Edinburgh, to Dublin twice and to Belfast. In Edinburgh he met Lord Pentland, Secretary of State for Scotland. As a 'social welfare' Liberal, Pentland was impressed by Geddes' exhibition and when he was appointed Governor of Madras in 1914, invited him to bring his exhibition to India.

Before he went, Geddes had a resounding international success in promoting his civic 'social gospel'. He took his Cities and Town Planning Exhibition to the Ghent World Exposition of 1913 to attend a congress organized within it: Le Premier Congres International et Exposition Comparée des Villes.[7] Sessions were in French, German, and English. Held under the looming shadow of world war, many found it one of the most exciting conferences they had ever experienced. It was a dramatic promotion of the Peace Movement. Not a town planning congress as such, it focused on cities across the world and their possible futures. The hope was that cities could form a 'Union Internationale des Villes' to share knowledge about best practices for the future since states were agents for war, not peace. It was attended by mayors, politicians, civil engineers, historians, economists, town planners, academics, agriculturists, city officials, philanthropists, scientists, doctors, and a phalanx of European architects including Unwin and Lanchester. Geddes' exhibition was well received, and he was awarded a gold medal.[8]

Geddes then left for India with his eldest son, Alastair, to take up Pentland's invitation—the challenge of working in India. It was not an unusual step in the world of social welfare work in the British Empire. Unease had been growing in Britain for some time about colonial rule and its deficiencies. There were increasing numbers of British organizations, volunteers, and professionals operating across the British Empire, but especially in India, including young doctors and nurses, social workers, educationalists, and public health experts. This generosity of spirit was a universally appreciated contribution from the West to the East and was seen as such by Indians. No politics was involved. Geddes had met leading Indians seeking just this kind of help, especially at the Exposition Universelle Internationale de 1900 in Paris. Most famous among them was Rabindranath Tagore, who was promoting his project for a new national university for India at Santiniketan in Bengal. Tagore got help from Geddes in designing the campus and even more from his younger son Arthur who worked tirelessly on the project with Leonard Elmhirst, philanthropist and co-worker.

In Paris, Tagore promised Geddes an introduction to the former missionary C.F. Andrews, now engaged in facilitating contacts between those from Britain wanting to engage in social welfare work in India and Indians. Since 1914, Andrews had been able to work more with Rabindranath Tagore and Gandhi, becoming close friends with both. These three men believed East and West could meet on a basis of goodwill through projects useful to India's future.[9] This was exactly what Geddes wanted to do. He had already found a kindred spirit at the Paris Exposition. Sir Jagadish Bose, a leading natural scientist, was raising funds for his Indian Scientific Institute in Calcutta. Supportive of each other in their different missions, Geddes and Bose became good friends. When Bose finally got his Institute in 1917, he asked Geddes to write his speech for the opening ceremony. Geddes himself, dressed in Indian clothes, was the only European present. In 1920, Geddes published a biography of Bose, celebrating his pioneering commitment to the future India, and raising the possibility that Indian-based research in the natural sciences might bring fresh insights to those working in the western tradition.

Geddes wanted to do the reverse: adapt his civic 'social gospel' for the people, the culture, the climate, and traditions of India. He was not going to India to boost Western planning practices and the methods of City Improvements Trusts. On the contrary, he believed his socio-biological approach could provide effective solutions for Indian problems. His Cities and Town Planning Exhibition would offer an idea of 'modernity' that would revivify Indian citizens to think about their future. Better public health and sanitation, cleaner water supplies, simpler plans for social housing and open spaces for the well-being of the people especially children, and finally conservation of historic buildings that could all become inspirational again in community life. Geddes saw this as social ecology—the links between living organisms and their surroundings.[10] This was a 'modernity' totally different from the 'Modernism' that was beginning to sweep Western architects and planners off their feet. Idealist? Yes, but not more than the Modern Movement in the first decades of the twentieth century. The split between these two visions of the future would become acute when India became an independent nation after the Second World War, led by a Western educated elite with the Congress Party determined to bury the past.

However, on reaching India in 1914, Geddes was shocked to find he had lost his Cities and Town Planning Exhibition, the cargo ship carrying it torpedoed by a German destroyer. But typically, Geddes turned this misfortune into an opportunity. As he had never been to India before, he was determined to visit as many cities as possible to learn as much about them as he could. Powers of acute observation were his greatest skill, honed over a lifetime of travel, analysing cities as he walked around them. He embarked on travel across the length and breadth of the continent. He particularly enjoyed the cities of the south: the lively streets, the colours and exuberance, the mixing of religious and spiritual concerns in daily life, especially the temples with their water tanks and gardens where people came to bathe, to meet, to pray. The Dravidian temples he found in abundance drew his greatest admiration for their magnificence: '[Even] the commonest street is given order and beauty by the simply pillared mantapam with which its vista so often terminates: or is raised to dignity even to sublimity, when it leads up to a mighty many storied Gopuram, with manifold exuberance of sculpture…'[11]

His travels encouraged his belief that his socio-biological approach would work in Indian cities. But with the loss of his exhibition, how was he going to proceed? Lanchester in London in 1914 came to his rescue, asking friends for material for a second Cities and Town Planning Exhibition to send to India. He returned himself to India in 1915 and was to join Geddes in Madras as Pentland had offered him a contract as Town Planner of Madras State. As this was his first task as Town Planner for Madras, Lanchester undertook a Geddesian style 'Survey' of the city of Madras. This was a benefit to Geddes. In all his subsequent work in India, he recommended planners should look at Lanchester's 'Survey of Madras' which he published as an example of the technique since he never had the time nor the team of assistants to do the work for each city he was planning. [12]

Lanchester also made sure that Geddes' first volume of reports for twelve small towns in Madras State was published. These reports were slight; Geddes had made notes after walking around them. But the volume earned him a commission from Bombay State. It was here that Geddes, visiting six towns in this British Presidency, first came up against hostility from British civil engineers. Five towns were small but the sixth, Ahmadabad, the 'Cottonopolis' of India, was more like a large Manchester than any other Indian city. The British engineers wanted more roads, the destruction of houses in their way, and the removal of the old city walls. Geddes tried to save the walls based on their historical importance. He lost the battle, but the plans he made for these six towns were reprinted in 1965, a sign that his ideas lived on for a long time afterwards.

He came up against a similar problem in a tiny independent state whose capital city was Baroda. Maharaja Gaekwad was a modernizer and had provided institutions and parks for the welfare of his people. But in the middle of Baroda was an ancient fort. It had become the business district, overcrowded, stifling in the hot season and with constant traffic congestion. The maharaja wanted to open it up and take the walls down. Geddes wanted the walls to stay. He wanted the 'old world' charm of the city to be preserved for citizens of the future. He offered alternatives: a new suburb for housing and economic development plans for the nearby village of Anandpura which could have been made to work. He was not successful. These failures, however, did not dent his reputation, and from 1916 to 1918 commissions poured in and he wrote many reports.

Reports for two cities in particular offer well known examples of his greatest successes. These were (three) Reports for Lucknow in the United Provinces, under British rule; the second, the most famous, his two-volume Report for Indore, a city within the Central India Agency, ruled by the Maharaja Holkar, Tukoji Rao III. In both he used his socio-biological approach and was determined to reach the citizens. His first visit to Lucknow in 1917 was to deal with heavy flooding during the monsoon. British engineers had filled tanks with rubble to obliterate the habitat of malarial mosquitoes. Geddes reopened the tanks and ensured the acquisition of many ducks to eat the mosquito larvae, one of his best socio-biological solutions. Also in Lucknow, he persuaded the British Chief Engineer to stop demolishing overcrowded housing: the only time he succeeded in changing a British official's mind! This generated supportive citizen responses to his work. He was able to create Lucknow's own 'City Exhibition' in the Council Chamber of the Town Hall with drawings and plans made by Lanchester from his Lucknow office. His final gift to Lucknow was a zoological park for the recreation and mental well-being of people and animals. It was enthusiastically received.

Geddes' work in Indore, carried out in 1917 and published in 1918, was on a much larger scale than Lucknow. He dedicated it to the memory of his wife and son, who both died in 1917, his wife dying of enteric fever in Darjeeling and his son on the Western Front just three months later. He worked like a man possessed. Indore was the central granary of India located on the central plateau. The storing of the grain encouraged rats and plagues were rife. Geddes ordered the amalgamation of the three grain stores to one site and the acquisition of many cats. Using his technical skills, Geddes read maps found in a council cupboard, left by the British Public Works Department, of a water scheme that had been constructed but not connected. Geddes was able to locate where to put standpipes, thereby connecting the system. The new water supply was a great boon and burnished his growing reputation. He was also able to use his skills in reading landscape and geography to plot the most desirable direction for future expansion of the city which in fact proved efficacious for the growth of the city over the next century.[13]

In 1917, he wanted to revitalize the people and their engagement with their city. He started with the road sweepers, the lowest status workers. He wanted them to understand their work was the most vital activity of all for the health and well-being of the city and to take pride in their work and keep the city clean. At Diwali, he organized a festival which became famous, as a part of which he held a competition for the cleanest street and rode the white elephant, as Maharaja for the day, with a procession through the cleanest one. At the end of the day, a bonfire burnt the effigy of a giant rat. This ceremony took place every year for more than a decade afterwards. The second volume of his Report gave considerable space to a project for a university for central India to be located in Indore.[14] He had been advocating for new universities for India for many years different from the universities of the West. He wanted more than just high-level specialist academic research and teaching. He wanted a synthesis of disciplines to build a holistic education for students. Such an institution should also offer practical training and skills of vital importance for cities and their future such as surveying, gardening, dealing with the care of rivers, etc.

His last significant achievement was his appointment to the first Chair in Sociology at Bombay University in 1919. He named it the Chair of Sociology and Civics. But he was still too busy on plans to devote enough time to the development of his work at the university. His career in India was coming towards an end. One of his last commissions was for Barra Bazar Improvement in Calcutta, a difficult brief to manage. The best analysis of his Report is in Partho Datta's, *Planning the City*.[15]

Notes

1. Patrick Geddes, *Cities in Evolution: An Introduction to the Town Planning Movement and to the Study of Civics,* London: Ernest Benn Ltd., 1915, pp. 60–83; repr., 1968, Introduction by Percy Johnson-Marshall.
2. Helen Meller, ed., *The Ideal City,* Leicester: Leicester University Press, 1979, pp. 75–183.
3. Ibid., pp. 67–174.
4. William Whyte, 'Introduction', *Transactions of the RIBA Town Planning Conference,* London, 1910.

5. P. Abercrombie in *The Interpreter: Geddes: The Man and his Gospel,* ed. Amelia Defries, London: George Routledge and Sons Ltd., 1927, pp. 322–3.
6. Jaqueline Tyrwhitt, ed., *Patrick Geddes in India,* London: Lund Humphries, 1947. Photos by Anthony Kenny, professional photographer for Condé Nast and Vogue, in India still waiting demobilization.
7. William Whyte, 'Introduction', *Ghent Planning Congress 1913,* 1913; repr., London and New York: Routledge, 2014.
8. Helen Meller 'Public and Private Enterprise: International Exhibitions and the Modern Town Planning Movement', *Planning Perspectives,* vol. 10, no. 3, July 1995, pp. 295–311.
9. Helen Meller, *Patrick Geddes, Social Evolutionist and City Planner,* London: Routledge, 1990, pp. 214–18.
10. Lydia Kallipoliti 'History of Ecological Design', *Research Encyclopaedia of Environmental Science,* Oxford: Oxford University Press, April 2018, pp. 1–60.
11. P. Geddes, 'The Temple Cities', *Modern Review,* vol. 25, 1919.
12. Geddes wrote about fifty reports but did not publish all of them. A collection of thirty-four published reports can now be found in the National Archives of Scotland, Edinburgh.
13. Ray Bromley, 'Introduction', *Town Planning towards City Development: A Report to the Durbar of Indore,* 2 vols; repr., Abingdon, Oxon: Routledge, 2018.
14. Ibid., pp. 239–42, 253–70.
15. Partho Datta, *Planning the City: Urbanisation and Reform in Calcutta, c1800–c1940,* Delhi: Tulika Books, 2012, pp. 256–63.

7

Modernizing Historic Cities in India

The Relevance of Patrick Geddes

A.G. KRISHNA MENON

PATRICK GEDDES (1854–1932) was a Scottish biologist, sociologist, geographer, and town planner, who thoughtfully conflated his varied disciplinary interests with his innate

*In 1990, my colleagues and I started a new School of Architecture in New Delhi to reform professional education. Its pedagogy emerged from the ideas I have discussed in this essay. The teaching of all subjects had to be reconceptualized, and to teach the History of Architecture to the undergraduate students of our fledgling School, we were fortunate that Narayani Gupta, already an established scholar of history, academic and pioneer of the heritage movement in Delhi, agreed to take the lead. She inspired our students to engage with the discipline as its stakeholders, by opening new perspectives for them to engage with and understand their historic architectural legacy.

She acquainted our students with the ideas of Patrick Geddes. To consolidate her initiative as an important tenet of the School's pedagogy, we proposed to establish a Geddes Study Centre at the School. We petitioned the British Council to gift us copies of his writings, publications and Town Planning Reports which would enable our students to access them for research. However, our experiment in architectural education failed, but that is another story. I am grateful that her engagement with our School provided me with a critical interlocutor to develop my ideas for integrating urban conservation into the practice of urban planning.

concern for the welfare of society. By so doing he developed a new language for urban planning, with a repertory of new subjects and protocols that persuasively challenged the quotidian disciplinary certitudes and goals of the urban planning of his time.

Biographers have described him as a messiah of 'humanist' urban development and influential social reformer, a 'practical genius, bold and ambitious, a precise observer and of penetrating insight'.[1] He was invited to India in 1915 to propagate his eclectic ideas, and the municipalities of the colonial and Princely States took this opportunity to seek his advice on how they could deal with local urban problems. These assignments enabled him to draft over fifty Town Planning Reports that further cemented his reputation as an iconic visionary and pragmatic town planner. In 1919, he also established the first Department of Sociology and Civics in the country, at Bombay University, which he nurtured until 1922. For these pioneering initiatives he is regarded as the father of Indian sociology and town planning.

Today his contributions are all but forgotten by the professional mainstream in India, with only a few acolytes who still consider his ideas germane or relevant. Nevertheless, he is routinely included in the syllabi of professional education and occasionally one comes across a reputed scholar who seriously engages with his ideas and suggests that they are appropriate to the resolution of contemporary urban problems.[2]

It would be simplistic to expect that, unmediated, the ideas he propagated at the turn of the last century are still able to deal with the complex problems of postcolonial urbanism. As Noah Hysler-Rubin noted: 'The general positive outlook on Geddes as a planner of good intentions, and the commonly positive approval of his plans and treatment of society, are changing with new readings of the work from more critical perspectives, although generally not those of planners.'[3]

Unfortunately, that caveat applies particularly to Indian professionals, because as Hysler-Rubin further points out, it would have entailed that they challenge 'the ideological and practical roots of modern town planning and its practice, providing much-needed critical tools for exposing hidden narratives and past agendas' that continue to dominate the disciplinary discourse.[4] This is the blind spot of the modern Indian profession; as in colonial times, it continues to uncritically rely on canonical urban planning knowledge generated by scholars remote from their urban context.

The broad understanding of the phenomenon of urbanization and many of the problems associated with it are universal, but its disciplinary axioms were developed by scholars in advanced industrial societies who had studied it empirically and then developed the protocols of urban planning in order to mitigate the problems it created. This body of knowledge is considered canonical, and was exported to much of the Global South, initially through colonization and now via globalization. This forms the foundation of disciplinary knowledge that the modern Indian profession relies on; had it, as Hysler-Rubin suggests, been critically verified by undertaking local self-reflexive studies, it would have exposed the 'hidden narratives and agendas' that subvert its objectives. It would have revealed that urbanization in India has different roots, and that many of the urban problems it generates are *sui generis*, necessitating the formulation of different urban planning strategies.

The problems of Indian cities emanate as much from the dynamics of the particular mix of traditional values and social practices rooted in society's civilizational culture, as from the unique characteristics of its post-Independence demography, economics, and politics. Geddes' 'penetrating insight' acknowledged these differences but the strategies he developed to resolve local urban problems for colonial civic authorities need to be re-examined by the postcolonial urban scholars and planners in the light of knowledge developed by modern interdisciplinary research.[5]

In essence, Geddes understood that the morphology and urbanism of Indian cities are interlinked and were the products of its own civilizational culture and defined the characteristics of indigenous urbanism. It is markedly different from that of Western cities, which is now more widely appreciated with the advent of cultural studies, whereby scholars have documented the correlation between the culture and built environment in diverse societies to create a rich body of literature on the subject.[6] Engaging with this sympathetically would have opened provocative possibilities for imagining an authentically indigenous modernity that would have satisfied the expectations of local societies: this was the 'humanistic' credo that Geddes hoped to propagate.

Today, however, any manifestation of indigenous urbanism is either studiously ignored by academics or treated with hostility by Indian professionals and civic authorities, thus replicating the attitude of colonial scholars and administrators. Yet this affinity has not been critically examined; rather than exploring the potential of indigenous modernism, the profession remains focused on following in lockstep, the first world narratives of modernity in an attempt to make Indian cities 'world-class'.[7]

Indian cities are complex entities and currently there are diverse narratives of their evolution and the development that are unfolding. At the periphery of the official gaze, other strategies of urban planning are being articulated, including the continued relevance of indigenous urbanism, but they have scarcely mediated postcolonial policy-making or piqued the curiosity of academic research, even though they offer compelling opportunities to contest the certitudes of canonical knowledge.

*

The characteristics of indigenous urbanism are a result of the evolution of pre-colonial settlements from the Indus Valley civilization, and have deep, and profound, cultural roots. At one end, these characteristics define the morphology of some of the most remarkable 'living' historic cities in the world, like Varanasi or Madurai, that continue to serve the functional and spiritual needs of modern society; and at the other, they underpin the rationale of 'unplanned' habitats, built in the interstices of contemporary planned developments. They constitute the 'soul' of the spatial imagination of pre-modern Indian society, and are so deeply ingrained that they continue to mediate many aspects of modern built environments as well. This has resulted in the Janus-faced characteristic of contemporary urbanism: the deep schism that exists between the personal preferences of residents and the professional expectations of urban planners, which has always confounded the objectives of postcolonial urban planning.

The seeds of this schism were planted over a century and half ago, when two diverse departments of the colonial government were established, one to construct new buildings and settlements, and the other to preserve the architectural legacy of the country. In July 1854, Lord Dalhousie established the Central Public Works Department (CPWD), to execute public works undertaken by the colonial government, and in 1861, Alexander Cunningham founded the Archaeological Survey of India (ASI) to preserve historic buildings in the country.

These two departments evolved independently by following British cultural and technical norms and standards. Over the years, the CPWD, and its cognate affiliates, city development authorities engaged with the needs of the built environment; in the process, they mediated the spatial imagination of society by valorizing British or 'modern' ways of building and planning, while the ASI mediated the temporal imagination by valorizing only 'dead' heritage buildings as exemplars of the country's civilizational legacy, thereby formally erasing the concept of cultural continuity. The protocols of the CPWD and the ASI decisively embedded two counterproductive propositions that have distorted the objectives of post-Independence urban development: first, pursuing the ideals of first world modernity; second, adopting the development versus conservation binary to determine the priorities in civic management. The postcolonial antipathy towards indigenous urbanism is now indelibly inscribed in the psyche of contemporary Indian architects and planners that it even determined the strategy to resolve the problems of the most venerated city in India, Varanasi, where the urban designer reflexively gutted its historic religious core in order to redevelop it in a 'modern' idiom and make it 'world-class'.[8]

Our postcolonial education system has subliminally perpetuated the belief that theory emanates from Western academia; the objective of academics (and professionals) outside the West is to simply apply it to define and resolve local urban problems. By and large, it has produced technicians, not self-reflexive urban planners who could have effectively engaged with the complex problems of Indian urbanization and thus arrived at more satisfactory strategies and outcomes. It is, therefore, not surprising that even in a resource-rich city like Delhi it is commonly believed that about 70 per cent of the development that has taken place had to be 'regularized' because it did not conform to the statutory Master Plan.

The Indian National Trust for Art and Cultural Heritage (INTACH), established in 1984, put the theoretical propositions underpinning postcolonial urban planning under critical scrutiny via the urban conservation projects they undertook and, in no small measure, contributed to redirecting the modern urban planner into according indigenous urbanism serious attention and value.

INTACH is a not-for-profit initiative of civil society interlocutors concerned about the rapid attrition of the country's rich cultural patrimony that lay outside the purview of the government. The ASI protects only about 3,600 Monuments of National Importance, which, together with those conserved by the state governments still account for a meagre 10,000 odd historic building that are officially protected. The rest, the hundreds of thousands 'unprotected' historic buildings are consequently cannibalized for building materials or outrightly destroyed to reclaim the land on which they stand for commercial profit.

INTACH has addressed this problem by broadening ASI's very limited definition of architectural heritage. It realized that attenuated protection policies, first of the colonial government, and now in independent India, not only severely restricted official initiatives to engage with cultural heritage, they also distorted both the spatial and temporal imaginations of society, which have contributed to the rapid depletion of the cultural patrimony in no small measure. It engaged with cultural heritage holistically by focusing on all its manifestations, immovable (architectural), movable (objects), natural (environment), intangible, including the crafts traditions, and also embarked on disseminating its work to the public, particularly school and college students, through its local Chapters (currently there are over 200 across the country) and education cell.

Over the forty plus years of its existence, INTACH's initiatives have had a profound impact on the cultural imagination of society, but this essay focuses on their engagement with historic cities and its influence on postcolonial urban planning and conservation.

By emphasizing the imperatives of documenting the unprotected built heritage around the country through the Chapters they vastly enhanced not only the number of historic buildings that are officially protected, but also expanded the categories of built heritage beyond the ASI's monument-centric definition. In Delhi, for instance, the

ASI protected only 174 monuments, but the Delhi Chapter listed 1,208 buildings and 27 historic settlements that have cultural significance. This listing became an effective tool for lobbying the state government to legally notify them as officially recognized heritage. Today the statutory Master Plan of Delhi has a separate section on protecting Delhi's heritage that identifies all 1,208 buildings, six historic settlements and three Archaeological Parks.[9] These initiatives have enabled INTACH to propagate and disseminate the significance of urban heritage as an important genre in urban planning.

Inter alia, INTACH undertook various projects to conserve historic settlements and leveraged its protocols to foreground the significance of protecting the characteristics of indigenous urbanism in the process of urban renewal. As there were no disciplinary protocols to guide them, the professionals undertook an immersive exercise to understand the problems of historic settlements and reify Geddes' ideas: that is, formulate culture-sensitive urban renewal strategies. As it turned out, this became an autodidactic process of learning, for they had to empirically question both the canonical gospels of urban planning that underpin statutory master plans, as well as the monument-centric protocols of ASI. They also had to dialogue and coordinate with various stakeholders, including civic authorities and their engineers and urban planners, local ASI officials, and politicians.

INTACH's urban conservation projects modified Geddes' prescriptions to suit postcolonial realities while using the protocols of 'diagnostic surveys' to 'forensically' study the morphological characteristics of historic settlements in order to appreciate their structural relationship with the social and cultural practices of the residents, before proposing minimal interventions by way of 'conservative surgery' to identify and resolve the problems and modernize and upgrade the quality of life of their residents. These projects have also had positive outcomes in terms of public policy, resulting in the initiation of several innovative urban renewal programmes, such as the Jawaharlal Nehru National Urban Renewal Mission in 2005 (JNNURM), and the National Heritage City Development and Augmentation Yojana in 2015 (HRIDAY), among others, thus bringing historic settlements within the ambit of the statutory development plans of cities.

That said, one needs to take note of a critical appraisal of HRIDAY projects that pointed out: 'However, many intentions of working in historic cultural and natural environments have, on the ground, translated to one-dimensional projects, not distinctly different from "beautification".' [10] This brings into focus the importance of reforming pedagogy of professional education. Indigenous urbanism in India needs to be studied and theorized in the manner that Christopher Alexander and Camillo Sitte engaged with pre-modern settlement patterns.[11] The objective of such pedagogic exercises would not be to replicate them, but take their evolution further.

The significance of developing post-Geddes strategies to engage with historic settlements in professional education is that they will foreground the potential benefits of developing non-Western narratives of modernizing historic Indian cities to create 'indigenous modernity'. These narratives can only be theorized by reforming academic pedagogy, which would, in turn, benefit urban planning in India by offering more compelling opportunities to positively and effectively deal with the unique characteristics of post-Independence urbanisation and urbanism. The relevance of Patrick Geddes must be assessed in view of this endeavour.

*

Three recent flagship projects of the national government to modernize historic cities throw into sharper relief the complexity of reforming postcolonial urban planning. Together, these initiatives by a powerful government eerily mirror the colonial visions and strategies to define India's urban future.

In Varanasi, the challenge of dealing with the dense urban fabric of the 'eternal city' was 'resolved' by demolishing large swathes of the built environment to create a grand landscaped plaza, directly linking the Vishwanath Temple to the ghats of the river Ganges. It was conceived by a well-known architect, clearly unfamiliar with the imperatives of sympathetically engaging with historic settlements, who nevertheless had to cater to the demands of a powerful political patron to 'modernize' this ancient city. Varanasi does indeed need to be upgraded, not by denigrating the genius of generations of local builders—who organically converted energy to culture—but by engaging with it and creating what I call an 'indigenous modernity'.

In Shahjahanabad, the greatest Mughal city, historic Chandni Chowk was proposed to be beautified and re-configured as a pedestrian street by another well-known architect. The civic intention to engage with the problems of historic cities was bold and exemplary, but here too, the strategies adopted were contentious. They ignored the cultural and historic significance of the site and outrageously proposed to locate several public toilets and electric transformers on the central verge, because 'there was no alternative'. It was only because of a timely protest by conservation professionals, together with judicial support, that this scheme was reluctantly modified. But the interventions demonstrated that respecting the protocols of heritage conservation can produce better results for all.

The third project, 'Redeveloping Central Vista', displays a similar disregard for conservation protocols, such as conducting a prior audit of the heritage status of this heritage precinct. Therefore, the proposal to redesign a colonial legacy into the symbol of 'modern India' is driven primarily by a political agenda. It is a greenfield project that will retain four heritage buildings, North and South Blocks, and the Parliament building, to be reused as museums, and the National Archives building for purposes yet to be decided. The primary purpose of the project is not to conserve the heritage characteristics of this precinct but to inscribe a new 'Indian' identity on this most iconic of public spaces in the city. The cost, both in monetary terms and cultural significance cannot be justified, its need, irrational.

There is considerable congruity between the three apparently different projects. Each seeks to inscribe a future for the historic city, not by conserving the significance of the past but by erasing it. Each displays a willful, and ironically, colonially rooted ignorance of the deep structure of civilizational genius that created these remarkable cities—one Hindu, another Islamic, and the third, colonial. This is worth discussing in the public domain because it is, after all, *our* heritage.

Notes

1. G. Slater, 'Illuminations…as by Flashes of Lightening', *The Sociological Review*, vol. 24, 1932, p. 37.
2. Indra Munshi, *Patrick Geddes' Contribution to Sociobiology and Urban Planning, Vision of A City*, London and New York: Routledge, 2023.
3. Noah Hysler-Rubin, *Patrick Geddes and Town Planning, A Critical View*, London and New York: Routledge, 2011, p. 3.
4. Ibid., p. 3.
5. For an overview of the problems of non-Western cities, see, David Satterthwaite, *Understanding Asian Cities*, Bangkok: Asian Coalition for Housing Rights, 2003. The cities studied were Beijing (China); Pune (India); Chiang Mai (Thailand); Phnom Penh (Cambodia); Karachi (Pakistan); Muntinlupa (Philippines); Hanoi (Vietnam); and Surabaya (Indonesia).
6. For a general discussion on this subject, see, Keith Diaz Moore, ed., *Culture—Meaning—Architecture, Critical Reflections on the*

Work of Amos Rapaport, London and New York: Routledge, 2019; first published, Surrey: Ashgate Publishing, 2000.

7. To understand the preoccupations of official policy-makers with the creation of 'world-class' cities, see, Devashish Dhar, *India's Blind Spot, Understanding and Managing our Cities*, Gurugram: Harper Collins Publishers, 2023.
8. For a critical study of the strategy to make Indian cities 'world-class', see, D. Asher Ghertner, *Rule By Aesthetics, World-Class City Making in Delhi,* New York: Oxford University Press, 2015.
9. Listing of the built heritage of Delhi is a work in progress and the number of Listed buildings is increasing following the data gathered through more surveys and research. But there have also been setbacks, the most prominent being the inability to compile a list of post-Independence buildings of significance because of government resistance to the idea.
10. Jigna Desai et al., eds., 'Way Forward, Editor's Notes', in *HRIDAY Reflections, A Monograph on Heritage City Development and Augmentation Yojana*, New Delhi: Ministry of Housing and Urban Affairs, Government of India, 2017, p. 161.
11. Christopher Alexander et al., *A New Theory of Urban Design*, New York and Oxford: Oxford University Press, 1987; Camillo Sitte, *Art of Building Cities According to its Artistic Fundamentals*, Westport, CT.: Hyperion Press, 1979.

8

Kinetic City

Issues for Urban Design in South Asia

RAHUL MEHROTRA

CITIES IN South Asia are characterized by physical and visual contradictions that coalesce in a landscape of incredible pluralism. Historically, particularly during the period of British colonization, the different worlds—whether economic, social, or cultural—of these cities occupied different spaces and operated under different rules—-the aim being to maximize control and minimize conflict between these opposing worlds.[1] However, today these worlds share the same space, but understand and use it differently.[2] Massive waves of distressed rural migration during the latter half of the 1900s triggered the convergence of these worlds into a singular, but multifaceted entity. This, coupled with the inadequate supply of urban land and the lack of the creation of new urban centres, resulted in extremely high densities in existing cities. Furthermore, with the emergence of a post-

*This article is based on an essay titled 'Negotiating the Static and Kinetic Cities' in *Urban Imaginaries*, ed. Andrea Huyssen, Durham: Duke University Press, 2007. I am delighted to offer this essay to Narayani Gupta's festschrift volume. I am grateful to Professor Gupta for having encouraged me to imagine the city as life in motion

industrial, service-based economy, the intertwining of these worlds within the same space is even greater.[3]

In this post-industrial scenario, cities in India have become critical sites for negotiation between elite and subaltern cultures. The new relationships between social classes in a post-industrial economy are quite different from those that existed in state-controlled economies.[4] The fragmentation of service and production locations has resulted in a new, bazaar-like urbanism, which has woven its presence through the entire urban landscape.[5] This is an urbanism created by those outside the elite domains of the formal modernity of the state. It is a 'pirate' modernity that slips under the laws of the city to simply survive, without any conscious attempt at constructing a counterculture.[6] With the retreat of the state through the 1980s–1990s (in different measures throughout South Asia), the space of the 'everyday' is where economic and cultural struggles are articulated. These common spaces have been largely excluded from the cultural discourses on globalization, which focus on elite domains of production in the city.[7]

Today, Indian cities are comprised of two components occupying the same physical space. The first is the Static City. Built of more permanent material such as concrete, steel and brick, it is comprehended as a two-dimensional entity on conventional city maps and is monumental in its presence. The second is the Kinetic City. Incomprehensible as a two-dimensional entity, it is perceived as a city in motion—a three-dimensional construct of incremental development. The Kinetic City is temporary in nature and often built with recycled material: plastic sheets, scrap metal, canvas, and waste wood. It constantly modifies and reinvents itself. The Kinetic City is not perceived by architecture, but by spaces, which hold associative values and supportive lives. Patterns of occupation determine its form and perception. It is an indigenous urbanism that has its 'local' logic. It is not necessarily the city of the poor, as most images might suggest; rather it is a temporal articulation and occupation of space which not only creates a richer sensibility of spatial occupation, but also suggests how spatial limits are expanded to include formally unimagined uses in dense urban conditions.[8]

The Kinetic City presents a compelling vision that potentially allows us to better understand the blurred lines of contemporary urbanism and the changing roles of people and spaces in urban society. The increasing concentrations of global flows have exacerbated the inequalities and spatial divisions of social classes. In this context, an architecture or urbanism of equality in an increasingly inequitable economic condition requires looking deeper to find a wide range of places to mark and commemorate the cultures of those excluded from the spaces of global flows. These don't necessarily lie in the formal production of architecture, but often challenge it. Here the idea of a city is an elastic urban condition, not a grand vision, but a 'grand adjustment'.

The Kinetic City, bazaar-like in form, can be seen as the symbolic image of the emerging urban South Asian condition. The processions, weddings, festivals, hawkers, street vendors, and slum dwellers or *Katchi Abadis*, all create an ever-transforming streetscape—a city in constant motion where the very physical fabric is characterized by the kinetic. The Static City, on the other hand, dependent on architecture for its representation is no longer the single image by which the city is read. Thus, architecture is not the 'spectacle' of the city nor does it even comprise the single dominant image of the city. In contrast, festivals such as Diwali, Dussehra, Navratri, Muharram, Durga Puja, Ganesh Chaturthi and many more, have emerged as the spectacles of the Kinetic City. Their presence on the everyday landscape pervades and dominates the popular visual culture of Indian cities. Festivals create a forum through which the fantasies of the subalterns are articulated and even organized into political action. In Mumbai for example, the popularity and growth of the Ganesh festival has been phenomenal.[9] During the festival, which occurs in August or September, numerous neighbourhoods transform temporarily with lights and decoration. New spaces are created to house the idol of Ganesh for ten days. During this festival period, family, neighbourhood, and city events mark the celebrations. On the last day, a large part of the city's population carries the idol in long processions ultimately to be immersed in the sea.

Each procession carries tableaux, depicting images of both local as well global concerns, with Lord Ganesh mediating the outcomes. This representation is not based on formal scriptures or predetermined rules; instead, human ingenuity breaches the boundaries between the local and the global, the historic and contemporary. They convey the hybrid urgencies of metropolitan India.[10] The neighbourhood processions weave through predetermined routes in the city. Each procession vies against other neighbourhood processions to showcase the intensity of their followings. Set against the backdrop of the Static City, the procession culminates with the immersion of the idol as it bids farewell amidst chants inviting Ganesh to resurrect his presence the following year.

Immersion becomes a metaphor for the spectacle of the city. As the clay idol dissolves in the water of the bay, the spectacle comes to a close. There are no static or permanent mechanisms to encode this spectacle. Here the memory of the city is an 'enacted' process—a temporal moment as opposed to buildings that contain the public memory as a static or permanent entity.[11] The city and its architecture are not synonymous and cannot contain a single meaning. Within the Kinetic City, meanings are not stable; spaces get consumed, reinterpreted, and recycled. The Kinetic City recycles the Static City to create a new spectacle.

This transformative ability of the Kinetic City becomes even more vivid in the events that play out at Mumbai's

Town Hall every year on 15 August, India's Independence Day. The Public Works Department (PWD) subverts the meaning and symbolism of the architecture of this classical building by reconfiguring it for an annual ceremony when the Governor of the State addresses the citizen. To ensure it is weather-protected from the monsoon rains, the PWD builds a structure, a sort of large porch, which attaches itself to the building. Built overnight in bamboo and cloth, the decorative trim and other ornamental highlights graft on to this classical building a local and perhaps traditional sensibility that momentarily transforms the architecture. The conservationists in the city protest each year decrying this as an abuse of the legislation that protects heritage buildings, but they ignore the fact that this as a reversible action, well within the bounds of even the holiest of preservationists' canons.[12] The intended image of this symbol of colonial power, a celebrated asset of the Static City, is subverted and re-colonized by the Kinetic City. The PWD alters the significance of this building momentarily to expand the margins of the Kinetic City.

This idea takes on a critical dimension when contemplating the preservation of the built environment in these contexts. Debates about the conservation of the Static City have often revolved around the idea of significance. This notion of 'cultural significance' as an all-encompassing idea is something that emerged clearly in the conservation debate in the 1980s. To be more precise, this notion of cultural significance first emerged in what is referred to as the Burra Charter—one of the many resolutions made by the International Charter for the Conservation and Restoration of Monuments and Sites (ICOMOS) to define and guide conservation practice. The Burra Charter (that was adopted at Burra, South Australia in 1979) defined cultural significance as the 'aesthetic, historic, scientific or social value for past, present and future generations.' Implicit in this definition is the belief that 'significance' is static. It is a definition that is 'object' centric (devoid of life) with its roots in the debate propagated by the antiquarians of the Renaissance.[13] What is the validity of such a notion where cultural memory is often an enacted process, as in the Kinetic City? Or where meanings are fluid like the Kinetic City itself and often complicated in postcolonial conditions by the fact that the creators and custodians of historic environments in the Static City belong to different cultures from those that created them?

What then is our cultural reading for the Kinetic City, which now forms a greater part of our urban reality? In this dynamic context, if the production or preservation of architecture or urban form must be informed by our reading of cultural significance, it will necessarily have to include the notion of 'constructing significance' both in the architectural as well as conservation debates.[14] In fact, an understanding that 'cultural significance' evolves, will truly clarify the role of the architect as an advocate of change (versus a preservationist who opposes change)—one who can engage with both the Kinetic and Static City on equal terms. Under such conditions, a draining of the symbolic import of the architectural landscape leads to a deepening of ties between architecture and contemporary realities and experiences. This understanding allows architecture and urban typologies to be transformed through intervention and placed in the service of contemporary life, realities, and emerging aspirations. Here, the Static City embraces the Kinetic City and is informed and remade by its logic.

The phenomenon of bazaars in Victorian arcades in the old Fort Area, Mumbai's historic district, is emblematic of this potential negotiation between the Static and Kinetic City. The original use of the arcades was two-fold. First, they provided spatial mediation between building and street. Second, the arcades were a perfect response to Bombay's climate. They serve as a zone protecting pedestrians from both the harsh sun and lashing rains. Today, with the informal bazaar occupying the arcade, its original intent is challenged. This emergent relationship of the arcade and bazaar not only forces a confrontation of uses and interest groups, but also demands new preservation approaches. For the average Mumbai resident, the hawker provides a wide range of goods at prices considerably lower than those found in local shops. Thus, the bazaar in the arcades that characterize the Fort Area are thriving businesses. For the elite and for conservationists, the Victorian core represents the old city centre, complete with monumental icons. In fact, as the city sprawls, dissipating the clarity of its form, these images, places, and icons acquire even greater meaning for preservationists as critical symbols of the city's historic image. Consequently, hawking is deemed illegal by city authorities that are constantly attempting to relocate the bazaars.

The challenge in Mumbai is to cope with the city's transformation, not by inducing or polarizing its dualism, but by attempting to reconcile these opposite conditions as being simultaneously valid. The existence of two worlds in the same space implies that we must accommodate and overlap varying uses, perceptions, and physical forms. For example, the arcades in the Fort Area are a special urban component that inherently possess a capacity for reinterpretation. As an architectural or urban design solution, they display an incredible resilience; they can accommodate new uses while keeping the illusion of their architecture intact.

One design solution might be to re-adapt the functioning of the arcades. They could be restructured to allow for easy pedestrian movement and accommodate hawkers at the same time. They could contain the amorphous bazaar encased in the illusion of the disciplined Victorian arcade. With this sort of planning, components of the city would have a greater ability to survive because they could be more adaptable to changing economic and social conditions. There are no total solutions in an urban landscape simultaneously charged with the duality between permanence and rapid transformation. At best, the city could constantly evolve and invent solutions for the present through safeguarding the crucial components of our historically important 'urban hardware'. Could 'Bazaars in Victorian Arcades' become an authentic symbol of an emergent reality of temporary adjustment?

Clearly the Static and Kinetic Cities go beyond their obvious differences to establish a much richer relationship both spatially and metaphorically than their physical manifestations would suggest. Here affinity and rejection are simultaneously played out in a state of equilibrium maintained by a seemingly irresolvable tension. The informal economy of the city vividly illustrates the collapsed and intertwined existence of the Static and Kinetic Cities. The *dabbawalas* (literally translated as 'tiffin men') are an example of this relationship between the formal and informal, the static and kinetic. The tiffin delivery service, which relies on the train system for transportation, costs approximately Rs.200 (four dollars) per month. A *dabbawala* picks up a lunch tiffin from a house anywhere in the city. Then through a complex system, she delivers the tiffin to one's place of work by lunchtime and returns it to the house later in the day. The *dabbawalas* deliver hundreds of thousands of lunch boxes every day. The efficiency of Mumbai's train system, the spine of the linear city, enables the complex informal system to work. *The dabbawalas* have innovatively set up a network that facilitates an informal system to take advantage of a formal infrastructure. The network involves the *dabba* or tiffin being exchanged up to four or five times between its pickup and return to the house in the evening. The average box travels about 30 km. each way. It is estimated that around 200,000 boxes are delivered around the city per day involving approximately 4,500 *dabbawalas.* In economic terms, the annual turnover amounts to roughly 50 million rupees or about a million dollars.[15]

Entrepreneurship in the Kinetic City is an autonomous and oral process that demonstrates the ability to fold the formal and informal into a symbiotic relationship. The *dabbawala,* like several other informal services that range from banking, money transfer, courier, and electronic bazaars, leverage community relationships and networks and deftly use the Static City and its infrastructure beyond its intended margins. These networks create a synergy that depends on mutual integration without the obsession of formalized structures. The Kinetic City is where the intersection of need (often reduced to survival) and unexploited potentials of existing infrastructure initiate new innovative services. The trains in Mumbai are emblematic of a kinetic space supporting and blurring the formal and the informal, slicing through these worlds while momentarily collapsing them into a singular entity. Here the self-consciousness about modernity and the regulations imposed by the Static City are suspended and redundant. The Kinetic City carries local wisdom into the contemporary world without fear of the modern, while the Static City aspires to erase the local and re-codify it in a written 'macro-moral' order.[16]

The issue of housing most vividly demonstrates the reordering process of the Kinetic City by the Static City. In Mumbai, for example, approximately 60 per cent of the city's population does not have access to formal housing. This population lives on approximately 10 per cent of the city's land in settlements that are locally referred to as slums. It is believed that about 70 per cent of the city's population works in the informal sector. This number has risen with the new liberal economy that curtails bargaining capacity through fragmenting labor in the cities. Despite its informal nature, this population's productivity allows Mumbai to be competitive on a global scale.[17] This subaltern population lives in the interstitial spaces of the cities—road edges, drainage channels (*nalla* spaces), edges of railway lines—and must engage in innovative means of negotiating everyday life. Dish antennas and a web of electrical wire and cables juxtapose these homes covered by plastic sheets or with walls made of empty drums. These developments represent a kaleidoscope of the past, present and future compressed into an organic fabric of alleys, dead ends and a labyrinth-like mysterious streetscape that constantly modifies and reinvents itself. The Kinetic City, like a twitching organism, locates and relocates itself through the city in perpetual motion. Flow, instability, and indeterminacy are basic to the Kinetic City. Regular demolitions exacerbate the tenuous occupation of land by the inhabitants of these settlements. The demolitions inhibit any investment the occupants might make in their physical living conditions. Thus, the Kinetic City is a fluid and dynamic city that is mobile and temporal (often as a strategy to defeat eviction) and leaves no ruins. It constantly recycles its resources leveraging great effect and presence with very little means.

This only heightens the growing contradictions in the islands of increasing concentration of wealth which are manifested physically in the gated communities throughout the city and the edge city suburbs. The popular metaphorical reference to 'making Bombay Shanghai'[18] is emblematic of the one-dimensional imagination that planners and politicians bring to bear on decisions about the city's development. An obvious extension of the Shanghai metaphor is the notion of remaking the city in a singular image and using architecture as the spectacle to represent a global aspiration. The radical transformation of the physical nature of the city is seen as the most immediate method to make the city viable for integration in a global network of cities and economies. New highways, flyovers, airports, corporate hotels, and convention centres (followed by a secondary development of museums, galleries, parks, and progressive urban regulations demonstrating further compliance with international urban standards) are all critical elements for the Static City to achieve this perceived integration. Such global implications also raise political questions that challenge the democratic processes of city governance.[19]

Ambiguity regarding the urban form of Mumbai and the dominant image of the city, prompts the question, 'Whose city is it anyway?' This question goes beyond the politics of occupation and challenges the processes by which the city is made. The making of the city is perhaps most critical when negotiating between the Static and Kinetic Cities; for it is also an effective point of intervention. Through the city-making process, globalization and its transgressions in the urban landscape are realized, but it is also how the Kinetic City can simultaneously resist or participate in globalization as well as reconfigure itself socially, culturally, and spatially.

The growing movement of slum associations and networks in Mumbai is a potent illustration of these points of effective intervention. These associations engage with the formal world of the Static City while mediating the inherent contradictions of issues of legality, informality, and the mobile and temporal strategies of the Kinetic City. The most successful of these movements is the alliance between an NGO, The Society for the Promotion of Area Resources (SPAARC), a Citizen Based Organization (CBO), The National Slum Dwellers Federation (NSDF), and the Mahila Milan, an organization of poor women. This alliance is essentially united in its concerns for securing land and access to urban infrastructure. It has successfully negotiated between the formal and informal worlds in the city and across national boundaries with a network of other alliances working with slum dwellers around the world. Besides representing efforts to reconstitute citizenship in cities, these efforts form what Arjun Appadurai refers to as 'deep democracy'. The depth refers to

> ...[a] model that produces poor communities able to engage in partnership with more powerful agencies—urban, regional,

national, and multilateral—that purport to be concerned with poverty and citizenship... vertical collaborations and partnerships with more powerful persons and organizations together form a mutually sustaining cycle of process. This is where depth and laterality become joint circuits along which pro-poor strategies can flow.[20]

It is through this restructuring of the city-making process that the Kinetic and Static Cities can be intertwined beyond the physical and better engage the inhabitants of the city.

The urbanism of Mumbai represents a fascinating intersection where the Kinetic City, a landscape of dystopia and yet a symbol of optimism, challenges the Static City, encoded in architecture, to reposition and remake the city.[21] The Kinetic City forces the Static City to re-engage itself in present conditions by dissolving its utopian project to fabricate multiple dialogues with its context. Could this become the basis for a rational discussion about co-existence? Or is the emergent urbanism of Mumbai inherently paradoxical where the co-existence of the Static and Kinetic Cities and their states of utopia and dystopia are inevitable? Can the spatial configuration for how this simultaneity occurs be formally imagined? The Kinetic City obviously cannot be seen as a design tool but rather as a demand that conceptions of urbanism create and facilitate environments that are versatile and flexible, robust, and ambiguous enough to allow this kinetic quality of the city to flourish. Perhaps the Kinetic City might be the tactical approach to take when dealing with the urbanism of the temporary, of high densities, and intensities? Despite these many potential disjunctures, what this reading of the city does celebrate is the dynamic and pluralist processes that make the urban Indian landscape. Within this urbanism, the Static and Kinetic cities necessarily co-exist and blur into an integral entity, even if momentarily, to create the margins for adjustment that their simultaneous existences demand.

Notes

1. Anthony King, *Colonial Urban Development: Culture, Social Power and Environment,* London: Routledge and Kegan Paul, 1976.
2. This unprecedented shift in demography has not only transformed the social make-up of Indian cities but has perpetuated an incomprehensible landscape charged with intense dualities—which are cultural, social, as well as economic. This new demography comprises mainly of rural migrants, who form the urban poor, bringing with them new skills, social values and cultural attitudes that not only determine their ability to survive in an urban environment, but also in the process are altering the very structure of the city! These different attitudes that influence the way the city is used and perceived is also emblematic of the more universal phenomenon of global flows that are transforming cities across the world and local resistances which emerge in landscapes characterized by uneven development. Furthermore, the presence of the urban poor makes explicit another crucial divide—between those that have access to the formal city and the infrastructure that goes with it, and those that do not have this access and therefore lack the basic amenities in the urban system.
3. Prasad Shetty, 'Stories of Entrepreneurship', research paper published for Sarai—CSDS, Short Term Independent Research Fellowship Programme, August 2005. The idea that distinct manufacturing zones and segregations spatially have now shifted to services and manufacturing occurring in fragmented areas in the city networked through the efficient transportation system the city offers.
4. Partha Chatterjee, 'Are Indian Cities becoming Bourgeois at Last?', in *Body, City: Siting Contemporary Culture in India,* Berlin: House of World Cultures and New Delhi: Tulika Books, 2003.
5. The fragmented nature of the new economy in Mumbai was well documented by Prasad Shetty, 'Stories of Entrepreneurship'. One of the interesting observations of the study had to do with the changing patterns of mobility along public transportation

and particularly the trains. It was observed that while the city's population between 1991 and 2001 grew by 22.4 per cent the train travel increased by 42.37 per cent (from 4.95 million to 6.4 million). This is largely due to the work and production patterns that are changing significantly. Small-scale operations and the growth of agents are now connecting nodes of manufacturing that are fragmented all over the landscape of the city.

6. Ravi Sundaram, 'Recycling Modernity: Pirate Electronic Cultures in India', in *Sarai Reader 01: The Public Domain,* New Delhi: CSDS, 2001.
7. Chatterjee, 'Are Indian Cities becoming Bourgeois at Last?'.
8. Weddings are an example of how the rich too are engaged in the making of the Kinetic City. The lack of formal spaces for weddings as the cultural outlet for ostentation has resulted in public open space being colonized temporarily for consumption by the rich as spaces for the spectacle of elaborate weddings. Often, very complex wedding sets are constructed and removed within twelve hours; here, a temporary spectacle is set up by the rich in the public domain for private consumption—again the margins of the urban system are expanded momentarily.
9. The Ganeshotsava (as it is referred to locally) in its present form was reinvented in the late nineteenth century by Lokamanya Tilak, as a symbol of resistance to the British colonial regime. Tilak took a domestic and private idiom of worship and translated it into a collective and public rite of self-assertion.
10. Ranjit Hoskote, 'Scenes from a Festival,' *The Hindu,* 14 January 2001.
11. Rahul Mehrotra, 'Bazaar City: A Metaphor for South Asian Urbanism', in *Kapital & Karma,* ed. Angelika Fitz et al., Vienna: Kunsthalle, 2002.
12. Conservation legislation was first introduced in Mumbai in 1995—the first of its kind in India. Over the last ten years of the existence of the legislation the debate about historic preservation or conservation (as is more commonly referred to

in Mumbai) has become a well-articulated one. A few NGOs in the city are actively involved in activism and advocacy to lobby for the protection of buildings that are listed. Unfortunately, most debates about the practice of conservation are biased towards British conservation practice on account of the largest number of Indian architects trained in conservation being from universities in the UK. They tend to bring a British centric view to the protection of colonial buildings often totally out of sync with contemporary Indian urban realities. Their benchmarks are British and European standards which often contribute to the drawing of conservation practice into the realm of the elite (banks, government agencies, etc.) and it being seen as an exclusionary activity.

13. These ideas were first presented at a seminar in Adelaide in July 2000 titled 'Cultural Significance: Construct or Criterion?' at the Center for Architecture and Middle Eastern Studies, University of Adelaide, Australia. I am grateful to Professor Peter Scriver for his inputs in developing these ideas.
14. For examples of works/projects that have attempted to translate these ideas refer to: Rahul Mehrotra, 'Planning for Conservation—Looking at Bombay's Historic Fort Area', *Future Anterior: Journal of Historic Preservation, History, Theory and Criticism*, vol. 1, no. 2, Fall 2004.
15. Vinay Venkatraman and Stefano Mirti, 'Network Design', *Domus*, vol. 887, December 2005, pp. 82–7.
16. Romi Khosla, *The Loneliness of a Long Distant Future: Dilemmas of Contemporary Architecture*, New Delhi: Tulika, 2002.
17. As organized manufacturing left the city of Mumbai skilled labour were left with no choice but to fend for themselves. Small manufacturing centres with agents working to network them have become the emergent paradigm. This system allows for an incredible web of distribution with the slums serving as centres of production.
18. Before Shanghai, till the late 1990s, Singapore was the metaphor for a successful city, and politicians tended to ask questions such as 'Why can't Mumbai become like Singapore?' The levels of hygiene, the cleanliness, the efficient functioning

all set in a tropical landscape was something Mumbai and its citizens could easily imagine happening to the city.

19. This is a political question because the two countries India and China have extremely different political systems. One an autocracy and the other a democracy. Big infrastructure projects or generally big moves in a city are difficult and slow in a democracy. Therefore the use of Singapore or Shanghai as a metaphor for the physical expression of Mumbai's aspiration is naïve, as it does not factor in the political system behind the expression.
20. Arjun Appadurai, 'Deep Democracy: Urban Governmentality and the Horizon of Politics', in *Environment and Urbanization*, vol. 13, no. 2, October 2001.
21. Charles Correa, the eminent Indian architect has described Mumbai as 'a Great City, Terrible Place'. In this expression, utopia is the cultural and economic landscape of the city and dystopia the physical landscape.

9

Reading the Town, Reading History

The Koil Olugu *and Srirangam in the Tamil Region*

RANJEETA DUTTA

Introduction

THE *KOIL OLUGU* or the chronicle of the Ranganathasvami temple at Srirangam provides an account of how the process of record keeping was systematized from the nineteenth century onwards. The time indicated in this context was after the three Carnatic wars in 1801 when the British East India Company established control over the region of Carnatic, including Tiruchirapalli, and Srirangam.[1] The three Carnatic wars fought between 1740 and 1763 involved several powers like the Marathas, Nawab of Arcot, Nizam of Hyderabad and his family, rulers of Tanjore and Mysore, the French East India

*I am grateful to Professor Susanne Rau, and Professor Jorg Rupke, the project directors of the DFG-funded project, 'Religion and Urbanity: Mutual Formations' at the Max Weber Kolleg for Advanced Cultural and Social Studies, University of Erfurt, Germany for providing me the opportunity for my research on Srirangam as a fellow from January to September 2020. I sincerely thank Dr Dhiman Debsarma, Research Associate, Centre for Regional Development, Jawaharlal Nehru University, New Delhi for making the map, 'The Tamil Region'; Inset: 'Srirangam and Surrounding Sites'.

Company based at Puducherry, and finally, the English East India Company based in erstwhile Madras (now Chennai). The wars ultimately established the domination of the English East India Company and paved the way for British colonial rule in India.

The *Olugu* narrates that sometime between July and August (Tamil month of Adi), the English East India Company's administration under its Collector, John Wallace decided to revive the customs and practices (*mamul*) that were suspended by Nizam ul Mulk, the erstwhile Carnatic ruler, who controlled the region and the temple for five years before the British annexation. With the help of his record keeper or the 'writer' Gajendra Rayar and interpreter, Seshachalam Aiyar, Wallace decided to earmark a sum of 41,000 rupees from the treasury to the temple of Ranganathasvami at Srirangam. The system continued till a dispute broke out between two rival sects of the Shrivaishnava community, the Vatakalais and the Tenkalais, regarding the control over the temple resources. Consequently, several important rituals were stalled.[2]

The temple priests, the functionaries, and perhaps the locals of the town of Srirangam gathered in the temple to resolve the crisis. We are further told that 'Wallace issued an order stating that the custom of the last two years of the Company's rule should be strictly followed and also commanded Velappa Mudali of the Devasthanam to send him a weekly report. This was announced by 'tom-tom' in the town'.[3] The dispute continued and Wallace summoned the Vatakalais and the temple functionaries who were Tenkalais and listened to their grievances. Each side claimed control over the temple and its resources based on the number of their respective followers in the town. Further, the Vatakalais asserted that the Tenkalai claim based on certain practised rituals and systems of worship could not be sustained as they were recently introduced and were never followed earlier. The Vatakalais also alleged that the Tenkalais had superimposed their sectarian mark or *namam* upon the Vatakalai *namam* on various sacred objects and shrines in the temple, thus appropriating the religious space. The *sthalattars* or the local temple functionaries who were Tenkalais outrightly rejected these allegations claiming an already prior presence of their systems of worship, rituals, and the Tenkalai mark. The narrative in the *Olugu* states that the Tenkalai claim was emboldened when the English record keeper or writer Gajendra Rayar said that everything could be asserted from his 'book' in which had been entered the accounts of the *sthalattar* of the temple. Referring to it he said that Sriranganatha was a Tenkalai God.[4] After confirming that all the past and contemporary temple leaders and functionaries were Tenkalais (even the Vatakalais finally agreed to the same), Wallace declared that the temple, its functionaries, and rituals would follow the system of the Tenkalais.[5] The narrative ends thus informing us about the process of record keeping:

> Velappa Mudaliar brought to the notice of Wallace all the Olugus that existed in the town and at the desire of the latter had the Olugus rewritten along with the events up to the days of Wallace and placed a copy of the same bearing the seal of the five (Stalattars), in the 'terku kallarai' (southern stone room) of the temple.[6]

The above narrative highlights the documentation of events and accounts, significant for record keeping as well as developing an archive that not only chronicled the events, daily life in the temple, and its accounts as history but also as a source of authentication at the time of conflict over rights and authorities between different stakeholders in the temple. This internal evidence of writing and documentation also informs us that there were many *olugus* or chronicles in the town and all were compiled, edited, or 'rewritten' and a 'copy' was attested with the seal of five temple functionaries, an important protocol for record keeping. This was a process of an archive in the making that involved the town, its residents, its temple, temple officials and functionaries, and the state with its set of scribes. It was also an assertion of a certain set of records over the previous ones, an attempt to rewrite the past and fashion the present in tandem with historical consciousness. Thus, apart from being a mere record maintained by the institution of the temple, the *Koil Olugu,* as is evident in the above narrative, was attempting to create an archive whose contents were of 'enduring value... stored for posterity and the use of others than those who created them'.[7]

The present essay will therefore analyse the *Koil Olugu* not as a source of history, providing evidence for the past; rather it will attempt to engage with the chronicle 'as a subject of inquiry', archiving the town, in this case, Srirangam. Endeavouring to create a certain kind of memory about the temple, and town life, the *Olugu* did not matter-of-factly record events and everyday life. Rather it recorded a particular worldview through an intersection between religion and urbanity, reflecting upon issues of identities, power, and negotiations. It is emphasized here that there was no one way of reading the town in history and no one way of perceiving the sacred. Apart from the *Koil Olugu,* the inscriptions on the temple walls, *prakaras* and the hagiographical and religious literature provide us with different perceptions of the urban, the town, and the temple.

The *Koil Olugu*: Urban Context and the Process of Redaction

As the river Kaveri meanders across the plains of Tamil Nadu, it branches into a tributary called the Coleroon at a short distance of 7 km. from the city of Tiruchirappalli. The two river streams encircling a small island from the north and south join a little later becoming the river Kaveri again, forming a delta near Thanjavur, and finally flowing into the

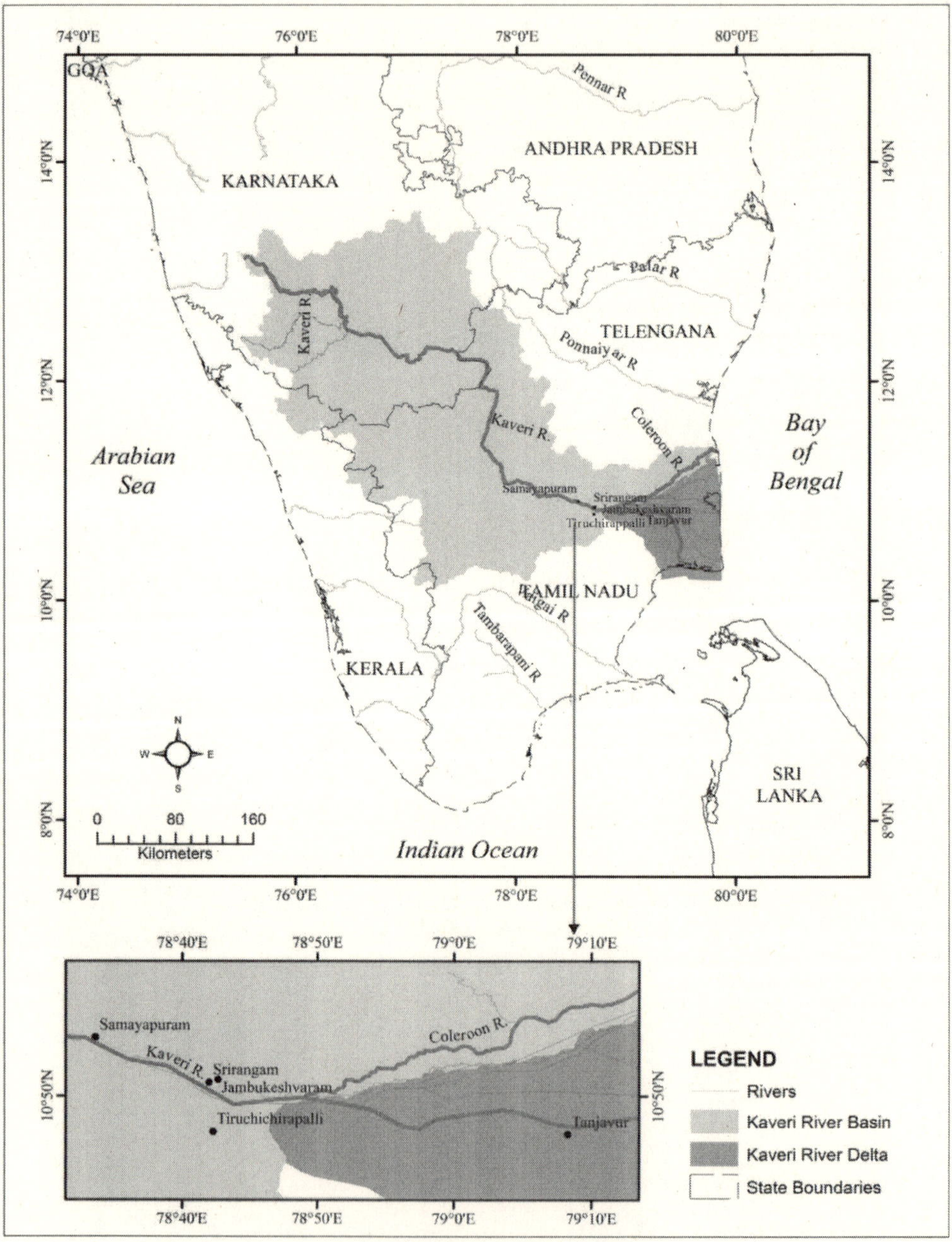

Map 9.1: The Tamil region; inset: Srirangam and surrounding sites

Source: Prepared by D. Dhiman Debsarma, Centre for the Study of Regional Development, JNU

Plate 9.1: The town of Srirangam

Source: Wikimedia Commons

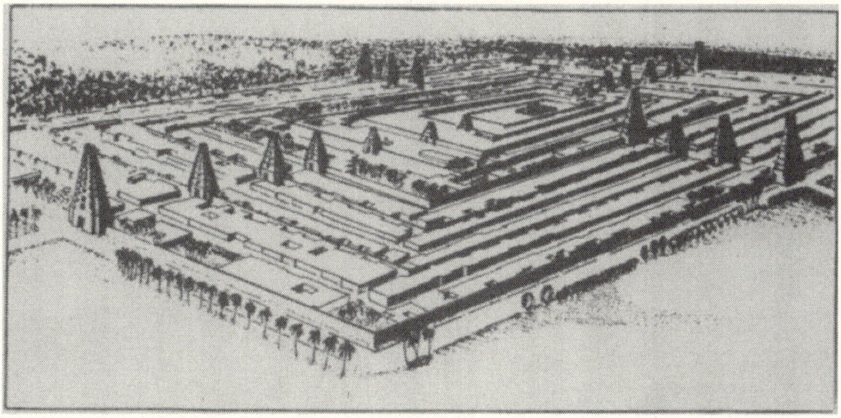

Figure 9.1: The seven *prakaras* or walled enclosures of the Ranganathasvami Temple, Srirangam

Source: https://dharmawiki.org/index.php/Srirangam

Bay of Bengal. The two rivers embrace a small island, the famous temple town of Srirangam or Thiruvarangam, known since ancient times as a sacred centre and in modern times as a hustling-bustling urban settlement. The monumental

Ranganathasvami temple, or Periya Koyil dedicated to Vishnu dominates the urban landscape with its towering gateways or *gopurams.* At a short distance, on the other side of the town is the Jambukeshvaram temple, or Tiruvanaikkaval dedicated to Shiva.[8] The two temples are important pilgrimage centres for the Shrivaishnava and Shaiva communities respectively, with approximately 2,000-year-old histories. Historically, the town settlements were mostly distributed within the seven walls or *prakaras* surrounding the Ranganathasvami temple, with each walled enclosure resembling ramparts, punctuated with four towering gateways or *gopurams.* The *prakaras* and the *gopurams* have been amongst the distinctive markers for Srirangam being labelled as a temple town.[9] However, the history writing on Srirangam somehow does not consider the Jambukeshvaram temple nor does it explore the relationship between the two religious structures and their devotees. This is a gap that needs to be filled up in future research.

The *Koil Olugu* demonstrates that the development of the town and the Ranganathasvami temple were almost synonymous with each other and religion played an important role in the production of urban space. It is one of the few texts that provided a long durée history of the Ranganathasvami temple starting from the epic-Puranic past and concluding in the early nineteenth century. The milieu in the *Olugu* narrative was undoubtedly influenced by the general historical context in which Srirangam evolved as a town.

Between the fifth and tenth centuries, the Vaishnava saints or the Alvars composed several devotional poems with Srirangam as a major sacred centre of Vishnu. Simultaneously, with the newly emerging state of the Cholas in the ninth century, Srirangam experienced agricultural activities with new peasant settlements that led to the expansion of a rich rural hinterland and a resource base for the urban processes at Srirangam. While the donations initially were not forthcoming, gradually by the eleventh to twelfth centuries donations of gold, paddy, cows, and land increased and these were invested in agriculture, with commercial and trading activities leading to an economy of circulation, exchange, and redistribution of commodities. The social background of the donors included a diverse population of peasants, tribes, pastoralists, artisans, merchants, religious functionaries, landed chiefs, and finally the state—all of whom registered their presence at Srirangam and participated in ritual activities of the Ranganathasvami temple. In addition, several donors also came from areas outside Srirangam, often as far as Malainadu (the present-day Kerala region).[10] Epigraphic evidence in the tenth century shows that the Ranganthasvami temple had four *prakaras*. This indicates the temple structure and the settlements around it, with diverse occupational and caste groups gradually migrating and settling here.[11] Consequently, the temple and the urban settlements within the *prakaras* witnessed repairs of older structures and the construction of newer ones.

The temple further became the centre of Vaishnava devotional activities, the context already described in the hymns of the later Alvars. This attributed importance to Srirangam as a pilgrimage centre, and visiting it was obligatory. This sacrality led to the introduction of temple rituals and festivals, especially the musical compilation and singing of the *Nalayira Divya Prabandham*, the corpus of the 4,000 hymns of the Alvars in the ninth and tenth centuries. From the twelfth century onwards, Ramanuja's exposition of the Shrivaishnava theology made Srirangam the centre of Shrivaishnava *acharyas* or religious leaders, and this was evident in the hagiographies, temple chronicles, and commentaries composed subsequently that delineated Srirangam and the Ranganathsvami temple as the reference point for the community.

The thirteenth and fourteenth centuries witnessed further development in the town and the temple. With the decline of the Cholas, the Kaveri delta region due to its rich resources attracted numerous warrior chieftains and major political powers, namely the Hoysalas (tenth to fourteenth centuries) from the Karnataka region, Pandyas (thirteenth to fifteenth centuries) from the Madurai region, Kakatiyas (twelfth to fourteenth centuries) from Warangal, Gajapatis (fifteenth to the sixteenth centuries) from Odisha, and finally, the Vijayanagara state (fourteenth to seventeenth centuries) from the northern Karnataka region to Srirangam, which now emerged as the centre of political as well as sacred geography. The town and the temple became loci of power, with control over them symbolizing an assertion of sovereignty. For instance, the Hoysalas established a second capital (the first one being Dwarasamudra in the southern Kannada region) in Kannanur, close to Srirangam. There is another instance of the Pandyan ruler, Jatavarman Sundara Pandya I (1250–68 CE) inscribing on the walls of the second *prakara* his victory over the Hoysalas, Cheras, and Cholas. Both instances highlighted that Srirangam town and the Ranganathasvami temple provided political spaces for legitimizing political authority.[12] The integration of the Kannada, Telugu, and Tamil linguistic regions under the Vijayanagara Empire from the fourteenth to the fifteenth centuries further accelerated the migration of traders, artisans, weavers, craftsmen, masons, peasants, and many occupational groups to Srirangam. As a result, the town witnessed hectic construction, repairs, and expansion of its built space.

Thus, the Ranganathasvami temple brought together political groups from far-off places, religious leaders, and common people within the economic and religious transactional network. The temple legitimized royal ideologies by applying the motif of a 'cosmological world-view' in which the ruler was attributed with divine origins. Simultaneous to these developments one finds the Shrivaisnava *acharyas* ranging from the monastic (*matha, mathadhipatis,* and *jiyars*) orders to influential families (*acharyapurushas*) flocking to the temple to consolidate their religious careers by developing their respective followings and patronage networks. The benefactions of political and mercantile groups were crucial. The religious leaders reciprocated by giving them temple honours like rights over portions of temple resources, and special participation in temple rituals and festivals that accorded privilege and prominence. Consequently, the social base of the temple functionaries expanded and included several non-brahmaṇas like the *Sattada Shrivaishnavas, ekangis, kaikkola mudalis,* and so on.[13] Thus, Srirangam, though a sacred centre, was complex and dynamic with sacrality as a significant part of its urbanity.

These processes of development of the town continued after the decline of the Vijayanagara power in the seventeenth and eighteenth centuries under the Nayakas of Tanjore and Madurai, the Marathas, the Nawabs of the Carnatic state, and finally the French and the English East India Companies, with the latter ultimately controlling the temple, town, and the entire region, thus setting the prelude to the establishment of colonial rule in the nineteenth century.

The *Koil Olugu* registered the changing historical context, weaving its narrative through the political history starting from the Cholas and ending with the English East India Company taking over the temple. It included details of various donations of different rulers, repairs, and construction works. The account is punctuated with activities of the Shrivaishnava religious leaders like the Alvars, *acharyas,* especially Ramanuja, and the *acharyapurushas* like the Uttama Nambis and disputations between them, and the politics of negotiation between the *acharyas* and the ruling elites, thus documenting a dynamic interaction between religion, politics, and urbanism. However, the *Olugu* was also situated within the framework of the Shrivaishnava textual tradition which in the fifteenth–sixteenth centuries, when *Olugu* in its various forms was being written, produced a genre of devotional literature, the *sthalapurana* dedicated to the history of temples and their locales to attract the pilgrims and their patronage. The *Olugu* in many ways had stylistic similarities with *sthalapuranas* in prefacing the narrative with epic-Puranic tropes that accorded sacred status from antiquity, the loss of the *vimana* (a pyramidal tower over the central shrine), and finally its recovery. Thus, we are told at the outset that Brahma worshipped the *vimana* in *satyaloka* (the highest heaven), and the Ikshvakus worshipped it in Ayodhya. Finally, Rama gifted it to Vibhishana 'who deposited it on the banks of Chandrapuṣkaraṇi, between the two Kaveri rivers', where it got buried under the sand, lost to posterity till the Chola ruler Dharmavarma at the behest of a divine intervention recovered it and rebuilt it.[14] Further, the language of the *Olugu* was Manipravala, a mixture of Tamil and Sanskrit, in which most of the Shrivaishnava texts like the hagiographies (*guruparamparas*), praise poems (*stotras*) and commentaries (*vyakhyanas*) were written. But unlike these texts, its tenor and quality were not literary, and the editor of the text, V.N. Hari Rao informs that the 'sentences were often fragmented with obscure words, meaning often vague and incoherent, making it difficult for an English translation'.[15]

An *olugu,* in general, recorded the day-to-day affairs and holdings of the temple. However, the internal evidence in the *Koil Oulgu* as discussed above informs us that there were several such records written by temple priests which were compiled, redacted, and edited into a single text in 1803 at the command of John Wallace, the collector of the British East India Company. According to Robert Sewell, the temple priests possessed this manuscript of the *Olugu* which contained a list of all the priests of the temples and details of its organization and administration.[16]

The fact that this single redacted manuscript was authorized by the five leading *sthalattars* 'belonging to a privileged family' in the presence of witnesses and kept in the safe custody of a group of temple priests highlights its value as an authoritative document that could not be tampered with and altered. Thus, the emphatic note in the *Olugu* about the nineteenth-century text as authentic and legitimate not only rendered the previous *olugus* redundant but also eliminated any difference that would challenge the redacted form. This process of rewriting history from the perspective of the nineteenth century by erasing multiple voices of the past was not only an attempt to create an archive that would be the only point of future reference, but it was also an initiative on the part of the five *sthalattars* to protect their interests and safeguard the benefits of their successors who belonged to the same *acharyic* lineage, thus ensuring uninterrupted hereditary domination over the temple resources.

The single-bound text referred to for this essay was based on the compilation, editing, and translation of the nineteenth-century manuscript in 1961 by V.N. Hari Rao, who also tells us that he used an original palm leaf manuscript and a paper version that he acquired from the Srirangam temple, both chronicling the events till 1803. Written by different accountants of the Srirangam temple storehouse in their handwriting, Rao writes that 'This was kept sealed and was referred to whenever there was a customary procedure of…, the temple rituals or honours. Thus it was a kind of diary kept by successive generations of temple accountants.'[17] Rao informs us further that there were two editions of the text which were published by Ananda Press and Umapati Guruprakasam Press in 1909 and were based on different manuscripts; however, the details in them were incomplete.[18] He fixes the date of the writing of the record to the twelfth century after the death of Ramanuja (d.1137 CE), based on the detailed narrative after the twelfth century compared to the sketchy one of the previous period.

The Temple and the Town in the *Koil Olugu*: An Interface Between Religion and Urbanity

The central idea of the *Koil Olugu* was the documentation of the history of the Ranganathasvami temple based on the role of select prominent *acharyas* in the administrative organization of the temple. These included ascetic leaders like Ramanuja, Sriranganarayan Jiyar, and Periya Nambi and householders belonging to the influential Shrivaishnava *acharyapurusha* lineage namely the Bhattars, Uttama Nambis, and Kandadais—all of whom possessed hereditary rights over the control of various temple offices. Therefore, the narratives on their activities, their relation with each other, the state and other temple functionaries were dominant. While the *Olugu* informs us about land grants and Ramanuja's 'Code of Udayavar' as the organizational prototype, it also gives prolific details about conflicts and negotiations over temple rights, resources, ritual performance, issues of succession to various offices, especially that of the *srikaryam* or temple manager and frequent reconfigurations of the administrative network, highlighting the challenges to and the vulnerability of the normative framework.[19] At the heart of these competing interests were the family of Uttama Nambis who appear recurrently in the narratives as trying to manipulate and negotiate the temple affairs on the one hand, and systematize the temple worship and enhance its resources mainly by soliciting land grants from the state on the other.[20] Notwithstanding these contestations, the *Olugu* details the reorganization of the temple administration, festivals and rituals, and frequent repair works done by various religious leaders.

However, the temple could not be deracinated from the town in which it was located. Therefore, for the *Olugu*, life inside the temple was not only connected with the urban space of Srirangam, but it perceived the town as a part of the institution of the temple, highlighting a relationship between religion and urbanity in which both interacted and influenced each other. In these narratives, Srirangam and its urbanism and the dynamism of a temple town that went beyond its sacred value were evident.

At the very outset, the *Olugu* gives us a glimpse of the seven *prakaras* with their names, and an impression of a hustling-bustling settlement with the last *prakara* described as 'the street full of storied houses'.[21] The narrative henceforth explains how the streets and gateways came to be named, thus familiarizing the reader with the setting where the events were to occur. For instance, Rajamahendra Street and the Aryabhattal gateway recur often as sites of significant activities later in the text, by which time one is already acquainted with them as the second *prakara* named after the Chola ruler, Rajamahendra Chola, in the eleventh century and the particular gateway which was constructed after the resolution of tensions between the Gaudadesa king (from outside the Tamil region) and temple authorities, respectively.[22]

The urban morphology of Srirangam in the *Olugu* comprised streets, gardens, shrines, *mandapams*, tanks, houses, and monastic establishments or *mathas*. These *mathas* in the *Olugu* were prominent sites of religious and political activities like settling disputes and bestowing honours and also were residences of powerful Shrivaishnava leaders like Ramanuja, Bhattar, Kuranarayana Jiyar, and Uttama Nambi. Thus, heading a *matha* was a prestigious entitlement. The *Koil Olugu* is full of descriptions of various streets through which the processions starting from the temple passed, connecting symbolically the entire town. These religious processions were a part of festivals that were celebrated in the temple and were delineated as spectacles in the *Olugu* involving the townspeople as spectators.[23] While the processions signified the movement within the town through a particular route, the descriptions of them by the *Olugu* show that they also became occasions for publicly bestowing honours, feeding devotees, and formally claiming villages in the vicinity or spaces in the town for the temple. These claims were legitimized either through the construction of shrines and pavilions, temporarily placing the festival deity, or conducting rituals and making formal arrangements for material exchange, rituals, and interactions. The description of several festivals, especially the Adhyayanotsava festival in which the 4,000 hymns of the Alvars were sung and enacted in a dance form and involved a large number of people, in the *Olugu* depicted how urban forms comprising a diverse population influenced the ritual activities and were in turn influenced by the temple activities.[24]

The *Olugu* details a continuous remapping of the urban space during festivals and processions. For instance, a boundary dispute between the Ranganathasvami and the Jambukeshvaram temple reconfigured the urban space for the Vaishnavas and Shaivas respectively.[25] This dispute was long-festering, with the Vaishnavas depicted as always having the upper hand till a flashpoint was reached.[26] We are told that on the eighth day of the Chittarai festival in the Tamil month of Panguni (mid-April to mid-May), the Ranganathasvami temple festival deity, the Perumal, entered the Shaiva area for the performance of a customary ritual of Ranganatha visiting the Shaiva goddess Akhilandeshwari, followed by washing of his feet in the tank (Jambu *tirtham*) of the Jambukeshvaram temple, and finally proceeding to a garden located along the banks of the river Coleroon. The *Olugu* reports that alleging trespassing into their area, the Shaivas obstructed the procession, killing one of the prominent Shrivaishnavas. The Shrivaishnava procession comprising the elephants, Perumal (the deity), *jiyars*, *parijans*, and dancers retaliated by reciting the Upanishads, raising the cry of victory, overwhelming the Shaivas and continuing towards the river Coleroon. The next year, the festival pageant performed its usual rituals and in addition, honoured those who had died in the clash on the boundary of the Shaivite territory and this agitated the Shaivas. Finally, the matter was taken to the Vijayanagara court where the Raya arbitrated between the Shaivas, the Shrivaishnavas whom Uttama Nambi represented, and the functionaries of both temples. A consensus was arrived at a common boundary area that remapped the procession route and demarcated the Vaishnava and Shaiva areas in this part of the town in the presence of various stakeholders. The account tells us that Uttama Nambi and the Shaivas struck a compromise and charted a boundary line leaving the Jambu *tirtham* and the Jambukeshvaram temple area much to the chagrin of the Shrivaishnava *mathadhipatis,* who finally relented. The Jambukeshvaram temple functionary 'requested a passage for their cattle promising a piece of land in exchange. Accordingly, the boundary stone was fixed… From that time the Perumal is taken to the boundary on the 8th day and not to the east (i.e. Jambukesvaram).'[27] V.N. Hari Rao, the editor of the text, dates this dispute to the fourteenth century.[28]

The physical location of Srirangam on the banks of the Kaveri with mangroves and forests finds reference when the river flooded the town, or when religious leaders from the temple built upon the river banks *mandapams* (pavilions) and cremation *ghats* for public use, and developed flower gardens for the supply of flowers to the temple.[29] The *Olugu* apprises us about raising the pavements, repairing the pillars and the walls, and two *gopurams* or the gateways of the second *prakara* due to seepage of water on the occasion of floods in the Kaveri every year at the initiative of Rajamahendra Chola.[30] However, these repair activities were embroiled in tensions. The *Olugu* tells us about a conflict between the villagers and the temple authorities when the latter wanted to dig a channel for diverting the flood water from the Kaveri. We are told that the *brahmans* (possibly Shaivas) protested by lying across the channel as their village land was being appropriated for this purpose. The temple authorities asserted themselves, forcibly built the channel, diverted the Kaveri waters, occupied the village land, and protected it by constructing sacred structures and introducing the performance and celebrations of rituals and festivals, with a stern enjoinment that defiling and transgressing them was a sacrilege.[31] Thus, controlling the flood water and minimizing the damage caused by it through repair activities also allowed the temple to extend itself into the urban space and its hinterland areas.

We find reference to constant repairs of the processional paths and building of tanks, monasteries, walls, and pavilions (*mandapams*), thereby rebuilding the urban space constantly.[32] It should be noted that most of the repairs and constructions were done at the behest of political patronage of the Cholas, Pandyas, Vijayanagara rulers, Nayakas, Nawabs of Arcot and Carnatic, and finally French and English East India Companies, thereby showing a nexus between religion, politics, and the town.

The lengthiest portion in the *Olugu* is dedicated to the arrival of Ramanuja to Srirangam, his zealous reforms called the 'Code of Udayavar' to reorganize the temple administration, the presence of powerful competing groups including the Uttama Nambis, their conspiracies against Ramanuja, and finally Ramanuja's steadfastness in overcoming the hostile opposition with the support of divine intervention.[33] We are told that after assuming the duty of *srikaryam,* Ramanuja discovered corruption in the accounts keeping and the collapse of administration. Consequently, he streamlined the system by introducing a new set of rituals, the celebration of festivals, especially the Adhyayanotsava festival and created an elaborate administrative structure by organizing the brahmana and non-brahmanas in groups of ten each, assigning them specific duties.[34] While the focus has been on the internal activities of the temple, the wider social base of temple functionaries that included a cross-section of the brahmana and non-brahmana groups, and the detailed assignment of specialized tasks indicates that for the *Olugu*, the people of the town had to be represented in the temple activities and the reforms of Ramanuja, which were already recorded in the Shrivaishnava texts, were significant in this respect. The *Olugu* not only cites the inclusion of temple non-brahmanas like shudras, *ekangis*, and *sattamudalis*, but it also provides details about the fourth group who were guards and the fifth group comprising sculptors, artisans, goldsmiths, blacksmiths, coppersmiths, washermen, handicraftsmen, potters, boatmen, and musicians.[35]

Thus, the *Koil Olugu* as a text presented its audience with a past that acquainted them with the practical aspects of the temple as an institution. The arrangement of events in a correct chronological manner was not its concern and expecting it to be would be akin to superimposing a modern worldview of time upon a historical text that has arranged the events following its aim. Undoubtedly, a sleight of hand in the *Olugu* placed certain events not according to their actual timeline but as a part of a narrative strategy that would impact the audience. For instance, the invasion of the Delhi Sultanate and attacks on the temple appear twice in the text.[36] In both cases, similar tropes are employed—disruption in worship and performance of festivals following the attack, looting and carrying away of the festival deity to Delhi followed by an adventurous recovery of the deity, and finally reinstalling it in its former place and resuming its worship under congenial circumstances. The first case involves a cross-section of people of the town ranging from a dancing girl to a washerman to temple servants and Kodavars and Irula tribes in the forests of Chandragiri at Tirupati, with an interesting event of the Sultan's daughter falling in love with the deity, making the arduous journey from Delhi to Srirangam, and finally merging with the god, thus establishing herself as an epitome of devotion or *bhakti.* The narrative is placed before a significant organizational intervention by the Shrivaishnava *acharya,* Nathamuni, perhaps attempting to contrast chaos with order. In the Shrivaishnava tradition which the *Olugu* also documents, Nathamuni is credited with collecting the hymns of the Alvars which were otherwise scattered and compiled, edited and put to music, thereby initiating a significant liturgical tradition in the temple. It should be noted that the dates of the first invasion of the Delhi Sultanate were between 1296 and 1314 CE under Sultan Alauddin Khilji (r.1296–1316 CE) and that of Nathamuni between the ninth and tenth century, an anachronism indeed if the *Olugu* is seen as a modern historical text with a sequential timeline. The second case is closer to the actual dates of the second invasion of the Delhi Sultanate under Mohammad bin Tughlaq (r.1324–51 CE) in the fourteenth century and has reference to the establishment of the Vijayanagara Empire (1336 CE) and the deity's reinstallation in the temple by the Vijayanagara general Goppana Udaiyar who brought the idol from Tirupati where it had finally taken refuge, travelling through Tirumaliruncholai in the southern parts and Melukote (presently in southern Karnataka) after its flight from Srirangam following the Turkish invasion.

Though the invasions of the Delhi Sultanate, the flight of the deity along with temple functionaries, and its subsequent reinstallation in the temple after peace returned, are mentioned in detail, these are not exceptions. The invasions by the Gajapatis of Odisha also led to the flight of the deity to Tirmularincolai and the suspension of worship in the temple. In all cases, the town of Srirangam was bound to be affected as we see how townspeople were motivated to save the deity.

However, the conflicts and negotiations within the temple and its manifestation in the town are the central focus of the history that the *Olugu* documented and not these invasions which were inserted to bolster the subsequent changes in the temple organization. The *Olugu* was creating a memory for the priestly community about how temple affairs were organized and the negotiation of conflicts that involved the religious leaders, the state and the town. Thus, it could be considered a ready reckoner for future temple functionaries who could use it, probably as a touchstone in case they encounter similar situations.

Conclusion

Narayani Gupta's pithy articles as a part of an eight-part series on *Reading a City* in *The Print* in 2019 and 2020 are an excellent sample of certain facets of urban history. [37] In this series, her third article on Srirangam informs us about Patrick Geddes, the famous Scottish town planner, coining the phrase 'temple-town' for the cities and towns in south India. Gupta in this write-up informs us that arguing for an Indian system of town planning, Geddes felt that the temple in these towns had a particular design that imparted a certain 'character and unity' to the urban morphology based on which the towns could be called temple towns.[38] The present essay while engaging with Geddes's idea of a temple-town points out that in addition to the urban layout and plan to study Srirangam, the *Koil Olugu* or the chronicle of the Ranganathasvami temple provided an alternate delineation of the town, while documenting the everyday life and the periodic matters in the temple.[39] The *Olugu* delineated the town and temple from the early period till around the eighteenth century presenting a complex dynamic urban form that disturbs the idyllic representation of Srirangam as an archetype of devotion and sacrality with the temple as an architectural exemplar.

Notes

1. The kingdom of the Carnatic comprised the region between the Eastern Ghats and the Bay of Bengal and included the modern states of Tamil Nadu and southern Andhra Pradesh. It was a part of the Madras Presidency and was for a while under the Nizams of Hyderabad. Tiruchirapalli and Srirangam were a part of the state of Carnatic.
2. The Vatakalais represent the Sanskritic tradition and give preference to the Sanskrit Vedas over the Dravida Vedas of the early Vaishnava saints, the Alvars. Kanchipuram in Tamil Nadu is their institutional centre, and Vedantadesika (traditional dates: *c.* 1268–1369 CE) is their spiritual preceptor. The Tenkalais, on the other hand, represent the Tamil tradition and regard the Dravida Vedas as their scriptures. Srirangam in Tamil Nadu is their centre and Manavaḷamamuni (traditional dates: *c.* 1370–1443 CE) is their religious leader. Both of them believe that the lineage of their respective leaders was the direct 'legitimate' line of descent from Ramanuja (traditional dates: *c.* 1017 to 1137 CE), the medieval saint and foremost leader of the Shrivaishnava community. See Ranjeeta Dutta, *From Hagiographies to Biographies. Ramanuja in Tradition and History*, New Delhi: Oxford University Press, 2014, p. 11.
3. V.N. Hari Rao, ed., *Kōil Oḷugu: The Chronicle of the Srirangam Temple with Historical Notes*, Madras: Rochouse and Sons, 1961, p. 203.
4. Ibid., pp. 203–4.
5. Ibid., pp. 202–5.
6. Ibid., p. 205.
7. Alexandra Walsham, 'The Social History of the Archive: Record Keeping in Early Modern Europe', *Past and Present*, vol. 230, November 2016, pp. 10, 13.
8. The Jambukeshvara temple is also large but has only one walled enclosure street, with settlements located outside the wall. Similarly, Madurai and Chidambaram in Tamil Nadu are two other temple towns with four and five *prakarams* respectively, with settlements situated outside the temples,

unlike Srirangam where the settlements fall mainly within the seven walls of the temple complex. For details, see Ranjeeta Dutta, 'Temple, Urban Landscape and Production of Space: Development of Srirangam in Early Modern Tamil Region', *Religion and the City in South Asia,* ed. Supriya Chaudhuri, Oxford, London, New York: Routledge, 2022, pp. 32–3.

9. On south Indian temple towns see James Heitzman, 'Temple Urbanism in Medieval South India', *The Journal of Asian Studies,* vol. 46, no. 4, 1987, pp. 791–826; George Michell, ed., *Temple Towns of Tamil Nadu,* Bombay: Marg Publications, 1993; R. Champakalakshmi, *Trade, Ideology and Urbanisation. South India 300 BC to AD 1300,* New Delhi: Oxford University Press, 1996.
10. Ranjeeta Dutta, 'Community, Religion, and Pilgrimage: The Growth of Śrīrangam in the Tamil Region', *Cities in Indian History,* ed. Pius Malekandathil and Yogesh Sharma, New Delhi: Primus, 2014, p. 468.
11. See Shri H.K. Narasimhasvami, ed., *South Indian Inscriptions, Volume XXIV (Inscriptions of Ranganathasvami Temple, Srirangam),* New Delhi: Archaeological Survey of India, 1982, no. 211–15, 222, 249.
12. Ibid., no. 195.
13. Burton Stein, 'Social Mobility and Medieval South Indian Hindu Sects', *Religious Movements in South Asia,* ed. David Lorenzen, Delhi: Oxford University Press, 2004, pp. 81–101; Dutta, *From Hagiographies to Biographies,* pp. 166–85.
14. *Kōil Oḷugu,* pp. 2–4.
15. Ibid., p. x.
16. Robert Sewell, *List of Antiquities,* vol. I, p. 268 in ibid.; also in K.V. Subrahmanya Aiyar, 'Koyilolugu', *The Indian Antiquary,* ed. Sir Richard Carnac Temple Bart and Devadatta Ramakrishna Bhandarkar, vol. XL, Bombay: British India Press, 1911, p. 131.
17. *Kōil Oḷugu,* p. viii.
18. Ibid, p. xv.
19. 'Code of Udayavar' means a set of reforms introduced by Ramanuja in the eleventh and twelfth centuries CE in the

administration of the Ranganathasvami temple at Srirangam. This was followed in other Shrivaishnava temples too. According to the Shrivaishnava tradition, Udayavar (one who owns everything) was the name given by the god at the temple in Srirangam, Ranganathasvami to Ramanuja when he migrated from Kanchipuram to Srirangam.

20. For instance, see, *Kōil Oḷugu,* pp. 145–52; pp. 155–62.
21. *Kōil Oḷugu,* p. 1.
22. Ibid., pp. 5–7.
23. Ibid., pp. 18–22.
24. Ibid., pp. 10–13.
25. Ibid., pp. 139–41.
26. Ibid., pp. 117–18.
27. Ibid. p. 141.
28. Ibid.
29. Ibid., p. 13.
30. Ibid., p. 4; pp. 174–5.
31. Ibid., pp. 118–20.
32. Ibid., p. 22; pp. 110–11.
33. Ibid., pp. 41–112.
34. Ibid., pp. 48–100.
35. Ibid., pp. 50–90, 96–9.
36. Ibid., pp. 24–38, 126–36.
37. Narayani Gupta, 'How Scotsman Patrick Geddes May Have Started India's Obsession with Vastu', *The Print,* 15 December 2019, see https://theprint.in/opinion/sahapedia/scotsman-patrick-geddes-started-india-obsession-with-vastu/332888/, 31 March 2024.
38. Patrick Geddes, 'The Temple Cities', *The Modern Review,* vol. 25, no. 3, pp. 213–22.
39. Jeannine Auboyer, *Sri Ranganathasvami Temple,* Srirangam: A Srirangam Temple Publication, 1968, p. 21.

10

The Former Capital

Mughal Legacy in Agra

SHAILAJA KATHURIA

THE MUGHAL capital moved from Agra to Delhi in 1648 and by the mid-eighteenth century a decentralization of Mughal rule had begun with governors of provinces establishing their own dynasties such as in Awadh and Hyderabad. This did not happen in Agra in any systematic or sustained way and it was only in the later part of the century that Agra saw a few decades of uninterrupted rule before British annexation.

Nadir Shah (in 1739) and Ahmad Shah Abdali (in 1756–7) were not the only raiders of Agra in the eighteenth century. The Bharatpur Jats under Suraj Mal invaded and plundered Agra in 1761. Political control of the region alternated between the Jats and Scindia Marathas till the mid-1780s when Mahadaji Scindia, as Mughal regent, conquered Agra and gradually became the de facto ruler.[1]

The defeat of Daulat Rao Scindia and the treaty of Surji Arjangaon in 1803 brought Agra and Delhi, together with all the possessions of Scindia north of the Chambal, into the hands of the British. This territory came to be known as the Conquered Districts and those areas acquired from the nawab of Awadh as the Ceded Districts. A board

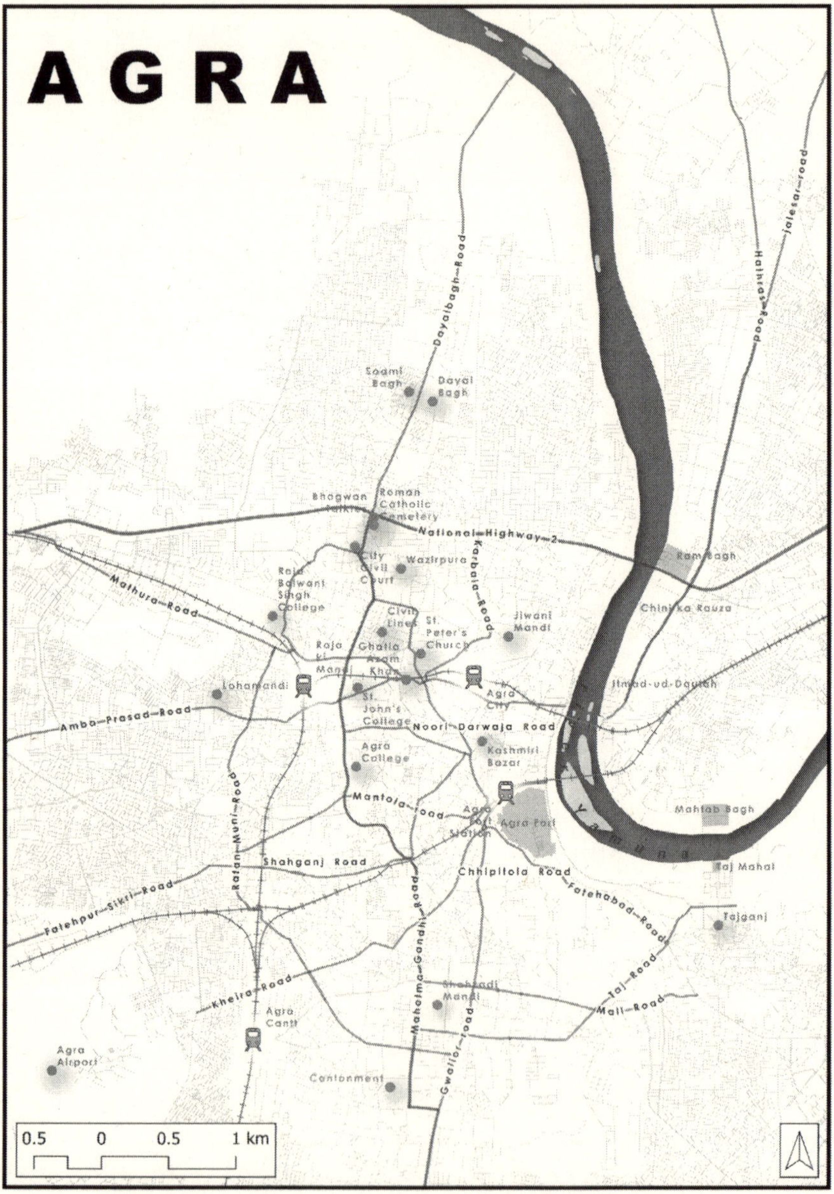

Map 10.1: Map of the city of Agra (*c.* twenty-first century) with some important landmarks, roads and localities (map drawn by Shubham Mishra)

Source: Map of Agra in *Agra Rambles and Recollections of Thomas Smith*, New Delhi: Chronicle Books, 2007

of Commissioners assumed control with the lieutenant governor as the president.[2]

Power and the City

Through this period the Mughal fort of Agra both resisted and fell to invaders several times. It was coveted for its strong defences and symbolic significance as the seat of government of the first capital of what had been a mighty empire and now lay open to invasion.

The shift of the capital to Delhi had led to a large-scale migration of the Mughal elite from Agra and a decline in the long-distance riverine and overland trade.[3] But constant military activity in the area and the large presence of soldiers in the fort and city created a demand for food and military supplies. Thomas Twining and Bayly mention the cannon foundries set up by the Marathas around Agra.[4] Lakshmichand, an eighteenth-century poet in his poem 'Agra ki Ghazal', describes a variety of bazaars in the city. In the immediate vicinity of the fort, in the Padshahi Chowk (enclosed market for the palace) which seems to have catered to the fort in Mughal times, a *gudari* or general market was held, selling everything from cheap cloth, sugar, and paper to swords and daggers.[5] Most likely, this bazaar served the new inhabitants of the fort and its neighbourhood, a large number of which were soldiers. The space for a palace bazaar was now taken by a general one.

Lakshmichand also writes of shows by 'madaris' (a caste which included those who trained animals such as monkeys and bears for street performances) in the same market.[6] Till the 1990s, when animal performances were banned in India, one could see bear trainers along the highway from Agra to Bharatpur. Clearly there was a large number of these itinerant performers in the region and the rise of Jat power in the Agra–Bharatpur belt eased mobility between the rural areas and the city and helped keep local markets alive in Agra.

The 'mandis' or markets for grain in Sikandra, Mubarak Sultan Ganj, Doria Ganj, and Fateh Ganj remained busy. The *Nakhasa* was a daily market for cattle and *Hajjam Mandi* was where the market for arms and ammunitions was located.[7]

Like many of the new dynastic chiefs in northern India, the Jats and Marathas gradually settled into a pattern of Mughal-style conspicuous consumption, thus reviving some industries producing luxury articles in Agra.[8] The Scindias assumed Mughal titles and continued to shop in Agra well after the British annexation. *Kalabatun* (gold and silver thread) and gold lace were frequently purchased by them and sometimes their request for the waiving of duties was granted by the new rulers.[9] It is well known that the Jats took marble, masons, and stone workers from Agra to build the magnificent palaces at Deeg.

After the British conquest in 1803, the Agra fort was taken over by military authorities who lost no time in 'renovating' it to suit their needs. The arches of the Dewan-i-Am were walled up and the area converted into an armoury.[10] Another portion of the fort was used to house the prison. Rows of military casemates were constructed in the quadrangle.[11] The Salimgarh palace which was the highest point in the fort was used as a canteen. Here too the archways were closed and a veranda added on one side. After the Allahabad fort capture, this was the second major Mughal fort to fall to the British and proved to be a valuable asset in subsequent years.

In addition to the fort, some villages to its south-west were also taken by the army and work was started on a cantonment. The 'Civil Lines' were built west of the old city and inhabited by the growing class of servants of the government. Agra became the capital of the North-West Provinces (NWP) in 1835 and soon had a Sadr Board of Revenue, a court, a civil hospital, and a government college.[12] Most of these were located on a road running parallel to the old city, later to be Drummond Road, now another Mahatma Gandhi Marg.

A universal concern and sometimes paranoia for the soldiers' health prompted more changes in sanitation, particularly in ventilation, water supply, and drainage.[13] An increasing number of venereal disease (VD) cases among the soldiers in Agra became an excuse for acquiring villages around the fort where prostitution was suspected to be rampant. Kachupur, Sultanpur, and Dhurera were quickly included in the Cantonment. The commanding officer declared that there was no cultivable land in these villages, so there was no obligation to pay compensation. However, the city bazaars were considered 'free of disease'.[14]

At the outbreak of the revolt in 1857, this was the only major fort held by the British between Lahore and Allahabad. Since it had been in their possession for half a century, there had been enough time to bolster its defences and make it more habitable. It was well stocked with grain reserves for up to 5,000 persons for a month-long siege.[15] As it turned out, it was used as a refuge for hundreds of Europeans and 'native' Christians[16] (of which there was a sizeable number) in the city.

In Agra, as in many places in northern India, the trading community had come out in support of the British. The grain merchants, in particular Lala Jyoti Prasad the contractor, kept the fort well supplied with provisions throughout the siege.[17] Although he had been accused of fraud in the 1840s, he was instantly forgiven by the desperate British army in 1857 and took the opportunity to return to favour.[18]

After the British regained control, retributive measures were not as brutal in Agra as they were in Delhi and Lucknow. For the Europeans and others, the haven of the fort had protected them from any large-scale massacre. However, Agra did see some destruction and change. The esplanade around the fort was extended and cleared of houses.[19] The gateway of Jahan Ara Begum's mosque outside the Delhi Gate of the fort was also pulled down.

The coming of the first railway line in the 1860s brought further changes in the morphology of the city. The Rajputana State Railway line cut right through the Tirpolia enclosure outside the fort and continued westward into the city.[20] The East India Railway reached Delhi in 1867 and had acquired the west bank of the Yamuna near Agra but it was only in 1908 that a bridge across the river gave them access to the city.

The *Padritolas* of Agra

In the few decades of Maratha rule in Agra some officials and nobles had been given jagirs (land grants) in and around the city by the rulers. It is interesting that the first government college in Agra city, though founded in 1823 by the local government, was begun from the proceeds of a rent-free grant made to Gangadhar Shastri, a *purohit* (senior priest) of the Scindia chiefs and a *padre* of sorts. The villages were Jhandari and Chaumuha in Agra and Iglas in Aligarh. The government decided that while one-fourth of the income from this jagir should go to Gangadhar's descendants, the rest should be used for educational causes. The two funds at Aligarh and Agra were merged and the Agra College was established from the remaining funds.[21]

Although English as a language was taught along with Hindi, Sanskrit, Arabic, and Persian, it was only after the government adopted it as the official language in 1837, that the number of students studying the language increased in the college. It was then converted into an Anglo-Oriental College.[22]

Akbar had made a land grant to the Jesuit mission in Agra in the late sixteenth century and by 1600 he had a church built which is still known popularly as Akbar's church. It is part of one of the oldest Catholic mission settlements in northern India. The locality came to be known as *Padritola* (locality of padres or priests).

This was the age of European military adventurers who helped 'modernize' the armies of the warring chiefs. Among them, Walter Reinhardt, Benoit de Boigne, John Hessing, and Jean Baptiste Filose had lived and served in Agra as commanders of forces under the Marathas, Jats, and Mughals.[23] In spite of their constantly changing loyalties and masters, some, like Reinhardt and Filose are still known for their philanthropy in Agra. Akbar's church was destroyed and rebuilt twice. Reinhardt and his wife, Begum Samru, contributed to its rebuilding in 1769 and Begum Samru made many subsequent donations to its renovations. It was here that she was baptized in 1781.[24] Later in 1835, Filose donated money for the church's extension. Filose owned a substantial amount of land in Agra and donated land for St. Peter's College in 1841.[25] Agra being the main diocese with an ancient Mughal cemetery, Reinhardt and Hessing were buried there. Hessing's tomb is a replica of the Taj Mahal in red sandstone.

Several missionary schools and colleges were founded in Agra in the first half of the nineteenth century. Among them were the St. Peter's Roman Catholic School (1846) and St. Patrick's (1842) begun by the Jesus and Mary nuns and later St. John's College (1852) founded by the Anglican mission.

Protestant missionary activity began in Agra in the early 1800s, but in the famine of 1837, Agra suffered greatly. creating over 2,000 orphans. Most were sent to institutions in Benares and Kanpur and a few hundred were admitted in the Anglican Church Missionary Society's orphanage in Agra. This was located in the compound of Akbar's mausoleum in Sikandra and the building of the tomb of Akbar's wife Maryam Zamani was used for the purpose. The mistaken assumption that Maryam Zamani was a Christian was the justification that was given by the CMS for their choice of this location. In the following years, most of the orphan children were converted, making this one of the largest convert establishments in the area.

A printing press was set up in the orphanage as a means of employment for the inmates and a source of income for the institution. It soon took on work for the government, earning enough profit to support the orphanage and later fund the establishment of St. John's College in 1852. The press was completely destroyed in the revolt of 1857 as the inmates took refuge in the fort.[26]

Conservation and Care

In 1871, the Archaeological Department took on the functions of conservation and repair and later, survey. This new role combined with a growing awareness of the historicity and beauty of Agra's old structures led to systematic repairs and actual restoration beginning in the 1870s.

The most important work was done in the fort both in a real and symbolic way. Large sections of the fort were evacuated and repairs carried out. The military casemates were removed and the cloisters restored, as were the arches of the Diwan-i-Am. The modern road was closed and the road between the two main entrances of the quadrangle of the Jehangiri Mahal was reopened.[27]

The Akbarabadi mosque and the Jama Masjid built respectively by Shahjahan's wife Akbarabadi Begum and his daughter Jahan Ara Begum were repaired and handed over to the local community in the 1860s.[28]

The 'Rauza' of Tajganj

In 2022, the Supreme Court of India ruled that shops within a 500 m. radius of the Taj Mahal were to be removed or 'restricted'. Most of the traders affected were in the Tajganj bazaar adjoining the mausoleum. The ruling provoked widespread protests and in November of the same year, the order was withdrawn.[29] Questions are now being asked about the propriety of the celebration of the annual 'Urs' ceremony of Shahjahan and Mumtaz at a protected monument.

When it was built, the Taj was conceived as a part of a complex of a shrine known in contemporary sources as 'Rauza-i-Munavvara' (tomb of light), a garden, and the area of Mumtazabad or Tajganj as it is known as today. The income from thirty villages had been assigned for the upkeep of the tomb and the imperial structures in Mumtazabad which had markets, *serais* (inns), and residences.[30]

Nazir Akbarabadi (1735–1830) the poet and resident of Tajganj, Agra, titled one of his poems describing the beauty of the Taj, 'Tajganj Ka Rauza' (The Shrine of Tajganj). To him it was not only the grand mausoleum of a Mughal queen and king but also a local *mazhar.* The beautiful white marble imperial building that visitors were already coming to see and admire in the nineteenth century, the shrine and the bazaar were a part of the same ecosystem.

Today, Tajganj houses a number of shops selling marble inlay handicrafts and *karkhanas* or workshops of marble workers which are now located in many places in the city. The lapidaries of Agra were employed to repair the marble inlay in the Taj by the British from the early nineteenth century. The name of Parshuram, an Agra lapidary comes up frequently in the colonial sources, and his services seemed to have been used extensively.[31] Before that, the French commandant of the Agra fort under the Marathas, General De Boigne, also tried to persuade his masters to renovate some portions of the Taj. The Taj was the only Mughal building in Agra which brought out such expressions of empathy from the Europeans until the 1880s, when the Archaeological Department began its work.

Celebration, Subversion, Resurgence and Nazir, Smith, Tanvir

After the shift of the capital to Delhi, Agra never really had a king's court around which cultural activities were centred through a system of patronage. Perhaps it was this decentralization of culture that produced poets like Nazir.

There is no better source of information on the city's popular culture and the everyday life of its people than his poems. Most were written in the vernacular 'Brajbhasha'. He wrote several poems on local festivals such as 'Kanhaiyaji Ka Janam', 'Baldevji Ka Mela', 'Basant', and 'Holi'. There are long poems on vegetables and fruit like cucumbers and melons, on sweets like 'Til ke Laddu' (a sesame-seed sweet), on dancers, gypsies, and street performers like the *madaris* with animals that Lakshmichand wrote about. In his poem on a popular monsoon swimming festival in the Yamuna in Agra, he proudly recounts how the swimming race attracts swimmers and spectators of all classes, making this event a great leveller.

By the late nineteenth century there was a substantial class of professionals and educated persons who were entering government service. Of these some had political ambitions and had begun to use public events such as the festivals Nazir wrote of, to try and create larger community identities based on sweeping generalizations of religion.[32] The 'Pairaki' or swimming festival was one such event. In 1888, there were two such festivals held, one which was the traditional and more inclusive one and the other which had been extended to include religious ceremonies.[33] However, Agra did not witness the kind of disturbances that other towns did in the province and in the 1890s the efforts of an able District Magistrate A.W. Cruickshank helped ease the situation. The Sitla temple fair and the Muharram procession in 1890 and later were attended by people from all communities.[34]

Nazir's interweaving of people, occasion, event, and locale supplied the perfect metaphor to at least two others in the twentieth century: Thomas Smith, journalist, Agra resident and chronicler, and Habib Tanvir the playwright and dramatist in his play *Agra Bazaar*.

Like Nazir, Smith was not only an observer but a participant and intrinsic part of the subjects he wrote about in his newspaper column. Like Nazir, he wrote about *mohallas* (localities), streets, and *bazaars*. Some of his eminent contemporaries like him were chroniclers of Agra and wrote interesting tales and anecdotes on some of the lesser-known historical buildings of Agra. He was descended from a military adventurer who had served in the Mughal and Maratha armies and lived in the Ghatia Azam Khan locality near Padritola, a neighbourhood which his ancestors shared with the Filoses. Smith's great contribution lay in popularizing the history and contemporary culture of Agra. He even wrote a story on the old Catholic cemetery in Padritola where he lies buried with so many of the subjects of his compositions.

It is significant that Habib Tanvir chose Nazir's poems and characters which were adapted for his play 'Agra Bazaar'. Once again one sees vegetable sellers, shopkeepers, street performers, courtesans, and others. This was written in the early 1950s but the story was set in the eighteenth century. This play was cleverly written in such a way that the social conditions presented in it remained relevant in the twentieth century as well.

Travellers from all over the world had been coming to see the Taj long before this most visible symbol of Mughal legacy and of India put Agra on the world tourism map, a place still held by it today. Equally, what is both ironic and fascinating is that this splendid Mughal capital became the subject of a robust popular culture literature epitomized in Nazir's poems, Smith's articles and Tanvir's play.

Here I will quote an English translation of an excerpt from 'Agra Bazaar'—the dialogue between a *madari* and his performing monkey:

Madari: Now tell me, how did Nadir Shah attack Delhi? (The monkey hits the madari with a stick.) Hey, you will kill the entire city of Delhi! Stop it, Bade Mian, stop it!
Madari: Well, how did Ahmed Shah Abdali attack Delhi? (The monkey hits the madari again.) Yes, yes, yes, you will destroy the whole country. Bade Mian, stop it!
Madari: And how did Surajmal Jat pounce on Agra city? (The monkey repeats the action) Oho, oho, he is dead. Stop it, Bade Miyan, stop it!
Madari: Okay tell me, how did foreigners come to India? (The monkey mimics begging.)
Madari: And what did Lat Saheb (Lord Saheb i.e. Robert Clive) do in the battle of Pilasi? (The monkey mimics shooting a gun using the stick).
Madari: Oh-ho, and what happened in Bengal? (The monkey holds its stomach and feigns weakness.) There was a famine. (The monkey lies down.)
Madari: People died of hunger. And what is our condition? (The monkey beats its stomach again.) And what will be our condition tomorrow? (The monkey falls). Then what should we do? (The monkey goes to the people and lies down with his head at their feet.) Salute! (The monkey salutes)

The dynamic cosmopolis of Nazir's Agra and Akbar's Akbarabad had become a universal metaphor.

Notes

1. Dharma Bhanu Srivastava, *The Province of Agra. Its History and Administration,* Agra: Shiva Lal Agarwala and Co., 1979, Chap. 1, pp. 15–20.

2. Ibid., p. 23.
3. C.A. Bayly, *Rulers, Townsmen and Bazaars. North Indian Society in the Age of Expansion, 1770–1870*, Cambridge: Cambridge University Press, 1983, p. 63.
4. Ibid., p. 56.
5. R.C. Sharma, 'Agra in the First Quarter of the Eighteenth Century', Lecture delivered on 7 December 1985 to the Agra Archaeological Society.
6. Ibid.
7. H.K. Naqvi, *Urban Centres and Industries in Upper India, 1556–1803*, Bombay: Asia Publishing House, 1968, Section on Commerce and Markets.
8. Bayly, *Rulers, Townsmen and Bazaars*, pp. 147, 209, 460.
9. Foreign Political Consultations, National Archives of India, NAI, 15 and 26 March 1812, 25 June 1813.
10. Military Dept Proceedings (NAI), 14 August 1806, 24 December 1806, 19 February 1807, 6 August 1810.
11. Military Department Proceedings (NAI), 21 November 1808, 12 September 1809, 6 August 1810, no. 90–1, 22 February 1811, No. 108.
12. Srivastava, *The Province of Agra. Its History and Administration*, pp. 126–64.
13. Military Dept Proceedings (NAI), 7 February 1845, no. 75–6, no. 9–13, p. 619; 4 June 1847, no. 131–2; 16 July 1847, no. 64–5.
14. Agra District Series (Uttar Pradesh State Archives, UPSA) 1858, Transfer of Mauza Kachupur and Sultanpur to Cantonment.
15. Military Dept Proceedings (NAI), 19 June 1857, no. 126–7.
16. Military Dept Proceedings (NAI), 14 August 1857, Agra District Series (UPSA) June 1857, Box no. 6.
17. Military Department Proceedings (NAI), June 1857; Bayly, *Rulers, Townsmen and Bazaars*, p. 363; J.W. Kaye, *A History of the Great Revolt*, vol. 3, London: W.H. Allen and Co., 1877, p. 399.
18. Military Department Proceedings (NAI), June 1857; Bayly, *Rulers, Townsmen and Bazaars*, p. 363.
19. Agra District Series (UPSA), Revenue Dept. 1858, Box 7.
20. PWD Railways (NAI), March 1872 no. 50–2, April 1872, no. 18–30, July 1873, no. 58–73.

21. Agra District Series (UPSA), no. 138, 1821.
22. Srivastava, *The Province of Agra,* Chap. 10. pp. 346–8.
23. Herbert Crompton, *A Particular Account of the European Military Adventurers of Hindustan 1784–1803,* London: T.F. Unwin, 1892, p. 8.
24. Thomas Smith, *Rambles and Recollections of Thomas Smith,* New Delhi: Chronicle Books, 2007, p. 27.
25. Smith, *Rambles and Recollections,* p. 59.
26. Avril Ann Powell, *Muslims and Missionaries in Pre-Mutiny India,* London: Routledge, 1993, pp. 160–3. F.J Mcbride, *Sikandra, 1840–1940,* Sikandra, Agra: Sikandra Press, 1940, pp. 13–14; Home Public Proceedings (NAI) 7 Aug 1832, No. 74.
27. Home Public Proceedings (NAI), May 1872, no. 10–12, July–October 1872, Archaeological Department Report, 1871–2 on Delhi and Agra by A.C.L Carlyle, Archaeological Survey of India, Delhi.
28. Agra District Series (UPSA), BR 1 May 1861–29 July 1861 and Agra Regional Archives (ARA) Revenue Dept, 1869, File no. J 24/37, Box 9.
29. Siraj Qureshi, 'SC Withdraws Order Restricting Business within 500-metre of Taj Mahal', *India Today,* 10 November 2022, see https://www.indiatoday.in/cities/agra/story/supreme-court-withdraw-order-restricting-business-taj-mahal-2295638-2022-11-10, accessed 9 July 2024.
30. Catherine B. Asher, *The New Cambridge History of India, Architecture of Mughal India,* Cambridge: Cambridge University Press India, 1995, p. 210.
31. Home Public Proceedings (NAI), 17 June 1824, no. 29 and Selections from NWP records, second series, vol. 1, 1869.
32. Sandria B. Freitag, *Agra in the 1880s: Communitas and Public Arenas in Collective Action and Community: Public Arenas and the Emergence of Communalism in North India,* Berkeley: University of California Press, 1989, pp. 146–7.
33. Ibid., pp. 140–1.
34. Ibid., p. 146. Newspaper report from Mufid-i-Am, 10 July 1893 and 1 September 1899.

11

Urban Profile in Late Medieval Punjab

INDU BANGA

PROFESSOR NARAYANI GUPTA is one of those few distinguished historians who are committed equally to teaching and research and who have a pronounced social conscience, with active involvement in causes like school education and conservation of architecture. She has been involved in design and urban planning too. She is full of ideas and her style of writing is evocative and smooth. Her gentleness and humanity are endearing, and her integrity and firmness evoke respect.

My earliest impressions of Narayani go back to the mid-1960s when I was doing MA at the Panjab University, Chandigarh. I remember her as a bright young teacher of history, participating in the History Teaching Workshop organized by Professor J.S. Grewal and (Dr) John C.B. Webster. One of the resource persons happened to be Dr Partha Sarathi Gupta. I have memories of some of the women participants teasing him, and Narayani taking it good-naturedly. What struck me then was her earnestness and sincerity about the teaching of history. One could have anticipated her deep involvement subsequently with the reform of history syllabi at the university and school levels, especially with the National Council of Educational Research and Training. Her address at the History Teachers Conference at the Panjab University in March 2008 is still remembered.

My professional association with Narayani began in February 1978 when she came to Guru Nanak Dev University, Amritsar where I was teaching then. She had been invited to participate in an international seminar on urban history organized by Professor J.S. Grewal as the director of the UGC project on 'Urbanisation in the Upper Bari Doab, 1700–1947'. In 1975, he had produced a pioneering study of medieval Batala located in this sub-region. This book was somewhat misleadingly titled, *In the By-Lanes of History: Some Persian Documents from a Punjab Town*. The UGC project, with which I was associated as deputy director, reconstructed the history of a dozen small towns on the bases of Persian accounts, British sources, municipal records, and field work.

Narayani had by then obtained her PhD from Delhi University on her thesis on 'Urban Government in Delhi, 1863–1925'. She had put together several kinds of exciting evidence scattered in and outside Delhi, making use of theoretical insights and fascinating empirical data. She could at once grasp the significance of the urban history project being pursued by the Department at Amritsar. She pointed this out to Dr Atiya Habeeb Kidwai, a regional geographer whose work on colonial urbanization in Calcutta and its hinterland is eminently characterized by a historical approach. Among the other participants from outside were Professors S. Nurul Hasan, S.C. Misra, V.D. Divekar, Stanley K. Shultz, and Dr Shereen Ratnagar.

The contributions ranged from theoretical propositions and historiographical surveys to empirical studies of the Indian urban scene from pre-historic to modern periods, in regional and subcontinental perspectives. Discussions were stimulating, like a journey of discovery on which we had embarked together. Historians had taken longer than other social scientists to seriously study the urban phenomena.

Everyone responded enthusiastically to Narayani's suggestion that an informal group should be formed to promote the study of urban history. In his concluding remarks, Professor S. Nurul Hasan proposed that an Urban History Group may be formed with a token membership fee of Rs.10, and that Professor J.S. Grewal may act as its convener and prepare a draft constitution.

After its informal meetings at Hyderabad in 1978 and Waltair in 1979, the General Body of this group met at Bombay in 1980, alongside the Indian History Congress session. The proposed constitution was discussed clause by clause and approved, with Professor S. Nurul Hasan in the chair. This group was registered as the Urban History Association of India (UHAI), with Professor Hasan elected as president and Professor Grewal as secretary. The eminent historians who later became its presidents were Professors Satish Chandra, S.C. Misra, Irfan Habib, Ravinder Kumar, and J.S. Grewal. Professor Grewal and I remained associated with the UHAI in different capacities. As a member of its executive, Narayani remained in the company of distinguished historians and geographers. From amongst the latter, the UHAI received the most consistent support from Professor Atiya Habeeb Kidwai.

For over two decades, the UHAI organized its symposium on the third day of the annual session of the Indian History Congress, which attracted a large number of young scholars. The symposia papers published as Occasional Papers covered the entire span of Indian history, as did the newsletters and bibliographies of the UHAI. Its seminars held at Amritsar, Baroda, Chandigarh, and Shimla were attended by historians and other social scientists, administrators, and town planners. Even scholars of literature took interest in its programmes. There was a noticeable increase in the number of papers on urban history brought to the Indian History Congress sessions. Courses in urban history were introduced in some Indian universities like Jawaharlal Nehru University, Guru Nanak Dev University, and the Panjab University. The anthologies published by the UHAI in association with Manohar—*Calcutta: Foundation and Development of a Colonial Metropolis* (1991), *The City in Indian History* (2005), and *Ports and their Hinterlands, 1700–1950* (2019)—were well received.

Narayani was among those few scholars who lent crucial and consistent academic support to the UHAI. She edited the volume entitled, *Craftsmen and Merchants: Essays in South Indian Urbanism* (1993) which, incidentally, has contributions by R. Champakalakshmi, Vijaya Ramaswamy, and Sanjay Subrahmanyam. The Occasional Papers Series brought out her own longish essay as *Towers, Tanks and Temples: Some Aspects of Urbanism in South India: Eighteenth and Nineteenth Centuries* (1983). Her perceptive paper on 'Pondicherry in the Nineteenth Century: A Port Without a Hinterland' was presented at the UHAI seminar on ports and their hinterlands. It may be added that Narayani's multi-faceted work on urban history is interdisciplinary and comparative in approach, covering a broad canvas. She skillfully uses a large variety of sources in different languages, including French. Her insightful analysis is combined with unobtrusive theoretical underpinnings and fascinating detail about facets of Indian urbanism. My essay in this volume dedicated to Narayani should appropriately relate to our common interest in urban history.

Introduction

The late onset of colonial rule in the Punjab in 1849 provides a window into the late medieval urban universe. It is axiomatic that the term 'urban' is used for a settlement which is distinct from 'rural'. In his *Char Bagh-i Panjab* completed in 1849, Ganesh Das, a hereditary *qanungo* of Gujrat in the time of Ranjit Singh (1780–1839), uses three terms for urban centres of different sizes: *qasba, shahr,* and *balda,* broadly denoting small and middling towns and the city. Despite differences in size and diversities of various kinds, urban centres shared certain common attributes. They had an externally delimited and internally divided space, and a much higher density and heterogeneity of population than villages. Generally, more people were engaged in rendering service of some sort; they were followed in numbers by those engaged in manufactures. The proportion of those dependent on agriculture was the smallest, and it was related inversely to the size of the centre (smaller the centre, larger the proportion of landed elements). An average urban centre performed administrative, economic, social, and cultural functions for its own population and the surrounding areas. Its hinterland was constituted by the neighbouring countryside, but its commercial linkages extended to the other towns and cities in the region and, in some cases, even outside. Some kind of local management of different urban segments, generally under the overall control of the state's representative, was an integral feature of the urban situation.

The existing studies of urbanization in the Punjab plains have identified over 150 urban centres in the early nineteenth century. Over 60 per cent of these, including Amritsar and Lahore and the other major centres, were located in the fertile and populous upper parts of the interfluves (*doabs*) and the Bist Jalandhar. Loosely referred to as the central Punjab, this area constituted the core of the supra-regional state of Ranjit Singh. It had remained under Sikh rule, that is of Ranjit Singh and his Sikh predecessors, for nearly a century. This period saw the decline of some old towns, but the scale of revival, expansion, and foundation of new urban centres was much larger. In fact, urbanization in the sense of increase in the number and size of urban centres, and decentralization of political power in the sense of large numbers of autonomous foci of power, went together in the last quarter of the eighteenth century. The new rulers vied with one another in attracting traders, artisans, and other people to their capitals which numbered around three score in the central Punjab. While absorbing these in his expanding state, Ranjit Singh continued to give impetus to urbanization.

Amritsar grew to be the largest city in the region under Ranjit Singh. It had a substantial segment of religious functionaries, particularly those related to the Golden Temple, renovated and gold-plated in the 1820s. The city was also a seat of traditional learning and medicine, and its *akharas* (establishments of the Udasi *sadhs*) were well-known. As an *entrepôt,* its manufactures and markets were more specialized and its traders and financiers better organized. The city had some Marwari traders too. Comparatively, and as the seat of government, Lahore had more state functionaries, more military personnel, more professional people and more of the service-performing groups. The number of its artisans, traders, and financiers was next only to that of Amritsar. Both cities had a visible presence of the members of the ruling class composed of top echelons of the civil and military officers and the middle ranking functionaries from varied backgrounds, but dominated by Jats and Khatris, respectively among Sikhs and Hindus. However, rather than the twin capitals of Amritsar and Lahore, the middling towns like Jalandhar, Batala, and Gujrat were more reliable indicators of the stable elements in the urban universe in the pre-colonial period.

Structure of Urban Population

Located in the most fertile tract of the region, Jalandhar was large enough by medieval standards to have been the headquarters of a small province in the state of Ranjit Singh, and later the divisional headquarters in the British Punjab. According to the earliest census of Jalandhar taken by the

British in 1848–9, in a population of around 22,800, there were several well-marked occupational categories. Those engaged in trade and commerce comprised of wholesalers (in grain, *gur*, cotton, and silk), retailers, petty shop-keepers, peddlers, confectioners, money-lenders (*sahukars*), money-changers (*sarrafs*), commission agents (*arhtiyas*), brokers (*dalals*), and weighmen. Together with their dependents, they constituted 14 per cent of the town's population. Among the hereditary craftsmen with considerable refinement and specialization of tasks were weavers, embroiderers, dyers, cloth printers, gold and silver smiths, blacksmiths, metal-vessel makers, potters, and leather-workers. Then, there were oil-seed crushers, *gur*-makers, wine-distillers, and tobacco-processors. The town had at least one unit of book binders, besides makers of soap, bows, bangles, *hukkas*, perfumes, ropes, and baskets. There also were masons, carpenters, barbers, water-carriers, tailors, tinners, wheat grinders, grain parchers, and scavengers. Their services were probably required more within the town. Collectively, the hereditary craftsmen and service-performing groups accounted for over a third of the town's population. The unskilled labourers and porters apparently functioned mostly in the markets of Jalandhar. They, together with their dependents and the domestic servants in general, constituted about 15 per cent of the town's population. In a relatively smaller proportion existed the religious functionaries like *mujawars* (keepers of shrines), *pirzadas, maulvis, purohits, granthis, ragis, rababis*, Nihangs, and the Udasis. Fifteen charitable grantees holding revenue-grants in the neighbouring countryside too were residing in the town. Among the professional people were the scribes, accountants, *padhas* (teachers of arithmetic and Lande script), and the teachers and practitioners of the traditional systems of medicine. Integral to the social scene were the courtesans, common prostitutes, minstrels (*bhats*), drum-beaters, beggars, eunuchs, faqirs, and the like.

Turning to the religious and ethnic composition of the population of Jalandhar, the presence of the votaries of the three major religions in the region is well established. Numerically, Muslims constituted the majority, and among them the Sunnis, followed at a distance by the Shias. Then, there were Hindus and Sikhs of different sectarian affiliations–mainly Shaivas, Vaishnavas, and the Shaktas and the orthodox Sikhs, Udasis and Nihangs. Ethnically, among Muslims, there were the Pathans, Shaikhs, Sayyads, Mughals, Arains, Gujjars, Kashmiris, and hereditary occupational categories. Hindus were dominated by the Khatris belonging to fifteen sub-castes in the town, followed by Suds, Banias, Aroras and brahmans, besides a host of low-castes and untouchables. Among the Sikhs, some Jats, but mostly Khatris and Aroras, and some occupational categories like the Tarkhans (carpenters) lived in Jalandhar.

An essential element in this urban universe was that of the state's representatives—the *nazim*, or the *kardar*, supported by the *qazi* and the *mutasaddis* (accountants), besides the *thanadar* with his *sipahis* and *chaukidars*. The *patwaris* and *qanungos* exercising jurisdiction over the neighbouring villages and *parganas* also resided in the town. The state functionaries worked in association with the locally influential persons (*panches*), or the representatives of different residential localities and trades.

There is sufficient evidence to suggest that the other middling urban centres in central Punjab, such as Batala in the upper Bari Doab (between the rivers Beas and Ravi) and Gujrat in the Chaj Doab (between the rivers Chenab and Jhelum), had a broadly similar occupational and social profile. There was a sprinkling of Jains in towns like Ludhiana, Hoshiarpur, Phagwara and some other places. By contrast, and as noted earlier, because of the much larger size of their populations, the cities of Amritsar and Lahore had a more complex social structure.

Organization of Urban Space

The structure of urban population and the organization of urban space went together. It is possible to discern the broad pattern of a middling town, which was delimited by a wall with a number of gates, connecting it with the countryside and the neighbouring urban centres. Thus, Gujrat had five gates, Jalandhar had eight, and Batala had twelve. Incidentally, Amritsar and Lahore had twelve and thirteen gates respectively, but their number in an average town varied between four and six. Generally, two main streets cutting across at right angles traversed the town. At their intersection was located the main market place or the *chowk*. The fortress and the *jama* mosque were located nearby. The other mosques, *takias* (resting places of *faqirs*), temples and the *imambara* (the Shia place of assembly and mourning for Imam Husain and martyrs of Karbala) were dispersed in different localities. Several specialized and general markets branched off from the primary roads. These roads had the residences of the well-to-do shopkeepers above the shops, though the predominant residential form was that of the *muhalla* occupying the space between these roads.

Several structures outside the walls like burial and cremation grounds, *eidgah* where the Eid prayers were offered and the *sarai* (resting place for travellers), tanks, gardens, and orchards, besides *khanqahs* (Sufi establishments), *takias,* and temples remained integral to the town's life. The shrines of local deities like Shitala (goddess of smallpox), Shani, and Vrinda (wife of the demon Jalandhar) too were located outside the walls. In addition, Jalandhar had a dozen settlements, apparently enclosed localities, which were called *kots* or *bastis.* There were some enclosures of the untouchables along the wall, besides settlements of market gardeners and the habitations of the brick-makers. The urban universe on both sides of the walls was oriented towards the *chowk*, and was dominated, regulated, and taxed by the local representative of the state who generally resided in a walled mansion (*haveli*) or a fortress.

Turning to the *muhallas*, or 'blocks of houses opening on to a square', these were self-contained localities, generally with their own gate, lanes and by-lanes, place of worship, source of water (a single- or double-wheel Persian well), and some kind of social mechanism to regulate life in the *muhalla*. Jalandhar had thirty-two such separate localities in the walled area, while the number of the known *muhallas* in Batala, was at least two dozen. In Jalandhar and Batala, *muhallas* were reported to be 'closed' localities, whereas in Gujrat, they had 'usually two openings, a lane leading in at one end and leading out at the other', though some *muhallas* 'ended blindly'. Their sizes and, therefore, the number of houses as well as the width of lanes varied. For example, the largest *muhalla* in Jalandhar, Muhalla-Qazian, had 642 houses, and the smallest, Muhalla Arain had 10 houses only. Sometimes the term *kucha* was used for a lane (*gali*) with a few houses (or shops), like Kucha-i-Din Muhammad in Batala. The width of lanes was from 4 to 10 ft. in Jalandhar, but in Batala some lanes were barely 3 ft. wide, and were locally known as the *bheeri* (narrow) *gali*, allowing just one person to pass comfortably at a time. The *muhallas* in Jalandhar were named differently—after a numerically dominant caste (Sud-an, Sehgal-an and Malk-an), dominant profession (Mujawar-an, Julahi-an, Kamangar-an); ethnic category (Jat, Arain, Shaikh); a prominent morphological feature (a *qila*, a *tahli* or *sheesham* tree); and individual founders (Muhalla Sayyad Kabir, Kot Buland Khan). The pattern was broadly similar in other centres. In Batala, however, three localities were named after the place of origin of the inhabitants (Hamdani-an, Bukhari-an, Multani-an). Batala had several *kots* or walled localities on the sides but within the town's wall, which was in marked contrast to the situation of a dozen localities (*bastis*) outside the wall in Jalandhar.

There were around 6,500 closely spaced houses in Jalandhar. Of these, around 3,000 were *pucca*, and 3,500 *kacha* houses. The latter, presumably, were single storey structures inhabited by the poorer sections on both sides of the wall. The *havelis* (mansions) of the rich in Batala had four or even five storeys, while the ordinary people lived in single or double storey houses. Because of the limited space in the walled area, expansion of the *pucca* houses was mostly vertical by storeys, and the houses of the well-to-do on an average had three storeys, and sometimes a basement as well. The essential features of these town houses were: (i) a platform called *thara* on both sides of the main door; (ii) a vestibule called *deorhi* into which the main door opened; (iii) reception area or *baithak*; (iv) cooking space or separate kitchen; (v) bathing space on the ground floor; (vi) latrine on the roof (*kotha*); (vii) provision for storing water, brought in by the hereditary water carrier (generally called the *jheewar* or the *bhishti*); and rooms for sleeping, storage etc. The actual use of space varied with seasons, moving to the lower floors in summers, and using upper floors in winters. The roof was used differently by the season as well as the time of the day.

Prakash Tandon provides interesting insights into the different uses of the platform and the vestibule in Gujrat: 'Women sat there in the afternoons, spinning, sewing, embroidering, and gossiping or quarrelling. From their respective tharas they could talk to each other without leaving their domain. Upon the thara the itinerant merchants spread their wares while the women looked at them from their windows above coming down only if they became interested.'

Men, however, used the *thara* when they came to condole a death. The vestibule was similarly put to different uses. Women went inside the door to view the dead body for the last time. On the occasion of a wedding, it was the *deorhi* where the bride took her last farewell from her parents, and where she was received on reaching her new home.

Urban Social Relations

The delimited urban space and its separate but closely spaced *muhallas,* markets, and houses bred their own peculiar social institutions and relations. Entering the urban social scene through the *muhalla,* the distinctive urban feature, we find that its people interacted with one another and outsiders at several levels. At the level of the family, the available evidence points to the existence of the joint family within the house, though the near relations had residential units in the same *muhalla,* or in an adjacent one. The basis of the joint family apparently was the property—both urban and rural, besides the family business, a shop or a particular trade. The meaningful unit of larger social interaction, especially for purposes of marriage and commensality, was the *biradari* (brotherhood) of the sub-caste, clan, or the particular occupational category which cut across *muhallas,* and even the boundaries of the town, though the town probably remained the effective operational unit. The people coming from outside to reside in the town tended to join the local *biradari* which provided a framework of mutual support in marriages and death, and also functioned as a means of social control. The *biradari* generally met in a *muhalla* square, and through its leaders (*panches, chaudharis*) dealt with matters concerning its individual members as well as relations with other *biradaris* and the representatives of the state.

Life in the *muhalla* was dependent on the services of several occupational categories, but the regular relations of mutual support and dependence probably existed with the *jheevar* (*bhishti*) or the water-carrier, the *chuhra* (*khakhrobe*) or the scavenger, the *dhobi* or the washerman, and the *nai* (*hajjam*) or the barber, the last playing an important role in betrothals as well. These service providers were differently located in the urban space which varied from town to town. For example, water-carriers were living outside the town wall in Batala, but they were scattered in different *muhallas* in Gujrat and Jalandhar. Scavengers lived on the outskirts of some *muhallas* in the two towns, but outside the wall in Batala. The washermen had their own street in a relatively central location in Batala, and the barbers had their own streets in three *muhallas*. The professional priests (*purohits*) apparently were scattered in localities with a large presence of non-Muslims. These service-providers were paid in both kind and cash, probably more of the latter. Their services, with the obvious exception of those of the religious functionaries, were shared by all the social and religious groups in the town.

The internal configuration of *muhallas* had interesting variations. Because of the larger proportion of Muslims in the total as well as urban population in the region, there were more Muslim *muhallas*. For example, their number was twenty-two in Jalandhar against nine Hindu and one Sikh *muhalla*. The town was broadly divided into Muslim and Hindu (including Sikh) localities. This was even more true of Batala and Gujrat. Yet, by the middle of the nineteenth century, and as a result of purchase, mortgage, gift, exchange, and migration for which substantial documentary and literary evidence is available, most localities came to have mixed neighbourhoods in terms of religious affiliation and class composition. Thus, the neighbouring houses in different *muhallas* in Jalandhar were occupied by people from different caste and occupational backgrounds such as brahmans, Khatris, Arains (Muslim vegetable gardeners), weavers, carpenters, and washermen. In Batala, a Muslim washerman, tailor, or Shaikh (a respectable Muslim convert) could be the next-door neighbour of a Khatri, or the latter could have a brahman, a goldsmith, and a barber as his next-door neighbour, besides Khatris from other sub-castes. The neighbourhood was even more varied in bazaars: a Khatri shopkeeper could have in the adjacent shops a Khatri, a brahman, a Shaikh, or a cloth printer (*chhapagar*); while a Shaikh could have a Khatri, a Bania, a brahman, and a burnisher of metal (*saiqaigar*). This of course would be more true of general markets. Thus, in spite of the provisions of the *shariat*, there were several attestations by Muslims on behalf of non-Muslims in the judicial documents from Batala.

In fact, people from different backgrounds interacted with one another in the judicial framework provided by the state. In the legal transactions in the court of the *qazi*, which was operating through Sikh rule, affinities based on birth and kinship appear to have been relegated to the background. Even the people belonging to the same kin group (as that of the Bhandari Khatris of Batala) preferred to formalize their transfer of property in the court of the *qazi*. Women too figure in these legal transactions as principals. Formal transactions were resorted to by the Bhandari Khatris while giving accommodation on rent to a Muslim potter, a carpenter, and a water-carrier, or mortgaging a three-storey *haveli* to a Muslim dyer, or a shop to a Muslim vegetable-seller. There is evidence to suggest that moneylending flourished with protection from the state of Ranjit Singh, and covered a cross section of the urban society as creditors and debtors. Evidently, the limited and congested urban space necessitated social interaction among people of different backgrounds, which demanded relaxation in the application of the provisions of the Islamic law.

Cultural Life

For purposes of social and cultural interaction, the categories based on broad religious affiliation appear to be less meaningful than those based on caste, clan, and occupation.

The Shias had a visible presence in Batala in three *muhallas*, having their mosques and two *imambaras*, and taking out two *tazia* processions in mourning. Similarly, different social and occupational categories among Sunnis had their own mosques which were a part of their daily existence. Even the streets of tailors and blacksmiths had their own mosques in Batala. Conversely, the Hindu Khatris and Sunars living in adjacent *muhallas* in Gujrat hardly had any social intercourse. The Sikh Jats (probably agriculturists) occupying a *muhalla* in Jalandhar did not have much social interaction with the shop-keeping Khatri and Arora Sikhs scattered in other *muhallas*, let alone the Sikh carpenters. The leather-workers, scavengers and some other segments among the occupational categories had their own deities, modes of worship, and community life.

Nevertheless, certain structural and cultural features tended to bring people from different sectional backgrounds together as Muslims, Hindus and Sikhs. The focal points that drew a cross section of Muslims were the *jama* mosque, the *eidgah*, and the *khanqahs*. Sunnis and even non-Muslims participated in the *tazia* processions in Batala. The *khanqahs* attracted non-Muslims too. Likewise, the sectarian differences between Shaivas, Shaktas, and Vaishnavas among Hindus do not appear to have meant much to the towns people. Despite dedicating temples to particular incarnations of Vishnu, or to Shiva and the Goddess, Hindus generally venerated gods and goddesses of the brahmanical pantheon. The large numerical presence of Muslims in the town as well as the region also made the internal sectional differences less significant in the day-to-day life of non-Muslims in the Punjab. At any rate, all Hindus celebrated the festivals of Diwali, Holi, and Dussehra.

However, some fine shades are noticeable in relations to urban structure. Diwali was celebrated mainly at the level of the joint family, extending to the *muhalla* and the main market; Holi appears to have been centred on the *muhalla*;

while Dussehra cut across *muhallas*, drawing people from different parts of the town to the staging of Ramlila as well as to its concluding function. A religious discourse (*katha*) too attracted a cross section of the non-Muslims. All Sikhs celebrated Diwali, but showed veneration to the *Guru Granth Sahib*, and accorded special sanctity to the gurdwaras associated with the gurus. Further, a cross-section of the towns people visited the shrines of local deities situated generally outside the walls.

In fact, formal religious affiliations appeared to be irrelevant in some other areas of cultural life like the seasonal festivals of Lohri, Basant, and Baisakhi. As the winter festival, Lohri in all probability drew people for the *muhalla* level celebration. Heralding the spring by kite-flying, Basant cut across *muhallas*; its scale and colourfulness incidentally was rather unique to Lahore. The Baisakhi fair marking the arrival of the new harvest in April, was held outside the town, attracting people from diverse backgrounds. In Gujrat, it drew men and women from the town as well as the countryside to the bank of the river Chenab; the people of Batala went to the tank; and the Lahauris went to the river Ravi. There were other such local fairs attracting people to a temple, a *khanqah*, a final resting place (*rauza* or *samadhi*), and a tank in the vicinity of the town. At the inception of colonial rule, fifty annual fairs were reported to be held in the upper Bari Doab, the small tract in which Batala is located.

Within the town, the forms of spending leisure time and of entertainment and recreation cut across sectional and class differences. Visits to gardens, tombs, *khanqahs* and *samadhis* by men and even women during their hours of leisure have been noticed in the sources. All sections of society appear to have been entertained by the professional entertainers like the *mirasis* (Muslim minstrels and drum beaters), *bhands* (jesters), *behroopias* (mimics), *bazigars* (acrobats), *madaris* (jugglers), *saperas* (snake-charmers), and *raasdharis* (actors).

The other forms of recreation associated with the urban people were kite-flying (to which a reference has been made), pigeon-flying, cock-fights, camel-fights (mainly in the south-western arid area), quail-fights, partridge fights, and wrestling and exercises, besides chess and dice. However, with the exception of the last, these forms provided entertainment largely to men. Women filled their leisure hours by gossip and mock fights. Ritual mourning in a sing-song manner in a gathering of women, and conducted professionally by a woman, was more a source of entertainment and, perhaps, catharsis. Visits to temples and gurdwaras or to a *khanqah* was equally a relief from domestic drudgery. The other high points in the women's lives were the ceremonies related to birth and marriage, and some exclusively women's customs like the *kanagat* (public abuse and ridicule of men of other *muhallas*) and the *moh mahi* (public teasing of men) among Hindu women of Amritsar.

Prostitution, a typically urban institution, catered to people from various social and cultural backgrounds. In Jalandhar, prostitutes and their associates lived in five different *muhallas* located on the sides. There was a courtesan's lane in Gujrat, and a prostitutes' *bazaar* in Muzaffargarh. It seems that they had a recognized place and function in urban society, and were not treated with contempt or prudery. Even respectable Khatri women in Gujrat did not hesitate to exchange pleasantries with the local prostitutes who happened to be Muslim. Prostitutes were broadly graded according to their skill and talent, as singing girls (*tawaifs*) nautch girls, special courtesans, and common prostitutes. It may be relevant to add that their localities in Amritsar were called the Bazaar-i-Kanjran (Kanjars were custodians of prostitutes) and the Bazaar-i-Mughlan, both located inside the walls, and Lahore had a rather large and bustling locality called the Hira Mandi in the walled area. It is likely that men from the countryside also visited the prostitutes in urban centres.

Urban–Rural Interaction

As a matter of fact, urban centres had various kinds of links with the countryside. Their hinterland probably extended to a radius that could be covered by a day's journey or a little more. Socially, the *biradari* linked the urban and rural populations among Khatris, and the Nai also helped in aligning the families living in urban and rural areas. Probably, the craftsmen working in a town belonged to the same social circuit as the artisans in the neighbouring villages, albeit generally with a higher level of refinement. The religious establishments in the town often drew the rural people, while the religious grantees enjoying revenue-free lands in the countryside preferred to reside in the town as noted earlier. Some temples in Batala were affiliated to the *matths* in the villages of Pindori and Dhianpur, situated at a distance of about 40 km.; their followers often stayed in these temples on visiting the town. The peddler and the moneylender were the usual conduits through whom the manufactured goods, salt, and other finer and rarer articles as well as credit reached the ruralites. The interaction between the rural and urban population was apparently most intense at the time of fairs and harvests.

The villages in the hinterland were administratively controlled from the town. Their inhabitants paid revenues to the state's representatives generally residing in the town, and occasionally had recourse to the *qazi*'s court. Most of all, the food, raw materials, and labour for the urbanities came from villages on a regular basis; in famines, however, more artisans and potential labourers than food and raw materials came into the town. Above all, the town extracted the rural surplus as tax and share of the intermediaries, besides rent and perquisites of the non-cultivating landed classes and charitable grantees. On the whole, it was an unequal relationship in the sense that what the town obtained was far more tangible than what it gave in terms of goods, ideas and law and order. This relationship has been termed 'parasitical' by Marx, though compared to the period of colonial rule in the Punjab region (1849–1947), this was an 'easygoing parasitism', to borrow an expression from Braudel.

Moreover, analytically, it may not be enough to say that the town as a whole exploited the countryside. People and groups in urban and rural areas were affected differently by various modes of urban-rural interaction. While the urban poor can be equated with the landless labourers in the rural areas, the landlords in villages as well as the moneylenders and the commission agents (*arhtiyas*) had more in common with the privileged sections in the towns. There probably was an unconscious alliance between the urban elites and the rural rich who generally managed to get the maximum accommodation from the state functionaries in the assessment and collection of land revenue and the administration of justice and police. In the pre-colonial times the town did siphon off a large share of the rural resources, but the exploitative influence of the dominant economic and political interests in urban areas remained relatively limited, given the technology and the means of transportation. By and large, the state allowed the urban processes to take their own course, subject mainly to its administrative needs of collection of taxes and maintenance of law and order.

In Retrospect

The dominant impression from this reconstruction of urban profile in the three upper *doabs* of the region is that of interaction across castes, clans and creeds and, to a certain extent, classes in the *muhalla*, the market place, and across the *muhallas* and the town walls. One's location in the urban space was perhaps as meaningful in daily life as other affiliations. Apparently, the consciousness of belonging to a monolithic community was not pronounced, whether among Muslims who were numerically dominant, or among Hindus and Sikhs who, together, were less in number in the first provincial census taken by the British in 1855. Thus, absolute numbers did not seem to count much in social relations or politics. It is not without significance that the available sources from the late eighteenth and early nineteenth centuries are silent about instances of marked tension between religious groups as Shaivas and Vaishnavas, or as Sunnis and Shias, or, for that matter, as Muslims and non-Muslims. This phenomenon of cultural co-existence and social acceptance of the other can be explained in terms partly of the organization of urban space and partly of the priorities of the pre-colonial state which promoted peaceful co-existence among its subjects.

It may be relevant to note that the watchwords for the Sikh rulers were justice, moderation, accommodation, and consensus. A great importance came to be attached to the people's will, and its expression through the *muhalla* panchayats in urban areas. It was at the invitation of a cross-section of the notables of Lahore that the young and energetic Ranjit Singh could easily occupy Lahore in 1799. Consent and accommodation appear to have remained his guiding principles too, which benefited people across religious, caste and class lines, and encouraged them to identify themselves with the state. This could be seen as the beginning of the process of secularization of consciousness and politics which, however, seems to have been arrested under colonial rule. It may be relevant to add that when this state succumbed to British imperialism, its epitaph was written in Punjabi by a Muslim poet, Shah Muhammad, who referred to the Anglo-Sikh War (1845–6) as a war between 'Hind' and 'Punjab' (*Jang Hind Panjab*): Hindus (including Sikhs) and Muslims had been living happily together until a 'disaster struck them in the form of a third community' (the British), laments the poet.

References

Banga, Indu, ed., *Five Punjabi Centuries: Polity, Economy, Society and Culture, c. 1500–1990*, New Delhi: Manohar, 2000.

——, ed., *The City in Indian History: Urban Demography, Society and Politics*, New Delhi: Manohar, 2005.

——, 'Urban-Rural Interaction: The Upper Bari Doab (c.1550–1900)', in *Five Thousand Years of Urbanization: The Punjab Region*, ed. Reeta Grewal, New Delhi: Manohar, 2005, pp. 129–44.

——, 'Raj-Khalsa: Ideology and Praxis', *Journal of Punjab Studies*, Special Issue on Guru Gobind Singh, vol. 15, no. 1–2, 2008, pp. 33–64.

——, *The Agrarian System of the Sikhs: Late Eighteenth and Early Nineteenth Century*, New Delhi: Manohar, 2019.

Chandra, Satish, *Fernand Braudel on Towns*, Occasional Papers, Chandigarh: Urban History Association of India, 1992.

Gauba, Anand, *Amritsar: A Study in Urban History* (*1840–1947*), Jalandhar: ABS Publications, 1988.

Grewal, J.S., *In the By-Lanes of History: Some Persian Documents from a Punjab Town*, Shimla: Indian Institute of Advanced Study, 1975.

——, 'Urban Economic Life', in *Maharaja Ranjit Singh: The State and Society*, ed. Indu Banga and J.S. Grewal, Amritsar: Guru Nanak Dev University, 2001, pp. 211–20.

——, 'Batala as a Medieval Town', in *Precolonial and Colonial Punjab: Society, Economy, Politics and Culture*, ed. Reeta Grewal and Sheena Pall, New Delhi: Manohar, 2005, pp. 113–42.

Grewal, J.S. and Indu Banga, eds., *Studies in Urban History*, Amritsar: Guru Nanak Dev University, 1981.

——, *Civil and Military Affairs of Maharaja Ranjit Singh: A Study of 450 Orders in Persian*, Amritsar: Guru Nanak Dev University, 1987.

——, tr. and ed., *Early Nineteenth Century Punjab: From Ganesh Das's Char Bagh-i Panjab*, Amritsar: Guru Nanak Dev University; 2nd edn., New Delhi: Routledge, 2016.

Grewal, J.S. and Veena Sachdeva, 'Urbanization in the Mughal Province of Lahore (*c.*1550–1850)', in *Five Thousand Years of Urbanization: The Punjab Region*, ed. Reeta Grewal, New Delhi: Manohar/Institute of Punjab Studies, 2005, pp. 107–27.

Grewal, Reeta, 'Polity, Economy and Urbanization: Early 19th Century Punjab', *Journal of Regional History*, vol. IV, 1983, pp. 56–72.

Jyoti, Kanchan, 'Jullundur 1846–1947: An Urban History', Ph.D. thesis, GNDU, Amritsar, 1988.

Latif, Syed Muhammad, *Lahore—Its History, Architectural Remains and Antiquities*, Lahore: n.p., 1892.

Misra, S.C., 'Some Aspects of the Self-Administering Institutions in Medieval Indian Towns', *Studies in Urban History*, ed. J.S. Grewal and Indu Banga, Amritsar: Guru Nanak Dev University, 1981, pp. 80–90.

Nevile, Pran, *Lahore: A Sentimental Journey*, New Delhi: Harper Collins Publishers, 1997.

Sharma, Harish Chandra, 'Artisans', in *Maharaja Ranjit Singh: The State and Society*, ed. Indu Banga and J.S. Grewal, Amritsar: Guru Nanak Dev University, 2001, pp. 236–45.

Singh, Chetan, *Region and Empire: Panjab in the Seventeenth Century*, New Delhi: Oxford University Press, 1991.

Tandon, Prakash, *Punjabi Century, 1857–1947*, New Delhi: Orient Paperbacks, 1961.

12

The Life of Dead Bodies

Corporeality and Memory in Pre-Independence Bombay

JIM MASSELOS

DEATH EVOKES a whole range of feelings. There are the traumas and emotions associated with dying; religious beliefs which surround the end of an existence; and ritual and custom about the disposal of the dead. Surrounding the dead person are the circumstances and the historical moment of death as well as the personality of the departed and the role he or she played in life. Other elements might well be added, but these are enough to indicate the depth of issues which flood the subject. This paper is not concerned with these issues as such nor, despite its title, is it about notions of transmigration, life after death, or resurrection.[1] The concern is not with the transcendent but with the mundane—with, specifically, the body after death, and memory of the body.

The dead body has both presence and corporeality. From the time of death to the disposal of the corpse, the presence of the dead body sets up a countervailing necessity—to ensure its proper and rapid disposal. The need to dispose of the body enjoins a set of actions: in this sense the body constitutes a source of potency, a demand for action derived from its very corporeality and the consequences of its decaying biological presence. These set up imperatives which are reinforced by the emotional and religious feelings of the survivors. In crisis situations the imperatives are even further intensified, and may result in dispute and conflict that is immediate and unplanned. The body's very corporeality has a potency that cannot be ignored.

The second aspect I will consider follows from when the body transmutes after its disposal; losing its corporeality, it transforms into memory. It is the persona the body once had which is what is significant. Within the framework of the public sphere this too may have equally significant consequences as the memory of the person acquires an autonomy and a life through its use as an active and changing symbolic field.

Presence and Corporeality

After a person dies the corporeality of the body sets up a number of imperatives. The body is to be cremated, buried, or exposed as quickly as possible, appropriately and with respect. Disposal should be rapid, preferably on the same day and in a proper place, in a cemetery, tower, or cremation ground, according to the practices of the religion, caste, or community of the dead person. This is the ideal and, in most cases, there are no problems. But, of course, ideals are just that, ideals which are not necessarily always followed. Even religious strictures might not be universally observed as the nineteenth century experience in Bombay demonstrates.

Religion, despite the texts, was not necessarily or always the prime determinant of how a body was handled: in 1871 the Municipal Commissioner reported that some 6,000 Hindu corpses out of a total 10,500 Hindu dead were being buried in Bombay rather than cremated.[2] Among them were very young children who by custom were buried as indeed were Dalits and other lower caste Hindus but the majority were buried because their relatives or friends could not afford the cost of cremation. Poverty, according to the report, overrode religion in determining the method to be adopted—the prime consideration seemingly being to ensure speedy and adequate disposal—not what religion decreed.

Subsequently, in the last decades of the nineteenth century the Government took up the matter and in conjunction with committees of community leaders worked on improving the conditions of the burial and burning grounds as well as reducing the costs involved in their use. The result was to establish more grounds and improve accessibility. The government view that cremation was the superior method in handling the dead thus coincided with religious imperatives, and culminated in an increased percentage of Hindu cremations in Bombay by the beginning of the twentieth century.

For Muslims where burial was the preferred method, the situation was complicated by the existence of specific cemeteries for particular groups. There were burial grounds for Moguls, Kutchi Memoms, Daudi Borahs, Konkani Muslims, Khojas and others, as well as more general ones for Sunnis and Shias. The grounds were often privately owned and controlled by community/caste *jamats*, often themselves under the control of religious and sectarian leaders. The community or the leader thus determined access to cemeteries, a potent source of power should the need arise. In most cases there was no need for it to be exercised, access to the graveyards was usually automatic, amicable, and unquestioned. But when dissension existed, the matter of access could become contentious.

During an extended dispute in the early 1850s Khoja opponents to the Aga Khan were denied entry to the Khoja burial ground and to their family vaults. Again, in 1862 the excommunication of a Khoja 'reform party' translated into exclusion from all caste property. Two months later, in October, after a death among the reformers, force was used to prevent the reformers from entering the *jamatkhana* to complete their funeral ceremonies. The following month when the brother of one of the leading dissidents died it was only after the police intervened that the mourners gained entry and were able to complete their funeral ceremonies.[3]

Given the conflicting priorities posed by the dead body and by the caste/sectarian dispute, the imperatives of the situation ensured that the only outcome could be that of heightened confrontation. The relatives were driven by the absolute need to observe the appropriate procedures and would not compromise. For the opponents, on the other hand, the situation provided an unprecedented opportunity to enforce their authority and punish recalcitrant members. For those in control of the caste assets the dead body was merely an object through which an example could be made; the death enabled an unmistakable display of power not otherwise readily available. For the mourners the body demanded a course of action they had no choice but to follow: it placed them in a tactically weak position in regard to their opponents but also contradictorily gave them a strong emotional cause. Surrounding the body then was conflict between custom about the proper disposal of the dead and denial of that custom for purposes unconnected with the death itself; and conflict over the actual attempt to bury the body properly. The necessary part of all this was the body in its transition state from death to dispersal; its specific corporeality rather than the person himself or anything he or she had been. The body became a symbol of the caste/group of which he had been a member when living and a symbol also of family relations with that group. It was the physical state that was important here not what the dead person may have done in life. It was both the vulnerability of the dead and the power of the dead body which came into play.

Similar considerations recur in the somewhat different circumstance of riots. During riots the nature of urban space and its accessibility alters. Rioters, in their attacks on people and places, assert control over urban space and access to it. Free movement is limited and public space retreats and becomes contentious. In addition, of course, the civil authority itself sets limits on movement, police patrol the streets and may impose day and night curfews. Given all this what about the people who happened to die while the riots were raging? What happened when it became necessary in such parlous circumstance to bury or cremate the dead? The bodies were still subject to the imperatives of death, to the need for quick disposal and in accordance with custom and religion. How did the dissolution of public space in the time of riot affect the process of disposal and the ability to get the body to the burial or cremation grounds? The congruence of riot, the fluctuations in the control of the streets, the amorphousness and uncertainties of just who controlled what, and the overall lack of safety presented difficulties at a time when there was widespread disorder and movement was perilous, foolhardy, or just plain aggressive.

An example of what was involved appears in that series of incidents spread over three days now collectively known as the Parsi-Muslim Riots of 1874.[4] They began when Muslims attacked Parsi fire temples and other Parsi property after the noon Friday prayers. On the third day, on Sunday 15 February, two funeral processions, one of Sidis and the other described in the reports only as 'Bombay Mohammedans' or 'Bombay Mussulmans' congregated in Bhendy Bazaar and proceeded together towards the Muslim burial grounds at Sonapore. The joint procession was 'perfectly orderly';[5] the Bombay Muslims were quiet while the Sidis made some noise, shouting 'Deen, Deen'[6] or 'La Illa Il Lalla'.[7] The noise was apparently not excessive and conformed with the usual practice at Sidi funerals which 'always have a great deal of shouting and singing'.[8] The size of the procession was however unusual. Usually such processions numbered from about 20 to a 100 people as had been the case with two such processions the previous day which had about 20 to 25 people.[9] The Sunday procession was significantly larger but just how much larger is unclear. Evidence given later in court as to the number varied from a low of 250–300[10] to a high of about 400[11] with one witness opting for 500–700.[12] Just how the large size is to be interpreted remains unclear: did it indicate an aggressive intent to attack Parsis or, given the heightened tensions of the day, were the numbers defensive and intended to insure the safety of the funerals. During the progress of the procession but before violence broke out, a police superintendent had asked one of the men why there were so many Muslims in the procession and had been answered 'There were only a few with a funeral yesterday, and they were obstructed by the Parsees', a version similar to what had been earlier reported to the superintendent by his own policemen.[13] The numbers on the Sunday probably were to protect the procession against Parsi obstruction.

The route taken may similarly be given an ambiguous interpretation. Starting from a Muslim area the procession tracked through Hindu sections and finally wandered through Agiary Lane and Breach Candy Road in order to get to the Muslim burial grounds at Sonapore. This was a Parsi dominated area with its own fire temple. However, the area adjoined the burial grounds and Parsi houses in fact looked down into them. The areas were juxtaposed and there was no easy route which could have avoided the Parsi concentration.

When the processions arrived in the grounds, they separated and went to the section appropriate to their group. The Sidis sat down and waited for the grave digging to be finished. It was then that some 200–300 Parsis gathered on the other side of the wall in front of the fire temple. They hurled stones across the wall at the Sidis some of whom jumped over it to retaliate. Sidi elders tried to restrain the younger men, as did the police who had come across the procession en route and had then accompanied it. A melee ensued but ended when the Parsis fled into their houses. Later, after the burials were concluded the Sidis and Muslims went to the Masjid for the usual post burial ceremonies. Some 700–800 Parsis were waiting there for them. A thin police line tried to hold the rival groups apart but both Muslims and Parsis pushed through it and a deadly fight resulted.[14] Subsequently, 30 Muslims and 8 Parsis were tried for rioting.

The Sonapore riots illustrate a number of points. On the part of the Muslims, they began their procession through the town without seeking police protection. They were not going to allow themselves to be affected by any riot situation since it was necessary they bury their dead. On the way they met the police who accompanied them to maintain order. Some of the Muslims seem to have carried sticks though whether this was for protection or for offensive action is unclear. On the other hand, the joint procession was not aggressive as it went through the streets and the primary objective would seem to have been to get to the burial grounds. There is little evidence to support an interpretation of intent to attack the Parsi houses and the fire temple. Most of the evidence supports a reading that the primary imperative was to bury the two bodies. That a disturbance resulted was due more to the hostility and aggression of the Parsis who read the situation differently and who believed that they were defending themselves and what was theirs. The brunt of police evidence in the court trials was that Muslims did nothing to incite the attacks.[15]

Rumours had been rife among Parsis on the previous night that Muslims intended to come in large numbers with a funeral procession or to use it as a cover by which to attack the fire temple.[16] On the Saturday night Parsis sought police protection and their *shetias* also employed some seventy-five Ghatis and Pardesis to protect the Hormusjee Wadia Fire Temple.[17] For the Parsis then the Muslim procession was threatening. They were not even convinced that the processions were truly funeral processions—some witnesses in the subsequent trial claimed that one of the biers did not contain a dead body but was filled with sticks to be used in a pre-planned attack on the fire temple. Convincing evidence was not produced to support the claim.

In the tense situation following the first two days of street violence the appearance of any procession would have been ominous given the background circumstances. But that the Sunday procession was large made it more alien and hostile. Just how ominous it was comes through in the subsequent evidence given by a share broker who considered it

> the largest Mussulman procession I have ever seen. Generally there are 25 or 30 men in a Seedie procession. There were about 400 or 500 persons in the procession of Sunday, the 15th. They were armed with sticks. Members of funeral processions do not carry sticks. The procession was a little disorderly ... They were singing and shouting *deen, deen*. They were passing as if going to a battle. There was no European officer with them. I was alarmed.[18]

That the shouting may have been an expression of customary practice or defensive show did not concern the Parsis who by this stage could only read the situation in polarized terms. All the signals as far as they were concerned were alien, strange and as such could be nothing but hostile. They read the behaviour as aggressive and threatening and saw the funeral as a charade, a guise, whereby they could more easily be attacked. This was no funeral procession as far as they were concerned or, if it was, it had purposes other than burial.

For the Parsis, the processions were aggressive and the dead bodies which were their raison d'etre were irrelevant. For the Muslims, the core need was to bury the dead whatever other agendas may have been involved. It would seem clear from the evidence given at the Sonapore riot trials that there were indeed dead bodies in the funeral procession and that the Muslims were driven by the imperatives of death to undertake burial as soon as possible. Whether there was a further aggressive intent, as the Parsis feared, is another matter but at the least the ongoing riot situation was responsible for the larger than usual funeral procession. As to the dead people themselves they hardly figured at all. They were not even named in the Sonapore Riot Trials. Their importance was that they were Muslim bodies, i.e. that they belonged to one religion rather than another in a time of extreme polarization and communal hostility. They were reduced to communal ciphers in a tangle of street conflicts regardless of the feelings of the mourners, the relatives, and friends of the dead. In the late nineteenth century there was another kind of incident involving dead bodies. Here, though, the concern was with maintaining the integrity of the body as a whole, with showing respect for the physical integrity of the dead, with maintaining the corpse intact, with retaining its corporeality. There is also a sub-text of hostility to Western medicine and its practices in the example which follows. But there is also, as in the Sonapore riots, typification of bodies by social stereotype—by religion and community

In 1875 a stable hand was kicked in the head by a horse and died a couple of days later. Immediately after the inquest, students from Grant Medical College were given reluctant permission by the educated members of the boy's caste-like group, the Moguls, to conduct a post-mortem on his body. The boy's friends however peered through the shutters of the dissecting room and saw him being cut up. They went to nearby Bhendy Bazaar, collected a group of fifty others and rushed into the dissecting room 'with a terrific shout. The [medical] students were panic-stricken and fled in all directions. The enraged Moguls had nothing to fling at the fugitives, but seizing hold of the scalp, the liver, the disjointed limb etc. [of the dead boy], they used these freely as missiles.'[19]

The incident is replete with symbolism. Although it has parallels with nineteenth century anti-dissection riots in

Britain in that it encapsulates the conflict between personal and scientific values, the incident is also about tyrannies and insensitivities. It is however ironic that in an incident which began as a defence of the dead body's autonomy and as an assertion of the dignity of the body as a whole, it ended with using parts of that body as missiles to attack the dissectors. It was to be another two decades before the issue of body integrity again surfaced. In 1891 a committee of the city's leading Muslims began to liaise with Grant Medical College authorities about the dissection of unclaimed Muslim bodies.[20] The head of the hospital made it a condition for further discussion that a Muslim public meeting should unanimously resolve to support the handing over of such bodies to appropriate Muslims. A meeting was accordingly convened in the Jama Masjid at the end of October 1892 under the chairmanship of the Kazi of Bombay, Kazi Sahib Shaik Mahomed Murghay, who voiced the concern about what was happening to the unclaimed corpses. He pointed out the bodies were dissected by students at the J.J. Hospital and their remains, as segments and parts, were bundled up with others of different sects and all were buried together.[21] The procedure, he pointed out, was 'calculated to hurt the religious feelings of the people'.[22] The meeting supported the resolutions unanimously and decided to send a deputation to the government through the Surgeon-General and submit their objections in a letter. Specifically, they objected to dissection itself; to the promiscuous burial of Muslim body parts along with others of different sects; and to Muslim bodies being touched by 'infidel' hands. The letter argued it was immaterial that the stopping of Muslim bodies for dissection might affect medical teaching in the College.[23]

The issue had already been canvassed in the government offices before the deputation arrived and salient points had been established—at least from a British and imperial viewpoint. In response to the earlier approaches from the

Muslim committee the Senior Medical Officer in charge of the J.J. Hospital had maintained in January 1892 that the bodies were always treated in an orderly manner under the superintendence of a Mahommedan official.[24] The acting principal of the Grant Medical College in September 1892 was concerned that if the Muslim claim to the bodies was allowed then other communities would follow and none would be available for dissection. Parsis had already objected and none of their bodies was available for use.[25] By December 1892 the principal of the College had decided that the Muslim committee were 'agitators' who were best handled by ignoring them.[26] By this stage it was also beginning to be clear that the College had no legal authority to keep dead bodies and dissect them.[27]

The Surgeon-General in commenting on the deputation in late February 1893 noticed its 'highly respectable' character and its fourteen JPs. He noted that the practice of dissection operated in Calcutta, Madras, Lahore, Poona, Ahmedabad, and Hyderabad and had not been questioned previously except in the case of the Parsis. He suggested Bombay Muslims were 'jealous of the Parsees' in this matter. As to the issue of interference in religion and religious prohibition of dissection, a point made by the deputation, he could not find any indication in the Koran that the dissection of Muslim bodies was unlawful. Some religious books had been cited by the deputation such as the *Durrul Mukhtar* (Constantinople), *Fatawa Alumgiri* (Delhi), and the *Ruddal Mohtur* (Constantinople)[28] but the Surgeon-General considered 'even these do so only in an indirect way'.[29] Since the hospitals could supply other bodies for dissection, i.e. those who were not Parsis or Muslims, he favoured approving the Muslim request but wanted them to be charged for the treatment of the body. Finally, the government resolved that it could not refuse to Muslims what had been conceded to Parsis—or even to Hindus should they ask for it. Muslim bodies were to be handed over unconditionally to appropriate Muslim authorities and there was to be no charge for medical expenses, since they were not levied on unclaimed Parsi bodies.[30]

Religion aside, what the Muslims had strongly objected to was that they had been receiving bodies for burial which had been cut up and incomplete—a head had been missing in one instance. But the question of religious sensibility and the handling by outsiders of a dead body was equally significant. The issue had another airing later in 1893 when the question was raised as to whether the post-mortem examination of Parsis and Muslims was allowed. An enquiry from the Surgeon-General to community leaders evoked strong responses.[31] Sir Jamsetjee Jeejeebhoy noted that Parsis objected more to the pollution of post-mortem touch than to post-mortem medical examination as such but 'in the present state of their religious belief and intellectual advancement, it is inexpedient and undesirable' to submit Parsi bodies to post-mortem examination except as required by law.[32] As for the Muslims, Murghay chaired another public meeting which unanimously resolved that it would be 'a grave sin' against Mohammedan laws and regulations to permit post mortem examination.[33]

Parsis and Muslims were both concerned with the body, with maintaining its corporeal physical integrity, and with conforming to religious and social attitudes which surrounded the dead. The official position could see only the deleterious effect the reduction of post mortems and dissections would have on medical training. A minute of February 1893 emphasized the priority of promoting anatomy study in Bombay and the way in which the removal of unclaimed Muslim bodies from dissection would inhibit the training of Indian surgeons in Bombay: 'This will be unfortunate, but it will be due to the shortsightedness of natives themselves, not of us who are trying to fit them for this as well as for other professions'.[34] Governor Harris concurred and wanted the correspondence published in order to show 'one at least of the difficulties that lie in the way of an extension of medical education in this country',[35] but the matter was not pursued. It was realized that if the matter were publicized other communities would lay claim to their bodies and the difficulties would be further increased for medical education.[36] The matter was finally settled in November with a government resolution.[37]

There was a postscript to these discussions in a request from Murghay, this time writing as President of the Majlise Taide Amvat La-varisie Islamie of Bombay in August 1894, that Muslims be permitted to pay for a building in the J.J. Hospital compound so that Muslim dead bodies could be kept separate from those of other castes and creeds. Separate accommodation was 'essential on religious grounds', he argued, but—and probably this was a sop to European prejudices and current western medical fancies—it was also required on 'sanitary principles' which would reduce the 'chance of contagious exhalations likely to affect the Sanitation of the Hospital itself'.[38]

The case for separate mortuaries was strong: Parsis already had their own mortuary and there was, the Surgeon-General noted, a need for a new mortuary with separate sections for Hindus, Muslims, and Christians. He recommended that the Muslim suggestion be accepted[39] but eventually, on PWD advice that such a decision would later prove awkward, the government did not accept the request. Instead it would in the near future build a new sectional mortuary and at its own expense.[40]

In death, as in life, bodies were thus to remain separate. Caste and sectarian distinctions were to be maintained. Dead bodies were still affected by the taboos of separation entertained by the living. The identity of the dead was marked by the distinctiveness gained from their having been members of one group rather than another when alive. The body remained after death part of the group of which it had been a member while living and it was this characteristic which was basic to its existence as a dead body.

In the examples I have given here the important issue in terms of entry into the burial grounds of the Khoja dissidents or of the burial of Muslims during the 1874 riots or what happened to the parts of the dead bodies was assertion of membership of a distinctive social group—in the first that of a caste-like group and in the other two that of a religious community, the Muslims. Kin ties, though presumably obviously important to the mourners, were less relevant in the conflicts over the burial. The body in life as in death retained membership of the primary social group as defined by caste-like characteristics and then by religion. Equally important and interlinked were religious requirements and rituals; here the social and the religious merged. But as the dissection example suggests, at issue also was a strong underlying concern for the dignity of the body after death and the maintenance of its physical integrity as a whole. Though religion was used to justify the opposition to dissection and body partition the fact that these were unclaimed bodies, bodies without relatives or friends, suggests that the concern was to maintain basic human dignity after death among people who were more akin as members of the same religious grouping than ones who were not. The dead body had a continued existence, a quasi-life which required consideration much as a living body would require. The dead in this sense had a physical presence and a corporeality as expressed through the membership of social groups rather than as individuals.

Persona and Memory

There were of course other times when it was individuals as themselves who were important and were remembered after death, for something they had achieved or represented. Their pasts, their life, continued to resonate after they died.

Most families remember their dead relatives and continue to do so at least for a couple of generations. Specific rituals enshrine and reinforce the memory of family ancestors and parents. Such private memory and practice may be mimicked in the public commemoration of people who in life had been pre-eminent. In addition, the memory of the dead may be used for public purposes and ongoing agendas and deliberately so by drawing on the family praxis of mourning and remembering.

Take the example of Babu Ganu and how his death was used to maintain the ongoing rage in the Congress campaign of civil disobedience against British rule. He was a Congress volunteer who died in December 1930 while picketing a warehouse of foreign goods in Kalbadevi.[41] Rumours spread quickly that he had been killed by a truck although the police claimed he had fallen in a melee on the site and had accidentally struck his head. Whatever precisely happened is irrelevant here. What is important is how quickly he became a martyr to the nationalist cause. Shops in the area immediately closed in protest over his death. By evening flowers and incense marked the spot where he died and it became a site of pilgrimage. His photo was installed there and a small lamp was lit, in conformity with death rituals. Bonfires were also lit near the spot and men passing by were required to take off their hats as a sign of respect. The police objected to the observances and to Babu Ganu's enshrinement and soon established a routine of opposition and destruction. The police would come and remove the lamp, the flowers and incense, and extinguish the bonfires. But as soon as they left, new lamps, flowers, and incense would be reinstalled and new bonfires lit. There was also violence when the police lath-charged the crowds of people who had come to pay homage at the spot.

There had been a major confrontation between the authorities and the nationalists during the funeral procession. On the day after he had died, Babu Ganu's funeral procession set out for the burning grounds, shouting slogans like *Inquilab Zindabad, Babu Ganu Zindabad, Bharatma Ho Azad* (Free Mother India), *Pardeshi Ho Barbad* (May foreigners be ruined). It was a large procession of perhaps 20,000 people.[42] On the way it suddenly changed direction and headed for Chowpatty. The police stopped it near Opera House and a small section pushed through only to be stopped by a police bayonet charge. The rest of the procession sat down on the road in true satyagraha fashion and refused to move. In the bylanes police lathi-charged crowds that were gathering. Eventually troops were brought in and kept at the ready inside the theatre. Meanwhile Congress leaders negotiated with the police and agreed to take the procession to the cremation grounds. In the events of the day some thirty people were wounded while elsewhere lathi charges connected with the demonstrations resulted in at least another thirteen injuries. In the process, over the two or three days after his death, Babu Ganu was adopted officially by the Congress as one of its martyrs and a year later the Bombay Pradesh Congress Committee decided to observe 12 December as Babu Ganu Day, and requested the All India Congress Committee (AICC) to order a similar observance of his death throughout India.

Babu Ganu thus became a symbol of opposition, a martyr, a brave satyagrahi, a cult figure who represented the values of the nation as against the power of the Raj. It was his action, that of satyagraha, and his death in the cause of resistance that made him a martyr and made him remembered. His death, not his life, was what was critical in his transformation from unknown Congress volunteer to martyr and in his being remembered. Nationalist songs may have helped the process in that they were currently eulogizing the need for bravery and the willingness to die.

Perhaps they helped provide the context in which to locate Babu Ganu and the emotions through which to see him. The virtue of struggle, the primacy of nation and love for the nation, and willingness to give up everything for the nation were the kinds of sentiments they repeated again and again in chorus after chorus. Some went further and sang of the need to die for the nation. Such urging may have provided the readings to place Babu Ganu in the context of his martyrdom. Take for instance one of the songs, 'For the Martyrs', with its affirmation of the almost magical powers derived from death in the national cause:

The blood of the martyrs will accomplish wonders.
These will go on shedding the blood of the heart [lit. the liver]
We shall never retreat being afraid,
We shall always continue to advance our step forward.[43]

Another made the point that country was more important than living:

In the service of the country let life remain or not.
For the love of the country let this glory remain or not.
…
Brothers, do not err in your duty through the fear of life;
The work will remain whether man remains or not.[44]

During the events of Ganu's procession death ceremonies had fused with nationalist agitation; the expression of nationalist opposition and the build-up of mass support occurred through rituals associated with death: the burning lamp, the incense and the flowers. It also occurred through the large funeral procession that accompanied him to his cremation. The attempt to take the procession to Chowpatty sought to link him with the *samadhi* of Tilak who had been cremated there a decade earlier; it associated him with the pantheon of nationalist leaders, and reinforced the connotations associating the Chowpatty space with nationalist memory and even sanctity.

That memory was indeed potent. The public cremation of Lokamanya Tilak on the sands of Chowpatty in August 1920 had been a massive testament to his enormous popularity and his potency as a fiery nationalist leader. Enormous crowds commemorated his achievement and his leadership by joining in the largest funeral procession that had been seen in the city. Until that time the procession that had accompanied Dadabhai Naoroji's remains to the Towers of Silence on Malabar Hill had been the largest, but Tilak's was even bigger. Whereas Dadabhai's had been mainly of the English educated and the elites of the city, the Lokamanya's had a more catholic composition, working class as well as educated, and people from the suburbs and outside Bombay as well as from within the city.[45] Two special trains had even run from Poona to bring mourners to Bombay. Tilak's body, seated in a palanquin, with pall bearers who included Gandhi, Shaukat Ali, and Saifuddin Kitchlew, headed a procession that was a mile and a half long with at least two lakh people in it, apart from all the many thousands who crowded every vantage point on the route from the Sardar Griha to the seaside to take their last darshan. The procession moved slowly and stopped frequently as people offered it flowers. As was later to be the case with Babu Ganu, Tilak was there as a representative of the Indian nation in its opposition to the British Raj, and there were people of all castes, religions and communities, Muslims, Hindus, Parsis and Christians in the crowd. Among the worthies present in the procession other than Gandhi, Shaukat Ali, and Kitchlew were Paranjpye, Jamnadas, and Banker.[46]

Tilak's potency had been asserted earlier when enormous crowds had come to see his body before it was carried away in procession. The numbers had been so large many had been unable to see him. The situation was described thus:

People had begun to flock near Sardar Griha from 7 in the morning and by 8 o'clock there was no room for anybody to go up to catch his last sight. His body had, therefore, to be brought out and put on the balcony so that it could be witnessed from the road. Thousands satisfied themselves by such a sight from [a] distance, but even after seeing him they were not inclined to give way to others and they stood there as firm as a rock. Such an abounding love they had for him! The crowd increased at every moment and it grew so tremendous that although the funeral procession was timed to start at 1 it could not be started till 2 p.m.[47]

The public commemoration had of course happened at a particularly eventful moment—the planned beginning of Gandhi's first non-cooperation campaign. The enormous crowds may have already been excited by what he had scheduled and thus the Tilak procession may have had a further underlay of complex associations and feelings apart from those specifically surrounding the death itself. The procession may thus have also been in part an expression of the aroused emotions around the campaign while it was on the surface purely a commemoration of the popularity of one of the most potent personalities Maharashtra had produced. His public cremation signalled his importance and the way in which he was regarded. It also provided a spot, his *samadhi*, which was thereafter to have significance as a revered and perhaps sacral space in the configuration of the mental landscape of the city. This was of course why the Babu Ganu procession had tried to go there rather than to the usual cremation grounds.

It was not Tilak's religion or caste membership that was uppermost in this acknowledgment of his stature; it was his political leadership, his articulation of the idea of the nation as opposed to the force of the Raj. His body was not a pawn in a caste or sectarian or religious dispute and the physical presence of his corpse was not used to make a point in a limited battle between rival social groups in the way we have seen operate in the first section of this paper. These matters were not relevant to what Tilak was about. But, of course, in a different sense the memory of Tilak was part of a battle—with the British Raj.

The idiom of the funeral procession and its nationalist message was taken up elsewhere in the country in mourning Tilak's death. For instance, in Maharashtra at Satara, bazaars closed immediately when the news reached the town. Thousands joined a mourning procession with the Lokamanya's picture carried in a palanquin to the confluence of the rivers. There everyone bathed and speeches in praise of Hindu-Muslim unity were made. The following day the whole city observed a fast.[48] Calcutta similarly had its mourning procession, a monster one almost as large as Bombay's with over a lakh people in the procession walking through teeming rain, barefoot and bareheaded to the Ganges bathing ghat. Tilak's photo was carried in *vimanas* on men's shoulders. Women from buildings en route showered the procession with flowers and coins; and virtually everyone on the streets bowed as it passed by and doffed their hats. When it arrived at the ghats the Hindus bathed and Muslims participated in the subsequent meeting.[49]

The funeral procession had thus multiplied itself and extended its range to cover most of the country. Though the actual procession taking the dead body to the place of cremation in Bombay remained the central event, it was not the only procession. It repeated itself in numerous processions in different places throughout the country. They were as serious and as reverential as was the initial one in Bombay with Tilak's body. They followed the mourning ritual much as in Bombay, but using a photo to represent the body. It was what Tilak stood for that was important and either his photo or his body could symbolize that importance. Apart from geographical spread, the numerous processions were national in their joint adherence to the symbol of the nation which Tilak represented. The funeral procession itself became part of the armoury of nationalism and the nation. It also became part of the techniques of struggle and was adopted in the nationalist struggle for other leaders when they died. Others who were killed in the struggle, not necessarily in Bombay, were similarly accorded mourning processions as in May 1930 when Bombay Muslims and Congress volunteers mourned the deaths of those martyrs killed in Peshawar.[50] So was the observance of Motilal Nehru's Shradha Day in February 1931 with its processions, hartal, and picketing.[51] The funeral procession and the anniversary of the procession both became part of the story of struggle.

But for Tilak, so massive a nationwide commemoration could not be allowed to be dissipated; it was too potent a symbol. In subsequent nationalist campaigns the remembrance of the day of his death became part of the nationalist panoply of resistance. Tilak Day became part of the techniques of opposition and was observed regularly for example during the civil disobedience campaign.

In 1930, a group of Congress volunteers laid flowers on the spot where Tilak had been cremated and then led a procession singing national songs and waving national flags towards the Fort area. It was stopped opposite the Victoria Terminus station and by then numbered 'many thousands', and was far too large, the police commissioner decided, it was to be dispersed 'without the use of considerable force'.[52] He therefore allowed them to stay there through the night. Early the next morning there were about 8,000 satyagrahis on the road but the number had begun to increase around daylight beginning with the arrival of several Prabhat Feri groups. The police ordered them to disperse around 7 a.m. and those that would not leave were attacked with lathis and a few were arrested.[53] News of what had happened spread quickly around the city, a partial hartal followed in which shops, markets, schools, colleges, and some mills closed. In this sense Tilak lived on in opposition and as struggle.

When the Congress was not in resistance mode but chose to work with or as government, Tilak Day was given another flavour. Thus in 1937 although there were the usual processions, meetings, and flag salutations, they had a different point. Congress had decided to form a government in Bombay and Tilak's Anniversary Day became Congress Office Acceptance Day.[54] The format was thus remarkably resilient to changes in the tactical situation and different elements in Tilak's own career were emphasized according to the circumstances of the times.

As to Chowpatty, Tilak's *samadhi* became a special space which articulated both the personality of the leader and what he had stood for in opposing the Raj. The *samadhi* embodied the memory, articulated it, and made it a reality in the ongoing struggle. Apart from unplanned incidents like that of Babu Ganu there were more structured attempts subsequently to use it as a location for the cremation of other national leaders. Permission was sought from the authorities to cremate Vithalbhai Patel there in 1934 but the government would not agree. Nor did the Congress government after Independence permit the cremation of Dr Ambedkar on the sands of Chowpatty either. Bombay as a result did not have a series of *samadhis* on Chowpatty which would link urban space with the memory of a range of leaders. Only Tilak was thus remembered.

In conclusion I have argued that the funeral procession had become absorbed into the vocabulary of nationalist agitation and in the celebration of the nation. Subsequent processions mimicked the primary, the original procession just as it in its turn drew on the practices of familial funeral processions. They celebrated the ideas and values of the dead person but those very values were applied to meet the existing situation, the tactical and logistic needs of specific campaigns and the climate of ideas in which they were happening. The corporeality of the body itself, the factor of decay, which provided the need for the initial procession became subsumed by ideas surrounding what the person had been and had represented. The procession became a celebration of the dead person, and presented him as a symbol which could be interpreted in many different ways and used actively in ongoing situations. The procession was made active by the needs of the day, just as the initial procession had summarized the needs of the time in which the death had occurred.

Notes

1. For a recent study of Hindu theories of death see Shyam Ghosh, *Hindu Concept of Life and Death (as Portrayed in Vedas, Brahmanas, Aranyakas, Upanisads, Smrtis, Puranas and Epics)*, New Delhi: Munshiram Manoharlal, 1989.
2. Cited in Mr Barrow's report, c.1881, reproduced in L.W. Michael, comp., *The History of the Municipal Corporation of the City of Bombay*, Bombay: Union Press, 1902, p. 291.
3. Jim Masselos, 'The Khojas of Bombay: The Defining of Formal Membership Criteria During the Nineteenth Century', in *Caste and Social Stratification among the Muslims*, ed. Imtiaz Ahmed, Delhi: Manohar, 1973, pp. 1–20.
4. The analysis which follows is based on the *Times of India* verbatim newspaper reports of the trials of rioters as reprinted *in toto* as an appendix, 'Reports of the Proceedings in the Police and High Courts' to *The Memorial of the Parsee Inhabitants of the City of Bombay, in the East Indies, to the Most Noble the Marquis of Salisbury, Her Majesty's Principal Secretary of State for India in Council*, Bombay: Bombay Gazette Press, 1874. Hereafter the reference will be given as TI [date], Appendix.
5. Mr Branson's defence summation in TI 7 April 1874, Appendix, p. 39.
6. Evidence, amongst many others, of Ramsing Gungasing, temple sepoy, TI 7 April 1874, Appendix, p. 35.
7. Evidence of Dhunjeebhoy Eduljee clerk, TI 7 April 1874, Appendix, p. 35.

8. Evidence of Police Inspector Austin, TI 2 April 1874, Appendix, p. 21.
9. Evidence of Ardasir Bomanjee, clerk, TI 7 April 1874, Appendix, p. 36.
10. Evidence of Police Inspector Austin, TI 2 April 1874, Appendix, p. 21.
11. Evidence of Thomas Mills, superintendent of police, C division, TI 1 April 1874, Appendix, p. 18.
12. Evidence of Ardasir Bomanjee, clerk, TI 7 April 1874, Appendix, p. 36.
13. Evidence of Thomas Mills, superintendent of police, C division, TI 1 April 1874, Appendix, p. 19.
14. Mr Branson's defence summation, TI 4 April 1874, Appendix, pp. 26–7.
15. See amongst others the evidence of Henry John Brewin, police constable, TI 2 April 1874, Appendix, p. 22.
16. Brewin's evidence, ibid., p. 23 and Ferguson's defence summation, TI 6 April 1874, Appendix, p. 29.
17. Evidence of Cowasjee Eduljee Patel, company secretary, TI 7 April 1874, Appendix, p. 37.
18. Evidence of Hurilal Pranjeewandas, TI 7 April 1874, Appendix, p. 36.
19. *Bombay Gazette*, 7 December 1874.
20. The honorary secretaries were Mirza Hoosein Khan, Mir Safaraz Ali and Nacoda Goolum Hoosein Rogay. TI, 1 November 1892.
21. Report of meeting in ibid.
22. Speech reprinted in TI, 4 November 1892.
23. Letter of Kazi Shaik Mahomed Morghay, Kazi of Bombay, and 53 others, 23 February 1893 in Maharashtra State Archives, General Dept., vol. 63, 1893, pp. 6–7.
24. Letter of W. Gray, 9 January 1892 in ibid., p. 12.
25. Letter to Surgeon-General, 7 September 1892, in ibid., pp. 10–10A.
26. Letter of 5 December 1892 to Secretary to Surgeon-general in ibid., p. 24.

27. Minute, ibid., p. 46.
28. Ibid., pp. 69–74.
29. Letter of Surgeon-general, 25 February 1893 in ibid., pp. 2–3.
30. Two minutes dated 18 March 1893 and reply to Muslim deputation, 29 March 1893 in ibid., pp. 79–86.
31. Letter of 8 September 1893 in ibid, p. 102.
32. Ibid., p. 105.
33. Ibid., p. 106.
34. 18 February 1893, in ibid., p. 80.
35. 11 November 1893 in ibid., pp. 120–1.
36. Minute of 'HB', 11 November 1893, p. 121A and Harris minute of 12 November 1893.
37. General Department Resolution 4112 of 17 November 1893 in ibid., p. 125.
38. Letter of 28 August 1894 in Maharashtra State Archives, General Dept., vol. 64, 1893, pp. 13–14.
39. Letter of 18 September 1894 in ibid., p. 25.
40. General Dept. Resolution 4380 of 23 November 1894 in ibid.
41. Jim Masselos, 'Audiences, Actors and Congress Dramas: Crowd Events in Bombay City in 1930', in *South Asia*, vol. VIII, no. 1–2, June–December 1985, pp. 78–9.
42. Bombay Police Commissioner confidential report of 13 December 1930 in Maharashtra State Archives, Home Dept. Special 750(76)/1930, p. 11.
43. The poem in government translation appears in Maharashtra State Archives, Home Dept. Poll. File 332 of 1930, pp. 7–8.
44. 'Our duty' in ibid., p. 9. See also Jim Masselos, 'Controlling the Prabhat Pheris: Bombay 1930–1931', in *The City in Action. Bombay Struggles for Power*, New Delhi: Oxford University Press, 2007.
45. *Indian Social Reformer*, 8 August 1920, p. 1.
46. *Bombay Chronicle*, 2 August 1920, p. 11.
47. Ibid.
48. *Bombay Chronicle*, 3 August 1920, p. 7.
49. Ibid.
50. Commissioner of Police, 31 May 1930, in Maharashtra State Archives, Home Dept. Special 750(26)/1930. pp. 33–5.

51. Special Secret Telegram to Secretary of State, 14 February 1931 in Maharashtra State Archives, Home Dept. Special 750(39) VII/1930, pp. 115–17.
52. Special Department report to Secretary of State, 2 August 1930 in Maharashtra State Archives, Home Dept. Special 750(39)-III/1930, p. 5.
53. See also the fuller report of the Commissioner of Police, 2 August 1930, in Maharashtra State Archives, Home Dept. Special 750(26)/1930, p. 93.
54. J.B. Irwin, Home Dept (Special), Govt. of Bombay to Home Dept., Govt. of India, 16/18 August 1937, in India Office Records, L/P&J/5/155, fol. 139.

13

Memory, Space and History

KRISHNA KUMAR

CHARLES DICKENS and Mahatma Gandhi could afford to be boldly critical of the railways. Dickens did so in several places, most sharply in *Dombey and Son*, which was was first serialized in 1846–8. Although steam locomotives had been around since 1825, the railway network was still expanding at the time Dickens was writing. The narrative of this book covers the period of the mid-1830s when land surveys, the necessary clearing of spaces—including graveyards—and the laying of tracks were underway in the area around Camden Town in London. Dickens singles out the construction for bitter criticism of the displacement and destruction it involved. The changes that Dickens saw coming into the life of people with the spread of 'railway mania' form the undercurrent in the story of *Dombey and Son* and other works. The moral vision that guides the plot permits it to push a villainous character—for whom no available instrument of justice seemed sufficient—under the mighty wheels of the railway engine.

Gandhi's treatment of the railways in *Hind Swaraj* is no less harsh, but it is located in a different, broader critique of colonialism and modern civilization. The ninth chapter of *Hind Swaraj* has a long critique of the railways which starts with these words: '...but for the railways, the English could not have such a hold on India as they have'.[1] The analysis covers both the external and the internal impacts on Indian society, its economy, and culture. It is also a moral critique. Even if you discount his wider canvas, you sense the drive to dismiss any possibility of a balanced view of the railway network that was still in its expanding phase in India when *Hind Swaraj* was written. Gandhi saw in the railways not merely a carrier of disease, but also a colonial design to drain India of its resources. The railways destroyed the self-reliant local economies that existed earlier, Gandhi argues. The criticism of railways forms a part of his general swipe at modern institutions such as courts and hospitals, and the professions they depend on, i.e. lawyers and doctors. Just as he practiced law and made it the instrument of his politics, he travelled tirelessly in trains, making them the means of embracing India's diversity. His writings and his life make him a practitioner of critical modernity, rather than a Luddite.

No one today can publicly empathize with the attitude and feelings Dickens and Gandhi expressed in their different ways. Writing on this theme would surely lose readers if the writer did not disown outright any Luddite traces in his thoughts about development and national progress that the railways symbolize. This was not so for Maharaja Pratap Singh. Legend has it that he did not let the railways pass through Tikamgarh, his capital. Born in 1854, he came to the throne of the Orchha state and died in 1930. It is during his long reign, which started in 1874 and lasted for more than half a century, that the capital of the Orchha state might have become part of the Indian railway network. Why it did not is an interesting subject of speculation and legend. Growing up in Tikamgarh was hardly possible without frequent encounters with a mixture of legend and history dating back to the reign of Pratap Singh and his modernist successor Vir Singh (1930–56), a patron of hockey, Hindi and girls' education among other things. His predecessor, Pratap Singh, was believed to have been the designer of irrigation works and bridges. There was a popular legend that he refused to grant permission to British engineers to carry out surveys for building rail tracks through his kingdom. No one knows if there was truth in this, but if you look at the railway map, it shows the railway passing through the northern tip of the state at the tiny station of the long-abandoned capital, Orchha, now a tourist spot busily served by huge SUVs from nearby Jhansi. The capital of the Orchha state had shifted to Tikamgarh two centuries before this branch line railway was built.

Tikamgarh town is now on the railway map. The popular BJP politician of the district, Uma Bharati, is given credit for accomplishing this feat. The Tikamgarh station became functional in 2010. Although Uma Bharati's political fortunes are no longer in ascendance, the popular belief regarding her role in bringing the railway to Tikamgarh is sure to last for a while. People believe that without her persistent pressure, the railway ministry would not have pursued the Khajuraho line project. At the time Uma was lobbying for this project, she represented the Khajuraho constituency in Parliament which combined Tikamgarh and Chhatarpur districts. This railway line joins Lalitpur with Khajuraho.

The opening of this line made an immediate impact on passengers' choice between bus and train. The train fare for Lalitpur is one-fourth of the bus fare. The same is true in the case of the bus fare from Tikamgarh to Chhatarpur although this route was never as busy as the Lalitpur route. The difference in fare made buses unviable, so their number came drastically down within weeks of the train's inauguration. Initially, there was just one train, and it offered merely two rounds in a day. People were willing to wait for it for hours—the fare difference apparently mattered so much. This was a clear indication of the economic status of the vast majority of the people of our region. I took this passenger train for the first time in 2014. It was jam-packed. Since then, this original passenger train has been replaced by others that join Bhopal with Khajuraho, Mumbai with Allahabad and Barauni, and Khajuraho with Kurukshetra via New Delhi. Tikamgarh is now comfortably ensconced on the national railway map. The pre-railway history of transport in Tikamgarh has now closed and a new era has begun. Historians will not face the usual problem of dating the transition. The problem of interpreting the transition will, however, remain.

There was a time not so long ago when it used to take one day for a letter posted in Delhi to reach Tikamgarh. That is how things were till the early 1980s. As I used the word 'post' I realize I am already into history and not just memory. Nowadays, it is used only in hyphenated settings like 'post-modern'. It is now covered by 'mail' which includes both the old postal messages and its electronic reincarnation. Ironically, the names of trains that had the specific task of carrying postal material were known as 'Mails'. They were just as fast if not faster than express trains. In the case of Tikamgarh, post came by the Panjab Mail. It connected Bombay with Ferozepur and started in 1914. Its schedule has not changed much. It touched Lalitpur towards the evening on its way to Bombay and at noon on its way back. It had a compartment for sorting letters and other material while the train was running. That is how and why letters arrived so fast to Tikamgarh. However, this was not the only train to carry mail.

Among buses too, there was a distinction between the ones carrying dak and others: the dak bus was more reliable to leave on time. One dak bus waited at the Lalitpur railway station all night to leave at the crack of dawn. For me it was the best choice during the early 1970s when I started my teaching career at Delhi University. I frequently went home, taking the night train—Pathankot (later Amritsar)-Dadar (Bombay) Express. One walked out of the station, turned right into a lane (which actually led to Devgarh where the mighty Betwa River flows beside Gupta period caves) and found the first bus for Tikamgarh standing there. At times, one had to wake up the conductor sleeping inside. Sacks of dak were loaded on the roof before the bus departed. That is how a letter posted in Delhi the previous day got delivered in Tikamgarh the next day. Post for smaller places and villages in our district was also in these sacks. The era of mail being sorted in trains, and unloaded at all stations as the trains reached them, came to a sudden end when Madhav Rao Scindia became the railway minister under Rajiv Gandhi in the mid-1980s. In the early dawn of liberalization, all public sector services like the railways had to smarten up by shedding unprofitable services like sorting mail in a designated compartment.

The dak bus took over two hours to cover the 36 mi.—or 56 km., the unit that became a common measure through the 1970s. Others took slightly longer. The route was flanked by trees and crossed several rivers, the last one being the Jamdar. Crossing it, one started preparing for arrival. The first sign of Tikamgarh was Tagore Hall, built as part of the local college in Tagore's birth centenary year. A glimpse of the *bada talab* (big tank/lake) came next, and as the bus drove along its bank, the majestic college building appeared on the horizon. It was once the queen's summer palace built during Pratap Singh's reign. Its huge basement served as the library. It was cool throughout the year without any form of air-conditioning. Past the college, the bus crossed the Shiv temple and then the town surrounded the passengers.

This familiar landscape changed when I took the train from Lalitpur the first time a few years ago. There was, of course, no change in the basic mnemonics. The location of Lalitpur with reference to Tikamgarh was the same as before, i.e. Lalitpur was west of Tikamgarh, so the bus as well as the train travel eastward. However, the bus entered from the south-west corner of the town, whereas the train enters from the north-west corner. This change usurps the memory of arrival by bus. As time passes, that memory will fade from the collective mind. Nothing seemed familiar as I got off the train and looked for an auto or an e-rickshaw. The train station was on a ridge created in order to enable the tracks to stay flat. It seemed as if it was a new town. That too was true in many aspects. In earlier visits I took the changes occurring in the town in my stride, but this time they struck me as vital. Old memory and the images it held was situated in spatial details. The new landscape created for the railway line did not allow me to sustain that old memory.

A new layer came in and settled on the old memory, marking my encounter with a historical shift in Tikamgarh's relationship with the world, its economy and cultural holdings. Some of these holdings had already become irrelevant; now, the rest slipped out of the contemporary. The train gave a powerful historic blow to bring in the new and ring out the remaining old. In his classic work on human geography, P. Vidal de la Blache wrote that 'the human element is the essential part of all geography'.[2] Let me add to those fine words: 'memory is the core of being human'. How we remember a place shapes our relation with it. That is why it is important to pause and think before altering a space, to determine whether you have worked out all aspects of the impact the alteration would have.

The value of remembering the dak bus lies in the perspective it offers on matters like speed and communication. The speed at which mail could reach Tikamgarh and its hinterland had slowed down long before the arrival of railways. It is still very slow, and the expected compensation by electronic communication has not materialized as yet. A similar contradiction can be noticed in cinema. Between the early 1950s and the 1980s, cinema expanded its reach in Tikamgarh town, and then it vanished. No simple history or speculation can reveal the 'full' story. Netflix has not changed the geography of access to films in Tikamgarh in any notable manner. Between small town prosperity and culture lie a number of social mysteries that memory alone guides us to notice, and the hope that history will one day replace memory with more sound or reliable knowledge of the past has not arisen yet. To the extent higher education might serve as the local mother of historical knowledge, we have no reason to be optimistic. In fact, tracing the fate of higher education that unfolded in district towns like Tikamgarh in the final decades of the last century would require more specialized space and treatment than would a study of transport and communication.

Memory and space are so closely associated that one cannot think about memory without recalling or imagining the space registered in it. If the space changes, memory can hardly survive by itself. Space, in this context, is the shape a landscape has taken under changing social conditions. The recent redesigning of New Delhi's Central Vista is a nationally significant case wherein memory of the previous version is all one might expect to survive, if only to guide the historian dependent on extant photographs to track the so-called historical forces that made every possible kind of challenge to the alterations irrelevant. More modest but equally instructive would be an investigation of any foot track passing, for example, through farmland or a forest. How it shaped people's lives is something historians might hardly notice, let alone recognize, without the aid of the memory of an interregnum—separating the original pathway from whatever replaced it—that some people might be in a position to offer.

As an academic discipline, history evokes pride among its scholars by the fact of being based on evidence. But there are regimes that specialize in destroying all evidence. History and its institutional aides like museums and archives look after breaks in memory, enabling it to gracefully, harmlessly fade. The objects on display hang free of the spaces they occupied in their original context. In some cases, where memories were strong and significant, they may turn into folklore and myth, and these forms may well be challenged or contradicted by history. One can rightly say that history lets you move on, bowing to its forces. The railway is doubtless one of these forces; it is partly a tool and partly the energy the tool needs in order to do its work. It is as powerful as roads, with the difference that while a road permits several kinds of vehicles and pedestrians to use it, a railway track is choosy. Perhaps that is a reason why its imprint on a landscape is deeper and its dislocating capacity with reference to memory is greater.

Geographically, Lalitpur, belongs to Uttar Pradesh whereas Tikamgarh is in Madhya Pradesh. Lalitpur is a salient town, i.e. landlocked in an alien administrative and political neighbourhood. Its relationship with Tikamgarh was tied up with a frequent bus service. There were eighteen of them, from early morning to late in the night. That relationship has now been snapped for me, and the mental map that arriving home by bus from Lalitpur formed is now fading away. It would be correct, but inadequate, to say that my memory in this case is evoking nostalgia. All, including unpleasant, memories have an element of nostalgia in them, and this one is no exception. However, the time when a particular, geographically rooted memory reaches the end of its life-period, so to say (i.e. when it is related to an ongoing phenomenon), is historically significant.

Though the new train service also comes from Lalitpur, it arrives in Tikamgarh from the opposite, northern end of the town. It has created a new memory page for the young. They will grow up in a new landscape. Not just Lalitpur, Bhopal too will now enter a new relationship with Tikamgarh. Earlier, one boarded the Delhi–Bombay trains from Lalitpur to go to Bhopal. Now, the new Mahamana Madan Mohan Malviya Express that links Bhopal to Khajuraho passes through Tikamgarh. Its relationship with the neighbouring Chattarpur too has changed as its bus route has lost its popularity and relevance, except for people going to smaller places on the route. Not all changes in the human geography of the region can be interpreted at present; they will take years to unfold.

Joining the railway map is seen as a harbinger of 'development' in the focused sense in which the term is currently used—to indicate a decisive economic shift. After two decades of BJP rule in MP, the public ethos of Tikamgarh has fully absorbed the message of 'vikas' conveyed in election after election and in between elections. Since 2014, Tikamgarh has been served by the so-called double-engine sarkar, i.e. the engines of like-minded governments at the Centre and in the State. Now that real engines are passing through the district and the town headquarters, perhaps Tikamgarh will swim out of the category of 'most backward districts' in India where it has so far been sitting comfortably with 249 others. One sense in which its backwardness makes sense to me is its opaqueness. No study exists to show how exactly its economy has fared since Independence. All the things one knows on account of being around have no statistical backing.

Migration is a fine example. While living in Delhi, I met numerous people who belonged to my district. They had moved to Delhi in search of livelihood, as labourers, masons, rickshaw pullers, gardeners, vendors, and so on. One such person, Ganeshi, used to sit on the sidewalk near the gate of Miranda House, selling American corn. Her husband had failed to find regular work, and her children were struggling at school. She can hardly count as a sample for making sense of Tikamgarh's economy, but there is no denying that she was one of the tens of thousands who leave the district every year looking for work. Poverty is crucial to any understanding of Tikamgarh. Will it decline now with the coming of trains, or will they speed up emigration is a good question. If pursued, it will help us distinguish between developmentalists and Gandhians in any group of scholars.

The history of railways in India is a fascinating subject of study, both in geography and economics. There is no reason for it to miss out politics, but it does. That the railways were a part of empire-building is well documented and accepted, even though Gandhi's interpretation continues to look a bit over the top. In his *India Conquered,* Jon Wilson says that 'railways only became a vehicle for asserting imperial power haphazardly and belatedly'.[3] The continued expansion of the railways in the twenty-first century is not a purely economic story. Political leaders who successfully lobby for the inclusion of their region in the railway map do attain political mileage. The cost is seldom calculated with reference to the benefit the inclusion would bring, partly because the benefit is hard to estimate without taking into account the question who would benefit most. On this question depends the character of the social change that the railways bring. The post-railway social topography may not be empirically shown to be linked to the railway as such, whereas the effects on the ecology are clearer. The drainage system is directly affected and flooding of rivers is known to be a familiar consequence. Denudation of the forest cover is another oft noticed result. No one can argue that Maharaja Pratap Singh of Orchha, who is believed to have denied the British railway engineers the permission to survey his state, anticipated these problems. He was perhaps simply being wary, or perhaps he was a vernacular Luddite. Historians are unlikely to identify his motive even if they find some worth in the question.

All I can think of are memories, but they will not suffice to assemble a history, including economic history that would prove whether Tikamgarh has become more prosperous since my childhood. Its isolation from the railways kept its exports and imports somewhat sluggish, dependent as they were on roads and trucks. In fact, roads were also few and a lot of villages were linked by foot tracks. The network of roads has become denser of late, but buses are not the only mode of commuting anymore. Motorcycles and jeeps or cars providing inter-village connectivity have multiplied. This also means that the cost of moving around has gone up considerably. On the Lalitpur road where the number of buses has come down drastically, a return trip to Kundeshwar can cost anywhere from 50 to 300 rupees, depending on the number of people available at a given moment to share seats. One might argue that the vehicles available as rural taxis create work opportunities. That is literally true, but the term 'opportunity' does not seem right to describe the compulsions under which frustrated young men take to this service industry. One wishes they had some options. The only option for many is to migrate to bigger cities and try their luck there.

Geography bears witness to the depredation that mining has caused to the landscape of our district. The signs had begun to surface several decades ago when the soap stone found in the hills across the district had begun to be exported—in trucks that led to ships sailing to Europe where companies needed it for various chemical products. The mining became so rampant that entire hills shown on the topographical map started to disappear. Export of wheat, soya bean and ginger had destinations within India. Then there were older, minor exports like fish and mangoes. With the train's arrival, both export and imports will swell. They already have. The richer residents of the town are now consumers of every conceivable luxury item required in everyday life, for special days, feasts and weddings. For the first time in the history of Tikamgarh, one sees gigantic sixteen-wheeled trucks pounding through the main artery of the town, itself barely wide enough to accommodate the cows, bulls, cycles, rickshaws and e-rickshaws, autos, motorcycles, cars and, of course, pedestrians. Whatever may be on those trucks, no one knows the monetary balance between exports and imports, but it does not matter whether we know or can estimate it. The basic fact is that mineral exports are irreplaceable. So are the jungles, most of which have already disappeared. Economic historians of the future will perhaps have more in-depth knowledge of Bundelkhand, but for now it seems certain that the arrival of the railways will enhance Tikamgarh's consumption capacity and its resource export.

The railways need to be studied in terms of their impact in different regions and sub-regions. They contribute to the growth of cities, especially coastal cities, but habitations in the hinterland use railways to drain their natural and human resources. The railways have become symbols of progress and development, like flyovers, four-lane highways in the mountains, the sleek Vande Bharat carriages. Those who use them are not necessarily the ones addressed in election speeches enumerating and describing development projects. The late President of India, K.R. Narayanan, had expressed his hope in one of his Republic Day addresses that designers of flyovers would leave some space for safe, usable pedestrian crossing ways. In Hathras district of Uttar Pradesh, the young Dalit woman who was raped and murdered a few years ago had stopped attending her primary school when a flyover came between her home and the school.

A differentiated economic history of 'backward' districts may show the railways in varying shades. After the radical change they wreak in landscapes and older public memories, curiosity about the pre-railway past tends to become rare, especially in the absence of any local content in the school curriculum. Physically too, that past becomes untraceable; mentally, it becomes irretrievable. I wonder if archeological investigation is possible in older geographical forms and their relation with human activity. For a 'backward' region like mine, who will do such an investigation or provide grants for it? The teaching of history in such regions is fully committed to cultivating loyalty to larger political units of territory and their development. This orientation is unlikely to affect the local oblivion even if the ongoing demand for a dialect-based state called Bundelkhand is one day conceded by political leaders in power who recently broke the district into two. The northern part, called Nivari, according to Wikipedia has the status of being the smallest district of MP. Its separation has further reduced Tikamgarh's revenue sources, taking away the relatively prosperous block of Prithvipur. The dictum in development planners appears to be: the backward shall move back further.

The general anxiety at a station that greets the arrival of an awaited train has been a familiar subject of essays that several generations of students have written as part of their English composition skill. It must be a rare student who decoded the noisiness and determined the contribution of the poor—both passengers and vendors—in creating the busyness. As the diesel engine pulling the Khajuraho-Kurukshetra Express crossed the outer signal of my town, its headlight pierced through the evening dust and the horn blew loud. I started moving along the platform towards my reserved compartment and noticed a bustle among the village women who had been resting on the bare floor of the platform, with *gatharis* serving as pillows. They quickly placed the *gatharis* on their head and their babies on the hip, then started running toward the few general coaches whose doors were open. Two tea vendors went up and down the long train, announcing their fleeting presence in a nasal rendering of the old, old term *chai*. For the two or three minutes it took me to locate and enter my bogey, it seemed as if a whole century had withdrawn its long and slow, forward movement. Amidst the radical changes that my old town and its rural surroundings are now going through, Kipling's world peeped in, creating more than a momentary vision wherein the tough everyday economy of men and women mixes with trumpeted political dreams. This is how in *Kim*, Rudyard Kipling had captured the moment of a train's arrival in Lahore station: '...the 325 south bound roared in. The sleepers sprang to life, and the station filled with clamour and shoutings, cries of water and sweetmeat vendors, shouts of native policemen, and shrill yells of women gathering up their baskets, their families, and their husbands.'[4]

Kim, as we know, was first published in 1901.

Notes

1. M.K. Gandhi, *Hind Swaraj,* Cambridge: Cambridge University Press, 1909; repr., 1991.
2. P. Vidal de la Blache, *Principles of Human Geography,* tr. in English, London: Constable, 1926.
3. John Wilson, *India Conquered,* London: Simon & Schuster, 2016.
4. Rudyard Kipling, *Kim,* New York: Macmillan, 1901; repr., New York: Dell, 1992.

14

City-making in 'Imperial' and 'Colonial' Capitals

A Scaffolding for Urban History (Delhi and Calcutta, 1690–1857)

ATIYA HABEEB KIDWAI

'Imperial' capital cities predate the 'colonial' capital city in India. In the late seventeenth century, paradoxically, when one of the most classic examples of a Mughal imperial capital city was taking shape on the western flanks of the river Yamuna, a tributary of the river Ganges, a colonial settlement, which later replaced this imperial capital, was creeping out of its embryonic form on the eastern flanks of the same Ganges. It would be interesting to compare the city-making processes around ascribed urban functions, form, and structure of the Mughal 'capital city' of Shahjahanabad representing a 'home-grown imperialism', with Calcutta, a 'colonial capital' representing 'implanted colonialism'.

I attempt in this paper to understand these cities not as a distinct structural entity, 'in itself, for itself' but as an 'enterprise' reflective of the system in which they appeared. Shajahanabad, as Delhi, was named, was the epitome of the Mughal design of a capital city while Calcutta grossly embodied symbols of colonial penetration and domination.

These cities ordered their realms and assigned their meaning in society through two different albeit hegemonic regimes, one established and indigenous and the other expansionary, colonial and foreign. The spatial and societal consequences of these regimes and the often-contradictory functional requirements of various groups representing them created and perpetuated a specific built environment and a specific form of urbanism during different phases of their development.

There is a vibrant debate in Urban Geography on how we conceptualize and research trans-local, trans-temporal urbanism under different politico-economic regimes and theoretical traditions and on how we interrogate and compare urban politics, life, economy, and culture. Inter-urban comparison of the components within cities brings out the diversity inherent in them more explicitly and helps us to build a theorization of urbanism more attuned to the similarities and differences that define urban complexity and diversity. Every city creates a unique configuration of materialities, ideation, and socio-economic processes. We need to find entry points that explain how and why particular forms of urbanism co-exist, contradict, and overlap with others, and also, what are the patterns of similarity and interconnectedness between cities in terms of similar experiences, components, and subsystems.

We begin with unpacking the different politico-economic and socio-cultural meanings prescribed to 'capital' and 'colonial capital' cities. These prescribed meanings have been historically embedded in the types of relationships that existed between the 'ruler' and the 'ruled' in the medieval world; the 'colonizer' and the 'colonized' in the phase of early modern Western colonization, and the 'dominant' and the 'dependent' in the present epoch defined by an increasingly interdependent and internationalized economy and the emergence of new capitalistic politico-economic and technological powers. These relationships have differently impacted the evolutionary processes of cities created by them or in which they have been embedded.

There are three concepts which circumscribe our discussion in this paper, viz., city-making, urban form, and urban function. City-making is a process, both planned and organic. While tracing this process we have to factor in a large number of issues and events, some crucial and complex, others elementary but basic. These pertain to the city's *raison d'etre*; its genesis; the organizing principles of its form and functions; the power structure and politico-economic forces it has symbolized and articulated; the conundrum of cultural values, beliefs and institutions that have governed the provision of human and social needs within it; the role of community and hierarchy in patterning its everyday rhythm, *ad infinitum.*

'City-making' is a provocative term. It hints at a utopian ambition to 'make' a perfect city, but city-making can also be layering as in old legendary cities that have created a layered character that would be impossible to 'make'. It requires drawing together the strands of physical place, society, and economy. Within the evolving framework of streets, spaces, and buildings, the city is ultimately shaped by the urban content, the activity, the people and the exchange of ideas, services and goods. City-making revolves around historically ascribed functions which lend cities their form and structure. The urban form is the spatial configuration of fixed elements which describe a city's physical characteristics and morphological attributes. It refers to the size, shape, and configuration of an urban area or its parts. How the urban form is structured depends on the scale of the urban area. Urban form does not simply relate to physical features but also encompasses non-physical aspects linked to economic, social, and political processes which to a great extent determine both the social environment and social interaction.[1] Urban functions of the city are conceptualized in the context of its social, economic and institutional needs and its interaction with other settlements and its hinterland.

The paper is divided into three sections. Section 1 forms the backdrop and gives a brief discussion on the *raison d'etre* and the genesis of Shahjahanabad and Calcutta, two capital cities formed contemporaneously for two different reasons, one political and the other economic. In Section 2 the key urban apparatuses of the two capitals as well as their processes of growth under two different regimes will be discussed and compared because Shahjahanabad was a planned imperial capital city while on the other hand Calcutta grew organically, gradually, and hesitantly as a trading post and only later transformed itself into an imperial capital. A chronological tracing of the growth and formation of the two cities, one which was 'indigenous and imperial', and the other which was 'implanted and colonial' led us to an understanding of the similarities and differences in their city-making processes. These will be summarized in Section 3 as the concluding remarks.

The *Raison d'etre* and the Genesis

Shahjahanabad was created as the imperial capital of the Mughal Empire by Shahjahan in 1639, while Calcutta was born as a rudimentary Indo-English settlement and trading post in 1690. Shahjahanabad was located on the medieval 'gateway' route to India while Calcutta was the colonial 'gateway' for its seaborne trade in its resources.

Shahjahanabad was the seventh of the seven cities of Delhi which came up and declined between 1000 BC and the seventeenth century. It lay in a strategic triangle of which two sides were formed by the *tor*-splattered undulations of the Delhi Ridge which is a culminating spur of the ancient denuded Aravali Hills of Rajasthan, the third side was formed by the river Yamuna. In earlier times the only route to India for traders and marching armies from the north-west penetrated through this triangle. The early Mughal rulers realized the importance of Delhi and paid frequent ceremonial visits to the city but preferred to rule India from Agra. Shahjahan had also continued to rule from Agra but had visited Delhi thrice in the five years between 1634 and 1638. He had perhaps been toying with the idea of founding a new capital to distinguish his era and to rule from a place which was less congested and less overbuilt than what Agra had become by his time. In 1639 he instructed his engineers, architects, and astrologers to choose a location between Agra and Lahore. The choice was 'Hazrat Delhi', the seat of the earlier Muslim empires and the centre of Islam in India.

It was a coincidence of historic importance that just three years before the establishment of Shahjahanabad, the British East India Company had started its 'drainage trade' with India in 1636. The Company had obtained royal permission to trade and establish factories (trading posts) in Bengal.[2] Almost half a century later, in 1690, it amalgamated three villages into a settlement, which was known as Calcutta and was the hub of its trade. Historians and chroniclers are divided in their views about the genesis as well as the selection of the site of Calcutta. The opinion of most British chronicles is that Calcutta grew on a site the selection of which was by chance and that it was nurtured by the Englishmen and local Indians did not have much to do with it.[3] This, however, is not corroborated by historical facts. The Company's trade had been initially based in Hughli and encouraged by the 'miserable and feeble' condition of Bengal the Company had valiantly prophesied the 'foundation of a large, well-grounded and sure English dominion in India for all time to come'.[4]

Job Charnock, the English Agent in Madras, responded to this prophecy and forgetting his earlier two reversals in Bengal sailed again, armed with his experience of three decades of navigating the Hughli River. He moored his boats on 24 August

1690 near Sutanati, a small village situated on the malarious unhealthy swamps along the east coast of the river and the location became the site around which the future capital of British India and its premier port developed. The Company servants, squatting on the goodwill of the local zamindar, bought the land and now become zamindars themselves.[5]

Qila-e-Mubarak (Red Fort)–Shahjahanabad

Shahjahanabad rose like a 'phoenix from the fire'.[6] Calcutta was almost 'chance-directed, chance-erected'.[7] Shahjahanabad was a planned project while Calcutta in most parts grew almost organically responding to population growth and the proliferation of urban functions. We outline here their early decades of growth and urban formation. The discussion will centre around their cores, i.e. their symbolic citadels, their key urban institutions, and areas which individualized their evolution.

The Mughal capital city was centred around its 'citadel' which comprised its fort, its palace, and its court. Shahjahan entered his new capital, which was a full-blown representation of the Mughal 'patrimonial system'[8] on 19 April 1648.

The notion of kingship of the later Mughals was influenced by Akbar, the ruler for whom the *Badshah* (emperor) was the pivot of authority and that authority had to be visibly articulated and manifested. The *Umara* (Mughal nobles) were next in importance and their presence was a prerequisite for a place to be recognized as a capital.[9]

The Citadel, *Qila-e-Mubarak* (Red Fort), was the emperor's palace-cum-fort and represented a harmonious fusion of Persian and Timurid elements but also 'appropriated and adapted indigenous practices prevalent in the subcontinent in the repertoire of instruments of power assertion'.[10] It had majesty, grandeur, and magnificence without an overpowering monumentality. Called the 'paradise' on earth, it was resplendent with gardens, palaces, water bodies, mosques, temples, and bazaars and accommodated some 3,000 people. It was the first Mughal palace fort designed according to an octagonal grid pattern. Shahjahanabad remained the seat of the Mughal Empire for more than thirty years until 1681 when Aurangzeb, who had been crowned king in 1658, left the north Indian part of his empire and never came back. About 200 years later, after the failed Mutiny against the British in 1857, the last Mughal emperor, Bahadur Shah Zafar, left the fort by the same gate from which Shahjahan had entered it.

Fort William: The Citadel of Calcutta

The East India Company, having found a footing in their settlement around Sutanati, by now known as Calcutta (anglicized version of Kalikata), had to ensure its security. The rebellion of the Maharaja of Burdwan in 1697 provided an excuse. A simple rectangular structure fortified at each corner with bastions was built to accommodate the private houses of the English Governor, factors, and writers. This 'citadel' called Fort William was connected to the old settlement. In the development of Indo-European towns in the seventeenth and eighteenth centuries in India, the progress was from the factory (trading post) to fortification and thence to the expansion of territory around the initial settlement. This was necessary because a fortified town was vulnerable to being besieged. Local rulers could cut off vital food suppliers or put pressure by harassing those of their subjects who lived near the town and who worked for the Europeans.[11]

Fort William, situated on the eastern banks of the River Hooghly, the major distributary of the River Ganges, covered an area (70 hectares) much smaller than the area of the Shahjahanabad Red Fort (103 hectares). The permission to construct the fort was granted by Mughal Emperor Aurangzeb in 1701 though it was named after King William III. This enclosure accommodated a modest Government House and the factory. The victory of the Company in the Battle of Plassey in 1757 rooted it in the region and it built a new fort south of the old one for which substantial alterations were made in the town. The Indian dwellings along the river bank were cleared for the fort and the tiger-infested jungle at Govindpur was cleared to provide open land called the *Maidan* for a free view and firing space. The fort was conceived as a complete European town with apartments, barracks, offices, and stores for 10,000 people but it was nowhere like the Mughal citadel in scale, opulence, and design.

A turn of circumstances was to change all this. The quashing of the Indian 'Mutiny' of 1857 in Shahjahanabad by the British was the catalyst. The powers operating from the unimposing citadel of Fort William, established just a century ago, were now set to rule India while the entourage of the Mughal Emperor walked out of their magnificent *Qila-e-Mubarak* after an ignominious defeat.

Shahjahanabad: An Imperial Plan

The city of Shahjahanabad skirted the citadel of the Red Fort on three sides. Spread over 569 ha., it was designed for a population of 60,000. It was enclosed by a wall and could be approached through seven major gates from which radiated highways to all parts of the empire. Its plan is considered by some to be analogous to a manlike macrocosm, the head is the citadel of the palace-fort; the spine radiating from the fort is the main axis of Chandni Chowk, which was used for both ceremonial and functional purposes; the heart is the Jama Masjid, the main Friday mosque; the organs are the dwellings and institutional buildings; the ribs are the streets; and, the city wall is the skin.[12]

Shahjahanabad was the capital of the patrimonial-bureaucratic empire, a type of state which characterized the Asian empires from about 1400 to 1750. The patrimonial-bureaucratic emperor 'dominated the social, economic, and cultural life of the city, and he dominated its built form as well'.[13] The city was an extension of the imperial mansion as the layout of the buildings and gardens, and the shops in the city copied the layout of the buildings within the palace complex. From the macro-perspective, the sovereign city was the kingdom in miniature. The emperor intended that his command of the city with respect to power, obedience, resources, and influence should be 'symbolic' of the influence that he and his subordinates exercised over the empire.[14]

The city was planned to have different identified areas earmarked with specific uses and trades. It had two distinct parts: the 'special', exclusively for the nobility and the rich; and the 'ordinary', where the common man lived and everyday affairs were transacted. The central axis, Chandni Chowk, divided the city into two unequal halves. The gardens, *serais*, ghats, and *hammams* were in the northern half, whereas in the southern half were situated most of the residential *mohallas* (neighbourhoods) where different craft communities lived along narrow and labyrinthine *galis* and *kuchas* (lanes and bye-lanes), many of which radiated from the main streets. Retailing, manufacturing, and living formed a close symbiosis.[15] The *mohallas* were interspersed by the mansions of the rich or by royal monuments. Some rich *ameers* lived near the fort in large *havelis* (mansions) built around open courts. The less affluent *ameers* and rich merchants had comparatively smaller houses with a lesser show of marble. The farther one went away from the fort the plainer and smaller the houses became. The mandis and grain *gunjs* (markets), wine shops and slaughterhouses were located along the circumference of the wall. The poorer artisans and other workers lived in huts along the wall. The city, being walled, did not have much space to accommodate the increasing population and in later years encroached into the open spaces and spilled onto the pavements.

While the Mughal builders adhered to an overall plan, the citizens were free to choose the built environment of their neighbourhoods. 'The Mughal system of planning was based on give and take. Private enterprise and individual initiative also became part of planning'.[16]

The royal planners decided sites and designs of walls, gates, the major avenues and laid down certain design rules for the street frontages of shops along streets, but the design of houses, *katras* and *mohallas* was left to individual choice. 'In every mohalla or locality, building activity was locally negotiated with your neighbours'.[17]

For more than thirty years, Shahjahanabad thrived as the capital of the Mughal Empire and was one of the most beautiful cities of the Orient. It was also a commercial centre and cultural hub that celebrated Urdu and Persian poetry, painting, music, food, and jewellery. During Shahjahan's reign, the capital had become a treasure trove of vast wealth. The city, however, lost its lustre during the reign of Aurangzeb who crowned himself emperor in 1658 in Shahjahanabad after imprisoning his father and shifting him to Agra. Aurangzeb left Delhi soon after and shifted the imperial capital to Aurangabad in the Deccan. Shahjahanabad was raided by the Marathas who controlled it from 1772 to 1803. They flew their flag over the Red Fort from 1788 to 1803 until they lost the battle of Delhi to the British. In 1803 Shahjahanabad and the territory around it came under the control of the British East India Company. The Company became the *de facto* ruler of the city, while the emperor and the royal family continued to live in the palace complex, the *qila.* A string of weak emperors, wars of succession, and coups by noblemen heralded the irrevocable weakening of Mughal power and of Shahjahanabad.[18]

The City Of Calcutta: A Gradual Physical Intrusion

Between 1700 and the 1770s, the settlement, catering essentially to the maritime activities of the English merchants, remained a 'straightforward business-like unit set and organized solely by the demands of commerce'.[19] In 1700 the Court of Directors had urged the Company servants to develop the settlement of Calcutta as a mercantile centre by attracting the more prosperous and better-established Armenian traders and Indian merchant and banking families to settle in the city to facilitate their trading activities.[20] This was a necessity because the Company had to deal in the coin of the country but was prohibited by the terms of its charter from itself acting as a banker.[21]

The settlement gradually began to grow and take shape. By 1707 the Englishmen lived in the centre and the Indians in the north. Sandwiched between these two localities were the slums of the Portuguese who had begun to migrate here after the destruction of their settlement at Bandel. They were soon to outnumber the English population, four to one, making Portuguese the *lingua franca* of the town for nearly a century.[22]

At the beginning of the eighteenth century, while Shahjahanabad prospered, most of Calcutta was still rural in appearance and was surrounded by deep jungles.[23] The European parts were 'built without order… the builders… taking what ground best pleased them'.[24] Their houses were not elegant but were useful. There were no carriages as there were no carriage roads in the city. The native areas consisted mainly of huts and a variety of shops and warehouses.[25] There was very little manufacturing activity in the town as the government discouraged ingenuity and industry in the populace. The foundation of the port was laid in 1700, and by 1716 it was shipping 10,000 tons of goods.

Socially the barrier between the Englishmen and the Indians until now was a barrier of religion and culture rather than of racial superiority or even language. Many of the company servants including Job Charnock took Indian wives and adopted Indian recreations and habits. However, the texture of all social interaction was ultimately decided by mercantile interests. The most representative sights of Calcutta of these days are depicted in many of the paintings and etchings of the period—British traders in square riggers anchored off the wharves at Hughli, Englishmen in tail-coats and high black silk hats; English ladies in long dresses; Indian men standing ashore in loin cloth; Indian women with babies astride their hips gravely watching the scene—two cultures meeting along the banks of a river.

In 1717 the Company obtained from the Mughal Emperor confirmation of all their former privileges[26] and permission to purchase thirty-eight villages extending on both sides of the Hughli for a distance of 10 mi. The land with the British in Calcutta now covered an area of 685 hectares (1,692 acres), considerably larger than Madras and Bombay established much earlier.[27] The urban built-up area, however, was very small and accommodated a population between 10,000 to 12,000. Within the next thirty years, the population of the settlement increased tremendously and in 1750 it was as large as Amsterdam (200,000) though still much smaller than London (675,000). The architecture of the British buildings was inspired by the English Renaissance but the settlement had very little civic dignity, with irregular streets which were nothing more than winding alleys. Until the end of the 1770s most parts of the city were still very unpretentious.[28]

The city-making processes in Calcutta changed very significantly following the victory of the British East India Company in the Battle of Plassey in 1757. The Company took charge of Bengal in 1772 and over the next hundred years vast territories in the rest of the Indian subcontinent, including Burma came under their control.

Calcutta became increasingly opulent and economically important through its entrepôt trade towards the close of the eighteenth century. Its opulence lay in its commerce. It was inhabited by many private English and Indian merchants who supplied the company with enough commodities to load fifty or sixty big ships yearly for long-distance trade and scores of smaller vessels to adjacent countries.[29] Merchant adventurers, 'men without either national or moral principles, competing with each other in a gigantic scramble for wealth and riches now flocked Calcutta'.[30] This trade both ruined Bengal and took the Company to the brink of bankruptcy and invited the first intervention by the British government in its territorial affairs through the Regulating Act of 1774. Henceforth, private trade was prohibited, a centralized administration was established and a Governor-General was appointed in the Presidency of Fort William (Calcutta). In 1775 a royal *farman* was obtained which granted the jagirdari of 24 Parganas to the Company in perpetuity which gave the city both space and security of tenure to expand.

The town, which had yet not been strictly delineated in space or greatly differentiated in appearance, was gradually sharply demarcated into 'European' and 'native' towns. Since the English now wielded supreme power in Bengal, the Council no longer felt it necessary to encourage the immigration of non-Europeans to Calcutta. They began to formulate plans for a more exclusive English town which contained only residences of the gentlemen in which English society lived, free from contact with the people of other religions and nationalities.[31] The texture of social life in Calcutta acquired new nuances. Social interaction, both amongst the Europeans themselves and between them and the native population changed. The Company servants settled in the pattern of

English family life in a patchwork of individual households living a life full of luxury and leisure with the fortunes easily acquired by private trade. Calcutta, functionally, however, remained but a trading factory, 'a valuable one but affording little promise of its future greatness'.[32]

The Decline of the Mughals and the Imperialization of the Colonial Capital

As the eighteenth century slid into the nineteenth, Shahjahanabad reached its nadir, while Calcutta, reflecting the imperial splendour and British pageantry reached a new zenith. In the Battle of Delhi, fought in 1803, the British East India Company gained control of Shahjahanabad as well as the territory around it. Just twenty-eight years after the Company had secured permanent land tenure in Calcutta through a Mughal *farman* in 1775, it became the *de facto* ruler of the Mughal capital. The emperor and the royal family were allowed to live in the palace complex, the *Qila*, which now was just their residence and no more the centre of their royal power.

Three visibly distinct morphological and social divisions had formed in Calcutta by the last quarter of the eighteenth century. The north was 'native' ('Black') and the south was 'European' ('White'). The separation was typical of any Asiatic or African city where the Europeans had settled. The only difference in Calcutta was that the native towns were separated by an ethnically heterogeneous buffer zone populated by Armenians and Portuguese who were socially segregated from the Europeans. The buffer zone, in physical appearance, was, however, no better than the 'native' town. The Indian population was gradually forced out of the central and southern-eastern parts of the town. Disasters of all kinds also helped in this clearing process.[33]

Calcutta's urban form towards the end of the eighteenth century was dictated by its social structure, defence needs, climatic considerations, and the aesthetics of the new power. The principle of the enclosed town was abandoned. An exclusively British enclave was carved out with a vista provided by the Central Park (the *Maidan*) and the Esplanade, along and around which large houses and the wealth and power of the town were concentrated. The newly added Supreme Court (1774), the Writers Building (1780), the Calcutta Madrasah (1784), the Asiatic Society (1784), the General Bank of India (1786), the St. John's Church (1788) glorified the city. Palace rose after palace, built with an obsession for classic porticoes, columns, and balustrades. Calcutta came to be considered not only the 'handsomest town in Asia but one of the finest in the world'.[34]

A strict arrangement of streets was followed from the 1780s as distances increased and wheeled transport became a necessity. Contemporary maps show that this arrangement in the European 'White' section of the town was achieved using certain streets that helped acquire a semblance of a grid-iron pattern. Aaron Upjohn's detailed map (1792–3), brings out the regularity of the pattern followed by the main streets of Calcutta. This pattern had an unmistakable 'non-Indian perspective'.[35] The rest of the town consisted of an irregular network of lanes and by-lanes.

The physical expansion of the 'Native' town continued to follow a layout pattern characteristic of Indian towns. Such had also been the case with Shahjahanabad. Local social and economic situations, usually very diverse, did not permit uniform districts and quarters to develop, as was characteristic of London and other English towns.[36]

The localities in this part of the town were non-descript and only one house belonging to Raja Nabu Kissen was identified by name. The street pattern consisted of a network of lanes and bye-lanes. Their irregularity showed that they had arisen spontaneously out of contingent necessity without any regard for public convenience or any control by the authorities. Small commerce intermingled with residences. The houses of the *baboos* (mainly salaried middle classes) were uniformly built in the form of a hollow square.[37] The mass of the labouring class lived in huts. Agricultural and vacant land was visible everywhere.

The houses of the wealthy Indians, belonging essentially to the trading class, were on the waterfront. The local landlords had turned into small *rajas,* thanks to the Permanent Settlement. They frequently resided in their mansions in Calcutta and became the progenitors of the '*bhadralok*' culture. These new Indian elites were associated with the British in trade, shipping, land development, government and educational institutions.

The early decades of the nineteenth century saw the establishment of Calcutta as the centre of an expanding empire and the capital for conquerors. The accession of Lord Wellesley as the third Governor General of India ensured that Calcutta 'lost no time in assuming the trapping and pomp appropriate to its position'.[38]

The 'Mutiny' of 1857 changed the political setup in the country. The East India Company was liquidated, Victoria was proclaimed Queen Empress and the Governor General was turned into her Viceroy. Calcutta was chosen as the capital of British India. Shahjahanabad lost its Emperor and its citadel and the areas around it lost their lustre. Calcutta now was the '*Urbs Prima*' of the country and the second city of the British Empire, both in terms of population and wealth.

Concluding Remarks

It is interesting to note that in both Shahjahanabad and Calcutta which had very different historical trajectories, *raison d'etre,* form and functions, the social spaces sometimes followed similar rules of construction but remained quite differentiated. In the making of these capital cities, we observe that:

i) In both cities there was a 'dominant' social group which provided a containing spatial matrix into which it inserted other 'dependent' groups. In the case of Shahjahanabad, it was the Mughal royalty and in the case of Calcutta it was initially the 'white' trader and later the 'white' ruler. This insertion was based on the convenience accruing from the proximity of the 'dependent' group as well as on 'congregational instinct'.

ii) 'Territory' which gives a sense of place, identity, and belonging frequently formed the base on which a distinctive social milieu developed in both cities. There was a very perceptive spatial expression of 'territoriality' to communicate space ownership or occupancy of an area by social groups. This expression became very stark when 'dominant' groups claimed 'territory' as 'turf'. The 'citadels' or the 'white city' at the city level and *mohallas, katras, paras,* and *tolis* at the neighbourhood level defined territoriality in Shahjahanabad and Calcutta.

iii) Urban space was conceptualized as an active arena in Shahjahanabad from its inception through a plan; whereas in Calcutta social, economic, and political processes spatially played out according to circumstance. This differentiated the evolution and the pattern of their urban development.

iv) The spatial pattern of 'segregation' and 'congregation' depends on the degree of assimilation determined by external factors such as attitude and institutional discrimination by the 'dominant' group. 'Segregation', was more pronounced in Calcutta, while in Shajahanabad 'congregation' was built in the city plan through planned neighbourhoods, religious institutions, the ceremonial avenue, and bazaars.

v) Residential clustering of social, occupational or religious groups took place in these capitals both due to positive and negative causes. Positive, because its members wished to preserve their own group identity or lifestyle; and negative, because of the 'otherness' of the 'other' based on class, culture, ethnicity, race and religion. This has been demonstrated in two papers, one on Shahjahanabad by Shuji Yamane, et.al.[39] based on extensive fieldwork and the other on Calcutta by

Kidwai and Nandy (2011)[40] based on primary data from the Censuses of 1876 and 1901.[41]

It would be interesting to compare the impact of the new power dispensation after 1857 on city-making processes in the two cities with reversed roles. Shahjahanabad was made a capital city again while Calcutta was assigned the role of a regional metropolis for the eastern part of the country. The macro city-level changes brought about by their changed functions have been visible in their form and structure and have been well documented. What has remained quite unchanged and less understood is the 'congregational' urban universe of the so-called historic 'native' town with neighbourhoods still somewhat linked to the past in both cities. This resilience needs to be understood and protected because in it lies the hope for a socially sustainable development of these cities.

Notes

1. N. Dempsey, et al., 'Elements of Urban Form' in *Dimensions of the Sustainable Cities,* ed. C. Jones and M. Jenks, London: Springer, 2010, pp. 21–51.
2. C. Stewart, *History of Bengal,* Calcutta: Black, Parry and Co., 1912, p. 143.
3. A.H. Kidwai, *Gateway Cities of Asia—Calcutta 1800–1981,* New Delhi: Project Report, Indian Council of Social Science Research, 1987.
4. India Office Records, Letter Book no. 9, Dispatch to Bombay, 11 September 1689.
5. P.T. Nair, *Calcutta in the 17th Century,* Calcutta: FKLM Pvt. Ltd., 1986.
6. W. Dalrymple, *City of Djinns: A Year in Delhi,* New Delhi: Penguin Books, 2004.
7. Rudyard Kipling, *Rudyard Kipling's Verse (1815–1918),* inclusive edition, London: Garden City, New York and Toronto: Doubleday, Page and Company, 1922.

8. S.P. Blake, 'Cityscape of an Imperial Capital: Shahjahanabad in 1739', in *Delhi Through the Ages*, Delhi: Oxford University Press, 1986.
9. C.M. Sinopoli, 'Monumentality and Mobility in Mughal Capitals', *Asian Perspectives*, vol. 33, no. 2, 1994, pp. 293–308.
10. Necipoğlu Gülru, 'Framing the Gaze in Ottoman, Safavid, and Mughal Palaces', *Ars Orientalis*, vol. 23, 1993, pp. 303–42.
11. K. Ballhatchet, 'The Development of an Indo-European Town in Mughal India: Tranquebar in the Seventeenth and Eighteenth Centuries', in *Changing South Asia: City and Culture*, ed. D.D. Taylor, London: School of Oriental and African Studies, University of London, 1984.
12. S.P. Blake, *Shajahanabad; The Sovereign City in Mughal India, 1639–1739*, New Delhi: Cambridge University Press, 1993.
13. Ibid.
14. Ibid.
15. E. Ehlers and T. Krafft, *Shahjahanabad/Old Delhi: Tradition and Colonial Change*, New Delhi: Manohar, 2003.
16. S. Liddle, 'Shahjahanabad: How a Planned City Came Undone', *Hindustan Times*, 1 March 2024, see https://www.hindustantimes.com/delhi-news/shahjahanabad-how-a-planned-city-came-undone/story-z7Gg3imYzCjCQQP3CBuZCO.html, accessed July 2024.
17. Ibid.
18. K.B. Brown, 'Did Aurangzeb Ban Music? Questions for the Historiography of his Reign', *Modern Asian Studies*, vol. 41, no. 1, January 2007, p. 79. doi:10.1017/S0026749X05002313. S2CID 145371208.
19. H.E.A. Cotton, *Calcutta Old and New*, Calcutta: W. Newman and Company, 1907, p. 11.
20. R. Pearson, *Eastern Interlude: A Social History of the European Community in Calcutta*, Calcutta: Thacker, Spink and Co. Ltd., 1933, p. 26.
21. Ibid., p. 39.
22. Ibid., p. 43.
23. S.W. Goode, *Municipal Calcutta*, Edinburgh: T&A Constable, 1916, p. 4.

24. Cotton, *Calcutta Old and New*, p. 24.
25. Pearson, *Eastern Interlude*, p. 71.
26. J.C. Sinha, *Economic Annals of Bengal*, London: Macmillan, 1927, p. 5.
27. A.K. Ray, *A Short History of Calcutta, Town and Suburbs*, Calcutta: Ridhi, 1982, p. 100.
28. J.R. Martin, *Notes on the Medical Topography of Calcutta*, vol. VI, part II, 1837, p. 38, repr., in A. Mitra, *Calcutta City*, Census of India, 1951.
29. Ibid., p. 39.
30. P. Woodruff, *The Men Who Ruled India*, vol. I, London: Jonathan Cape, 1954, p. 106.
31. Pearson, *Eastern Interlude*, p. 100.
32. Martin, *Notes on the Medical Topography of Calcutta.*
33. S. Nilsson, *European Architecture in India, 1750–1850*, London: Faber & Faber, 1969, p. 67.
34. Grandpre, L. De, *Voyage Dans L'Inde et Au Bengale* (1789), tr. in English as *Voyage in the Indian Ocean and to Bengal*, London: G. and J. Robinson, 1801.
35. Nilsson, *European Architecture*, p. 66.
36. K. Blechynden, *Calcutta, Past and Present*, London: W. Thacker and Co., 1906, p. 83.
37. Martin, 'Medical Topography of Calcutta', p. 141; Cotton, *Calcutta Old and New*, p. 166.
38. Cotton, *Calcutta Old and New*, p. 166.
39. Shuji Funo Yamane and Takashi Ikejiri, 'Space Formation and Transformation of the Urban Tissue of Old Delhi, India', *Journal of Asian Architecture and Building Engineering*, vol. 7, no. 2, 2008, pp. 217–24, DOI: 10.3130/jaabe.7.217, retrieved from https://doi.org/10.3130/jaabe.7.217
40. A.H. Kidwai and K. Nandy, 'Social Spaces in the Colonial "Native" Towns: Calcutta in the Late Nineteenth Century', Project Report, New Delhi: Mimeo, DSA, CSRD, JNU, 2011.
41. H. Beverley, *Report on the Census of the Town of Calcutta*, Calcutta: Bengal Secretariat Press, 1876.

15

Marsiya-e-Dehli-e-marhum

Mourning a Lost World

SWAPNA LIDDLE

THE REVOLT of 1857 looms large as a catastrophic event in the history of Delhi. On 11 May that year, soldiers who had mutinied in Meerut rode into Delhi and persuaded many sections of the city's population, including the emperor Bahadur Shah II, to join them in upturning British rule, killing or driving out British administrators, army personnel, and British and European civilians who were assumed to be sympathetic to the regime. By doing this they upset a status quo that had existed since 1803, under which the city had been administered by the East India Company, while the Mughal emperor and royal family continued to live in the palace (known to us today as the Red Fort)—a still influential presence.

For a little over four months the city was an important centre of a revolt that swept through large parts of north and central India. This was a difficult time, particularly after

**Marsiya-e-Dehli-e-marhum* is the title of a very popular *shahr ashob* by Altaf Husain Hali, composed in the 1870s, which opens with the couplet: *tazkira dehli e marhum ka ae dost na chhed; na suna jayega humse yeh fasana hargiz* ('do not speak of the departed Delhi my friend! This is a story I cannot bear to hear').

mid-June when a British force regrouped and took up its position on the Ridge, the high ground overlooking the city. The face-off between the British outside and the forces inside the city lasted for three months, until mid-September when the British reconquered the city. This brought an even greater calamity on the city. Apart from combatants that held out against the invading force and were killed in the fighting, civilians were killed in the crossfire, or fled Delhi to escape the fighting and bombardment, only to be subsequently rounded up to face the firing squad or the gallows, under a blanket assumption that they had supported the revolt. In particular, the British held the Muslims responsible for the revolt, and treated them especially harshly. Many had their properties confiscated, and while non-Muslims were allowed to return and take up residence in the city after some months, Muslims were not allowed to do so till late 1859.

Even when peace returned, the city had changed in significant ways. The Mughal court had been extinguished, with the exile of Bahadur Shah, and the death or exile and/or expropriation of other members of the royal family. A similar fate had befallen many others of the Muslim landed and service elite of the city. 1857 also destroyed institutions such as the Delhi College—the city's first Western-style institution of higher learning. The city, founded in the seventeenth century and named 'Shahjahanabad' by its founder, Shahjahan, was also changed physically. There were extensive demolitions, some motivated by a need for security—for instance to provide a clear line of fire around the Red Fort, and within it to make way for stationing troops. Others were consciously aimed at replacing Mughal landmarks with British colonial ones—the square known as Chandni Chowk with its shops and an adjoining *serai* commissioned by the princess Jahanara in the seventeenth century, were replaced with a clock tower and a Town Hall.

In the several decades to come there would be a memorialization of the world that had been destroyed by the Revolt and its aftermath, constituting a significant body of literature in Urdu. These writings, mostly in the form of poetry and memoirs, have been very influential in shaping popular ideas of what late Mughal Delhi had been like, but equally significantly they should be read for what they tell us about the memorialists and their times. How did they picture the lost world of pre-1857 Delhi? What aspects of it did they mourn? This essay will analyse a selection of this literature from the 1860s to the 1930s, to understand the contexts in which these often shifting evaluations of a lost world were made.

The earliest published writing in this category is a book of poetry, *Fughan e Dehli*[1] published in 1863. It was an anthology of verses composed by several different poets, in a genre known as *shahr ashob,* literally 'ruined city'. While these verses concentrated on the calamity of the revolt and the destruction it had wrought, implicit in them were certain assumptions about the nature of the culture and society that had been destroyed. A theme the poets dwelt upon was the ruination of the elite, particularly the Muslim elite, who not only suffered the violence of re-conquest, but also the looting and confiscation of their properties.

These were heart-rending tales of the high born, raised in homes where they lacked for nothing, suddenly being thrown out on the street; of the Mughal royal family, descendants of one of the most powerful dynasties of history, being reduced to penury. To drive home the point, and emphasize the contrast between their fortunes before and after 1857, the prosperity of the earlier period was exaggerated. A picture of a luxurious lifestyle enjoyed by the elite was painted to contrast it with the poverty of the period that followed. The Mughal court was described as being at the pinnacle of authority, such as in these lines by Mohammad Ali 'Tashna':

woh takht e saltanat, woh bargah e sultani,
ke jis mein baithte the aake zill e subhani
paron se sar pe huma karta tha magasrani,
baja is auj pe tha dava e sulaimani
....
zohal ki aankh padi ittefaq se nagaah,
tamam ho gaya taraj mulk o maal o jaah[2]

That throne of the empire, the court of the emperor
In which the shadow of God came and sat
The huma bird used its wings as a flywhisk overhead
Rightly it laid claim to being the equal of Solomon's throne
.....
An unlucky star shone on it suddenly
All was plundered—the territory, the wealth, the power.

These images of a powerful empire suddenly laid low were clearly exaggerations, penned for effect. In fact, the Mughal Empire had ceased to exist long before 1857. What had lingered on was an impoverished court and a descendant of the Mughal dynasty who was dependent on the East India Company even for his paltry allowance.

'Tashna' also mourned a departed literary culture:

ghazal ka zikr na charcha kisi yagane se
mazaq e sher o sukhan uthh gaya zamane se[3]

No mention of the ghazal, or talk of it among friends
The taste for poetry has left the world.

Though framed as an effect of the revolt, this crisis in poetry writing had a longer history, and was the result of social and cultural changes that had been taking place under colonial rule. In the *shahr ashob* poetry however, there was little room for such nuance. The revolt was held responsible for every loss, every regrettable change.

Generally, the *shahr ashob* poets praised the culture of pre-1857 Delhi in hyperbolic terms—the place where the most learned, the most talented and refined people made their home. There were however some instances where the revolt itself was seen as a punishment from heaven on a decadent and ungodly lifestyle. Thus, Hafiz Ghulam Dastgir 'Mubin' wrote:

hai! kya kya na zamane ke kiye makruhat
nach aur rang mein din raat guzare auqat
aish mein mahv rahe, bhul gaye saum o salwat
zar ki ulfat mein ada bhi na kiye haj o zakat
zulm goron ne kiya na sitam kalon ne
hum to barbad kiya apne hi amalon ne[4]

Which abominations of this world did we not commit!
We were sunk day and night in dance and pleasure
Prayers and fasting were forgotten in the preoccupation with pleasure
In the love for money, we forgot the Haj and almsgiving
Not by the oppressions of the white man, nor the tyranny of the black man
We have been destroyed by our own actions.

In the *shahr ashob* poetry, the primary aim of which was to evoke strong emotions, the world that was destroyed in 1857 was deliberately outlined in exaggerated terms, sometimes contradictory, to contrast with what came after. It was a literary device rather than an exercise in painting a realistic picture of the past. In contrast, a work that appeared more than two decades later—*Bazm e Aakhir*—by Mohammad Faizuddin,[5] claimed to capture the details of the Mughal court as it had been during the reigns of the last two Mughal emperors, Akbar II (r.1806–37) and Bahadur Shah II (r.1837–57). The narrative consisted of detailed descriptions of the daily routines of the emperor and his family, their lifestyle, special customs and festive occasions, even their distinctive language and idioms.

In *Bazm e Aakhir* the declared emphasis was on authenticity and accuracy. The book included an endorsement by a prince of the royal family, certifying that Faizuddin had spent many years in the royal palace as an employee, and therefore was a trustworthy chronicler.[6] The use of the present tense throughout the narrative helped to strengthen the impression of an authentic account. Appearing nearly three decades after the passing of the Mughal court, it addressed a generation too young to have known those times, as well as the vast majority who had in any case not been privy to the everyday goings on in the palace.

Given its claims, Faizuddin's account is in many ways unreal, often through the omission of important details. For instance, the description of 'the court of justice' shows the emperor dispensing justice in court as if it were in the administration of an empire. In fact, the last two Mughal emperors had no jurisdiction outside the palace, and beyond their own extended family and household.[7] Similarly, the detailed description of the ceremonies on the anniversary of the emperor's accession to the throne, completely erases the British officials who were in fact an important presence on such occasions. Far from acknowledging the reality where even the accession of a particular candidate for the throne had to be endorsed by the government of the East India Company, the reader is encouraged to picture the Mughal empire in its heyday.[8]

Faizuddin, who had been closely connected to the Mughal court, was understandably inclined to present a romanticized and idealized picture, particularly as it was an institution so suddenly and cruelly uprooted. But there was another writer who had also seen the pre-Revolt world, who had little stake in the Mughal court. Mohammad Zakaullah had been a student of the Delhi College, committed to its project of imparting a modern education, and inspired by his teacher, Master Ram Chander, who had an interest in social reform as well as modern science. Moreover, following the Revolt, Zakaullah came to be closely associated with Syed Ahmad Khan and his project for modernization and reform of Muslim society and culture, centred at Aligarh.

Zakaullah's writings on pre-Revolt Delhi as he remembered it consist of several essays published in various magazines.[9] In contrast to *Bazm e Aakhir*, they give us a look at the city outside the palace. In one essay he writes of the Urdu newspapers that were published from the city beginning in the 1830s, telling his readers with pride that modern Urdu journalism began in Delhi.[10] In another long essay on the fairs and festivals of Delhi[11] we see that unlike Faizuddin, Zakaullah's approach is more strictly that of a historian, meticulously recording change, with 1857 as a landmark date. He describes changes in ways of celebrating popular festivals, or in the locales of fairs, or in some cases the entire discontinuance of a practice. He also notes cases in which there has been no change.

Moreover, Zakaullah is not nostalgic about the past. For instance, he does not regret the passing of customs that involved large expenditures of money. He credits changing mores to enlightenment, particularly that which was gained through Western education, which he celebrates. Thus, he writes that before the Revolt there used to be more elaborate lighting of homes during Diwali, and adds, 'the reason for the decrease in lighting is the enlightenment which the Hindus have gained through an English education.'[12]

In another essay, this time a history of some major mosques and other places of worship,[13] Zakaullah is again a dispassionate chronicler. He describes the Akbarabadi Masjid, the biggest mosque in Shahjahanabad after the Jama Masjid, and simply states that the British authorities saw fit to demolish it as a security measure after the Revolt. As for the demolition of many of the buildings around the Jama Masjid, he celebrates it, as having finally revealed the beauty of the mosque to view. The only time regret creeps into his narrative is when he speaks of the deterioration in relations between Muslims and Hindus after the Revolt. He notes with sadness:

> Before the revolt, though Delhi was governed by the Company, there was nominally a Muslim emperor too, who employed several Hindus and Muslims. In working together people of different faiths become friends, and therefore in the city Hindus and Muslims bore affection towards one another, and were famous for their unity. But once the revolt happened and the emperor was no longer there, the bond of affection between Hindus and Muslims also was broken.[14]

Faizuddin and Zakaullah were the last to write of the Delhi of the last Mughal emperor and the East India Company from personal memory. This was, however, by no means an end to the writing on the subject. In fact, particularly in the 1920s and 30s there was a spate of such accounts by different authors, often first appearing in popular literary magazines, later republished in book form and avidly consumed by a wide readership.[15] Most of them continue to be in print today, and some have been translated into English.[16]

Reading these, one is immediately struck by how these authors approach their subject. None of them choose to show us the Delhi that Zakaullah gave us a glimpse of—the Delhi of modern journalism, or of institutions like the Delhi College. Instead, the most popular theme was that covered by Faizuddin—of the Mughal emperor, his court, and household. Though this generation of writers was too young to have personal memories of the time, a number of them attributed their information to an older generation.

One of these was Nasir Nazir 'Firaq' Dehlvi (*Lal Qile ki ek Jhalak*),[17] who drew his information from accounts passed down in the family from a close family friend, a woman who had worked in a responsible position in the royal kitchens for many years. His account is full of details of life in the palace, particularly in its more secluded areas, but it also provides a view of historical events and people in the palace and the city. Thus, unlike in Faizuddin's account, the British officials are not blacked out, and the assessment of the Mughal-

British relationship is largely accurate. It is worth noting that Firaq's general assessment of British rule was positive, and at one point he explicitly praises the material benefits it has brought—the railways, good roads, the postal system, timely payment of the salaries of government employees. This outlook probably made it easier for Firaq to be more objective about the late Mughal court and culture.

A somewhat different perspective was that of Wazir Hasan Dehlvi (*Dilli ka Akhiri Deedar*). Wazir Hasan too speaks in large part through the words of an old lady who he describes as a 'Mughalani'. Aghai Begum however does not restrict herself to relating an account of the Mughal palace and its ways. At each step she takes the opportunity to comment on modern society and culture, invariably comparing it unfavourably to that of the past. She criticises the low necklines, sleeveless kurtas, and high heels of modern women who turn up their noses at old fashions, and risk ruining their reputations by emulating foreign fashions. She is disparaging of modern marriages, where, according to her, 'husbands and wives go their separate ways every evening'.[18] In contrast she praises the women of the Mughal era, where even the courtesans were so refined that the young were sent to learn etiquette from them.[19]

It is not just contemporary social mores that Aghai Begum is critical of. She deplores the loss of Hindu-Muslim unity, which she says was a feature of the old times.[20] She also points out that, nowadays, despite there being plentiful rain and abundant crops, there is repeated famine. This is because, to quote her, 'whatever we have is taken away in sackfuls'.[21] Earlier, in her words 'the wealth of the home remained in the home'.[22] This is obviously a critique of the drain of wealth under British rule, which Wazir Hasan could express indirectly through the words of Aghai Begum. This is clearly a polemical point. The supposed contrast with late Mughal rule is misleading, because the period she speaks of was already a time when the British ruled Delhi and India.

There are other points at which it becomes clear that Wazir Hasan's narrative is more a critique of British rule than anything else. In this account, late Mughal Delhi is made to stand for an ideal era before the advent of British rule. In a long passage in the introduction to the book he writes: 'The life of Delhi was its grace—it was raised on the milk of Asiatic culture, played in the lap of empire, grew up with knowledge and skills, all the glories from Raja Bharat to the house of Timur (i.e. the Mughals) took shape on this land.'[23] Sadly, this idyllic state gave way to a period of disunities, which allowed 'the world' which had been eyeing the 'golden bird', to pounce:

> 1857 came as a doomsday, the empire expired in the lap of the pure hearted emperor, the flickering lamp of the Timurid court flared one last time and then was extinguished. Those who were its beloved, and its lovers, some fled such that they could never return; many were killed; and those few who were left, were outnumbered in the flood of outsiders...when the people of Delhi did not survive, how could Delhi have survived?[24]

In this skilfully written passage, Wazir Hasan achieves remarkable feats of elision. The long and slow transition from the Mughal empire at its height to British control is compressed into the single event of 1857, which becomes the watershed moment between one empire and another. The fate of Delhi after the brutal suppression of the Revolt becomes the story of the colonial conquest of the country. Within Delhi, Wazir Hasan seems to merge the lament for the changes brought about following the Revolt—such as the emigration of many Muslims, with more recent changes. Aghai Begum laments, 'Dilli was from the people of Dilli,... now the city is not Dilli but Dehli, a place of outsiders',[25] and we assume that she is talking of the changes brought about after the Revolt. Yet Wazir Hasan open his narrative thus: 'With every step time moves forward. If today one wishes to make better cities than Delhi, they can be made. Bricks and stones are available, the masons are there, there are better amenities. But Delhi was never about bricks and stones...'[26]

When speaking of new and better cities of bricks and stones, was Wazir Hasan thinking of the grand capital city of New Delhi that was coming up next door?

The Delhi of the Mughals, Shahjahanabad, had been ravaged in 1857, its political and cultural importance permanently eroded in the period that followed. 1912 brought new changes. The shifting of the British Indian capital from Calcutta to Delhi not only brought in a fresh wave of 'outsiders', but set in motion the process of building a new capital city, which threatened to overshadow whatever remained of the Mughal city. The formal inauguration of New Delhi in February 1931 finally relegated Shahjahanabad to the status of 'Old Delhi', reinforcing its marginalization.

We should probably place the new wave of memorialization of late Mughal Delhi that gained momentum in the 1920s and 30s in this context. Wazir Hasan repeatedly bemoans the passing of a rich culture, at one point saying: 'Whether it was the domestic life of the Delhi of old, or its manners, social interactions and etiquette, all were steeped in "culture" [in English in the original].'[27] One suspects that this is less an elegy to a late Mughal Delhi long past, and more an anxiety about the changes anticipated by a new modernity brought to the doors of Delhi by the new capital, and the sudden appearance of many 'outsiders' who came with the new political role of the city.

The master of such elegiac writings of this time was Rashid ul Khairi, popularly known as '*musavvir e gham*', the 'painter of sorrows'. One of his most popular works, *Naubat e Panj Rozah,* follows other such writings in giving a fairly standard account of the Mughal court as it was in its last years. Unlike say, Faizuddin or Firaq, however, he is not concerned with establishing the authenticity of the picture he paints. The main aim of his work is to mourn the passing of a culture of refinement, courtesy and kindness, that permeated a world presided over by the last Mughal emperor. By his own admission his work is a tribute to the memory of a benevolent, gentle, moral, but ultimately tragic ruler, and by extension, an elegy to Mughal Shahjahanabad. In his introduction he writes: 'Oh Badshah! Who sleeps in a deep grave, these flowers (of my words) are a respectful offering at your grave, which is before me in my imagination, and I say—"Badshah! Shahjahanabad has been laid waste!"'[28]

His descriptions of Bahadur Shah in his court and household are occasions to mount a defence of old 'Eastern' values against the charges of those influenced by the 'West' and its standards. In a typical passage he begins: 'O worshippers of the West, your ideas are true and your opinion correct! Who am I to contradict them? This is your age, your style, your day and your night. I do not wish to intrude with my laments of an old tale. But do look to this scene of the palace...', and he goes on to give an example of the benevolence of Bahadur Shah.[29] It is this dialogue between the moral universe of Bahadur Shah's Delhi and the degradation of the twentieth century that is at the heart of Rashid ul Khairi's lament. Though he mourns the passing of the Mughal court, for him 1857 does not really represent a turning point between an idyllic world and its ruination. For, he says:

> The Badshah was no longer there, but those who had beheld him were still there; the assembly of the night had risen, but the piles of the ashes of the moths were still there ... till eight or ten years into the new century...one could see an occasional face in some neighbourhood, whose white beard was a relic of that convivial gathering.[30]

Thus, for Rashid ul Khairi it is the second decade of the twentieth century that truly marks the destruction of the old world and its values. He relates the change to the passing of the last of a generation that had imbibed the culture of the Mughal court, and the rise of the education and values of the 'West'. Interestingly however, much of his angst is directed at the physical signs of New Delhi that he sees around him. He comments on the changed face of Feroze Shah Kotla, which has been spruced up:

> of which every person is full of praise and eulogies, for this reason that it was earlier a ruin and now it is a garden; a garden these days means a 'park' [original in English]. The enclosing walls, the ruins of the madrasa and the eastern walls survive, but in the middle there is mostly green grass and gravel paths. And not just Kotla, all of Delhi has changed ... those seeing it may praise this splendour, but each spade of this new construction and each shovel of this progress has fallen as a blow on the hearts of the people of Delhi.[31]

At first sight Rashid ul Khairi's writing is a lament for a world destroyed by the Revolt as much as the *shahr ashob* poetry of the immediate post-Revolt period was. After all, the stated intent of all these works, from Faizuddin's in the 1880s to the many written in the 1920s and 1930s, was to write about that world. There were, however, significant shifts that set apart the writing of each period from the other. The *shahr ashob* poets mourned the exile of the Mughal emperor, the physical destruction of Shahjahanabad, and above all the impoverishment and marginalization of their own class—the service and intellectual Muslim elite. These direct results of the Revolt were a very recent trauma, which found expression in poetry. The writings of Zakaullah and Faizuddin, who had also lived through the Revolt, but were writing several years later, were qualitatively different. Theirs was an attempt to capture their own memories of the world as it had been before 1857, for the benefit of posterity. Though their emphasis differed, Faizuddin concentrating on the Mughal court and Zakaullah largely on the city outside it, their approach was similar—to dispassionately present the past.

What prompted them to write when they did, many years after the Revolt? It may have been the passage of time itself, and the realization that they were of the last generation that carried such first-hand memories, and if they were not to be lost, they must be written down and shared. Is it also possible, at least in the case of Faizuddin, that the desire to recall the Mughal court was a response to more recent political developments? Queen Victoria's assumption of the title of 'Empress of India', or 'Kaiser e Hind' had been announced with the great fanfare of a 'durbar', modelled on Mughal durbars or assemblages, in 1877. The event had been held in Delhi, hundreds of miles from the capital Calcutta, because her Viceroy, Lytton, had desired an event 'which conspicuously places Her authority upon that ancient throne of the Moguls, with which the imaginations and traditions of your Majesty's Indian subjects associate the splendour of supreme power.'[32]

For the British government this was an important step in their project to promote the image of Queen Victoria as a benevolent, motherly ruler, devoted to the interests of her Indian subjects. This had led to an intensive blitz of propaganda, which reached a crescendo with the event of 1877. Maybe Faizuddin felt that this was the time to remember the Mughals, when they were sought to be replaced by an English empress in the Indian imagination.

The writers of the second to fourth decades of the twentieth century—Firaq Dehlvi, Wazir Hasan, Rashid ul Khairi, another very popular writer not discussed here, Khwaja Hasan Nizami, and several others—had no personal memories of the trauma of 1857 or of the world it had destroyed. Yet they all chose to write about it, often in a style heavy with nostalgia. They mourned a lost world with an intensity that was no less than the anguish of the *shahr ashob* poets precisely because the loss was as immediate and personal for them as it had been for the latter. They mourned the loss of old ways of life and a culture that was being eroded by Western education and values, they chafed under colonial rule, but probably it was the supersession of the Mughal capital—Shahjahanabad, by the building of a new British capital on the very soil of Delhi—that was the most immediate and palpable loss.

To that extent the Mughal court, the culture of Delhi before 1857, were somewhat incidental to the concerns of the works written in the twentieth century. Rashid ul Khairi's attempt to extend the persistence of the 'old ways' into the early twentieth century by reference to those 'who had seen the emperor' is not really convincing. It is clear that the Mughal emperor, or Shahjahanabad under Mughal rule, and specially the tragedy of 1857, had become metaphors through which feelings of loss and nostalgia could be expressed.

Notes

1. Tafazzul Husain Khan 'Kaukab' Dehlavi, ed., *Fughan e Dehli*, Noida: Navrang Kitab Ghar, 2007.
2. Ibid., pp. 61–2.
3. Ibid., p. 64.
4. Ibid., pp. 100–1.
5. Munshi Mohammad Faizuddin, *Bazm e Aakhir*, Delhi: Armughan e Dehli press, 1885.
6. Ibid., pp. 103–4.
7. Ibid., p. 12.
8. Ibid., pp. 2, 8–33.
9. A short selection may be found in Maulvi Mohammad Zakaullah, *Intekhab e Mazamin*, Lucknow: Uttar Pradesh Urdu Academy, 1983.
10. 'Dehli ke qadeem Urdu akhbar', see ibid. pp. 59–63.
11. 'Dehli ke mele aur tyohar', see ibid. pp. 64–79.
12. Ibid., p. 74.
13. 'Dehli ke masajid o moabid ki sarguzasht', in ibid. pp. 80–122.
14. Ibid., pp. 110–11.
15. Those discussed in this essay are, Nasir Nazir 'Firaq' Dehlvi, *Lal Qile ki ek Jhalak*, Delhi: Imperial Printing Press, n.d.; Wazir

Hasan Dehlvi, *Dilli ka Akhiri Deedar*, Delhi: Delhi Printing Works, 1934; Rashid ul Khairi, *Naubat e Panj Rozah*, Delhi: Ismat Book Agency, 1928.

16. Of the works mentioned in this essay, *Bazm e Aakhir* has recently seen two translations; Ather Farouqui, tr., *Bazm-i Aakhir: The Last Gathering—A Vivid Portrait of Life in the Red Fort*, New Delhi: Roli Books, 2021; and also as part of Rana Safvi, *City of My Heart: Accounts of Love, Loss and Betrayal in Nineteenth-Century Delhi*, Gurugram: Hachette India, 2018. The latter also includes a translation of Wazir Hasan's *Dilli ka Akhiri Deedar*.
17. 'Firaq' Dehlvi, *Lal Qile ki ek Jhalak, passim.*
18. Wazir Hasan Dehlvi, *Dilli ka Akhiri Deedar*, pp. 53–4.
19. Ibid., p. 78.
20. Ibid., pp. 92–3.
21. Ibid., p. 68.
22. Ibid.
23. Ibid., pp. 7–8.
24. Ibid., pp. 8–9.
25. Ibid., p. 67.
26. Ibid., p. 7.
27. Ibid., p. 40.
28. Rashid ul Khairi, *Naubat e Panj Rozah*, p. 7.
29. Ibid., p. 16.
30. Ibid., p. 109.
31. Ibid., pp. 67–8.
32. Lytton to Disraeli, 20 April 1876, in Miles Taylor, *The English Maharani: Queen Victoria and India*, Kindle edn., New Delhi: Penguin Random House India, 2018, p. 187.

16

The Asaf Ali Trial

A Little-known Episode in Delhi's Nascent Nationalism

T.C.A. RAGHAVAN

THE BEGINNING of Asaf Ali's legal career coincides with a gradual change in Delhi from being a sleepy political backwater to gaining a sense of itself as the imperial capital.[1] Politics here would gradually acquire a new optical value and symbolic power. While this process may well have begun by the time he returned from England in 1912 as a qualified barrister, it was to gather more traction with the outbreak of the war. By 1915, Muslim intellectual opinion in the city was charged up on account of the Ottoman Empire's terminal crisis, its successive military defeats and loss of territory and, most of all, by the fact that the British were fighting against it in the World War. Asaf Ali thus felt a 'marked change in the political atmosphere' with a 'wave of excitement and indignation among the Musalmans'.[2] He saw Muslim politics, hitherto 'timid, petty and narrow', taking 'giant strides forward'. Abul Kalam with his publication *Al Hilal* in Calcutta and Mohammad Ali with *Comrade* and *Hamdard* in Delhi were amongst those voicing this opinion even as 'prayers were commonly said in Mosques for Turkey's victory'.[3] He knew both editors well and was part of their circle in which the physician M.A. Ansari was also a leading light. Ansari, about 8–9 years older than the young Asaf, was already in a sense his mentor, a role that he would continue to play till his death. While in England Asaf had forged close friendships with Sarojini Naidu, the poet who was making a name for herself in public life in India, and with Syud Hossain, a law student like himself but someone actually more interested in journalism than a career at the bar. These friendships widened Asaf's horizons and gave him a sense of life in the public gaze and even opened the possibility of a life in politics.[4] Yet for a number of reasons it was not on a Khilafatist platform that Asaf Ali would make his initial mark in Delhi's nascent anti-colonial politics.[5]

By 1917 we find Asaf determined to immerse himself in Delhi's public and political life such as it existed then. Two factors provided a platform for his new role. First, in February 1917 the formidable Mrs Annie Besant established a branch of the Home Rule League in Delhi and Asaf was one of its early members. The branch in Delhi marked a change for the city. After initial enthusiasm over Khilafat, ever since Muhammad Ali's internment in May 1915 the city had entered a quietist phase as if slipping back to its original character as a political backwater despite its new status as the imperial capital. The establishment of the branch of the Home Rule League in Delhi provided some political activity. Dr M.A. Ansari was an early enthusiast and his reputation on account of the Turkish medical mission drew others in.[6]

Asaf's law practice and activism on issues taken up by the Home Rule League gradually became his principal preoccupation. Despite his privileged status as an England qualified barrister, settling down to legal work in the district courts in Delhi was not easy. At one stage, soon after he started regular practice, he wrote to Syud Hossain about his colleagues in the bar and the experience of legal work in a subordinate court: 'I am more than ever disgusted with this miserable profession and the country in which it flourishes in its lowest form. Only a villain of the deepest dye can succeed in this profession in this part of the world. The members of this learned class actually swindle people.'[7]

This was perhaps no more than the fulminations of an idealistic young man frustrated at the reality he confronted in the grind of day-to-day work, and part of the inevitable process of settling into a new profession. More significantly, his public speaking skills were starting to attract attention as the growing activism of the Delhi branch of the Home Rule League meant frequently held public meetings 'to ventilate grievances and carry on educative political propaganda for self-government'.[8] 'I became', Asaf wrote somewhat immodestly, 'the League's star turn',[9] but perhaps this was also an indication of how fledgling politics was in Delhi at the time, outside of the polemics of the Ali Brothers which was entirely addressed to a Muslim audience and centring around the fate of the Ottomans. The Home Rule League believed it was a broader church and also took up local issues accordingly. Asaf also tried to develop his own particular speaking style. He would make sure that a speech would have at most four or five principal points, and each would be so developed so that it culminated with a carefully chosen Persian or Urdu verse from a well-known master to bring the audience to cheers. This was well suited to Delhi's Urdu speaking milieu and he recalled that '(m)eetings swelled to thousands, sometimes as much as 30,000'.[10] This may have well been an exaggeration but to Asaf it certainly appeared that 'a new spirit was released and Delhi was now becoming politically conscious'.[11]

Secondly, in addition to the Home Rule League activities and his legal practice, Asaf began to write regularly in newspapers and magazines which added to his profile and supplemented his income. He had been a regular contributor to local Urdu magazines, but acquired a larger audience after Syud's return to India towards the end of 1916 when he joined the famous *Bombay Chronicle.* The *Bombay Chronicle* was then edited by the legendary B.G. Horniman, and Asaf began to write regularly for it in English. Under Horniman it had become the vehicle for conveying news and comments with a nationalist tinge and was quite distinct from the official and establishment view usually taken by the *Times of India.* For Asaf writing in its pages was the ideal way to convey to a larger audience news about what was happening in Delhi in terms of the activities of the Home Rule League, popular and nationalist expectations from the local government and in general voicing the frustrations of its articulate citizens.

At that time the default mode for those in politics, or in public life also meant being circumspect. The general tenor of the times was to be extra cautious about not openly crossing officialdom and taking particular care not to come to the adverse notice of English officials or give them cause for offence. Just how sensitive the official establishment could be to transgressions is illustrated by an episode in mid-1917. The background relates to a follower of Annie Besant—Leonora Gmeiner, principal of the Indraprastha Girls School, later to become a leading Delhi women's college. Gmeiner, an Australian, had lived in India since the 1890s and was active in the Home Rule League's activities in Delhi. Her activism soon led to official disapproval and at one stage Malcolm Hailey, the then Chief Commissioner of Delhi, warned her that she risked losing the government's financial support to her school unless she desisted with her involvement with the Home Rule League. Asaf's journalistic forays in the *Bombay Chronicle* in fact began with this episode—in support of 'the decencies of public life'.[12] The *Bombay Chronicle* editorialized on the issue and, Asaf writes, 'Haileyism was added to the vocabulary of political polemics'. Much of what the *Bombay Chronicle* published on the issue came from Asaf—now both a journalist as well as an activist in these proceedings. More significantly perhaps with the issue being aired in the media, public financial contributions to the school swelled and the matter acquired some local notice and even notoriety.

Shortly afterwards the Delhi government was informed that Asaf had made a speech in which he had reportedly described this particular action—that of the Chief Commissioner threatening to withdraw government support for Gmeiner's school unless she toed the line—as an 'act of folly'. In Asaf's recollection this phrase 'disregarded the restraints of those days' but 'the audience applauded me to the echo'. Asaf wrote: 'I knew now what was wrong with our public life. It was not the people who lacked the spirit of self-assertion'. He meant that it was leaders who were timid. A few days later he received an invitation to meet a senior English official who conveyed to Asaf that he had 'used some expressions which it was not usual in public controversies to use'. Asaf's speech had been in Urdu and he had used the Urdu term *himakat* to describe the Chief Commissioner's action. This was translated and conveyed to the authorities by the plain clothes police monitoring the event as 'idiocy' or 'dunderheadedness' and that the term 'conveyed some impression of contempt'. In the interview Asaf responded, as he informed Syud in a letter, that he had 'not exceeded the limits of parliamentary expressions' since *himakat* only meant 'unwisdom' and his audience had understood it as such.[13] The officer responded that he 'did not think that in the Parliament anybody ever called a public servant a fool'. Asaf's response was that the meaning being ascribed to the term used was wrong and therefore wrong information about him had been circulated. During this 'interview' precedents from the English Parliament were discussed including those set by Winston Churchill and Lloyd George.[14] In Asaf's record of the conversation his English interlocuter 'admitted that Mr Lloyd George had, when he began his vigorous speeches 10 or 11 years ago made some startling departures in polemics, but even the expressions he had used were not stronger than the expression I had used in my speech!'

Asaf wrote to Syud that he had responded that while 'I could not help being surprised at the flattering comparison' but Lloyd George and Winston Churchill 'had been called a pair of ugly ducklings' and 'foul mouthed tub thumpers',[15] i.e. it was not as if British practice was above board.

This exchange, unimportant in itself, is nevertheless revealing of the politics of the time. Such verbal duels and ambivalent speeches were the stuff of the moderate politics of early Indian nationalism. What is significant is how quickly this and also the mood of the times was changing. For Asaf the takeaway from his interview was 'the narrow limits within which public speech making is ... confined'. If, he wrote: 'fair criticism must stop short at compliments and ambiguous references to the defects of administration, the public must ever remain in the dark'.

Each of these details would be printed in detail in the *Bombay Chronicle* in columns entitled 'Imperial Delhi'. Local activism on issues such as refusal of official permission to hold public meetings, the routes to be taken by Dusshera and Moharram processions, the excessive police and intelligence scrutiny of the Delhi Home Rule League activities, etc., thus each became vehicles for campaigns in the press against the local authorities and against 'Haileyism'.[16] On the Indraprastha School and the Miss Gmeiner issue, the *Bombay Chronicle* under 'Imperial Delhi' editorialized: '...the circumstances of the onslaught at that wholly innocuous and admittedly admirable institution... [throw] a flood of light on the manners and mentality of those who have the run of India's metropolis, the capital selected by the King Emperor himself...' [17]

That issue of the newspaper also carried a long letter from 'Bar at Law'—one of the names Asaf employed for his letters which in effect were columns to the *Chronicle*. The lengthy letter covered a wide range of complaints: 'the abnormal activity of CID agents in relation to the Home Rule League'; the exclusion of Indraprastha school girls from a function on the King's birthday which illustrated the 'craven stupidity of the sycophants but also the peevish and childish spirit of the authorities responsible'; that 'more than half of Chandni Chowk has been denuded of trees'—'one act of blind philistinism has reduced the best street of Delhi to a state of intolerable ugliness'.[18] The latter point—that of the trees being removed from Chandni Chowk—had in particular incensed Asaf, a citizen of Delhi to the core. This project itself was not a new one and dated back to the 1912 assassination attempt on the then Viceroy when he entered Chandni Chowk in a ceremonial procession and the trees were believed to have provided cover to the assassin. The failed attempt had not drawn much support in Delhi and given its overall political dormancy had even shocked most people. Asaf had referred to the attempt as having 'evoked much condemnation'. But the trees being felled now certainly upset him:

> Oh! Syud it is heart rending to see the entire avenue of trees in the Chandni Chowk hewed down! It is wanton vandalism. There is no knowing where they will stop. The matter is of more than local interest—they are blotting out history...Fancy even the Hindus have permitted their sacred pipal trees to be removed by the roots.[19]

A visit by the Secretary of State for India in November 1917 found Asaf being given the responsibility of drafting a representation to the government on behalf of Delhi's leading citizens. Asaf says he was impatient with the 'footling local demands' it contained but found that he did not have much flexibility in changing the substance of the text. The preamble though was his to write as he wished and 'I worked into it a reference to Delhi as "the cradle and grave of mighty empires" and also the hope of "the termination of India's non age"', meaning its servitude and political acquiescence. Left to himself, he wrote, 'I would have urged self-determination and full self-government'.[20] That the Secretary of State was not given the opportunity to attend a public reception intended in his honour was the opportunity for more articles, editorials, and letters. Much of this was a play on words and a showing of literary excellence aimed at British officialdom.

The point perhaps was that for Asaf and those like him, no Englishman could count himself automatically as their superior: their own education and more importantly their English qualifications and experience of living in England ensured that. It was this sense of equality which also underwrote their nationalism at the time and from it also came a mood of defiance which others, less well endowed, would have found both something to admire as also something to envy. At one stage, responding to a communication from the Government of Delhi which did not address him correctly because it did not add 'Esquire' after his name, Asaf was to write to the Chief Commissioner and drew his attention:

> to an omission in the said order, accidently I presume and is I am sure, the result of the clerk's scanty familiarity with polite forms of address. I suppose it is needless for me to observe that members of the English bar are entitled to the same form of address as members of the Civil Service, the omission of which may not be altogether free from unnecessary misinterpretation.

Needless to say, this letter was as much for a general audience as for the addressee since it was published in full in the *Bombay Chronicle*.[21] The only Indians entitled to have 'Esquire' added after their names while being addressed in correspondence were members of the Indian Civil Service and barristers, i.e. those who were also members of an English bar.

This sense that he was no less than any Englishman in India and in fact was better, comes through in other ways not least demonstrating his command of English and knowledge of English mores and then using this to contrast the arbitrariness of the local bureaucracy with the high standards expected from 'true' English behaviour. This was in many ways the hallmark of nationalism in India as it had developed till then and is best summed up by a 1901 book by a pioneer of Indian nationalism—Dadabhai Naoroji (1825–1917)—titled *Poverty and Un-British Rule in India.* This view that the colonial state in its actions was not 'British enough' is certainly something Asaf consistently put forward in this early phase of his public life and it is fair to assume that this was not only for tactical reasons. Having recently returned from England, he saw no reason why English standards could not be upheld in India. We get an illustration of this in July 1917 when a public meeting was planned by the Delhi Home Rule League to protest an internment order on Mrs Annie Besant by the Government of Madras. Asaf Ali was served with an order withholding permission to hold such a meeting. His response was a long letter to the *Chronicle*—it took up almost half a page of the broadsheet:[22]

> The Chief Commissioner has shown that means are not lacking, if a bureaucrat takes it into his head to display disregard of constitutional rights of the people... Do they realize they are doing the greatest *disservice* to the cause of the empire in thus ruthlessly alienating the sympathies of which they stand in sore need?

Possibly the intention was to underline that his critique was not just some local level grievance but the articulation of a point of view that was wider and sought to cut through the claims of racial superiority:

> If the World struggle is for the assertion and reaffirmation of the Rights of Man, if the world war is raging to vanquish despotism... no deviation is possible for the government of India from the principles for which the world is fighting the Central Powers. You cannot profess one formula in the West and act contrariwise in the East. But I have infinite faith in the British democracy with which we will have to deal ultimately. A bureaucrat may strike a discordant note here, or a misguided official may sound a discordant note

there, but the heart of the British democracy beats true to the noble impulses of Humanity...[23]

As 1918 progressed the momentum of politics in Delhi had moved up a gear and Asaf writes, '[it] had shattered the nerves of the Delhi administration'. With the forthcoming Indian National Congress session to be held in Delhi, efforts to mobilize support, raise funds, and enroll supporters moved up several notches with the local administration clearly not amused. He and Neki Ram Sharma, an upcoming politician and powerful orator from nearby Bhiwani, were barred from addressing public meetings under the Defence of India Rules. The order served on him referred to the 'reasonable grounds for believing that Asaf Ali, Barrister at Law, Delhi, has acted and is about to act in manner prejudicial to public safety and to the Defence of British India' and that he should 'refrain from addressing public meeting in the Delhi province'.[24] The order was served on him on 12 June and was immediately the subject of numerous column inches in the form of news reports, both Asaf's commentaries, and angry editorials in the *Bombay Chronicle*. Both Asaf and Neki Ram attended meetings thereafter—but sat through them quietly—regularly evoking a huge response as 'dumb speakers'. In one meeting both were billed to speak but did not while occupying their designated places as speakers. Asaf became in the *Chronicle* the 'muzzled speaker' who got a 'record ovation'. The meeting itself was to highlight the conditions of Indians in South Africa but this local issue concerning someone those gathered knew clearly animated proceedings. The reading of the Chief Commissioner's order against Asaf Ali and Neki Ram was greeted with 'deafening cries of shame'.[25] For the *Chronicle* the gag order was an opportunity to further develop its critique of 'Haileyism' in reference to the Chief Commissioner of Delhi W.M. Hailey and the column 'Imperial Delhi' noted that this 'reactionary bureaucrat has supplied a fresh illustration of his worst tendencies'.

Asaf, however, wanted to push this particular envelope further and, lawyer that he was, soon detected a loophole in the order in that it related to 'public' and not to 'private' gatherings. He felt, therefore, that a meeting held indoors and limited to registered members of the Home Rule League would not fall within the ambit of the ban order. Some other lawyers advised against this. Asaf knew he was going to cross a line. The opportunity was there as Home Rule League Day was on 16 June 1918.

A meeting was thereafter publicized for members of the Home Rule League to be addressed by Asaf Ali and Neki Ram Sharma and naturally, 'The announcement created a sensation', seen clearly as an act of defiance of the recently issued order.[26] At the entry to the Laxminarain Dharmshala—the building in Chandni Chowk where the meeting was to be held—arrangements were also made to enroll new members to the League! The Laxminarain Dharmshala was incidentally the site of many Home Rule League meetings and was regarded as its 'storm centre'.[27] In Asaf's later recollection on the day of the meeting 'several hundred new members were enrolled at the gate'[28] and the audience finally consisted of a thousand or more including several plainclothes policemen. At the time however he was at pains to emphasize how strictly he was acting within the limits of the permissible and the meeting was entirely a private affair confined only to members of the League, some of whom may have joined just before the meeting. Entry to the hall where the meeting was held was also strictly controlled to keep non-members out.

Clearly Asaf was setting the administration up for a public fall and it fell into the trap. He was arrested some twenty days later, on 6 July and he recollected being 'filled with a strange feeling of elation'. Possibly for him his actions were a vindication of his personal integrity after the blows his reputation had received in the past three years and he had embarked on this risky venture for precisely that reason: 'This was my baptism and I could not henceforth be denied the genuineness of my credentials'. His mother 'tense but seemingly calm and dignified' was the most affected: 'You are my only child. Did I bring you up for this day? May God protect you'. Brushes with authority for middle class Muslims in Delhi were always accompanied by trepidation: the elders in his family, still haunted by the events of 1857, 'used to tremble at the very mention of anti-government agitation.'[29] But this issue was now a public spectacle and the press and the *Bombay Chronicle* in particular made it into an all-India show. Asaf's mother was interviewed and was perhaps tutored on what to say. The paper quoted her to the effect that 'This was the first happiness she has known since she became a widow at the age of 20 some 30 years ago'; and that 'her son is doing his best for the constitutional freedom of India and no sacrifice is too great for that righteous cause'.[30]

Possibly the *Chronicle* also found a public hungry for gestures of defiance and no detail of the arrest was too small to be printed—and Asaf was to provide graphic detail for its reports. Taken to the Kotwali, the old city's historic police station, it was revealed to him that 'I was sitting only a few paces from the cell in which Ghalib the poet is said to have been confined once...'[31] News of the arrest was described as follows:

> Uncommon sensation and indignation prevails in Delhi. The general belief in his innocence and the unjust action of the authorities in molesting the most popular leader of public opinion have won the overwhelming enthusiasm for Mr. Asaf Ali. A public committee for the defence has been immediately instituted with Rs 10,000 as a nucleus.[32]

Asaf was bailed out quickly which was disappointing 'since it took the elation of martyrdom down by many pegs'. His aim however really was a 'forensic duel' in a courtroom and he aimed to make as much capital out of this in the media and elsewhere as possible.[33] The *Bombay Chronicle* connection now played a major role and as the trial grew closer, space in the newspaper devoted to the case grew from some columns to whole pages and more. Messages of support and sympathy poured in from across the country and a senior Counsel from Bombay was engaged to conduct the defence. When the trial began on 18 July the 'Court room was packed to capacity and large crowds filled the court compound'; 'Coming out of the Court Mr Asaf Ali was greeted with copious showers of rose petals and cheers and shouts of "Vande Mataram" punctuated the intervals between the court room and the car'.[34]

Asaf did not venture into this contest without several serious concerns: being found guilty could mean conviction for at least a few months if not longer, possible debarring and loss of his career. The stakes were now much higher than a letter or an article in a newspaper. He was advised by many of his friends to look for a way out: 'It was alright for the Tilaks and the Mrs Besants, whom the people had supported with hundreds of thousands and showered gifts on but not for you at the start of the only career left.'[35]

Certainly, he had received a heads up and an implied warning from the Public Prosecutor in Delhi of the difficulties he would face and also a suggestion that he could seek a way out. Asaf stuck to his guns but went through many anxious moments. There was also the more than occasional despondency at the weak support he thought he was getting in Delhi: 'I meet with sniggers not infrequently! They think I am being tried for treason and therefore they must not be seen talking to me or sympathizing with me.' We also find him writing to Syud—'I write to warn you not to put any faith in the high-sounding names'. In the first flush of enthusiasm after his arrest numerous persons had pledged financial contributions but he noted of the Defense fund of Rs.10,000 nucleus expected 'actually only Rs.1,840 has been promised of which only Rs.75 has been collected so far. They are all talking a lot but no work done'. [36] What hurt more—and for this Asaf blamed a clique in Aligarh—was a spurious story being circulated to the effect that the entire prosecution was a sham and a conspiracy: 'Just think those dammed *Bahanchouds* of the Aligarh sect who call my trial also "a move by the government to restore me to public confidence"'. 'Who will expect me to have patience with such *Madharchouds*?' he asked.[37] But in contrast to the lukewarm response in Delhi, support in the rest of the country was strong. Telegrams of support from important leaders including Mrs Annie Beasant poured in. Horniman's message from Bombay ended: 'Stick to your Guns'.[38]

As the trial commenced on 18 July and continued for the next 10 days, the *Bombay Chronicle* maintained its detailed coverage.[39] The criminal proceedings against a barrister were significant enough to attract attention outside nationalist circles. The *Times of India* also reported on it in some detail.[40] The magistrate hearing the case, George Spence had to be brought from another province as the Delhi officers could not be expected to pronounce on the infringement of their own government's order. Asaf's lawyer was imported from Bombay—thanks largely to the support of the *Bombay Chronicle.* The defence's argument was that the Delhi administration held a grudge against Asaf for his writings criticizing them in the *Bombay Chronicle;* but the case really hinged on what constituted a public meeting as opposed to a private gathering. The judgement found the accused 'contumacious' i.e. someone stubbornly and willfully disobedient to authority but also had to concede that there had been no infringement of the Chief Commissioner's order as the meeting was not 'public' but a 'private' one and there was therefore no alternative but to acquit. In one account Spence was given a punishment posting thereafter.[41] In any event, his career in the longer term does not appear to have suffered and he was Law Secretary to the Government of India in the 1940s and Asaf would meet him in the Central Legislative Assembly.

The verdict was an emphatic victory for the two defendants. The technicality or the loophole Asaf had identified, had worked. 'We were wildly cheered and garlanded and walked out on a carpet of rose petals in the court compound. And I suddenly became well known in the country'. The *Bombay Chronicle* later put together all its reporting and editorializing on the case and the judgment in the form of a little booklet titled *The Asaf Ali Trial* and it was advertised for sale in the paper for months afterwards. The nature of the case, the support of the *Bombay Chronicle*'s editor Horniman, and perhaps most of all the presence of Syud, who wrote the introduction to the book, meant that Asaf's had not been a silent struggle.

Asaf had staked a great deal and possibly had done so thinking that he needed to play the high stakes game to fully clear his name from the blow his reputation had taken from Mohammad Ali's charge of being an informer. The ordeal and the final judgement in his favour certainly marked a step forward but did not change everything and reservations about him persisted in the Congress hierarchy. He wrote to Syud: '... persecution cannot be tolerated after a certain limit ... I feel sick and disgusted'. But there was support also for him: 'I think Akka means to do her best for me, but I feel uncertain about the result'.[42] Akka—Sarojini Naidu—was already a person of importance in the Congress hierarchy.

Notwithstanding such doubts, victory in a legal 'forensic duel' that he had set up may well have strengthened a belief that the way ahead for him lay in more of this: constitutional and legal battles in the full glare of publicity in which the finer points of law and fair play were contested and victory came from knowledge, skill and finesse and not necessarily the application of force. For someone like him, equal to India's rulers in knowledge and education, nationalism also meant demonstrating your personal worth, even your superiority and the political task ahead could be to accumulate incremental gains like this. But such thoughts existed perhaps in the background and would assert themselves only gradually for the period that lay ahead for the next four years or so was one of mobilization, agitation and of more demonstrative and less clinical action as the anti-Rowlatt and then Khilafat protests irrevocably changed Delhi's political landscape. Yet his trial was also, perhaps to an extent unknown to him then, a stage in Delhi's political evolution and his victory a minor landmark for the incipient national movement.

Notes

1. I have dealt with Asaf Ali's (1888–1953) life and career in greater length in *Circles of Freedom: Friendship, Love and Loyalty in the Indian National Struggle,* New Delhi, Juggernaut, 2024. Narayani Gupta's *Delhi between Two Empires, 1803–1931: Society, Government and Urban Growth,* Delhi: Oxford University Press, 1981, remains the classic text documenting the change in Delhi from the end of the first decade of the twentieth century.
2. G.N.S. Raghavan, ed., *M Asaf Ali Memoirs: The Emergence of Modern India,* New Delhi: Ajanta Publications, 1994, p. 116 (henceforth Asaf Ali, *Memoirs*).
3. Ibid.
4. Details of these friendships can be found in Raghavan, *Circles of Freedom.*
5. For reasons of space, I am unable to go into these reasons here, but the details are in ibid. In brief Mohammad Ali accused Asaf of being a police informer. The former's high stature consolidated further by his subsequent internment meant a considerable, even if as it turned out temporary, reputational damage for the young Asaf Ali. He 'lay low' for about two years after this on the advice of other friends and then gradually re-entered public life through the Home Rule League branch set up in Delhi.

6. For the Medical Mission in assistance of the Ottomans and M.A. Ansari's role in it see Mushirul Hasan, *M. A. Ansari: Gandhi's Infallible Guide,* New Delhi: Manohar, 2010.
7. Asaf Ali to Syud Hossain, June 17, Syud Hossain papers, Prime Ministers Museum and Library. The year is not mentioned in the letter but it would appear to be 1916, some months before Syud Hossain himself returned to India and joined the *Bombay Chronicle.*
8. Asaf Ali, *Memoirs,* p. 127.
9. Ibid.
10. Ibid.
11. Ibid.
12. Ibid., p. 125.
13. A letter to the editor of the *Bombay Chronicle* sent by Asaf Ali to Syud Hossain dated 6 October 1917, Syud Hossain papers.
14. Ibid.
15. Ibid.
16. For instance, *Bombay Chronicle* 12 June 1917; 22 December 1917; 27 October 1917 amongst numerous others.
17. *Bombay Chronicle,* 12 June 1917.
18. Ibid.
19. Asaf Ali to Syud Hossain 21 May 1917, Syud Hossain Papers.
20. Asaf Ali, *Memoirs,* p. 128.
21. *Bombay Chronicle,* 18 June 1918.
22. *Bombay Chronicle,* 3 July 1917.
23. Ibid.
24. *Bombay Chronicle,* 17 June 1918.
25. Ibid.
26. Asaf Ali, *Memoirs,* p. 133.
27. Oral History Interview of Jugal Kishore Sharma, S. no. 177, Oral History Transcripts, Prime Ministers Museum and Library, p. 7.
28. Asaf Ali, *Memoirs,* p. 133.
29. Ibid., p. 134. For details of why the events of 1857 so haunted Asaf Ali's family see Raghavan, *Circles of Freedom,* pp. 18–20 and T.C.A. Raghavan, 'Asaf Ali's Haveli', *Open, the Magazine,* 11 August 2022, see https://openthemagazine.com/cover-story/asaf-alis-haveli/, accessed 10 July 2024.

30. *Bombay Chronicle,* 8 July 1918.
31. Ibid., 10 July 1918.
32. *Bombay Chronicle,* 8 July 1918.
33. Asaf Ali, *Memoirs,* p. 134.
34. *Bombay Chronicle,* 20 July 1918.
35. Asaf Ali, *Memoirs,* p. 136.
36. Asaf Ali to Syud Hossain, 10 July 1918, Syud Hossain Papers.
37. Asaf Ali to Syud Hossain, 9 July 1918, Syud Hossain Papers.
38. Asaf Ali, *Memoirs,* p. 135.
39. *Bombay Chronicle* 18 July 1918, 22 July 1918, 6 August 1918, 9 August 1918, 8 August 1918, 17 August 1918, 28 August 1918, 6 September 1918.
40. For instance, *Times of India,* 18 July 1918.
41. Oral History transcript, Jugal Kishore Khanna.
42. Asaf Ali to Syud Hossain, 9 October 1918, Syud Hossain Papers.

17

The Communist Party of India in Delhi

The First Decade

AMAR FAROOQUI

THE BEGINNINGS of the organized communist movement in Delhi may be traced back to the late 1930s, more than fifteen years after the foundation of the Communist Party of India. An 'Indian Communist Party' (Communist Party of India) had been founded at Tashkent in 1920. The lead in this was taken by communists from India, and revolutionary nationalists who were inspired by the October Revolution in Russia. The initiative had the backing of the Communist International and the Bolshevik government.[1] Tashkent was at this time the capital of the Turkestan Soviet Socialist Republic. A few years later, a conference of Indian communists was organized in Kanpur. This conference, held in 1925, was the first such gathering within India, and has been considered as the year of the actual foundation of the Communist Party of India (CPI).[2] However, after the split in the party in 1964, the Communist Party of India (Marxist), CPI (M), stated that 1920 should be taken as the date for the formation of the party. In his book *Myself and the Communist Party of India* (1969), the prominent CPI (M) leader Muzaffar Ahmad regarded the Kanpur conference as 'a disgraceful affair'.[3] In the second volume of *Documents of the History of the Communist Party of India* the editor G. Adhikari provided a detailed account of the Kanpur conference and reviewed the controversy regarding the foundation date of the CPI. He quoted a letter sent by the CPI to the Indonesian Communist Party before the split in which, replying to a query about the year in which the party was formed, the CPI secretariat stated that, 'It was in December 1925 that in a meeting of representatives of the various groups of communists in the country held at Kanpur that the Communist Party of India was formed'.[4] The letter was signed on behalf of the secretariat by B.T. Ranadive, who would later become one of the stalwarts of the CPI (M). The outline history of the party published by the CPI (M) recently on the occasion of the centenary of the formation of the CPI in Tashkent notes that, 'The Kanpur communist conference held from 26 to 28 December 1925, was the first meeting on Indian soil, where almost all the communist groups and elements had joined'.[5]

With the growing Left-wing radicalization of the anti-colonial struggle in the late 1920s, the British Indian government launched an offensive against communists, implicating leading communist and trade union activists in the Meerut Conspiracy Case in 1929. For over four years the top leadership of the CPI was in prison, making it difficult for the party to function effectively. It is only after the incarcerated communists began to be gradually released from 1933–4 onwards that the work of the party could be resumed, although it had to operate underground due to the continuing ban on its activities. In Delhi itself, several trade unionists and revolutionaries had been attracted to communist and socialist ideas, and were getting involved in radical mobilization against British rule. Some of these activists were employed in the textile mills located in Delhi. The city already had four mills in 1911 when the decision to shift the capital from Calcutta was announced. In 1920 G.D. Birla acquired the Hanuman and Mahadeo Spinning and Weaving Mills, renamed it the Birla Cotton Spinning and Weaving Mill, and expanded the enterprise by investing a large amount of capital in it.[6] In the latter half of the 1920s, Delhi Cloth and General Mills (DCM) added two new units to their existing establishment set up earlier. With the expansion of the textile industry, efforts began to be made to organize the workers. Two names figure in this early history of unionization, Sant Singh Yusuf and Baba Ramchander.[7] Anand Gupta in his history of the CPI in Delhi has put together the available information about the first generation of communists in the city, mostly based on documents in his personal collection.[8] According to Gupta, Baba Ramchander was born in the Etah district of the United Provinces, and migrated to Delhi in the 1920s where he was employed in the Birla Textile Mills (early 1930s). Before joining Birla Mills he had done odd jobs in various other cloth mills, so that he had contacts among textile workers across the city. He was among the organizers of a protest meeting against the execution of Bhagat Singh and his comrades on 23 March 1931, at Gandhi Ground, located opposite the Delhi railway station. The ground was a large open space which had become a popular venue for nationalist gatherings in this period. Baba was arrested soon after the meeting. Another trade union activist who had been working among textile workers in Delhi, Sant Singh Yusuf, had assisted Baba Ramchander in organizing the meeting at Gandhi Ground.[9]

Sant Singh Yusuf, who was to later emerge as one of the leading communist trade union leaders in Kanpur, had migrated from Punjab to Delhi at a very young age. He had worked in Birla Mills and DCM. He became part of the initial group of activists who were trying to organize workers, especially textile workers, in the city. Sant Singh (Chaddha) would adopt the name Sant Singh Yusuf, formally adding a part of his underground name (Muhammad Yusuf) to his original name; after Independence he contested elections with this name. His abilities as an organizer were noticed by the well-known trade unionist S.H. Jhabvala. Jhabvala was based in Bombay where he was connected with a large number of unions including the Girni Kamgar Union, and in 1927 was elected organizing secretary of the 'Council of Action' of the All India Trade Union Congress (AITUC).[10] During a brief stay in Delhi in 1927–8, mainly to attend the sixth session of the AITUC (March 1927) and the meeting of the AITUC executive (February 1928),[11] he helped form the (Delhi) Textile Labour Union along with Asaf Ali, Lala Shankar Lal, and Dr M.A. Ansari. The union was later affiliated to AITUC. This might have been the first union in Delhi to be granted affiliation. Sant Singh became secretary of the union in 1929. Shortly afterwards he lost his job due to his participation in a strike by textile workers that year.[12] This forced him to look for employment elsewhere, and he moved to Ahmedabad, having first shifted to Lahore where he was imprisoned for a while. Baba Ramchander too had relocated to Ahmedabad after he was dismissed, successively, from Birla Mills in Delhi and the Birla-owned textile mill in Gwalior. Together both of them began mobilizing workers in Ahmedabad. By 1938 Baba Ramchander was back in Delhi, while Sant Singh Yusuf had made Kanpur the base of his activities.

In Delhi, Baba Ramchander was active in the Sabzi Mandi area (where Birla Mills was located), and became ward secretary of the Congress. This is the time when, in early 1939, efforts were being made to form a Communist Party in Delhi. The central leadership of the party, which was now functioning under conditions of semi-legality, had deputed R.D. Bhardwaj to bring together communist activists in Delhi with the objective of constituting a party unit for the city and some of the neighbouring areas. Bhardwaj, who is unfortunately a forgotten figure today (he died of tuberculosis in 1948, at the age of 40), was instrumental in keeping the party organization at the centre alive while most of the party leaders were in prison in the Meerut Conspiracy Case. When the party was reorganized in 1935, Bhardwaj became a member of the newly constituted politburo (with P.C. Joshi as the general secretary). He was given charge of building the party in north India. The founding of the party in the United Provinces was to a great extent the result of his endeavours. It is in this context that a meeting of communists was convened in Delhi in July 1939. According to Gupta, the meeting was held at a dharamshala in Chandni Chowk.[13] Chandni Chowk would have been an obvious choice as this was the area with which the main coordinator in Delhi, Bahal Singh, was most familiar. Moreover, this was an area in which he had been mobilizing shop assistants and *thela* (handcart) drivers.[14] The Congress too had a strong presence in Chandni Chowk, with the Gandhi Ashram khadi outlet (perhaps Shuddh Khadi Bhandar?) becoming a regular meeting place. Apart from Bhardwaj and Bahal Singh, Baba Ramchander, Khushi Ram Mehta and two other communist activists were present in the meeting. Before this meeting, a small group of communists working among textile workers had met in December 1938 to discuss the possibility of forming a communist group.[15] The meeting was held in Sohanganj in the Sabzi Mandi area, not far from the Birla Mills. In other words, the July 1939 meeting was preceded by consultations among communists in Delhi, and some groundwork would already have been done before Bhardwaj met the Delhi comrades.

Khushi Ram Mehta was among the first communists in Delhi. He had served a sentence in the Andamans, having been convicted in the sensational Ooty Bank case. Mehta and his revolutionary comrades, led by Hazara Singh who was inspired by the Kirti Kisan Party and Bhagat Singh, had planned to rob the Ooty Bank in response to the claim of a senior colonial official that the subjects of Madras presidency were loyal to the British. In April 1933 they successfully deprived the bank of a large sum of money. However, the revolutionaries were apprehended, put on trial, and sentenced to transportation.[16] They were released in 1937 following the formation of Congress provincial ministries. While in the Andamans, Mehta became a member of the Communist Consolidation Committee in 1934. The Communist Consolidation Committee had brought together communist prisoners in the Andamans, and had attracted a large number of new members who were drawn towards communism through discussions with communist revolutionaries. In later years Mehta took enormous pride in the fact that his party card mentioned 1934 (while he was in prison) as the date of his joining the party.

An Organizing Committee (OC) for Delhi (including Rohtak, Gurgaon, and Alwar) was constituted at the meeting of July 1939. Bahal Singh became the secretary of the committee. This arrangement was approved by the central committee of the party. Although no record of the meeting is forthcoming, N.N. Manna in his published unfinished draft dealing with the early history of the party in Delhi, suggests that the OC consisted of three members. He has looked at some of the other relevant evidence, including some police reports, to elicit this information. The three members, according to Manna, were Bahal Singh, Baba Ramchander, and Sherjung.[17] Sherjung had recently joined the party after being released from jail. He had been sentenced to death in the so-called 'Ahmedgarh Dacoity Case'; the sentence was commuted to life imprisonment, later reduced to eight years. Thus, at the age of 31 he had already served a prison sentence of eight years.

Sherjung was a revolutionary who had taken part in an unsuccessful raid in 1929, at Ahmedgarh (near Ludhiana), on a train carrying government money. He subsequently gave himself up through a trusted intermediary who received the reward amount (which he handed over to his political associates).[18] Around 1925, Sherjung had come in contact with Bhagat Singh and joined the Hindustan Socialist Republican Association (HSRA). He was born and brought up in the Sirmaur state (the territories of which are now located in Himachal Pradesh) where his father was a high-level official.[19] He had been trained to be an expert marksman, was an accomplished hunter, and later used his skill effectively in the communal situation in Delhi during 1947, when he was deputed by Jawaharlal Nehru to help control rioting in parts of north Delhi and intervened to prevent violence in several instances. Soon after his release from prison, Sherjung got involved in trade union activities in Dehradun, and came close to communists such as Mahmuduzzafar who was active in the recently formed Progressive Writers' Association. He assisted Mahmuduzzafar with the newly launched Marxist journal in Urdu, *Chingari*.[20] He also began taking classes at study-circles organized in Delhi for textile workers, commuting frequently between Dehradun and Delhi.[21]

There are no figures for the actual membership of the Delhi party in 1939. Apart from the five members who attended the July meeting, we have about fifteen more names, mainly trade union cadre, but also referred to as communists by Manna and Gupta.[22] In any case it is unlikely that there were more than twenty members at this stage. It is not clear whether all of them had been formally inducted into the party. Some of them are likely to have been loosely associated with the party while being engaged in trade union work. We need to bear in mind that since the party was still illegal, it functioned as an underground organization. Therefore, great care was taken while making someone a formal member of the party. The tendency was to keep the numbers small and manageable. Many who were ideologically committed to communism and socialism did not necessarily become members of the party. They worked in mass organizations with the knowledge that these were connected with and guided by party members, most of whom were whole-time workers.

Bahal Singh is such an important figure in the early history of the anti-colonial struggle and the communist and working-class movements in Delhi that it is astonishing that he is so little known. The brief outline of his life and political work which follows is based on the account of his role in the history of the Delhi party in Manna's published draft, and Gupta's book. This is supplemented by some information derived from the recollections of my father, Muqimuddin Farooqi, who was brought into the party by Bahal Singh and worked with him for a few years before Bahal Singh's untimely death at the age of 36 in 1946—he died of tuberculosis, his condition having worsened due to complications caused by the long spells he was forced to spend in colonial prisons.

Bahal Singh came from a well-to-do family which was in the wholesale cloth business. The family establishment was located in the Katra Dhulia locality of Chandni Chowk.[23] Chandni Chowk was the main centre of the cloth trade in Delhi. His father, Guggan Mal Jain, perhaps had some link or at least sympathies with the Congress for which reason he does not seem to have objected much to his only son's activism, even allowing him to use the *barsati* above the shop as an office and meeting-place: 'On the roof above the shop of Shri Guggan Mal Jain there was a room with a large open space in front of the room. The room was covered with *gaddas & chaddars* [mattresses and sheets] with [bolster] pillows. This room was the centre of all political activities of Bahal Singh'.[24]

Soon after Bahal Singh completed his school education he began participating in programmes of the Congress. He accompanied some young workers to the crucial Lahore session in December 1929. As part of the preparations for the session Dr Satyapal had made an appeal for volunteers, and Bahal Singh and his comrades responded enthusiastically, travelling to Lahore ten days before the session to help with the arrangements as volunteers. Upon his return he enlisted as a satyagrahi in the Civil Disobedience Movement, and was arrested in 1930. He also took part in the movement when it was resumed in 1932. This time Bahal Singh was arrested and imprisoned for a year. It is possible that he became acquainted with Sant Singh during this agitation.[25] Following his release he turned towards more militant action. One of his initiatives at this time was the setting up of an enterprise called 'Vishnu Dyers and Drycleaners' in the Katra Neel locality of Chandni Chowk. This was in fact intended to be a centre of revolutionary activity. The tasks undertaken by him and his comrades included the manufacture of crude bombs. The establishment was disbanded after a police raid in which, fortunately for the revolutionaries, no incriminating evidence could be discovered.

With the formation of the Congress Socialist Party (CSP) in 1934 within the Congress, many activists found a platform for pursuing a more radical politics. Bahal Singh was among the younger members of the Congress who turned towards the CSP. This marked an important phase in his ideological evolution in the early 1930s, especially under the influence of Bhagat Singh. As is well known, the execution of Bhagat Singh, Rajguru, and Sukhdev had a profound impact on the youth, a significant section of which came under the influence of socialist ideas. Bahal Singh had already been associated with the Bharat Naujawan Sabha in the late 1920s, and now his political understanding underwent a further development so that he became a committed socialist and eventually a communist. An important role was played by in this by Satyavati, who had been engaged in organizing textile mill workers for some years, and coordinated the work of socialist groups in Delhi. Satyavati was a satyagrahi in the Civil Disobedience movement. She was imprisoned, and later released in 1932.[26] Aruna Asaf Ali was among the several young freedom fighters who were inspired by Satyavati, and her influence as a mentor was acknowledged by Aruna Asaf Ali in later years.[27] It may be mentioned that Satyavati's grandfather was the prominent Arya Samaj leader, Swami Shraddhananda. She passed away in 1945, at the age of 41, having contracted tuberculosis, the disease which killed Bahal Singh as well (and it may be recalled that tuberculosis was the cause of Bhardwaj's death too).

Satyavati and Bahal Singh revived the Textile Labour Union, which had been dormant for some time. In 1938 May Day was observed jointly by the union and the CSP. A large meeting was held at the Gandhi Ground on the occasion; Chanandeen of the *tanga* union presided over the function. We have names of several trade unionists who became part of the Textile Labour Union and mobilized workers in Birla Mills and DCM: Hardhyan Singh, Brij Kishan Chandiwala, Shiv Narayan Vats, Ramchandra Tyagi, Hukam Singh Rana, Kishan Lal Bharadwaj, Natha Ram (Natha Singh?),[28] Ramdeen Singh, Bhisham Singh, Shrikrishna Varma, and Ganpat Sharma.[29]

The period 1936–8 also saw the emergence of Chando Bibi as a prominent trade union leader in Delhi. Chando Bibi had migrated to Delhi from Calcutta, and first began working among *tanga* drivers. At the same time, she joined Satyavati and other trade-unionists in their efforts to organize textile workers. This was a time when the workers of Birla Mills and DCM were intensifying their struggles. For instance, in 1936 the Textile Labour Union gave a call for a strike to demand the reinstatement of twenty workers who had been dismissed by DCM. In December 1937 there was a move to organize a strike in Birla Mills. The attempt was unsuccessful as the main leaders were arrested by the administration before the strike could take place, and imprisoned. Then in January 1938, within a few weeks of the AITUC session in Delhi (1–3 January), there was a forty-day strike in Birla Mills.[30] Chando Bibi became an integral part of the collective leadership of textile unions. Simultaneously she was mobilizing workers in other sectors. Fred Munson's pioneering study of the history of printing unionism in Delhi has highlighted her contribution to the formation of unions in the printing industry. Chando Bibi worked closely with Ajit Das Gupta and Ram Chandra Sharma.[31] Sharma, who himself was a printing worker, rose to be one of the foremost leaders of the CPI in Delhi (he was already a prominent communist trade union leader in Kanpur before shifting to Delhi). Chando Bibi never joined the party. Her political trajectory was somewhat different: she became a member of the Revolutionary Socialist Party.

The Revolutionary Socialist Party (RSP) was formed in 1940 by Marxists among the Anushilan revolutionaries of Bengal ('Anushilan Marxists'), following serious differences with the CSP at the Ramgarh session of the Congress.[32] In Delhi, Chando Bibi along with Ajit Das Gupta broke with the communists after 1940. According to Munson, 'rivalry developed ... between the Communists on the one hand and Chandu [*sic*] Bibi and Ajit Das Gupta on the other'.[33] Yet Munson is not entirely clear about the reasons for the differences between Chando Bibi and Das Gupta, and the communists, which was their shift towards the RSP. He does nevertheless mention that the premises of the regional office of the RSP in Delhi (780, Ballimaran), were leased in the name of Chando Bibi.[34] For a few years after the formation of RSP, Chando Bibi continued to work together with the communists in the trade unions.[35] She was greatly respected for her dedication and capabilities. At the AITUC session in Delhi in 1938 she was the chairperson of the reception committee. She was elected as one of the vice-presidents at the Kanpur session of the AITUC in 1942.[36] More importantly, she was elected president of the provincial committee of the AITUC (PTUC) when it was constituted in January 1947. Representatives of both CPI and RSP unions participated in the conference which led to the formation of the Delhi PTUC. S.A. Dange was present at the conference. Muhammad

Yamin of the Delhi CPI was elected the general secretary. Yamin, from Delhi, had been active on the trade union front since 1940, and was instrumental in organizing the 1947 conference. He had earlier been inducted into the executive committee of the Delhi party (see below).[37]

By about 1936–7 there was a fairly large number of activists in Delhi who were attracted to communist principles and were ideologically closer to the CPI than they were to the amorphous socialist groups represented by the CSP. Bahal Singh had taken on the task of coordinating their work. He himself led several unions, the most important being the Kapra Shramjivi Sangh which was a trade union of shop assistants employed in establishments of wholesale cloth traders. The union was formed in 1937 and remained a formidable force till at least the 1970s. Of course, there was considerable overlap between communist trade-unionists and those who were part of the CSP. Many communists, under conditions of illegality, became members of the CSP and tried to steer it in the direction of Marxism. The association of the communists with the CSP did not, at least for the time being, lead to tensions in the case of Delhi. Rather, the CSP was able to tap into the networks of the communists who in turn were broadening their base among workers, making use of the opportunities that a political platform that could function openly, provided for their activities. This does not mean that the colonial administration was not aware of the presence of the communists in the CSP, and repression was severe with the outbreak of the war. This was the era of Linlithgow's brutal regime which lasted for seven long years (1936–43). Sherjung, for example, was imprisoned and sent to Deoli (in Rajasthan). Towards the end of 1940 Bahal Singh was arrested and jailed in Gujrat in Punjab. Here his health deteriorated. It worsened due to a serious error in the medical treatment given to him. Asaf Ali too was incarcerated in the same prison. Gupta refers to a letter written by Asaf Ali to

Sikandar Hayat Khan who was then prime minister of the provincial government in Punjab, urging him to release Bahal Singh due to his serious medical condition.[38] Whether it was Asaf Ali's letter or the faulty medication which induced the authorities to release him, we know that he was freed a few weeks before the completion of his term. His condition was so bad that he was immediately admitted to a hospital upon his arrival in Delhi. Bahal Singh never fully recovered, and further complications due to tuberculosis made it difficult for him to function normally after 1941.

Notwithstanding his frail condition, Bahal Singh laid the foundations of a strong party organization in Delhi in the years between 1941 and 1944. He was completely incapacitated after 1944. We need to bear in mind that following the invasion of the Soviet Union by Nazi Germany in 1941, and the shift in the position of the CPI with the People's War line at the end of 1941, it became relatively easier for the communists to engage in political activities more openly with the relaxation of restrictions on them. By the middle of 1942 the ban on the CPI had been removed, even as several of its leaders continued to languish in jail. These included Bhardwaj, who despite the efforts of the party was not released till 1943 when his medical condition worsened. He had to be taken directly to Bhowali and died a few years later. Manna tells us that soon after he (Manna) had shifted to Delhi from Allahabad, he was deputed by the party to escort Bahal Singh to the sanatorium in Bhowali (now in Uttarakhand): '[Bahal Singh] had been sent to Bhowali sanitorium for treatment where Communist leader Bhardwaj was convalescing. I had accompanied Bahal Singh to Bhowali, stayed for a day there and met Bhardwaj…'.[39]

The Delhi party held its first conference in 1944 (23–25 January). Gandhi Ground was the venue of the conference. The conference was inaugurated by Rahul Sankrityayan. The main organizational problem with which the conference had to deal was that of finding a suitable functionary who would be able to shoulder the responsibilities of the party secretary. As long as Bahal Singh was active, he had been the obvious choice. Things had now become difficult for him, and he could no longer take on this arduous task. In this moment, which signified his enormous achievement, it became necessary to elect some other leading activist as the secretary. Bahal Singh was present on the occasion; he was a member of the five-member presidium which conducted the conference. He supervised the arrangements, steered the proceedings and ensured that a team that was efficient and ideologically sound would continue the work of the party. A provincial executive committee was elected, comprising five full members (including Bahal Singh), and two candidate members.[40] Yagya Dutt Sharma (known as YD among his comrades) was elected the secretary, with Muqim Farooqi as joint secretary. YD Sharma had joined the party in 1940. He studied economics at St. Stephen's College, and became active in the students' movement. With his outstanding academic qualifications, he was able to get a teaching position in Ramjas College, but soon became a party whole-timer. Farooqi had been a student of history at St. Stephen's College, participated in the students' movement and became a member of the CPI in 1940. Both YD and Farooqi were inducted into the party by Bahal Singh.

In view of the organizational problems the party was facing due to the relentless onslaught against the communists following the outbreak of the war, the central leadership of the party had reconstituted the OC soon after Sherjung was arrested. Manna, who provides this information, does not mention the date.[41] In addition to Bahal Singh and Baba Ramchander, who were already members, Shiv Narayan Vats (who had attended the initial July 1939 meeting), YD and Farooqi were made members of the expanded OC. Bahal Singh remained the secretary. The decision to put forward the names of YD and Farooqi for the secretaryship and joint-secretaryship, respectively, in 1944, would have been based on an assessment by Bahal Singh and the central leadership of the capabilities of the two in the period between the reorganization of the OC and the first Delhi CPI conference. YD officiated as the secretary from 1941 onwards, when Bahal Singh was undergoing treatment. After the conference YD was prevented from functioning as secretary due to restrictions imposed on him earlier. In the middle of 1944, Yamin became the secretary for a short while, and Farooqi took over at the end of the year (he was already the joint-secretary).

By the time the conference took place, the Delhi party had its provincial office at Urdu Bazaar. When the ban was lifted, Bahal Singh began exploring the possibility of renting a sufficiently large space in Shahjahanabad for the party headquarters. A suitable place was found in Urdu Bazaar, located in the midst of bookshops, and conveniently situated on the main road leading from Darya Ganj to Jama Masjid. The building faced the mosque. The new office was inaugurated in January 1943. The office was on the first floor, and the terrace with a *barsati* was also part of the premises rented out to the party.[42] Initially the Delhi CPI had functioned from an office in Katra Shahanshahi in Chandni Chowk. This housed the offices of the Kapra Shramjivi Sangh and the Delhi unit of the All India Students' Federation as well. The Katra Shahanshahi premises continued to be the office of the Kapra Shramjivi Sangh.[43] Not far from the Urdu Bazaar office was the 'commune' in Darya Ganj. This was a small, rented house which had been let out to YD. He had taken it on rent when he began teaching at Ramjas College. Subsequently it was converted into a party 'commune', a collective dwelling for wholetime workers. Farooqi lived in the garage, while other comrades, who included Manna and Shakil Ahmed, stayed there for short periods of time. Shakil Ahmed had come to Delhi after graduating from Aligarh Muslim University, and was elected as one of the two candidate members of the executive committee in 1944. Comrades from other parts of the country who might be passing through Delhi, often stayed there. Manna tells us that the commune was the venue of the crucial central committee meeting of the CPI held in June 1947 on the eve of Independence. The commune was organized on the principles of a Gandhian ashram, with an emphasis on austerity and simple living. All inmates were expected to collectively share responsibilities of maintaining the commune.[44] In her memoir, *Kaifi and I*, Shaukat Azmi provides an endearing contemporary account of life in the Bombay (CPI) commune. She lived there for several years with Kaifi Azmi, [45] The headquarters of the party were in Bombay at this time.

In organizational terms, the 1944 conference marked the coming of age of the Delhi CPI. The first conference was the outcome of efforts of the preceding decade to build a communist movement in Delhi, against the backdrop of the anti-colonial struggle. The history of the early years of the CPI in Delhi is relatively unexplored. This brief sketch can only provide an outline which could be the basis of further research on the subject.

Notes

1. *CommunistParty@100: A History of the Party, 1920–1964*, New Delhi: CPI (M) Publication, 2021, pp. 13–16.
2. 'In the earliest phase, before the Kanpur Bolshevik Conspiracy Case in mid-1924, these groups [of revolutionaries who were attracted to communist ideas] were sought to be coordinated by the communist centre organised abroad on the basis of the Communist Party of India formed at Tashkent on 17 October 1920 by M.N. Roy and others soon after the Second Congress of the Communist International [1920]. These communist groups or their representatives came together at the First Indian

Conference at Kanpur at the end of December 1925, which was convened by Satyabhakta with his own ideas, but was taken over by the real communists rejecting his ideas'. G. Adhikari, ed., 'General Introduction', *Documents of the History of the Communist Party of India*, vol. I (1917–1922), Delhi: People's Publishing House, 1971, p. 2. Satyabhakta was a political maverick who later propounded ideas of 'Hindu Communism'. See Charu Gupta, '"Hindu Communism": Satyabhakta, Apocalypses and Utopian *Ram Rajya*', *The Indian Economic and Social History Review*, vol. 58, no. 2, 2021, pp. 213–48.

3. Muzaffar Ahmad, *Myself and the Communist Party of India, 1920–1929*, tr. from Bengali, Calcutta: National Book Agency, 1970, pp. 412–3.
4. G. Adhikari, ed., *Documents of the History of the Communist Party of India*, vol. II (1923–1925), Delhi: People's Publishing House, 1974, p. 609.
5. *CommunistParty@100*, p. 22.
6. Ankur Shukla, 'State Policies and Industrialisation in Delhi: 1921–1951', *IOSR Journal of Humanities and Social Science*, vol. 22, no. 6, ver. 13, 2017, p. 101.
7. Baba Ramchander is not to be confused with the peasant leader Baba Ramchandra of Awadh.
8. Anand Gupta, *Dilli ki Communist Party ka Itihas*, Delhi: Communist Party, 2007. Unfortunately, Gupta does not provide sufficient references in his book, though he had in his possession a large amount of material which he had painstakingly put together over several years. I have had the opportunity to go through some of the rare documents in his personal collection. However, I did not take down any notes at that time, something that I very much regret. I am unaware of the present status of this invaluable archive.
9. Gupta, *Dilli ki Communist Party*, p. 46.
10. Jyotishman Mudiar, 'The Meerut Trial: Labor, Internationalism and Cold War', *Journal of South Asian Studies*, vol. 8, no. 3, 2020, p. 126. See also, interview with S.H. Jhabvala (transcript), Centre of South Asian Studies, University of Cambridge, 10 May 1969, see https://www.s-asian.cam.ac.uk/archive/

audio/collection/s-h-jhabvala/, accessed 13 May 2024; Prem Sagar Gupta, *A Short History of the All-India Trade Union Congress (1920–1947)*, Delhi: AITUC Publication, 1980, pp. 113–14.

11. The AITUC held two sessions in 1927: in March 1927 at Delhi, and in November 1927 at Kanpur. Gupta, *Short History of the All-India Trade Union Congress*, pp. 82–94; 101–14. Mudiar mentions the presence of Jhabvala at Delhi in February 1928. Mudiar, 'The Meerut Trial', p. 126.
12. N.N. Manna, *CPI in Delhi: Its Role in the Struggle for Freedom and Trade Union Movement*, Delhi: People's Publishing House, 2011, p. 28. This small booklet is based on an incomplete, partly handwritten, manuscript and some rough notes of the author, and a portion of it comprises his reminiscences. Manna was secretary of the Delhi State Committee of the CPI from 1995 to 2002; he passed away in 2010. He was associated with the Delhi CPI as a full-timer since the late 1940s. This makes the booklet a unique source for the early history of the party.
13. Gupta, *Dilli ki Communist Party*, p. 132. The dharamshala, Lakshmi Narayan Dharamshala, is still extant.
14. At the 1938 session of the AITUC, held in Delhi, affiliation was given to five Delhi unions, including the Thela Union. Manna, *CPI in Delhi*, p. 43; Gupta, *Short History of the All-India Trade Union Congress*, pp. 297–9.
15. Manna, *CPI in Delhi*, p. 45.
16. Gupta provides a detailed account of the Ooty 'robbery', based on an interview with Mehta whom he knew very well personally. *Dilli ki Communist Party*, pp. 230–4. See also, Vikram Raj, 'Hazara Singh: Unsung Hero of the Freedom Struggle', *Frontline*, 16 September 2022 (online edition), see https://frontline.thehindu.com/society/hazara-singh-unsung-hero-of-indian-freedom-struggle/article65898628.ece, accessed 13 May 2024.
17. Manna, *CPI in Delhi*, pp. 66–7.
18. Gupta, *Dilli ki Communist Party*, pp. 251–2. There is a slight error in Sherjung's year of birth mentioned by Gupta (1904). I have gone by the date mentioned in some of the other sources (1906), including an article based on a volume

commemorating Sherjung, see Shriniwas Joshi, 'Sher Jung—the lion of Himachal Pradesh', *The Tribune*, 18 January 2015 (online), see https://www.tribuneindia.com/news/archive/features/sher-jung-the-lion-of-himachal-pradesh-31610, accessed 14 May 2024.

19. Rajendra Rajen, 'Sher Jung's Pivotal Role', *The Tribune*, 20 November 2020 (online), see https://www.tribuneindia.com/news/comment/sher-jungs-pivotal-role-452659, accessed 14 May 2024.
20. Gupta, *Dilli ki Communist Party*, p. 252.
21. Manna, *CPI in Delhi*, p. 45.
22. Manna has a list of fifteen names of those belonging to 'communist groups' in Delhi, *circa* 1938. *CPI in Delhi*, p. 65. Many of these names appear in Gupta's account as well.
23. The bomb hurled at Hardinge in 1912, injuring him, during his state-entry procession in the new capital, is supposed to have been thrown from the premises of the Punjab National Bank branch in Katra Dhulia.
24. Manna, *CPI in Delhi*, p. 28. Manna came to know Bahal Singh in the early 40s when he joined the All India Students' Federation (he was then studying in Allahabad University), and occasionally came to Delhi where his parents were staying. He would visit the party office in Katra Shahanshahi (in Chandni Chowk), which also served as the office of the Students' Federation, and be given some assignments pertaining to the organisation (p. 79). The offices of several unions would later be located in these premises. These included the Kapra Shramjivi Sangh, and the Municipal Workers' Union.
25. Manna, *CPI in Delhi*, p. 32. According to Manna, Sant Singh served his term in Multan jail.
26. Qurban Ali, 'Congress Socialist Party (CSP) at a Glance and Short Profiles Works [sic.] of its Leaders', *Lohia Today* (website), pp. 91–2, see https://lohiatoday.com/wp-content/uploads/2018/09/cspataglance.pdf, accessed 16 May 2024.
27. T.C.A. Raghavan, *Circles of Freedom: Friendship, Love and Loyalty in the Indian National Struggle*, New Delhi: Juggernaut, 2004, p. 186.

28. Manna in his list of trade-unionists active in the Textile Labour Union mentions Natha Singh, while Gupta's list has the name of Natha Ram. Manna, *CPI in Delhi*, p. 42; Gupta, *Dilli ki Communist Party*, p. 224. One might mention that Natha Singh, though not necessarily the same person, was later the secretary of the Shahdara district of the Delhi CPI for several years, and a senior member of the Provincial Executive Committee.
29. Gupta, *Dilli ki Communist Party*, p. 224.
30. Ibid., p. 122.
31. Fred C. Munson, 'Printing Unionism in Delhi', *Indian Journal of Industrial Relations*, vol. 3, no. 4, 1968, p. 419.
32. Buddhadeva Bhattacharya, *Origins of the Revolutionary Socialist Party*, Chapters 3 and 8, Marxist Internet Archive, see https://www.marxists.org/archive/bhattacharya/1982/origins-rsp/index.htm, accessed 16 May 2024.
33. Munson, 'Printing Unionism in Delhi', p. 419.
34. Ibid., p. 432.
35. It is pertinent that the umbrella trade union body linked to the RSP, United Trade Union Congress, was established only towards the end of the 1940s.
36. Gupta, *Short History of the All-India Trade Union Congress*, p. 376.
37. Yamin and his family left for Pakistan in 1951 and settled there.
38. Gupta, *Dilli ki Communist Party*, p. 172.
39. Manna, *CPI in Delhi*, p. 102.
40. The candidate members would not have had the right to vote in the executive.
41. Manna, *CPI in Delhi*, p. 71.
42. The *barsati* with its tin roof, provided accommodation to some of the party workers.
43. Gupta suggests that the office of Delhi unit of the Students' Federation was located in the residence-cum-office of Muqim Farooqi's elder brother, Abdullah Farooqi. Abdullah Farooqi was a Congress activist and had been jailed as a satyagrahi. He resided in Urdu Bazar, a stone's throw away from the new Delhi CPI office. Manna, however, categorically states that when he first went to the Katra Shahanshahi office in 1942,

the office 'was at that time the trade union office, the AISF office and office of the illegal CPI'. Gupta, *Dilli ki Communist Party*, p. 148; Manna, *CPI in Delhi*, p. 79.

44. Manna and Farooqi, between them, had to prepare morning tea and breakfast. While Farooqi was good at making tea, brewed in a fancy teapot (which must have been donated by some sympathiser), Manna's specialty was toasting slices of bread on a coal *angithi*. On most days this would have been the only breakfast.
45. Shaukat Kaifi, *Kaifi and I: A Memoir*, New Delhi: Zubaan, 2005.

18

Profiling Women's Political Activism in Delhi, 1930s–1940s

Snippets from Indraprastha College for Women, University of Delhi[1]

MEENA BHARGAVA

> *The world today seems to be in a sad turmoil...with the international dissension widening into a yawning gulf...with our own land having plunged in a ruinous state of affairs. Surely, this is the greatest crisis our country has ever faced...together we must strive and build up this beautiful land that is our home...yours and mine...*
>
> — *Pradeep*, Indraprastha College Magazine, 1948

THE ENTERPRISING efforts to educate women and empower them had begun by the mid-nineteenth century, yet as we approached the twentieth century, these endeavours were still shrouded in prejudice and several hurdles remained. Regardless, women and education were no strangers; the

*I am delighted to write this essay for Professor Narayani Gupta to celebrate her as a distinguished alumna of Indraprastha College, a faculty member of the College and erudite academician who tirelessly with affection and warmth has empowered and inspired generations of students, one being me.

bonds between the two existed, even though they were fixed and decided by the patriarchal order. In the given historical system, there was scarcely space for the critique of patriarchy or social institutions and religious practices. Notwithstanding, several women, undeterred by the conventional, rigid social norms, challenged the ancestral customary practices, created a public space for themselves and entered the contested terrain. To study political activism and public participation of women in the city of Delhi in the 1930s–40s, a period marked by an extensive struggle for freedom and its culmination, I study the experiences, responses, and reactions of women to the atrocities of the British government and how they coped with it, without diluting their radicalism or dampening their spirit of defiance. Talking about the trends in the women's movement in Delhi that overcame caste, class, and gender bias, thus establishing its primacy in national politics, I specifically focus on Indraprastha College for Women, University of Delhi, established in 1924 as the first women's college in Delhi and also the first women's college of the University of Delhi, for two reasons: to understand the movement for women's empowerment in India, the resistance and obstacles that it encountered but surmounted; and the pioneering role of women in national politics. The few snippets that I illustrate connect the College to the nation and its politics in the mid-twentieth century.

I begin by capturing the sentiments and emotions of two distinguished alumnae—Qurratulain Hyder[2] and Sharan Rani Backliwal[3]—to exemplify the ways in which Indraprastha College inspired them and influenced them and how the students of those days perceived the College, while the nation was in the throes of the freedom struggle and immediately after it achieved independence. I quote an excerpt from the conversation that I had with Qurratulain Hyder, a student of the College from 1941–5, on the occasion of the Platinum Jubilee of the College in 1999:

Sufi ke adarsho per yakin rakhne wale jin buzoorgo ne ye idara qayam kiya tha, ye college un adarsho ka muhafiz aur ayanadar tha... Talibat Hindustan ke mukhtalif hisse se aye the aur har firqae se taluq rakhte the, yeh ek khushbash mushtarka khandan tha...

Those who believed in Sufi principles and ideals, such respectable men had established this institution, this college was the protector and mirror of these principles...The students came from different parts of Hindustan and were in contact with every group and section of the people...this college was a happy joint family. (Translation mine).

The *buzoorgo* or respectable men that Qurratulain Hyder referred to were the founders of the College—philanthropists and reformers—who stood firmly defiant and strong to empower women. Significantly all of them were in the service of the British Government, yet they had no hesitation in taking up cudgels to confront the government even if at the cost of government grants to the College.

Sharan Rani Backliwal, a student of the College during 1947–53, in an interview in 2005, on the occasion of the release of my co-authored book, reflected upon the values that the College upheld: 'IP always believed in high ideals and we were taught never to compromise on this score... Dedicated teachers were on hand to guide...but not curb our youthful spirits. And simplicity of dress coupled with a modern mental outlook were the mark of our traditions...'

Towards Women's Empowerment

Institutional education was a rarity for women in pre-colonial India and until the mid-nineteenth century, *zenana* education or domestic instruction was the accepted norm. Women, confined to their homes, were taught to read religious scriptures, read and write the vernacular language, though the focus remained on learning the home craft and subjects of domestic and practical utility.[4] These patterns transformed gradually from the mid-nineteenth century with the efforts of Christian missionaries—the pioneers in women's education. Even as the nineteenth century social reformers contemplated the necessity of educating women, they were countered by traditions that were against the introduction of 'bookish learning' for women. There was also the fear of proselytization and exposure of women to 'harmful western influences' if they were sent to Christian missionary schools. Paradigms changed yet again from the 1850s as Indians initiated the opening of schools for girls, warding off the apprehensions of conversion. Essays and articles were written during this period to emphasize that women's education was a part of Indian tradition, that it was encouraged in ancient times and that contrary to being harmful, it was beneficial for women to be educated and that education would situate women in the 'modern world of the nation'.[5]

In Delhi, different denominations of missionaries established schools to impart English learning to girls. The school that is now known as Gange High School for girls was established by the Baptists in 1875, followed by the foundation of Victoria Boarding School for Christian girls in 1876. But the upper and middle-class Hindu and Muslim families abstained from sending their daughters to these institutions for fear of proselytization and subversion of their values. To mobilize the support of conservative Indian families in such circumstances and at a crucial juncture when the Swadeshi movement engendered anti-imperialist struggles throughout India, the Indraprastha School, the root of Indraprastha College, was founded in Delhi in 1904. The immediate problem of the School was to find women teachers equipped to teach various subjects. The insistence on the caste and gender of the teachers in those days is notable, not only in Indraprastha School but in all schools for girls. The obsession of the girls' parents with the caste and gender of the teachers dwindled by 1924 as the school matured into an intermediate college. The emphasis shifted to imparting knowledge in the vernacular language rather than in English to provide easy access to learning and exposure to new and varied ideas and global influences. Also, by then, male teachers were hired, regardless of their religion: Prof. Rama Deva to teach Hindi, Sanskrit, and Philosophy, Pandit Nand Kishore for Music, and a Muslim male teacher, Rahman-ul-Nisa to teach embroidery and needlework. The College continued to function from the premises of Indraprastha School located in Chhipiwara (near Jama Masjid) till it started bursting out of its seams and was moved to Chandrawali Bhawan in Civil Lines in 1931. Around the same time, the founder Principal of the College, Leonara Gmeiner, took a radical decision on the removal of the tradition of *purdah* and the early marriage of girls. By the 1930s, out of over 600 girls (from age 5 to 24 years) registered in both Indraprastha School and Indraprastha College, there were only two or three girls who could not withstand family pressure and were forced into marriage.

The distinct identity of the College was firmly established by 1932 with the initiation of the process of introducing degree classes. Till 1932, in the absence of any such classes, girls keen on pursuing higher studies joined co-educational institutions, many a times in defiance of their families, who remained indifferent to the aspirations of their daughters. A distinguishing feature of the College that had evolved by 1934–5 was its diverse demography and popularity irrespective of caste or religion; while the College had admitted only 5 students in 1924, the numbers showed a substantial increase to 71 by 1934; of these 9 were Muslims and 2 were Christians. As the college grew, its student body became more and more cosmopolitan and so did its management and the faculty, manifesting its secular and pluralistic credentials. Recognized as a degree college in 1937 by the University of Delhi along with several other colleges including St. Stephen's, Hindu, Ramjas, Anglo-Arabic (now Zakir Hussain College) and

Commercial College (now Shriram College of Commerce), Indraprastha College was equipped to provide instruction up to BA (Pass) in Humanities and Languages. It was later in 1945 with the introduction of BA (Hons) and MA classes that the College reached its complete stature as a liberal arts college, broadened further with the launching of Computer Science, Multimedia and Mass Communication (the only College to teach the discipline at the undergraduate level), Geography and Sociology. By 1937, Chandrawali Bhawan could not cope with the expanding number of students, especially those from outside Delhi. The efforts to acquire a spacious accommodation initiated as early as 1925 succeeded in August 1938 and the new premises, then known as 'Alipore House' (where the College is still located) was inaugurated on 7 February 1939.

Dared to Resist: The 1930s

Born in the milieu of the anti-imperialist national struggle for freedom, Indraprastha College stimulated not only national zeal but also political and social sensitivity amongst its students. The students, mostly from conservative, urban middle class families, had no hesitation in breaking away from the traditional, customary practices and participating freely in the processions, marches and picketing organized during the national movement. The political activism of the students and their reproving responses to the politics of the British government took different forms in the course of the freedom struggle. One such manifestation was the boycott by the students of the visit of Vicereine Doreen Linlithgow to the College in 1937 at a time when the college authorities were engaged in a dialogue with the government for the acquisition of a spacious building for the College and government grants for the purchase of it. The students stood firm to oppose any symbol of British authority. Markedly, neither the college management nor the faculty reprimanded them.

Gandhi's impact on young Indraprastha students was conspicuous. Radical rendering of non-violent 'passive resistance' as *satyagraha* or 'truth-force', a term that Gandhi had adopted almost two years before he composed *Hind Swaraj,* was remarkably instrumental, evident from their reactions to the Congress session at Lahore in 1929 and the Second Civil Disobedience Movement in March 1930. Responding to the call of *Poorna Swaraj* by the Congress at the Lahore session, the students of the College took the pledge of *Azadi,* circulated the Independence Day manifesto and hoisted the tri-colour flag of freedom on 26 January 1930 and continued do so annually.[6] The participation of women in the Second Civil Disobedience Movement, sparked off by Gandhi's Dandi March, was phenomenal. They picketed liquor and foreign cloth shops, led the khadi campaign and participated in political demonstrations and mass agitations. Intensely influenced by Gandhi and determined to make the movement successful in the city of Delhi, Satyawati, granddaughter of Swami Shraddhanand, mobilized women, prodded them to be *sabala* (strong), come out of their homes and participate in the freedom struggle.[7] As Satyawati organized the women of Delhi to picket shops and exhorted the wealthy women who came to bathe in the Yamuna River to abandon the use of foreign clothes,[8] a large number of students of Indraprastha College joined her to achieve the goal. Reacting to the cry of boycott of foreign clothes, Chameli Devi, an Indraprastha student led her peers to participate in the *holi* (as it was known then) or burning of the *videshi* clothes in *kutcha* Ghasi Ram, a lane in the walled city of Delhi. The students followed up the act in the back verandah of Indraprastha School, where the College was located in those days. The students of the College carried on the picketing and marched in procession through the lanes and by-lanes of Delhi, singing patriotic songs, beating drums and raising slogans. Further, they joined the students of Ramjas and Hindu colleges to observe complete *hartal* and burn the *videshi* garments. Visibly affected by Gandhi, many Indraprastha students took to wearing khadi, learnt to weave on the *charkha,* and made their own saris from *sut* or cotton thread.[9] These activities of the students of the College enfolded the events throughout India; *prabhat pheris,* meetings and picketing became a regular pan-Indian feature.

As the College shifted to Chandrawali Bhawan in 1933–4, the Girls Guide Company known as Number 4 Delhi Company acquired a prominent hold in the College activities. Disguised as a soft skill to build the personality and confidence of the students, it was in reality an attempt to inspire awe and support for British imperialism and the British monarch.[10] Notwithstanding, the Girls Guide Company of the College spurned the government order and in defiance formed a group called *zinnia patrol* that refused to salute the Union Jack or shout slogans in support of the King, thereby upsetting the authorities of the Girls Guide Company. Leonara Gmeiner, the Principal of the College, compelled to intervene, encountered unyielding, adamant students, yet she took no action against them, being a rebel and a freedom fighter herself.[11]

The defiance of Indraprastha students was bolstered by the visits to the College of politically active women like Sarojini Naidu and Satyawati. Emboldened, they violated the regulations of the College, jumped the College walls and cut lectures to listen to the national leaders like Gandhi and Nehru whenever they were in the vicinity.[12] Inspired by Gandhi's message to fight the caste system, the students of the College, unmindful of social taboos, visited the Harijan *basti* in the neighbourhood of Chandrawali Bhawan, imparted lessons in health, hygiene and science and taught the children of the *basti* in the College premises during their free classes.[13]

In the mid-1930s, to promote the practice of *ahimsa,* as announced by Gandhi, the Congress proposed training in self-defense for girls that included lessons in the use of hands or fists and at the most use of lathi. For the period 1936–8, Sarla Sharma, an Indraprastha student, was nominated the commander of a group of girls in Delhi who had volunteered to join classes in self-defense. This phase coincided with Congress protests against the 1919 massacre at Jallianwala Bagh. Indraprastha girls dressed in white khadi formed a large section of the procession that moved across Chandni Chowk, shouting anti-British slogans and singing:

Nahi Rakhni Nahi Rakhni, Zalim Sarkar Nahi Rakhni
Jallianwala Bagh Me Jakar Nihatha Mari
Nahi Rakhni Nahi Rakhni...[14]

Do not want to keep, do not want to keep, the cruel government, do not want to keep
They killed the unarmed in Jallianwala Bagh
Do not want to keep, do not want to keep...

To defy British imperialism and be deeply immersed in the national movement, several students joined the All India Students Federation (AISF) formed in 1936. Set to create social awareness among Indian students, the AISF represented all shades of ideologies—Congress, Communist, Socialist—yet it remained a united body of students. Divergences, nevertheless, arose with the growing influence of M.N. Roy's communist ideas. Though communism then was not acceptable in India, there were many staunch Gandhian and Congress abiding students, not only from Indraprastha but different parts of India as well, who came under its sway. At a time when communist women were active in the national struggle and relief work during the Bengal famine, the AISF established Girls Students Committee as a separate organization to mobilize militant young women all over India.[15] In Delhi, even though the mobilization was not as strong, several students including some from Indraprastha joined the committee. When I interviewed Sarla Sharma, the memory of her comrades and their activities was so fresh in her mind that she rattled off a number of names of those who, along with her, were active AISF members and supported the communist ideology. Reflecting with pride upon their activities, she narrated how they moved around on bicycles from college to college to distribute communist party literature. Nostalgic with lasting zest on her face, she recounted her experience with Prof. V.K.R.V. Rao of Delhi School of Economics. Apparently, when she gave him the party literature, he threw it on the ground, rejecting it. Undismayed and disregarding that he was a professor of an eminent institution, she censured him for being a fascist, ordered him to pick up the literature from the ground, pay 4 *annas* (the cost of it), read it, and discuss it even if he disagreed with it. Exuding pride, she said that he did as she had ordered, resulting in their enduring friendship though they differed ideologically.[16]

Deepened Aggression: The 1940s

The Cripps Mission had failed in 1942, arousing aggressive passions and fervid determination among most Indians to purge British power and seize independence. The volatile sentiments were ignited even further with the passing of the Quit India Resolution by the All India Congress Committee on 8 August 1942, calling for the withdrawal of the British from India and the intensification of non-violent mass struggle under the leadership of Gandhi. Barely a day after the announcement of the Quit India Movement, the Congress leaders were arrested on 9 August 1942 leading to protests, strikes, demonstrations, clash with the police and mass arrests. In Delhi, the students and teachers of the University of Delhi led by Professor V.K.R.V. Rao took out a procession soon after Gandhi went on a fast after his arrest. The atmosphere in the University was tense for several days, classes were not held and police reprisal was overwhelming against those who were found to be politically active.[17] The situation hardly appeared to be a deterrent; the belligerence and activism of women remained exceptional. In addition to participating in strikes and demonstrations, some women helped to organize peasant movements and when the government used measures against them, they went underground to continue their activities.[18] Taking the lead, Aruna Asaf Ali inspired and mobilized people by her bulletins and magazine *Inquilab,* which she edited with Ram Manohar Lohia even when she went underground to evade government repression and arrest. Reminiscing about their daring and the impact that Ali had on Indraprastha students, Rup Seth, a student of the College from 1940 to 1944, described the enthusiasm of students who assisted Aruna Asaf Ali in pasting anti-British posters on the walls of Delhi. Arrested for anti-government activities, as was the norm those days, the girls did not succumb; instead, 'the daredevils of Indraprastha College hoisted the tricolor in the premises of the jail'. Several students of the College who participated in the Quit India Movement and demanded civil liberties for all Indians were imprisoned for three to four months or even more and rusticated on release. Unnerved, the students appealed to the Vice-Chancellor for the annulment of the rustication order, which, to the advantage of the students, he considered sympathetically.[19] To protest against the arrest of the national leaders and demand their release, almost 10,000 students from the University of Delhi led by Indraprastha alumna Sarla Sharma marched passively. Notwithstanding their non-violent behaviour, the police reacted with a lathi charge and tear gas. Narrating her experiences of 1942, exuding ethereal calm and confidence, Sarla Sharma observed that the students those days were not cowed down by the fear of arrests, their targets were all the symbols that represented British authority and the students volunteered to court arrest.[20]

The students' movement in Delhi was further consolidated when the AISF mobilized the University students and gave a call for anti-British protests. Indraprastha students, nonchalant towards any binding rules or regulations, jumped the walls of the College to join the boys of St. Stephen's and Hindu College to participate in a procession in support of the Quit India Movement. Nostalgically recalling the event of 10 August 1942, Ajit Bhattacharya, then a student of St. Stephen's College related how the students of Indraprastha College assembled outside the gates of St. Stephen's College and exhorted the boys to join the procession in support of the arrested Congress leaders. Convinced by the girls' arguments, about half the students of St. Stephen's joined the demonstration. As the procession marched down Alipur Road en route to Indraprastha College, the gates of the latter were locked to prevent the remaining girls from joining. Unrelenting and adamant, Indraprastha students jumped the walls, shouted slogans and joined the procession that continued into the lanes and by-lanes of the old city of Shahjahanabad.[21] Throughout 1942, the students of Indraprastha remained engaged in strategizing and organizing strikes and demonstrations—a recurrent pattern noticed throughout the country. The Students Union of the College did not host any academic or entertainment programs all through the year. The unyielding and determined behaviour of the students can be gauged from yet another event of 1942. A student team from Indraprastha College sent to participate in the Olympics (now known as National Games) of 1942 had emerged successful as the runners-up in the netball competition. But the excitement of being runners-up soon transformed into aggression when they heard of the Quit India Movement and the arrest of national leaders. Spurning the accolades, the students shouted anti-British slogans and rallied against the arrest of national leaders. Lady Linlithgow, the Vicereine, present at the function and offended by the students' conduct, complained to the Governing Body. The members of the

Governing Body, in a dilemma, especially because they owed the College building—Alipore House—to the efforts of the Vicereine, instructed the College Principal to take strict disciplinary action against the students. Dismissing these warnings as unwarranted, the students remained unruffled and unfazed in their commitment to the cause of the nation.

The political activism and active participation of the students in the Quit India Movement led the British government to identify Indraprastha College as the centre of brewing trouble and protest. Imposing coercive measures and pressure tactics on the College as it had done in other parts of India, the Superintendent of Education threatened to withhold the government grant to the College and complained to the Governing Body about the 'indifferent discipline' in the College, referring ostensibly to the agitation of the students and their conviction and arrest in this regard.[22] Recognizing the importance of the government grant to the College, the Governing Body responded by advising the Principal to prepare an exhaustive report on the alleged misdemeanor of students. The Principal too understood the financial exigencies faced by the College, yet she pleaded on behalf of the students, arguing that their activities were impulsive and spontaneous and stood steadfast on not divulging the names of the students, thus extricating them from being victimized.[23] It is pertinent to note that notwithstanding the government threats, the Principal, Kalavati Gupta was relentless in her commitment to the national struggle and extended tacit and discreet support to the students.

Invigorated by the empathy and implicit consent of the principal, the students continued to participate in political deliberations and planning throughout 1942. The government, alerted by the nationalist activities in the College, persisted with its oppressive measures and threatened both Indraprastha and Ramjas College that unless order was restored in their respective colleges and the students resumed classes, the recurring maintenance grants provided by the Central Revenue Department would be cancelled for the financial year 1942–3.[24] Persistent in its persecutory and tyrannical policies towards the politically active students of the University of Delhi, the British government in September 1942 rescinded the wheat permit of the hostels of the three colleges—Indraprastha, Hindu and Commercial College (now Shri Ram College of Commerce)—without assigning any reasons for the order. It is worth noting that while there were more than a dozen hostels in the other colleges of the University, the wheat permit was cancelled for the hostels of only three colleges. With no rationale behind the order, it caused much resentment and widespread coverage in the media that termed it as a political move, a 'sort of omnibus vendetta for any sins of omission or commission' that the controller of wheat thought the students of these colleges may have committed individually or collectively.[25] The cut in the food supply to these hostels, however, continued till 1945. It appears that the cancellation of the wheat permit to Indraprastha College was caused by the participation of its students in the '*rakhi* expedition' or sending *rakhi* to their Muslim brethren to emphasize Hindu-Muslim amity and communal harmony.[26] This student action, as on several other occasions, did not meet the approval of the British government, which it saw as an attempt to fuel political unrest, especially since the government policies by 1942 had widened the gap between the two communities. Irrespective of the government order on the wheat cut, the emotional temper of the girls was hardly compromised, evident from the way the Students Union organized the Annual Day of the College in 1943. The Union, unperturbed by the rationing order that threatened to disrupt the co-curricular activities on the day, collected student contributions and successfully hosted the tea party as per the traditions of the College.

Even as the government stood challenged by student aggression and defiance, it exercised greater arbitrariness and oppression on the College, leaving the Governing Body with no alternative but to instruct the principal to restore order and dissuade the students from engaging in political bellicosity. Since 10 August 1942, in support of the Quit India Movement and to protest against the arrest of the national leaders, the students had cut classes even though they came to College, observed *hartal*, organized meetings in the campus, made fiery speeches, mobilized students for political activities and picketed classes against such students who attended them. Neither the principal nor the teachers could control the militant student activities. As a last resort, the principal felt compelled to write a letter of complaint to the parents of the students in September 1942, urging them to convince their daughters to either attend classes or withdraw from the College. The repeated letters of complaint written by the principal failed to have any impact on the parents or the students. The principal, of course, remained committed to not invoking the help of any 'outside body or to take any unpleasant step'.[27]

The events of 1942 had engendered dynamism, activism, and aggression in almost all students of Indraprastha College. Shanta Vashisht, an IP graduate of 1944 and a former practicing civil lawyer in Delhi, observed in an interview that in 1942 in an atmosphere surcharged with patriotism, both the teachers and the students were aroused by national fervour. Such was the extent of their involvement that when the political prisoners at Deoli camp went on hunger strike, the hostel kitchen remained closed, with the whole College observing a one-day hunger strike in support. The students missed no opportunity to organize endless political meetings, shout slogans, sing patriotic songs, and defy the British orders and ordinances. Narrating her experiences, yet another former student of the College, Protima Mukerji, commented that the Quit India Movement had transformed the students into 'miniature politicians, orating on the College platform and passing resolutions in support of the movement'. Nilima Chakravarty and Nirmala Prakash, both former students as well as faculty members, nostalgically remembered the student agitation of the 'stormy August days of 1942' and student defiance to the appeals of the then principal, K. Ranga Rao, who feared that any political activity on the College campus might incite the government to impose prohibitory orders on the College and withdraw its grant. Nirmala Prakash recalled that rejecting the pleas of the principal, she mobilized the students of the College and lectured to them for hours in the College lawns, urging them to join the demonstrations and strikes against the British government. In the same spirit, the students initiated the idea of opening a *charkha* association in the College under the aegis of the Social Service League of the Students Union. By 1944 *charkha* classes were consolidated and several *charkhas* were acquired.[28]

No appeals, persuasions or coaxing appeared to convince the students or undermine their rebellious, refractory spirit against symbols and representations of British power. Sceptical of the congenial attitude and reformist agenda of the British Vice-Chancellor, Sir Maurice Gwyer, Indraprastha students along with other students of the University of Delhi organized demonstrations and marches and sought his removal. The government reaction was as prevalent in other parts of India: police repression, teargas, and use of bullets. Three students of the University were also suspended for their radical activism, provoking the students yet again, who organized *hartals* and courted arrest and demanded the repeal of suspension orders.[29]

The political activism and unrestrained public participation of the students of the University of Delhi was once again noteworthy in 1945, the year of the INA trials, and the release of the national leaders arrested in 1942 during the Quit India Movement. Mobilizing the students and urging them to organize demonstrations to demand the release of INA soldiers, Sameeruddin Khan, a student of St. Stephen's College (1945–7), provoked the students to boycott classes, coordinated a protest march and pulled down the Union Jack from the flagstaff.[30] Instigated, students of Indraprastha College led marches, singing the popular INA song *Kadam Kadam Badhaya Ja.* The government, caught in the intense political movement, was compelled to release the INA soldiers, evoking unprecedented public euphoria throughout the nation.

The events of 1942 and 1945 had galvanized the nation into an even greater determination to drive out the British. Among the different strategies to express angst against the government, the IPTA's (Indian Peoples Theatre Association) plan was significantly atypical during the years 1943–7. Ostensibly critical of the British government, IPTA, a voluntary body with no financial resources, performed shadow plays and pantomimes. Since these plays were aimed at the government, the latter made every attempt to isolate them from the public and deny them publicity by disallowing the use of posters and microphones. Several students of Indraprastha College, particularly those who were members of the AISF, had joined IPTA. They accepted the challenge, mobilized the students through the Cultural Secretary of the Students Union of different colleges and motivated the students into watching IPTA plays and participate in IPTA ventures. To reach out to the larger public, they used newspapers to make posters and pasted them on the roads so that as people traversed these paths, they would read them and attend the IPTA activities.[31]

Reflecting on the experiences, reactions, and responses of women students of Indraprastha College for Women and of University of Delhi in general, let me describe how women power and resistance against the British government mounted from early 1946, more specifically from March 1946 when the British government sent the Cabinet Mission to India to negotiate the terms for the transfer of power. Pandit Jawaharlal Nehru formed an interim cabinet in October 1946 comprising members from both the Congress and the Muslim League. Even so, the jubilation at the thought of imminent independence was tarnished by communal riots that shook the nation from August 1946. While Gandhi toured East Bengal and Bihar to halt the riots and appeal for peace, and several Hindus and Muslims laid down their lives to wipe out communal hatred, women of all castes, class, party, and religion foregrounded the belief in 'universal womanhood' and struggle against communalism and partition.[32] Women from the AISF including a few from Indraprastha College were detained without trial for their anti-government activities and kept with the criminals. Sarla Sharma was one of the twenty-four women held in custody without trial in Delhi jail. Drawn into her past, as if living it again, she recounted that the students then had no regrets about the treatment meted to them in the prisons, they only felt elated and proud at the 'unified determination' of the Indians to fight for the nation's independence.[33]

Joining the nation-wide movement for communal amity, the Students Union of Indraprastha College engaged in various activities throughout 1946–7. The Entertainment Society of the Union celebrated the festivals of Diwali and Eid with equal ardour and passion; the Social Service League, on the other hand, took up the task of teaching the two languages, Hindi and Urdu, emphasizing the value and importance of both, to the children in the vicinity of the College; and the annual college magazine *Pradeep*, in 1946, carried articles by the students of the College urging for calm and tranquility and abandonment of communal carnage. The faculty of the College was not only supportive of student activism but also joined the demonstrations and processions against communal hatred and killings. Germane to the issue were the constraints that the teachers faced in those days. At the time of their appointment, they had to affirm that they would stay away from any national political activity. Nonetheless, they could rarely abstain, evident from the example of Nirmala Sherjung, a lecturer in the College. The principal's patronage further fortified them. Sherjung, a fighter and a revolutionary, observed that regardless of the assurances that she gave to the College, she participated in the demonstrations and processions in 1946–7. In one such procession, she was in the front row carrying a *mashal.* As the procession passed through the University, she was noticed by someone, who complained to the College authorities. When questioned by the principal, Sherjung, ostensibly keen to retain her job, denied having participated in the march. Considering that violation of the College code was unpardonable, the College management undertook the responsibility of investigation. One of the members of the management committee alleged that the complainant was a 'respectable' person, and his statement therefore ought to be deemed to be correct. The rejoinder of the principal in this regard was significant. Undaunted and firm, the principal rejected the contention saying that whatever be the status of the complainant, it was Sherjung's testimony that was of importance.[34]

Processions, demonstrations, appeals for communal harmony on the one hand and atrocious communal holocaust on the other characterized the years 1946–7. India was to be free but not united. The grief and pain of the killings and partition undermined the joy and ecstasy. The character of the city of Delhi changed with the huge influx of refugees. As refugee camps came up in different parts of the city, it had repercussions on the University as well. Even as the students of the University were taken to the Constituent Assembly for Independence Day celebrations, Indraprastha students organized separate festivities, illuminated the College building like all other public and official buildings and made financial contributions to the government fund towards the welfare of the refugees. The Social Service League of the College Students Union organized stitching and knitting of garments for the refugees, the raw material for which was provided by both the students and the teachers. To facilitate food supplies to the refugee camps, the League grew vegetables on a plot of land allotted by the principal within the College campus. In addition, to help the refugee students with books and other miscellaneous items, the Students Union arranged what they called the 'Poor Fund' and held a 'Fancy Fair', the proceeds of which were sent to the Prime Minister's Relief Fund for the benefit and betterment of the refugees. Co-curricular and academic activities like inter-college debates to promote harmony and peace and inculcate goodwill and comradeship among students of different institutions of the University and the city of Delhi at large were coordinated by the Debating and Literary Society of the College Union.

Partition affected the lives of millions; and women were the worst sufferers. The year 1947 was a haunting 'gendered narrative of displacement and dispossession...of the realignment of family, community and national identities' in which the people were compelled to accommodate to the 'dramatically altered reality that prevailed'.[35] The trauma of Partition and communalism that engulfed the city of Delhi did not spare the University and its students either. The students of the University of Delhi as of Indraprastha College responded with equanimity and sensitivity and continued to be active in public rallies and protests. Indraprastha students organized a procession from the College to Gandhi Maidan to Ramlila Grounds and another march to Azad Park in support of Gandhi when he went on fast to reinstate concord and peace. For her active involvement, Sarla Sharma was arrested yet again and kept in Delhi prison with criminals for five weeks in October 1947. The coercion and denial of fundamental rights by the independent Government of India appear inexplicable. Perhaps, it was a tactic to assert their power and counter the mad assassins!

As we understand and profile the sentiments of the youth and their political activism in the 1930–1940s, it appears appropriate not only in recalling those times but also the present, to quote Phyllis Wheatley, an African American poet:[36] 'In every human breast God has implanted a principle, which we call love of freedom; it is impatient of oppression, and pants for deliverance. The same principle lives in us...'

Notes

1. This chapter draws extensively from my book, co-authored with Kalyani Dutta, *Women, Education, and Politics: The Women's Movement and Delhi's Indraprastha College*, New Delhi: Oxford University Press, 2005; 2nd edn., 2015, published articles in journals and talks and seminars that I gave in different places. Also, the chapter owes a tremendous intellectual debt to the interview with Sarla Sharma, student of Indraprastha College, 1936–40. She was the granddaughter of one of the founder members of the College, Lala Jugal Kishore. A political activist and a Communist Party worker since the 1940s, she had several stints as Municipal Corporator of Delhi.
2. A celebrated Urdu novelist, short story writer and an academic who won many awards including Padma Bhushan (2005), Jnanpith Award (1989), Ghalib Award (1985), Soviet Land Nehru Award (1969) and Sahitya Akademi Award and Fellowship (1967 and 1994 respectively).
3. She was the first Indian woman instrumentalist and sarod maestro. A recipient of Padma Bhushan (2000), Padma Shri (1968), Sangeet Natak Akademi Award (1986), Sahitya Kala Parishad Award (1974) and several others, she was the only

woman instrumentalist to receive the title of 'National Artiste' from the Government of India in 2004.

4. Shaista Suhrawardy Ikramullah, *From Purdah to Parliament*, New Delhi: Oxford University Press, 2000, p. 27.
5. Partha Chatterjee, 'The Nation and its Women', in *A Subaltern Studies Reader, 1986–1995*, ed. Ranajit Guha, New Delhi: Oxford University Press, 1998, pp. 249, 253.
6. Interview with Sarla Sharma, 21–2 May 2010.
7. Sunaina Sharma and Madhu Kishwar, 'Toofani Satyawati: An Unsung Hero of Freedom Struggle', *Manushi*, no. 107, July–August 1998, p. 25.
8. Aparna Basu, 'The Role of Women in the Indian Struggle for Freedom', in *Indian Women: From Purdah to Modernity*, ed. B.R. Nanda, New Delhi: Vikas Publishing House, 1999, p. 27.
9. Interview with Sarla Sharma, 21–2 May 2010.
10. 'Delhi Girls' Education: Record of Progress of Indraprastha Girls' School', *The National Call*, 16 April 1934, Private Collections of Shri Narain Prasad, Chairman, Governing Body of Indraprastha College for Women (henceforth Private Collections of Shri Narain Prasad).
11. Interview with Sarla Sharma, 21–2 May 2010.
12. Interview with Prem Mukhi Saxena, a student of the College in 1935–9, 19 April 1999. She joined the College as a lecturer in the Department of History in 1942 and continued to serve till her retirement in 1986.
13. Sarla Sharma, 'Rashtriya Andolan Mein Indraprastha', in *The Golden Oriole, 1924–74*, Special Issue of the College Magazine to celebrate the Golden Jubilee of the College; also, Correspondence with Shanti Nigam, a student of Indraprastha School from 1929 and then of Indraprastha College during 1934–8.
14. Sarla Sharma, 'Sangeet Roopak, 1929–47', unpublished.
15. Kumari Jayawardene, *Feminism and Nationalism in the Third World*, New Delhi: Kali for Women, 1986, p. 106.
16. Interview with Sarla Sharma, 21–2 May 2010.
17. Aditya Bhattacharya, 'From an Ivory Tower', *The Stephanian*, vol. LXXXVIII, no. 1, Winter 1978–9, pp. 19–20.

18. Geraldine Forbes, *Women in Modern India*, The New Cambridge History of India, vol. IV, part 2, Cambridge: Cambridge University Press, 1996, p. 204.
19. Reminiscences of Alumnae—Rup Seth (1940–4), Pushpa Murgai (1942–5), and Vijaya Mehrotra (1941–7).
20. Interview with Sarla Sharma, 21–2 May 2010.
21. Bhattacharya, 'From an Ivory Tower', pp. 19–20.
22. From the Superintendent of Education to the Chairman of the Governing Body of Indraprastha College, Letter No. 7335, 10 December 1942, in Minutes of the Governing Body, 22 December 1942, Private Collections of Shri Narain Prasad.
23. Nirmala Sherjung, 'Sharing Some Experiences', a talk given on the occasion of Indraprastha College Alumnae Function, 10 February 1998.
24. From J.C. Chatterjee, Education Department to the Secretary, Ramjas College (undated), Principal's File—Miss Kalavati Gupta, 24 March 1939 to 3 March 1943, Private Collections of Shri Narain Prasad.
25. 'Preposterous: The "No Wheat Order"', *The National Call*, 3 September 1942, Private Collections of Shri Narain Prasad.
26. Ibid.
27. Letter of Kalavati Gupta, Principal, Indraprastha College for Women to the Parents/Guardians of Students, 7 September 1942, Private Collections of Shri Narain Prasad.
28. Interview with Shanta Vashisht in Nirmala Malhotra, 'Indraprastha College Fifty Years of Women's Education', *Femina*, 10 May 1974; Sucharita Sengupta, 'Down the Memory Lane', in *The Golden Oriole, 1924–74*; Protima Mukerji, 'Looking Back', Nilima Chakravarty, 'My Views regarding the College', and Nirmala Prakash, 'Recalling the Past', in *Pradeep 1950*, Special Issue of the College Magazine on the occasion of its Silver Jubilee.
29. Sharma, 'Rashtriya Andolan Mein Indraprastha'.
30. Bhattacharya, 'From an Ivory Tower', pp. 19–20.
31. Interview with Sarla Sharma, 21–2 May 2010. An AISF member and an IPTA activist, she was responsible for publicity in Chandni Chowk area, where she lived. She organized

newspaper posters and pasted them on the way to the Yamuna River so that as people crossed these roads for their morning bath, they would read the posters and attend IPTA functions.

32. Geraldine Forbes, *Women in Modern India*, pp. 221–2.
33. Interview with Sarla Sharma, 21–2 May 2010.
34. Sherjung, 'Sharing Some Experiences'.
35. Ritu Menon and Kamla Bhasin, 'Recovery, Rupture, Resistance: Indian State and Abduction of Women during Partition', *Economic and Political Weekly*, vol. 28, no. 17, April 1993, p. WS2.
36. Wheatley wrote poems combining piety with a concern for her people. Writing to the Mohegan Native American minister, Samson Occom in 1774, she penned a line that not only applied to African Americans but to all Americans struggling to be free.

19

Nizamuddin, History and Conservation

RATISH NANDA

IN 1990, I secured admission to study Architecture at the TVB School of Habitat Studies, ranked at the very bottom!

Being an innovative, progressive, and plain different architectural school, we had an 'Urban History' course in the first year taught by Dr Narayani Gupta. An assignment in the course encouraged us all to explore the history of our neighbourhood—and for me residing in the vicinity of Kotla neighbourhood, a supposedly quick assignment turned out to be something I obsessed over for the whole semester. Discovering fourteenth-century monuments and spending endless hours exploring, albeit failing the semester, gave my life a new direction. The rest as they say is history!

The brilliant teaching of a first semester subject coupled with over thirty years of hand holding turned me towards a path which I otherwise would not have taken.

It is thus both a great honour for me as well as an overwhelming challenge to write this essay.

700 Years of Heritage

The Nizamuddin area, comprising the Hazrat Nizamuddin Basti, Humayun's Tomb complex, Sunder Nursery,

Batashewala complex, and residential areas of Nizamuddin East and West is today recognized as one of the densest ensembles of medieval Islamic buildings anywhere in the world. Almost every dynasty to have ruled Delhi has left their mark here; the Il Bari Turks also known as the Slave dynasty, the Khaljis, the Tughlaqs, Lodhis, the Surs, and of course the Mughals built some of the finest buildings of their reign in this small geographical area that stood along the river Yamuna, until it receded eastwards in the nineteenth century.

It was Ghiyas ud din Balban who, as a prince, built his palace here in the mid-thirteenth century, before he ascended the throne in AD 1265, giving the area the name of Ghiyaspur. Lal Mahal, as his palace came to be known, was a fine building on a cruciform plan; a central dome and its remains are today the earliest surviving Islamic palace building in all of India. Lal Mahal seems to have seen the earliest recorded use of the dome and true arch in India. The principal building of the Lal Mahal today serves as a residence with the outer buildings demolished in 2008–9 to make way for a mosque extension by the Tablighi Jamaat.

The significance of the area today comes from Hazrat Nizamuddin Auliya, the revered fourteenth-century Sufi saint choosing to establish his khanqah in Ghiyaspur in an area marked by the confluence of the river Yamuna with its tributaries. The saint chose a spot along the river Yamuna to meditate and a *chillgah* was built for this purpose. It was abutting this structure that, two centuries later, Humayun's Mausoleum, the first of the grand dynastic mausolea of the Mughal dynasty was built.

The grand 'Jamaat Khana' mosque built here during Alauddin Khalji's reign (AD 1295–1315), remains, to date, one of the grandest structures in the complex. It was said to have been built to serve as the dargah or mausoleum of the saint. The construction of the baoli in AD 1320, would signify the presence of a significant population in Ghiyaspur or even a large volume of pilgrims visiting here to seek the blessings of Hazrat Nizamuddin Auliya. The Baoli would have served not only the drinking water needs of the local community and pilgrims but also would have been used for *wuzu* or ablutions prior to prayers at the mosque.

On his death, the saint was buried in the courtyard of the Jamaat Khana mosque, and the Ghiyaspur area began to be known after him as 'Nizamuddin'. For almost 700 years, pilgrims have been visiting the shrine of the saint and since it is considered auspicious to be buried near a saint's grave, five centuries of monumental tomb building can now be seen here—stretching to Nila Gumbad to the east, Golf Club monuments to the north, and the Sunder Nursery monuments to the north-east.

Within six months of the death of the saint, his favourite disciple, the great poet, Amir Khusrau too died, unable to bear the grief of the loss of his spiritual master. Hazrat Amir Khusrau (AD 1253–1325) is still remembered as a revered figure in the Indo-Persian cultural landscape of the South Asian subcontinent for over 700 years. In keeping with Sufi pluralistic traditions, he was without doubt, the most popular proponent of what has come to be called Hindustani culture, a fine synthesis of Hindu and Muslim elements into a syncretic whole. He was a devout follower of the Chishtiya order while being associated with the courts of at least seven sultans of Delhi, straddling the spiritual and mundane worlds with ease. Khusrau's grave received attention from each of the first four Mughal emperors—Babur gifted a marble headstone, Humayun added the red sandstone lattice enclosure (both inscribed with poetry in honour of Khusrau), Akbar is said to have built a domed mausoleum which Jahangir later replaced with a spectacular vaulted mausoleum.

It was Muhammad bin Tughlaq, a disciple of Hazrat Nizamuddin Auliya, who is said to have created a network of irrigation canals, now referred to as nallahs; the Barahpullah nallah marks the western and southern edge of the Nizamuddin area and this stretch has so far escaped being covered but now it houses an elevated road, built for the Commonwealth Games in 2010.

Two major buildings were built here during the Tughlaq era, the Kalan Masjid in AD 1370–1 and the tomb of Khan Jahan Junan Shah Tilangani, the prime minister of Firoz Shah Tughlaq. The mosque and tomb stand on the southern edge of Hazrat Nizamuddin Basti and originally stood within an enclosure of which only a few traces now remain. The tomb is understood to be the earliest octagonal tomb in India and the central chamber has now been conserved; efforts continue to rescue the seven verandahs of the mausoleum from occupation.

Structures were built surrounding the baoli of Hazrat Nizamuddin Auliya up till late Mughal times, with the southern arcade dating from AD 1379–80. Following the partial collapse of the baoli in 2008, a major conservation initiative was undertaken over a decade wherein eighteen families living atop the southern arcade have been provided alternate housing by the Aga Khan Trust for Culture. Until the collapse of the baoli, the Aga Khan Trust for Culture initiatives in the basti had been focused on socio-economic development projects—building education, sanitation and health infrastructure—amongst other similar activities. Conservation of the collapsed baoli, recognized by UNESCO with an Award of Excellence in 2021, also required building alternate houses for eighteen families.

The spate of tomb building in the area continued through the Lodhi period and even though some of the significant royal tombs of the Lodhi dynasty were built almost a mile west of the Dargah of Hazrat Nizmauddin Auliya, structures now known as Barahkhambha, Gol Gumbad, and Do Sirihya Gumbad were built within Hazrat Nizamuddin Basti.

It was with the coming of the Mughals that the Nizamuddin area was dotted with garden tombs; in fact this was the earliest Mughal era settlement in Delhi with Humayun's Purana Qila just north of here. The blue domed Nila Gumbad is without doubt the earliest building of the Mughal era to have been built in Delhi. Located a few yards south of Hazrat Nizamuddin's Chillgah, on a river island, the dome, tilework, and plasterwork are all reminiscent of Persian influence.

Sabz Burj, boasting of a gold and lapis painted ceiling and intricate decorative elements, is likely to have been built in AD 1530 by Humayun as a mausoleum for his mother.

Emperor Humayun chose to build his capital city, which he named, Dinpanah or 'refuge of the faithful' north of Hazrat Nizamuddin's Dargah. The city walls were only half built when Humayun was ousted by Sher Shah Sur who continued to build the fortifications and the citadel, now known as Purana Qila or Old Fort.

Dating from AD 1541 is the tomb of Bai Kokaldai, standing on the western edge of Hazrat Nizamuddin Baoli and presently partially used as a residence.

The sixteenth century Grand Trunk Road stretching from the eastern end of India to Peshawar and beyond in the west, passed through the Nizamuddin area, skirting the Lakkarwala Burj. With the river along the eastern edge and the GT Road passing through it Nizamuddin was located on major medieval transport arteries, allowing easy movement of people and building material. This stretch of the GT Road would have followed almost the same layout of the present Mathura Road with deviations introduced only during the building of British New Delhi.

Isa Khan Niyazi, a noble of influence at the court of Sher Shah Sur, was buried here in an octagonal garden enclosure in AD 1547–8. Isa Khan Niyazi's tomb enclosure was thus the culmination of the octagonal style of tomb building that commenced with the nearby tomb of Khan

Jahan Junan Shah Tilangani, 180 years earlier. Isa Khan's tomb enclosure more closely resembled the early fifteenth century tomb of Mubarak Shah Sayyid, in Kotla Mubarakpur, but is significantly more ornamental with the use of dressed sandstone for the façade of the mosque, elaborate finials, large scale use of ceramic tiles on the façade of the tomb, mosque and on the canopies and the highly ornamental plasterwork. It also pre-dates the Mughal era garden tombs including that of Emperor Humayun.

Conservation and landscape work at Isa Khan's tomb enclosure by the Aga Khan Trust for Culture, have revealed that the outer garden was treated as a sunken garden and over 4 ft. of earth is presently being removed to restore the original relationship of the tomb to its immediate setting. This would have been the earliest sunken garden in India, pre-dating Emperor Akbar's tomb in Sikandra, Agra—the most famous existent example—by over a century.

A small tomb, locally known as the Barber's Tomb, standing within the walled enclosure of Humayun's Mausoleum, is commonly believed to have been built following the latter, but as with the adjoining Nila Gumbad would pre-date Humayun's Mausoleum. It is well known that Humayun's Tomb was a place of pilgrimage for the royal Mughal family and it can be said with conviction that following the building of Humayun's Mausoleum other minor structures such as the Barber's Tomb would not be permitted to be built within the walled garden enclosure. The Barber's Tomb, despite lacking refined architectural details, demonstrates a shift in style from Persian influences such as in Nila Gumbad to assimilating local architectural traditions such as using the red-white contrast with sandstone and marble, seen earlier in Delhi at Alai Darwaza and Ghiyasuddin Tughlaq's tomb.

Humayun's Mausoleum was built between the river Yamuna on its east and the Grand Trunk Road to its west. Built in the 1560s under the patronage of his son Emperor

Akbar, the tomb of Humayun located in Delhi and standing within a walled garden enclosure of 26 acres, is the first of the grand dynastic mausoleums that were to become synonymous with the Mughal architectural style that reached its zenith a hundred years later with the construction of another Mughal tomb– the Taj Mahal. Humayun's garden-tomb is also called the 'dormitory of the Mughals' as in the cells are buried over 160 members of the Mughal family, all in uninscribed graves.

Humayun's Mausoleum dwarfs any tomb built in Delhi during the three centuries of Muslim rule that preceded the Mughals; Isa Khan's tomb, built only two decades before Humayun's tomb is minuscule in proportion. In fact, never before in the Islamic world had a mausoleum been built on such a scale. With red sandstone and white marble brought in from the Agra region in vast quantities, the 'architect', Mirak Mirza Ghiyath of Persian descent, who was invited by Akbar from Herat (present-day Afghanistan) created a striking red-white contrast by applying white 'marble-like' lime plaster on the parts of the façade not covered with stone, such as the domes of the four corner canopies and the faces of the lower niches.

The Holy Koran repeatedly promises the faithful, 'gardens below which rivers flow' as their final resting space and Humayun's Mausoleum was set amidst an enclosed garden inspired by the description of paradise. This was amongst the first gardens built on the plains of Hindustan and remains one of the earliest surviving char-baghs. Unfortunately, neglect in the eighteenth century and significant alterations through the nineteenth and twentieth centuries have disfigured the original Mughal intention.

In 1997, on the occasion of the fiftieth anniversary of India's independence, His Highness the Aga Khan gifted the restoration of the Humayun's Tomb Garden. As part of the garden restoration, craftsmen worked tirelessly to manually remove 3,000 truckloads of earth to restore the original levels and the garden-pathway relationship. Stone craftsmen, using traditional tools, hand chiselled 3000 m. of sandstone to edge the water channels and 3500 m. of pathway edging stone were manually lifted and reset, with most stones weighing over 1000 kg. The garden restoration culminated with the restoration of flowing water in the channels rebuilt to a 1:4000 slope, and the creation of a large rainwater harvesting system that was coupled with desilting of Mughal wells and the planting of 2,500 trees and plants favoured by the Mughals including mango, lemon, neem, hibiscus, and pomegranate.

Humayun's Mausoleum remained a place of pilgrimage for the Mughal emperors Akbar, Jahangir, and Shahjahan who made frequent visits to pay their respects. In fact, Humayun's Mausoleum continued to be used for burial well up to the mid-nineteenth century and the later Mughal emperors[1] like Muhammad Azam Shah, Jahandar Shah, Farrukhsiyar, Rafiuddaulah Rafiddarajat, Ahmad Shah, and Alamgir II are said to lie buried here.

While Humayun's Mausoleum was being built, just outside the western enclosure wall, two significant buildings—a tomb and mosque—known as Afsarwala Tomb and Mosque were also being constructed. It is not known who commissioned these or if they stood in an independent enclosure. Based on archaeological evidence, 'Arab Serai' dates later than Humayun's Mausoleum. A few hundred yards north of the Arab Serai was another Mughal Serai, known as Azimganj. Though today it is in a ruinous condition, nevertheless it is a significant Mughal era structure. It is quite possible that Azimganj Serai pre-dates Arab Serai and as such would be one of the earliest Mughal era structures in Delhi.

Following the building of Humayun's Tomb several prominent structures, mostly tombs, were built in the Nizamuddin area, especially during Akbar's reign. Atgah Khan, 'who was present when Humayun was defeated by Sher Shah Sur and aided the emperor in his escape from the field of battle'[2] was buried in AD 1566–7, in close proximity to the dargah of Hazrat Nizamuddin Auliya. His jewel-like tomb is covered with a unique inlay of tilework in marble but is rarely visited as the enclosure within which it stood has been encroached upon. Though protected by the Archaeological Survey of India (ASI), the crypt of Atgah Khan's Tomb is occupied by families, who, in order to create more 'living space amongst the dead' have clawed away at the foundations, putting both building and life in danger.

Atgah Khan's wife was the wet nurse of Emperor Akbar and Atgah Khan had risen to become the emperor's Vakil or Chancellor of the empire. His son, Mirza Aziz Kokaltash, foster brother of Emperor Akbar, was buried in AD 1623–4, in a unique marble tomb, in close proximity to his father's tomb, now known as Chausath Khambha on account of the sixty-four marble pillars supporting the twenty-five domed bays. The architectural style of the Chausath Khambha was no doubt inspired by the colonnaded halls of Persia such as the *Chihil Sutun* and in turn inspired the halls of public audience of the Mughal emperors such as the Diwan-i-aam in the Delhi Red Fort.

Another foster brother of Emperor Akbar, Zain Khan Koka, built his palace, Khas Mahal, in AD 1642–3. The structure would have been significant had it survived as a palace building in the greater Nizamuddin area, but was demolished in the twentieth century to build the residential neighbourhood of Sundar Nagar.

Other important sixteenth or early seventeenth century structures include the enclosed garden tombs of Bu Halima, the 'Batashewala' Complex, and the 'Sunderwala' complex.

The tomb of Muzaffar Husain Mirza, grandnephew of Emperor Humayun was built in AD 1603 and is today known as Bara Batashewala Mahal. The adjoining 'Sunderwala Mahal' is the only other example of the *hasht-bihisht* plan—a central tomb chamber surrounded by eight rooms. Another tomb, now known as Chotta Batashewala stands alongside Muzaffar Husain Mirza's tomb. At the turn of the twentieth century, the walled enclosure that housed these two tombs was given to Bharat Scouts and Guides. Their neglect, misuse, and vandalism led to the almost total destruction of Chotta Batashewala and the nearly complete demolition of the arcaded enclosure walls of the garden-tomb. Recent demolition of illegal structures built by the Bharat Scouts and Guides, who built dozens of buildings in the area used for a range of inappropriate activities including a commercial club, revealed an entire stretch of the Mughal era enclosure wall that had literally been built upon and has now been reconstructed.

The 'Sunderwala complex', another tomb-garden enclosure, includes the two tombs now known as Sunderwala Burj and Sunderwala Mahal and though it is today unknown who these were built for, the architectural style and the ornamentation within them allows us to date these to the sixteenth or seventeenth century, i.e. the early Mughal era. The two tombs 'originally stood within an enclosure 74 ft. x 610 ft. and entered through a lofty gateway.'[3] When Maulvi Zafar Hasan inspected the building in the 1920s he stated that 'the enclosure walls have disappeared but the gateway still stands'[4]—no trace of the gateway now remains.

It is not known who 'Bu Halima' was, but her tomb is entered through a lofty gateway standing opposite the western gateway of the Humayun's Tomb complex, off-centre to her own tomb, suggesting it dates immediately after the building of Humayun's Tomb. The southern end of the western wall of Bu Halima's garden enclosure culminated in the Isa Khan's Tomb enclosure until the 1920s when the British demolished a stretch of this wall to build an oval shaped 'carriageway' to access Humayun's Tomb, thereby destroying the original layout and character of this important Mughal enclosure. Excavations revealed foundations of the enclosure wall and allowed its reconstruction.

On the Tughlaq era canal which marked the western and southern edge of the Nizamuddin area was built the Barahpullah bridge, in the years 1611–12, indicating the high volume of travellers from or to the south, where the capital city of Agra was located.

Over half a century after the building of Humayun's Tomb, Khan-i-Khanan Abdur Rahim Khan, the Commander-in-Chief of Emperor Akbar, built a grand mausoleum for his wife, Mah Banu. Similar in design and scale to Humayun's Tomb, Khan-i-Khanan's tomb could have originally been sited in a walled garden of which no trace now remains. The marble cladding of the dome was removed in the mid-eighteenth century for use at Safdarjung's Tomb. The conservation of the ruinous mausoleum by the Aga Khan Trust for Culture with the support of the InterGlobe Foundation was coupled with celebrating the intangible heritage of *dohe* written by Rahim with publications, festivals, exhibitions and seminars.

Through the eighteenth and nineteenth centuries tomb building continued in the vicinity of the dargah, including a dozen mausolea built within the present-day Delhi Golf Club. Aga Khan Trust for Culture is now embarking on the conservation of these structures.

It is well known that the last Mughal emperor Bahadur Shah Zafar took refuge in Humayun's Mausoleum after the failure the Revolt of 1857 and he and his sons were arrested from here by the British troops. Following this there was a renewed interest in the site by the British and the Mughal layout—in poor condition as a result of over a century of using the walled garden for agriculture—was altered in parts by the British to make way for an 'English' landscape with circular carriageways and decorative flower beds. In the early twentieth century, Lord Curzon directed the historic sixteenth-century layout of the garden to be restored along with a major conservation effort at the mausoleum.

By the late nineteenth century the river Yamuna, along whose banks Humayun's Tomb had been built, receded eastwards and it seems the east pavilion of Humayun's Tomb was altered in this period. In the space vacated by the riverbed the railway tracks were laid replacing the transport functions of the river and forever segregating the Nizamuddin area from the river. The northern end of 'Platform 1' of the Nizamuddin railway station in fact is built over what was the eastern half of the Nila Gumbad walled garden enclosure.

Through the eighteenth and nineteenth century tomb building continued in the vicinity but the large garden-tombs were followed by smaller structures such as those dotting the Delhi Golf Club. The famous nineteenth century poet Mirza Ghalib was also buried in close proximity to the dargah of Hazrat Nizamuddin Auliya; his tomb and its setting has, in 2010 been sensitively landscaped to create a tranquil setting where *mushairas* can be held in the memory of the great poet.

Significant changes were carried out in the Nizamuddin area in the early twentieth century, together with the building of the capital city of New Delhi. The 67-acre Sunder Nursery was established here, to experiment with trees and plants to be planted in the new capital city, and several species brought in here from distant lands such as Australia are still found here. The layout of the GT Road was altered slightly to locate the significant Sabz Burj in a traffic island at the culmination of Lodhi Road and one of the artery roads emanating from the 'India Gate' circle. Within Humayun's Tomb complex the Isa Khan Enclosure and Bu Halima enclosure were bought from the villagers for conservation of the structures, yet the relocating of the principal entrance to Humayun's Tomb from the south to the west meant that the Bu Halima complex was partly demolished to build a road.

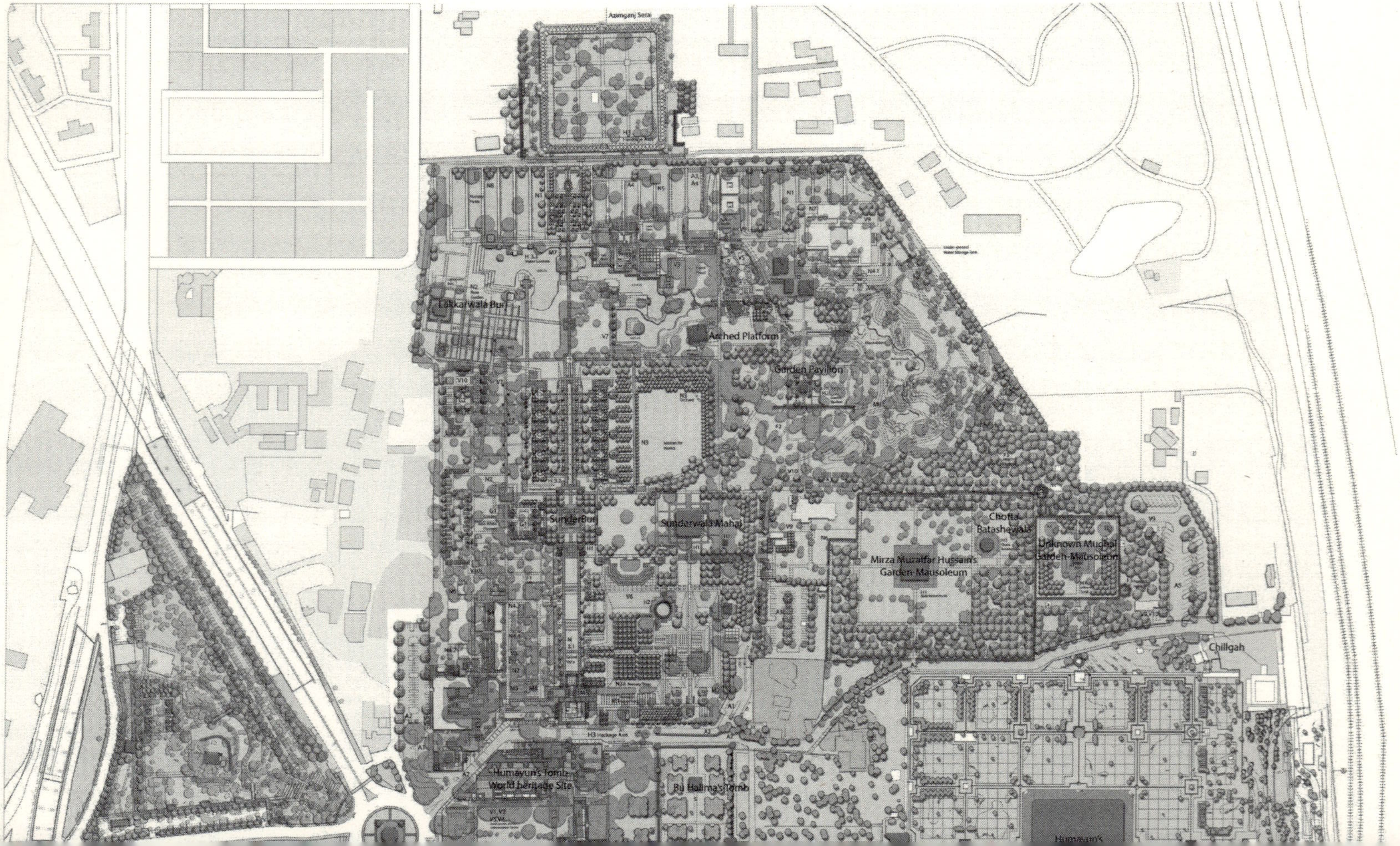
Azimganj Serai
Lakkarwala Burj
Arched Platform
Garden Pavilion
Sunder Burj
Sunderwala Mahal
Chotta Batashewala
Unknown Mughal Garden-Mausoleum
Mirza Muzaffar Hussain's Garden-Mausoleum
Chillgah
Humayun's Tomb World Heritage Site
Bu Halima's Tomb
Humayun's

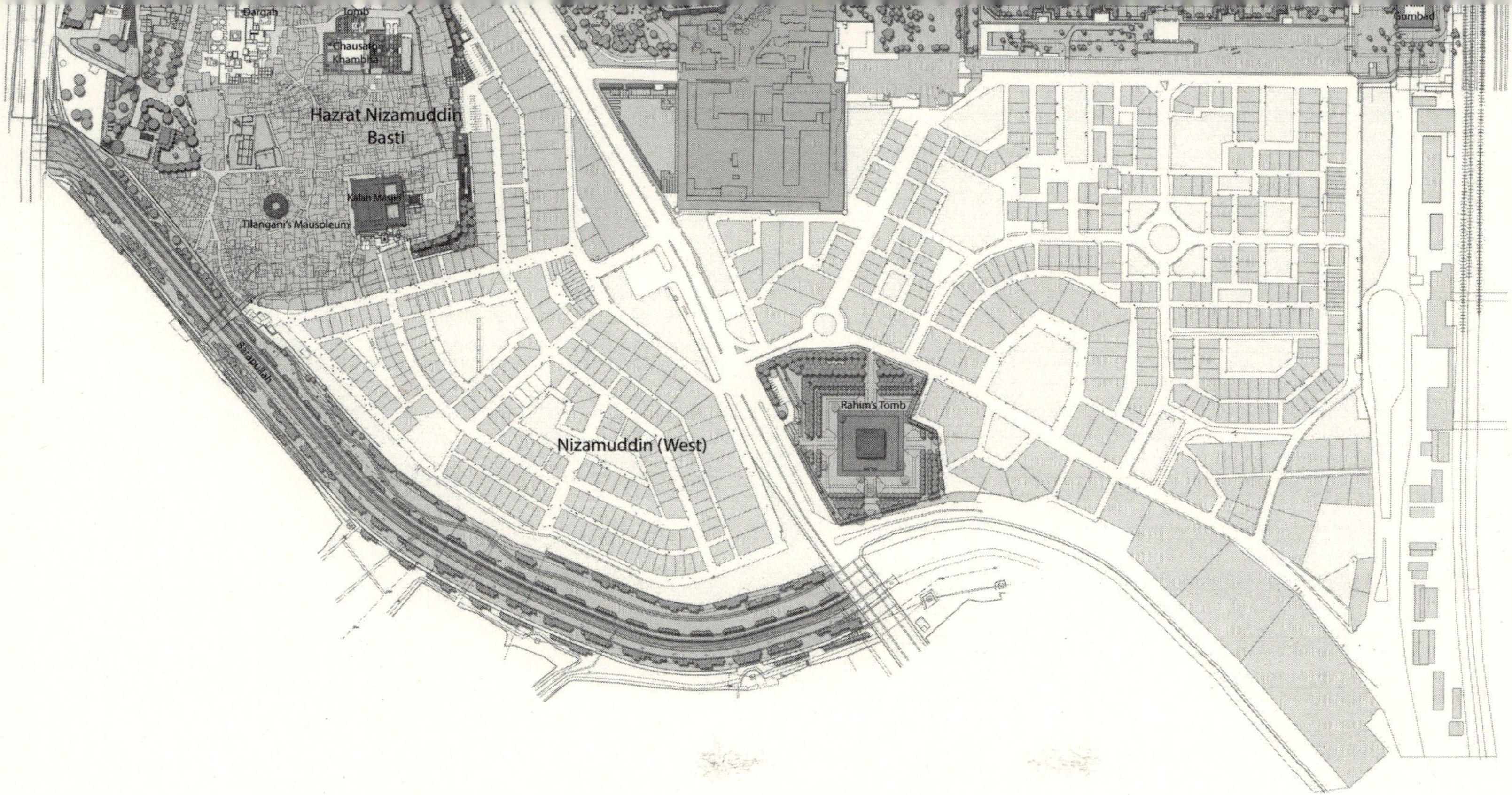

Map 19.1: Map of the area surrounding the tomb of Nizamuddin Auliya

Source: Author

Conservation

Though the British introduced a formal system of conservation in India with monuments considered to be of national importance acquired and protected by the newly established ASI, they, in the process destroyed traditional systems of conservation, followed here for centuries. The knowledge of master craftsmen was replaced by the inexperience of engineers, archaeologists, and architects in traditional building techniques. Inappropriate conservation methods not only allowed significant buildings to look like ruins in an English landscape but also accelerated the decay of structures with the use of modern materials.

Over a million kilograms of concrete was laid on the roof of Humayun's Tomb in the twentieth century and have only now been carefully removed. Lime plaster made way for cement, while iron doors, prison like in appearance, replaced wooden doors. The comparatively poorly built eighteenth and nineteenth century tombs were, as a result of poor conservation or neglect, in a ruinous condition by the mid-twentieth century when several were demolished to build the residential neighbourhoods that stand in the area today. These twentieth century 'repairs' have now all been removed, cement plaster replaced with over 200,000 sq. ft. of lime plaster on the walls.

Independence from British rule brought the bitter Partition and millions had to relocate. The Humayun's Tomb enclosure was used as a temporary refugee camp and in the harsh winter the wooden doors of the structure were used as firewood. Soon after Independence, the single archaeological zone that stretched from Purana Qila in the north to Khan-i-Khanan's Tomb in the south was sub-divided by creating the Zoo, Sunder Nursery, handing over the Batashewala Complex to the Bharat Scouts and Guides and the Arab Serai to the Industrial Training Institute. If the sixteenth century cultural landscape—stretching from Purana Qila in the north to Humayun's mausoleum in the south—was retained as a single contiguous green zone, it would today have compared with New York's Central Park in terms of scale.

A careful study of archival material also reveals that several important monuments were wilfully destroyed in the late twentieth century. In addition to the gateway of the Sunderwala Complex and Khas Mahal mentioned above, 'Nili Chattri' recommended for protection in the ASI listing by Maulvi Zafar Hasan was demolished by Delhi Public School, Mathura Road. Nili Chattri was the tomb of Naubat Khan, a noble in Emperor Akbar's court and the structure was described in the 1920s as follows. It 'stands within an enclosure ... which is entered by a gateway. The building is octagonal in plan ... the outer faces of all walls are lavishly adorned with tilework—blue, green, yellow and orange...'[5]

Also, it seems that in the twentieth century ornamental building elements like tiles, sandstone screens, stone finials, columns, and capitals, all of which were visible in archival images were removed from several monuments for the antique market. The finials on the canopies of Isa Khan's Tomb all went missing, as did lattice screens of Sunderwala Burj, Lakkarwala Burj, 'Unknown tomb' standing to the north of Humayun's Tomb, and the Bu Halima gateway. The sandstone facing Isa Khan Enclosure gateway, the Mughal pavilion that now stands in the Sunder Nursery were ruthlessly stripped.

Following the successful completion of the garden restoration in 2003, the ASI and the Aga Khan Trust for Culture entered into another agreement in July 2007, together with the Central Public Works Department and the Municipal Corporation of Delhi, to implement the 'Humayun's Tomb—Sunder Nursery—Hazrat Nizamuddin Basti Urban Renewal Initiative'. Powered by a non-profit public-private partnership between various agencies, the project is the first of its kind to combine conservation with environmental and socio-economic development while working with local communities and stakeholders establishing an archetype for participatory conservation-led development of historic cities.

Conservation of over sixty monuments has since been undertaken including community owned structures such as the Jamaat Khana mosque. These have required over 1.5 million human-days of work by master craftsmen—stone carvers, masons, carpenters, tile makers, amongst others.

With the sensitive landscaping of Sunder Nursery, re-integration of the Batashewala Complex with both Sunder Nursery and Humayun's Tomb—land recently restored to the ASI—and the possible reintegration of Nila Gumbad to the Humayun's Tomb complex by relocating the road presently segregating the two almost contemporary structures, the project enabled the expansion of the UNESCO designated World Heritage Site from the 26 acre Humayun's garden-tomb to almost 200 acres, including the garden tombs of Nila Gumbad, Lakkarwala Burj, Sundar Burj, Sunderwala Mahal, Isa Khan, Bu Halima, amongst others.

The vision of the project has been to conserve and develop the presently segregated albeit historically connected sites into one cohesive and integrated complex. The urban renewal initiative includes the conservation of monuments using traditional tools and building techniques, renewal of the surrounding spaces and environment, and sustainable socio-economic development to improve the quality of life of the resident community. Since 2018, the opening of Sunder Nursery to the public, with 1.15 million visitors in 2023 alone, has provided the people of Delhi a 90-acre green space with restored monuments, supplemented by visitor facilities and improved quality of life for local communities. We continue to work to preserve Nizamuddin's glorious built and cultural heritage in a setting worthy of its rich, historical past.[6]

The project has been recognized with several awards, including UNESCO Awards of Excellence for Conservation of Sunder Nursery Monuments (2020) and Nizamuddin Monuments (2021). The project has been able to fulfil 15 of the 17 Sustainable Development Goals and has received recognition for Sustainable Development from UNESCO for both the Sunder Nursery and Nizamuddin project areas.

Notes

1. Hasan Zafar, *Hindu and Muhammadan Monuments of Delhi*, vol. 2, no. 235, New Delhi: Archaeological Survey of India, 1919, p. 175.
2. Ibid.
3. Ibid., vol. 2, no. 149, p. 113.
4. Ibid., p. 175.
5. Ibid., vol. 2, no. 89, p. 56.
6. See http://www.nizamuddinrenewal.org.

PART III

THE CHALLENGES OF TEACHING AND LEARNING

20

Looking Back, Looking Ahead

Learning to Teach History to Undergraduates at Jamia Millia Islamia

PRABHAT KUMAR BASANT

THE JAMIA Millia Islamia, located in Delhi, attracts a large number of students from small towns and villages of north India. Education in Jamia is their first encounter with modernity at an intellectual level. Teaching history poses strange, unthought-of challenges. History is a modern discipline, which means that no book is too holy to be questioned, nor are there ideas that are holy cows. The classroom, thus, becomes a site of encounter between tradition and modernity. Teaching feels, sometimes, like 'One step forward, two steps back'.

I joined as a faculty member in the Department of History and Culture in 1989 after having taught in a Delhi University college for a few years. However, the classroom at Jamia presented a new set of challenges. I shall narrate my experiences in Jamia in the late eighties and early nineties.

University education for many of my students from non-descript towns and villages was a road to freedom, not merely

*I am grateful to Dr Bharati Jagannathan for reading the first draft and suggesting many changes.

in the larger ideational sense, but also from the tyranny of schools that mandated compulsory attendance and non-stop classes from morning to evening. I, too, was excited about the possibility of 'de-schooling' them. Steeped in ideas of dialogical communication, I imagined that I would start a conversation where students would speak and subvert the culture of silence. The study of history appeared an excellent entry into the world of ideas. The excitement of this tryst with the currents of historical imagination seemed self-evident. I walked to my first class; the classrooms allotted to me were structures called 'dumpoos': temporary, roundish, hut-like brick structures, with asbestos ceilings. I faced a slightly puzzled-looking set of about thirty students who occupied a set of dusty, half broken chairs and benches facing a fully broken blackboard. A slightly anti-climactic beginning for their first class in Jamia—mine too. I hastily introduced myself as their teacher and, after an awkward pause, launched into my rehearsed opening gambit: 'You could have opted for Political Science or Sociology. Why did you opt for History?'

They looked perplexed and were obstinately quiet. It required some amount of cajoling for one of them to make a confession, Sir, *sach sach bataayen*? (Sir! Shall I tell you the truth?). 'Of course', I said. After all, truth had such high value in academic discourse. *Sir kahin admission nahi milaa to kyaa karta... history mein aa gaye* (Sir, I could not get admission anywhere. There was nothing else to do... so joined history).

It was my turn to be tongue-tied. None of my readings on historical method and history as a vehicle for a career had prepared me for this encounter. Was it the suppressed subaltern voice? Was this the ambivalence of students towards the irrelevance of the kind of education they were getting? What became clear to me over the succeeding weeks was that history teaching in this class was not simply about teaching history. I was not ushering them into the discourse of history. The challenge was to find something to teach over the next twelve months which would be meaningful and relevant for these kids and which might also sound like history to me. I was not in the business of creating future historians, but I hoped I would be able to shape minds that would open out to possibilities of modern forms of knowledge. I was also hoping to see them grow into beautiful humans, perhaps, more sensitive, humane and loving. They were aware of something called history which they believed dealt with biographies of some great figures of the past. They had read about Asoka and Akbar. If I were to ask them what the difference between the two was, they would say that both were well-meaning, indeed, great monarchs. The only difference they could recall was that one was a converted Buddhist while the other was a Muslim. Were Ram or Yudhisthira figures of history? They would nod vigorously in affirmation. On being asked why they thought they were historical figures they would say that they had seen their pictures and watched the *Ramayana* and *Mahabharata* serials on television.

The students in Jamia represented a mix of young men and women largely from mofussil towns of north India, with a sprinkling from Delhi too. There were students who had studied in madarasas. Overall, they had had very little exposure to the social sciences. If India is a constellation of many worlds, this class definitely represented a pre-modern setting. They seemed to have sleep-walked through the dozen odd years of their schooling. Their assumptions about life, political mobilization, and social structure were a true reflection of their social backgrounds. The classroom became an encounter with modernity. By modernity I mean a way of looking at the world in which there are no holy books that cannot be scrutinized and put under the scalpel of historians. Books and prophets are pulled down from divinity and located in time and space. Modernity as an intellectual tradition is a method of changing ontologies. Any theoretical proposition that cannot explain one's reality is replaced by another set of ideas. Forty-five minutes seemed inadequate for handling the jumbled set of ideas that I needed to peddle as history. So, I devised the strategy of following up classroom teaching with 'Gup-shup'. A hot cup of tea proved to be a great ice breaker. Students who would not utter a word in the classroom would start chatting. Soon, we were joined by a larger number. Our discussions moved from history to life which, I soon realized, was far more important than the classroom. They would discuss Urdu poetry, Hindi short stories, cinema, politics, what it meant to be a Muslim, sports, and myriad other things like who beat up whom or debates about who the biggest bully in the university was. I discovered some talented students who turned out to be very good writers and poets. Some of them eventually moved into streams related to Mass Media. I was beginning to discover an unseen, unacknowledged world in the shadows of formal academics. It was just the beginning. Echoes of our chats reverberated in the classroom. Within a couple of months students began to talk freely in the classroom too.

I was deputed to teach another paper called Indian Religion and Culture to a mixed class of students from the sciences, social sciences, and humanities. It was a class of around 150 students who were expected to fit into a classroom with a seating capacity of about 70. Luckily, the classes began at 8:30 a.m. which was too early for at least half the students on any given day. Besides, many of those who turned up for the class tended to succumb to the delicious waves of the opiate called sleep. My primary challenge was to keep them awake.

'Indian Religion and Culture' was meant to introduce students to various religious traditions of India. It had chapters on the Harappan religion, the religion of the Vedas, Buddhism, Jainism, the religion of the Puranas, Christianity, Islam, and Sikhism. The syllabus was clearly innocent of anthropological traditions and did not have any section dealing with the Adivasi communities of the subcontinent.

Neither were the themes integrated to social history. As each of the units became a succession of pontifications about a set of principles considered integral to a religious tradition, I thought that a useful way of introducing belief systems could be the introduction of history into the narrative of religion.

Typically, people are open to questioning religious traditions of other communities. This paper, it appeared, could provide an opportunity to analyse religious ideas. I began with discussions on the idea of religion. It took a fair amount of effort to convince students that, traditionally, the word religion meant only one belief system. That for Brahminism, Christianity, or Islam everything outside the ambit of its own tradition was considered ignorance, darkness, sin, or a web of the devil. That it was only in the eighteenth century that the modern meaning of the word religion emerged where it referred not to a single religion but to a variety of belief systems. That people take their own religious beliefs as self-evident and given.

When I finally started on the formal chapters of the syllabus, I realized how mistaken I had been in estimating the impact of those introductory classes. I decided to read out passages from various holy books and let them speak for themselves. This was to be followed by a discussion on how historians attempt to understand the said religious tradition in the context of time and space.

Thus began a not-so-fruitful journey into understanding 'Indian religion and culture'. Trouble erupted when I began talking about the early Vedic communities. I had read out some beautiful prayers from the *Rig Veda* and gradually moved on to prayers like *Asato ma sadgamaya* (take me from untruth to truth) from the *Brhadaranyaka Upanishad*. The difficult part of the story began as I started introducing historians' accounts of early and later Vedic literature. Historians generally agree that the early Vedic literature was created by pastoral nomadic tribes. The difficult part was the word 'tribe'. The image of tribal communities in today's India is one of poor, backward, impoverished groups staying in forsaken corners. Worse, the British classification of many of them as 'Criminal Tribes' has left a lingering impact which has not disappeared entirely even today even though such derogatory categories have been removed by the government of India. Since prejudices persist beyond legislative acts, I was asked to 'show the passage from the Vedas where the Aryans are called "Tribesmen".' This got me tied into knots. I had to try to explain that words like Tribe, Class, Status and State, with their attendant connotations, were modern ideas. One cannot find many of these words in pre-modern texts. That we were unlikely to find a word like 'Tribe' in the Vedas. Rather, scholars in modern times use this term to refer to communities whose dominant form of organization is based on kinship rather than on political centralization. That history is a modern construction based on a careful reading of evidence surviving from the past did not cut much ice. Their idea of history was not the traces of the past that historians stitch together. The archaeological theory of knowledge where different artefacts found in different locations and different layers are brought together to create a coherent narrative called history was way beyond my capacity to explain. History to them was a solid three-dimensional entity made up of facts that spoke for itself. The only role that the historian had was to pull it like a rabbit out of the hat of the past. So, the net result of our chaotic discussion was more like a drawn cricket match because of shortage of time. The students—as well as I—sighed in relief.

The following chapters dealing with Buddhism and Jainism were easy because there were no Buddhists or Jains in the class. I could put these religious traditions on the block of historical analysis without any resistance. Although students were intrigued by the fact that these two religious traditions did not believe in the existence of an almighty god, I was able to bring these two within the ambit of social history. At the same time, I could underline the extraordinary emphasis on non-violence in both these heterodox traditions, particularly in Jainism. It was also easy to point out that these religious traditions attracted a large following because they connected to the needs of those times. I was trying to point out that to be able to understand a religious tradition it was important to examine the followers more than the founders. That every age would have produced great thinkers and spiritualists but not all achieved mass following. If the philosophers-preachers in some periods became founders of great religious traditions, it was not because they had discovered the final truth as believed by their followers. Rather, it was related to people discovering that their spiritual and material needs echoed in the calls of these prophets.

In about six months of teaching I had got the students talking, sometimes too loudly and far too frequently, in the classroom. Sometimes a student in high-octane performance mode would say something unwarranted and all hell would break loose because a large number of his or her classmates felt the need to oppose or defend the statement. Afraid that it might end in a fist fight I would signal the end of the class. I worried about such situations but I had let the genie out of the bottle. However, I persuaded myself that I was leading students towards a liberal democratic world where the public sphere spawned a democratic spirit and contending ideas co-existed.

The hollowness of my six months of teaching became obvious, however, when I started teaching Islam. I had covered the prescribed space of what the religion had to say about itself. I described the conditions in the Arab world and the life of Prophet Muhammed. As I began exploring uncharted spaces like the history of the Arabic language and the prehistory of many of the ideas found in the Quran, most of the class rose in one voice. '*Quran aasmani kitab hai. Usko itihas se nahin jod sakte*' (Quran was created in heaven. One cannot connect it with history). All my skills of persuasion failed to assuage the enraged students. I signalled the end of the class. The next day, I approached the topic gingerly. I tried to talk about the contending traditions of Islam, how Islam is understood differently by the Shia and Sunni traditions. But the students had smelled the rat. They insisted that a non-Muslim like me could have no understanding of Islam and should not be allowed to talk about it. Lest my perfidy cause further harm they spoke eloquently about the five cardinal principles of Islam. When one student ended his speech, another one would start and repeat the same things over and over again. So, I abandoned teaching Islam and moved on to other religious traditions like Sikhism.

The exercise of teaching 'Indian Religion and Culture' left me with a niggling suspicion—all the other religious traditions had been subjected to rigorous historical analysis. I had tried to understand religious traditions in historical context. I had also shared beautiful stories, songs. and philosophical observations that were part of each religious tradition. The idea was to create an understanding rather than pass judgement. However, many students were continuously making judgements. By not applying the scalpel of history on Islam I ended up reinforcing the view of the majority in my class that Islam was the real thing while other religions were superstition.

After a few years, the Department of History and Culture returned 'Indian Religion and Culture' to the University and it was allotted to other departments. Since then, I have taught students of my own department. There has been a distinct change in the quality and intake of students in the last twenty years. They are far better informed and far more open to the idea of history.

All of us remember examinations as the three crucial hours that define our future in academia or elsewhere. With so much focus on the 'final examination' it is inevitable that examinees would devise novel strategies to beat the system.

Most Indian invigilators are familiar with the small chits containing answers to questions expected to be asked in the examination. Discovering the cunningly concealed and even more surreptitiously consulted 'chits' is an activity worthy of Sherlock Holmes. Quick consultations with neighbours when the invigilator is perceived to be at a strategic distance is probably one of the great joys of our students. However, trouble for invigilators starts when this fine art comes to be perceived as a fundamental right, as it had in the Jamia of the eighties. Invigilators risked being waylaid—or worse—if they hindered them in the exercise of this right. Punishment was out of the question.

Thus, it came about that in my very first year in Jamia, my invigilation duty was enriched by an encounter with a skilled practitioner of the art form. He pulled out a bundle of papers, arranged them to his satisfaction on the table, and leisurely sat down to copy. With what were evidently outdated notions of my duty as invigilator, I took away the papers but allowed him to continue. He looked a little puzzled and sat restlessly for a while and glared at me intermittently. I tried to ignore him. After half an hour he walked up to me and told me in no uncertain terms that he would pull out some more chits and I should not bother him. He also pointed out that the other two invigilators were keeping a safe distance from him. I realized that the other invigilators had bought their peace and kept away from him. The young man—a strapping, muscular character, I must add—pulled out another sheaf of papers. I took them away. This time he banged the table and stormed out of the room. By the time the examination was over I could see about a dozen menacing and dangerous looking faces glaring at me from just beyond the door. One of my co-invigilators informed me helpfully that they had come for me. When I stepped out of the examination hall with a pile of answer scripts in my arms, one of the waiting toughies said, *Tumse baat karni hai* (I have something to say).

I said I would talk to them after submitting the scripts in the office. They let me, knowing full well that they occupied the sole exit from that building. I came back and was welcomed with choicest abuses.

'Naye aye ho?' (Have you joined recently?)

'Haan.'

'Sale Rahate kahan ho?' (Where do you stay?)

'Tum apane ghar ka pata de do. Agar peetanaa hi hai to mai tumhare ghar chala aataa hoon. Peetane se kyaa tumhari mushkilen khatma ho jayengi?' (Tell me your address. If you wish to beat me up, I shall come where you live. Will that solve your problem?).

They were a little puzzled by my eagerness to get beaten up. Amidst the confusion of abuses, I gathered that they represented the sports fraternity of Jamia. They told me that no one ever stopped them from writing their exams their own way. At that point, a distinguished looking elderly man passed by. They shouted some abuses in his direction. The gentleman pretended not to have heard them. I discovered later that he was the Proctor of the University. One of the toughies said that he was a national level hockey player. That he was a Centre Forward. I asked him, 'Do you demand that the goalkeeper be removed when you shoot the ball towards the goal post?' He saw the connection between playing fairly and writing an examination without copying. He persuaded the others to let me be. It turned out that the person I had prevented from cheating was a wrestler and the younger brother of some well-known Ustad. He parted with his friends hurling another round of abuses in my direction and a warning that if I interfered with him during his next paper, he would break my bones. Luckily for me, I did not encounter him again during that examination season. Some months later, I saw his pictures on posters in the university. He was contesting in the Students Union election.

This battle of nerves was an annual event until one of the Vice-Chancellors, with experience in handling insurgency in Jammu and Kashmir, put an end to it by harshly punishing a few students. I never stopped thanking him for what he achieved.

All of us who evaluate examination answer scripts have been amazed by the extraordinary inventiveness of our students. From Harappans living in caves before moving to trees, or that civilization's famously planned towns housing 'mandirs, masjids, gurdwaras and churches' next to one another, it is a short step to Asoka making tractors and pesticides available for his people, and even, in one case, of his having made rivers! Kalidasa, Kabir, Nanak, Birbal, Gandhi, Nehru, Bhagat Singh, and even Nawaz Sharif, can all be pressed, in a magical fusion of chronology, into serving the Mughal court, the bhakti movement or the national movement, as the requirement arises. I cannot resist sharing two favourites for their sheer alliterativeness:

पूर्व वैदिक काल में अंधविश्वास में अटूट विश्वास था।
(In the early Vedic period there was deep faith in superstition).
ईसा पूर्व में ईसा ने आकर शास्त्र विरोधी संप्रदायों को जन्म दिया।
(Jesus came in the period Before Christ and spawned heterodox sects).

These answers, however, hold certain lessons for us. When students fuse time and space, they are trying to create a viable script. They are working with notions of the past that have a tenacity well beyond the careful formulations of historians. Good kings built roads, worked for women's education and improvements in agriculture, and generally fought against the British. Under their rule, the sound of temple bells mingled seamlessly with the *azaan* from mosques, and, tellingly, there was no unemployment. Bad kings were inevitably drunkards and womanizers. Non-royal characters with which school history books are peppered were invariably worthy of reverence—why else would they have made it to the pages of books? Violence to chronology does not bother anyone; indeed, it is irrelevant to the larger narrative. The past is truly a foreign country.

If undergraduate students of history are unable to see any link between the academic discipline they study and the lives they lead, our contemporary public discourse is not surprising. The political dispensation today has no difficulty in creating a fictional past and embroidering it with fanciful details. We need to examine why our painstakingly researched histories are spurned by millions in favour of simplistic and patently fictional narratives. Our students' 'imaginative' answers are built on the bedrock of a larger social narrative of the past. Challenging it effectively is our challenge.

Jamia has gradually modernized over the decades. Many of the buildings are new; few people today even recall the 'dumpoos' where I began my journey. It has been my privilege and pleasure to teach, through all these years, some exceptionally bright and sensitive students. Examination halls are no longer the fraught spaces they were for invigilators. The student body is more diverse in certain ways but less so in others. Admission policies in Jamia have been affected by 'minority status' being conferred on the University. This means that a larger percentage of students are Muslim. It has also meant that Dalits and students from the North-East do not get any representation. However, the number of women students has increased noticeably. Girls are studying to chalk out their own careers and not to become presentable brides. The other change has been a massive shift to writing answers in English. When I joined the university, most of the students wrote their answers in Hindi and Urdu. Answers in English were rare. Now Urdu answer scripts have almost disappeared and there are only a handful of Hindi scripts. This invisible shift is part of larger processes that has nothing to do with the policies of the university or the government.

The political culture of the country over the last decade has forced students to examine their assumptions and agitate about their ideas. Thus, students expect classroom discussions to help them in their search for meanings. I typically began my classes with the statement, 'Babur won the battle of Panipat because God wanted it.' I would challenge the students to prove me wrong. They would find a variety of arguments to skirt the 'God argument', like human will and freedom. I would respond by asking if Babur could have won the battle if God did not want him to. Some of them would contend that the sources do not mention God's will to which I would answer that Babur, in his autobiography, clearly mentions that he won the battle by the grace of God. As such I was not being dishonest to 'facts' mentioned in the sources. This interchange invariably opened the students to the idea that history is a modern discipline that has banished God. It opened out many possibilities for the students. God had been crossed out not only by the explanations in history; all modern disciplines had a similar attitude. This, I hoped, would help them develop habits of mind where they could, and would question traditional assumptions about society, family, and politics. Another question I posed was intended to help them understand that they were part of the stream of history. I would ask them to name the father of Asoka. Many of them would promptly answer: 'Bindusara'. I would immediately respond by asking them to name their own ancestors who had lived in the time of Bindusara. The students would laugh but we would be immersed in the business of finding reasons why we did not know the names of our ancestors. Such exercises led them to visualize history as a history of power. It also led them to explore their own pasts. These exercises brought them face to face with subaltern notions of history. They felt connected with streams of the past that were peopled not only by kings and conquerors but also by their ancestors who were ordinary people like us and they were not dispensable details of history. During our 'Gup-shup' sessions, I would ask the students to imagine the life of their ancestor a hundred years ago. They wrote little but they felt that what they were studying was their own history. I hope it enlarged their vision and liberated them from the limiting vistas of tradition. As the number of students collecting for 'Gup-shup' swelled with the passing years, I felt rewarded by the affection of students. The political landscape of India has changed dramatically. We have tried to understand these changes as part of historical processes. Many students have been able to establish a dialogue with the ideas of Marx or Gandhi and discover their destinies. Some became social activists. Some girls hailing from conservative backgrounds sponsored Dalit students from their villages. These students have taken off and they will continue to enrich our worlds. Although there is a mismatch between tradition and modernity, the most humane and progressive aspects of tradition co-exist with modernity.

21

Knowing Narayani

SOHAIL HASHMI

I HAVE no idea when I first met Narayani, I honestly don't have the foggiest. What I know for certain is that I met her after I had read *Delhi Between the Two Empires.*

I read the book about twenty years ago, so let us say roughly around 2004 or 2005. When I did meet her for the first time I was already in awe of her scholarship and her attention to detail, all of which is in ample evidence in *Delhi Between the Two Empires.*

The two preceding paragraphs are a prologue to what follows and my encounters with Narayani will keep popping up as this narrative progresses.

Around 2004 I was working at Leap Years, a creative activity centre for children started by Rahul Bhandare. It was Rahul's idea to create a space where children could come after school and be in a secure environment to explore their creative urges—draw, paint, sing, dance, write, use cameras, act, and do all the things that are increasingly being moved beyond the pale of 'learning'.

I was introduced to Rahul by Shubha Mudgal and ended up looking after Leap Years. I could write reams on how the idea developed, how the centre came up and how it transformed the children who came to us and how happy were the parents who sent their children to Leap Years. But all that can be left for another occasion; this is about how I came to know Narayani. I met her because of some things that I had initiated at Leap Years and thereby hangs a tale or several tales.

Leap Years was located in the farm-houses area in Vasant Kunj and the children who came to us mostly lived in and around that part of Delhi. I looked after Leap Years as its director and the faculty consisted of talented and enthusiastic artists, actors, dancers, musicians, writers, and story tellers; today most of them are well-known names in their chosen fields.

I started a loosely structured activity called 'My World', I talked to the children about the world around them, took them on walks in the 'untamed' rocky neighbourhood of Vasant Kunj—Malikpur Kohi, Masoodpur and Mahipalpur—looking for abandoned nests, caterpillars, bugs, white-anthills, taken over by the hedgehog and the mongoose.

In my interactions with these young students, I realized that though they knew that all insects begin as eggs, hatch into caterpillars, pupate and then mature into butterflies, moths, etc., very few had seen a live caterpillar. They knew a whole lot of bird names but did not know what they looked like in real life. I also came to realize that they knew nothing of the city they were growing in.

When we were growing up, our parents took us around to see the city. We went to picnics at Hauz Khas, Qutub, Kotla Ferozeshah, the Okhla Barrage, and the mango orchards at Andheria Bagh.

Our father, who among other things also dabbled in archaeology, showed us the seven capitals in the order in which they had come up and we learnt how trabeated structures transformed into the corbelled arch and how the true arch and the dome arrived and transformed our architecture.

We were made to notice how with the expansion of the empire, Delhi quartz gave way to sandstone and marble and changed the look and feel of our monumental structures and the changes brought about during the colonial period were pointed out to us.

Our mother took us to participate in Shankar's on the spot painting competitions, to Sapru House to see the cinema of Charlie Chaplin and De Sica, to the Dolls Museum, National Museum, Crafts Museum, Rail Museum, and the Gallery of Modern Art. We joined Bal Bhawan, and began to learn to paint, dance, sing and act and to spend time in the Bal Bhawan Library.

My siblings and I benefited greatly from all this. Due to my restlessness and the habit of running away from school I learnt a few other things as well. Once I ran away with four of my classmates to spend an entire day at Tughlaqabad; the magnificent ruins continue to be my favourite to this day. A couple of years later five of us hitch-hiked to Bombay after our school finals. This wanderlust has remained with me and I continue to walk and travel and encourage others to do it all the time.

In college I had a friend from Ballimaran; he too loved to walk and very often we walked from the campus to his house, approaching his house in Gali Qasimjan from a different direction every time and that is how I came to know the narrow streets and by-lanes of the city of my ancestors and fell in love with Shahjahanabad.

Recalling all these activities, I realized the children who had joined Leap Years had no exposure to all these things and the principal reason was that their parents, caught as they were in the race to survive, had no time to spend with their kids. The schools were only interested in creating over-achievers and the children were being robbed of their curiosity and their childhood.

Day-in and day-out, the children were woken up in the morning to get ready, rush through breakfast, and run to catch the school bus. They returned to eat, rest a bit, go out to play under parental supervision, finish homework, have dinner, and sleep. Next morning repeat.

This went on for ten months or more. If the parents had leave from office and some money, everyone went to Singapore or Bangkok or else they went to spend time with grandparents. They grew up in a city, never knowing where they lived.

Leap Years tried to introduce them to Delhi and to childhood.

We took them to Sanjay Van and taught them how to sit silently without fidgeting and wait for the nilgai, the peacock, the partridge, quail, or the crow-pheasant to come out into the open. We took them to the scrub-land behind the farm houses to look for the caterpillars of the monarch butterfly on milkweed shrubs. We took them to the Science Museum, the Natural History Museum, the Dolls Museum, and the Railway Museum.

Every second Saturday, there was an outing and thus began the Discover Delhi Walks. The short excursions were not confined to the reserve forests and museums; every alternate outing was to some mediaeval ruins. Not to talk about kings and dates but to spend time amidst the ruins, to explore tunnels, walk down dry step wells, to hear the echoes of one's own voices under domes and to talk of things that interested the children, most of whom were just about 4 feet high, so they noticed things that we did not normally see and we ended up talking about what the children were seeing.

The kids began to enjoy these outings. We began to see these ruins from an entirely new perspective, from the perspective of a child and began to see details that we had not noticed before.

The children talked of these outings in their schools and with their parents and soon we had a delegation of parents wanting to come on Discover Delhi walks. One parent who worked with NDTV arranged for a breakfast-show focused on a walk in Mehrauli. I started getting enquiries and the walks with adults began. *Timeout Magazine* began to feature the walks, doing short write-ups and a photo or two and this small initiative eventually grew into 'Delhi Heritage Walks with Sohail Hashmi'.

This rather long-winded narrative is to foreground three things: one, that my walks were born in a place that had been created with children at its centre; two, that I had picked up little bits of history of Delhi in my childhood from what our parents had told us and shown us; and three, that I wanted to share the joy of the discoveries that I had made.

With the walks began my problems.

I have never studied history except as a subsidiary subject in college and that does not make you a historian. Even if you are only conducting heritage walks, you need to know the history of the place and when you are doing a walk for children you need to know much more, mere sketchy knowledge will not do, because children can ask the most unexpected questions.

Three unconnected things were to shape the content of my walks and this is how they unfolded.

One, finding Narayani—I had begun wandering through the Mehrauli area to get to know the places where one could take the children and was looking for material to read up about them.

I had Syed Ahmad Khan's *Asar us Sanadeed*, bought by my father in the 1950s and I read it for the first time, I went to the Urdu Academy and picked up Bashir Uddin Ahmad's *Waqeyaat-e-Daar-ul-Hukoomat Dehli* and a set of other books that dealt with Delhi, its history, culture, language, festivals, and communities. All this was in Urdu, some of the writing appeared dated and more than a little one sided.

I started looking for books on Delhi in English and that is when I came across *Delhi Between the Two Empires* and a little later Percival Spear's *Delhi, its Monuments and History*, updated by Narayani Gupta and Laura Sykes.

Narayani's *Delhi* made me look at Delhi from an entirely new perspective and I realized that there is a lot that one can do through the walks and that is what I have been trying to do.

Two, finding Indian National Trust for Art and Cultural Heritage (INTACH)—wandering through the Mehrauli Archeological Park, then called the Jamali Kamali area, I came across a little folder that someone had dropped and that is how I came to know about INTACH, the walks they organized, their efforts to preserve our built heritage and the extensive documentation of our built heritage that they had carried out.

I was to later, much later, meet K.T. Ravindran, A.G.K. Menon, and Swapna Liddle. These three people through their long association with INTACH and through their enviable body of work have contributed greatly to how some Dilliwalahs have learnt to appreciate and love their city. Much of what I know about Delhi, I owe to their putting up with great patience to my endless questions.

Whatever little I know about conservation, I have picked up in exchanges with A.G.K. Menon and with Ratish Nanda, a former student of Narayani and currently the Projects Director of the Aga Khan Trust for Culture. He is the man responsible for the restoration of Humayun's Tomb, the Tomb of Khan-e-Khanan, the Sunder Nursery restoration, and the Nizamuddin Urban renewal project.

Three, finding a peg to hang my tales on—I was now regularly taking children from Leap Years to places like Tughlaqabad, Hauz Khas, Adham Khan and Quli Khan's Mausolea, Jamali Kamali, and other places nearby. We were at the Rajon ki Baoli and I was telling the children, how a group of masons, who lived there till the early 1920s, had turned the interiors black with soot, because they cooked their food inside. A 9-year-old stopped me and out of the blue came the question that stumped me absolutely: 'Sir why do you only show us Muslim Buildings?'

It took me some time to come back with an answer that would make some sense to him and I said, Muslim kings ruled from Delhi for many centuries and they had built forts, palaces, mosques, and mausolea, just as in Jaipur and elsewhere Hindu Rajas built forts, palaces, many temples, and dharamshalas.

The question kept bothering me and I talked to the parents of the child to find out how a 9-year-old was looking at the world in these terms. One parent was a Tamil, the other a Malayali, theirs was an inter-caste marriage, they were not temple going and through their large circle of friends celebrated all festivals, including Christmas and Eid. The child was going to a 'progressive school'. They were as shocked as I was.

Where was this outlook being injected into the minds of little children? Both parents and I agreed that this tendency is becoming a part of our environment. The very air we breathe, carries this toxicity and we need to do something about it. Clearly what we have been able to do is not enough.

This innocent question—the child was unaware of its implications—was to trigger another question: can and should architecture be seen and described in denominational terms? Hindu architecture and Islamic architecture and if yes, then why don't we have Christian architecture? And this is the peg on which I learnt to hang my tales.

Just as we have discarded the periodization of history as Hindu, Muslim and British—categories created by the colonial discourse that had vitiated and continues to inform how we perceive our past—should we also not discard the architectural categories of Muslim and Hindu architecture?

It is these questions that led me to start looking at our architecture a little more closely—the defining elements of architecture, as also the finer embellishments.

A new world now began to unravel before me. Looking closely at the details generally missed, was something that Narayani made me do. One day I was telling her about my last trip to Tughlaqabad and she asked me, have you seen the Brahmi inscriptions at Tughlaqabad?

I had been to Tughlaqabad scores of times, but I had not noticed any Brahmi inscriptions. I asked her where and she said on the causeway leading to the mausoleum of Ghyasuddin Tughlaq. I reached there next morning and spent an hour looking for them and found twenty-four of them; I photographed them all. Some looked like text while others were more like symbols, axes, tridents, *damarus*—standalones or in combinations of tridents and *damarus* or tridents and axes. I took them to Narayani and after some inspection we realized that in all likelihood they were mason's marks and a few were probably names of masons.

She had seen them decades ago and remembered and I learned why you do not become a historian by conducting heritage walks. You have to study and learn the discipline.

The last almost two decades have been this exciting journey of discovery and learning and Narayani is one who has patiently indulged me and pointed my nose in the right direction. It was Narayani who came up with the idea of creating a loosely structured platform called 'Friends of ASI'. There were just four of us, Narayani, the conservation architect, Anisha Shekhar Mukherji, and my classmate from JNU, Kamala Menon, who was then at the Mother's School and I.

It was Narayani's idea to create this platform, where we could facilitate a dialogue between the residents of Begumpur and the Archaeological Survey of India (ASI). Kamala was able to involve the senior classes of the school, who were already working with the students of the local school in Begumpur, in this project.

The interaction with the village elders taught us that many of the villagers had till the late 1950s lived inside the mosque in the corridors and the prayer chamber. We met a retired Air Force officer, who was born there and an old woman who wanted to bring her chicken and goats and her cot to sleep inside the mosque. She had spent all her childhood and much of her youth living there and could not understand why she had been asked to move.

We realized that the villagers saw the ASI as someone who had asked them to move out and had permitted them to build their houses 50 yards away from the mosque. It was the same ASI that was now preventing them from adding even a single room to their homes because now the new construction limit was 100 metres.

More than anything else we came to realize that the ASI was not interested in a dialogue; they had the law on their side and they were happy with it.

While the effort lasted, we were able to access, from the ASI archives, several photographs of the mosque from a time when the villagers had lived inside. Anisha was then probably involved in restoring the Jantar Mantar and was familiar with the ASI archives. Narayani knew Dr Sengupta, the then Director General of ASI, at a personal level; all this certainly helped. We put up an exhibition of those photographs inside the mosque.

The exhibition caused a lot of excitement among the old residents. We had a fun-filled afternoon. The old residents spent a lot of time with their children and grandchildren, showing them the places where they had lived and where their cows and buffaloes had been tethered inside.

The kids from the Mother's School had learnt how to conduct a heritage walk and they led us through one. A group of budding filmmakers from the school made a short film on the history of the monuments in the area. The school organized a tree plantation drive at the Bijay Mandal and the village elders volunteered to look after the monuments, and the trees if ASI agreed to remove the rubble piled up after the last bout of conservation. The ASI did not remove the rubble and gradually the village elders too lost interest.

It was a long shot, but it was Narayani's enthusiasm that gave us the confidence that things can be made to move, the people can begin to own their heritage. All that is needed is a sympathetic ear and a positive attitude.

We keep talking about doing away with the legacy of colonialism. If we are a democracy, the first thing we need to do is to stop treating the people as enemies of the state or as chattel. We need to use our institutions and not our people. We need to consult them, involve them in all decisions, discuss issues with them and listen to them and this is as important in matters of heritage conservation as it is in everything else. We cannot pass laws without consulting those that are going to be impacted by those decisions. We cannot force laws down their throats instead of having a dialogue with them and evolving a genuine consensus. Our entire approach to the people needs to change; they are no longer subjects of a colonial power and the State is not their ruler, the State is there to serve them, not to lord over them. The vestiges of colonialism will not go away by merely changing names, they will be eradicated only when we do away with the mindset of the colonial masters.

There is another instance connected with how we deal with matters of heritage conservation, this time it was I who dragged Narayani into a project.

The new town hall was inaugurated on Jawaharlal Nehru Marg and a commissioner of the Municipal Corporation of Delhi (MCD) asked me for ideas in restoring the old Town Hall at Chandni Chowk and turning it into a cultural hub.

I got very excited and talked to Narayani about it and there we were again; Anisha too was dragged into it as was the food writer and old friend Rahul Verma.

We planned the resurrection of the Public Library that existed at the Town Hall in its initial days and suggested the creation of a research and reference section consisting of every book ever written about Delhi. We fleshed out plans for creating restaurants, food festivals, including festivals of the street foods of Delhi. The Town Hall would become a site for concerts, performances, and exhibitions.

Finally, all this was put together as a proper proposal, approved by MCD, and forwarded to the Government of India. It was approved and the first tranche of funding was sanctioned.

But before the funds were transferred, the government changed hands. The enthusiastic commissioner, who had listened to us patiently and had pushed the proposal with all the resources at his command because he saw merit in what we had suggested, was recalled to the centre, because he had completed his three-year tenure in Delhi. We, the untiring champions of lost causes were once again in search of new challenges.

Throughout this longish association, I do not know when it started, Narayani has been pushing me to do things, to speak in seminars and symposia, to write and to participate in events, while she sits there with an indulgent smile, not unlike a proud elder or a teacher. I still don't have the foggiest idea why she does it. It can't be due to anything that I have done. It is perhaps because she is 'like that only'?

Before I end this rather rambling piece, I have to recall one last episode that involves Narayani. I have to recall it because this is one act that ended differently, in partial success, from all the others that I have been associated with under the benign gaze of Narayani.

One day I got a call from Narayani. After the usual banter with which she prefaces all her conversations, she casually mentioned that she was editing a series on the UNESCO world heritage sites in India and if I would be interested in working on the project. She said the idea is to begin with a series aimed at junior school students, followed by a series for senior school students, and then for college students. There were to be six to begin with and she named them. I jumped at the idea and asked her if I could do Sanchi. She named the next lot, and I asked, can I do Bhimbetka.

Narayani said that the idea is to take a group of children to Sanchi, spend a day there with them listening to their questions and comments and create the text based on the children's conversation. This I thought was a brilliant idea and was sure no one had visualized a series on heritage like this.

I travelled to Sanchi, and a dear friend helped mobilize five children from a school for marginalized children, being run by a committed group of young people, and five children from a 'public school'. All the children had one thing in common, except for one girl who had been to Sanchi when she was 4 years, none of them had been to Sanchi, a mere 42 km. from Bhopal. A few from the 'public school' had however travelled abroad.

The conversations we had led to *Sanchi: Where Tigers Fly and Lions have Horns.* The five books that came out including Sanchi, Mahabalipuram, Keoladev Bird Sanctuary, Qutub Minar, and Victoria Terminus (now Chhatrapati Shivaji Terminus), were published in Hindi, English, Bangla, Tamil and Urdu. The book on the Qutub Minar was written by Narayani.

These were fantastic books. Had the series gone on to include one book on each world heritage site in India, manmade as well as natural and had the series grown to include three versions of each book, for junior school, senior school, and college level students, it would have made a phenomenal contribution to the students and adults getting to know their heritage and India in a very meaningful way.

After the first five books, we were told that work on the next lot would begin soon. It was planned that all these books would be published in all Indian languages.

It was not to be. No one knows why such great ideas are quickly forgotten while we continue to lament the absence of good reading material, even as children are constantly bombarded with strange imaginary histories.

As long as Narayani and people like her continue to think of ideas that would make history and heritage more accessible to those who live amidst all this, there is hope.

Knowing Narayani, she will think of something, I hope she includes me in her next enterprise.

22

Making History Accessible

Connecting the Past with People

NAVINA JAFA

THIS CHAPTER examines heritage walks and other public outreach activities, expounding on how these initiatives foster citizen engagement with local history and the more extensive Indian history. These efforts empower people to become informed and encourage them to participate proactively in their communities.

The Conservation Society of Delhi, established in 1985 under the guidance of the illustrious social reformer and freedom activist Kamaladevi Chattopadhyay, highlighted a deep-seated concern about the rapid transformation of Delhi's urban landscape. Professor Narayani Gupta, an active member of this group, spearheaded heritage walks as a maiden venture in India.

In the early 1990s, during a lively exchange in Professor Gupta's room at the Department of History and Culture, Jamia Millia Islamia University, she spoke about the transformative potential of heritage walks, saying that these were not merely outings with people interested in history, as outreach engagements of history along with other kinds of innovative activities could foster civic awareness on shared concerns such as gaining knowledge to appreciate the arboreal heritage and the stories of the landscapes of their city, such as significant roads in Delhi.

Years later, as a heritage professional with the Shahjahanabad Redevelopment Corporation, Government of Delhi, I found myself navigating the intricate lanes of Old Delhi's historic neighbourhoods on Sundays, week after week, equipped with portable public address systems. Here, amidst a populace including recent footpath migrants, the rallying cry in Hindi, 'Listen to the story of where you live', marked the beginning of each expedition. Subsequent surveys by the organization revealed a noticeable increase in the residents' sense of ownership over their humble abodes.

The growing number of historians transitioning into the mantle of heritage professionals assume a multifaceted role beyond mere 'tour guides'. They amalgamate the role of meticulous curator, adept performer, and community mobilizer in their avatars as public academics. This confluence of aptitudes endeavours to craft immersive historical narratives that resonate with the contemporary fabric of cities, thereby engendering a sense of custodianship over their shared heritage.

Wielding a discerning eye, the historian curator meticulously selects and articulates interpretive themes that animate the past, weaving a seamless tapestry that bridges bygone epochs with the present. This experiential journey through history in the form of heritage walks is not just recounted but 'performed', transmuting heritage into a living tableau that reverberates with the cadence of collective memory.

Integral to this narrative are the custodians of tradition, whose lived experiences enrich the heritage scape. A holistic comprehension of heritage necessitates appreciating the symbiotic relationship between monuments and the surrounding ecology. Take, for instance, an initiative in Srinagar that illustrates the importance of elements in an ecosystem and one of history's many purposes for public outreach programmes. An eminent organization, Women in Security, Conflict Management and Peace (WISCOMP), employs heritage walks once in a while for peacebuilding in diverse parts, including Kashmir.[1] The organization aims to influence processes of cultural change by incorporating a series of heritage walks to locations that embody a shared history. These walks assist participants in looking beyond the notion of a conflict between people of different faiths and exploring the symbols within their faith traditions that promote intercultural understanding, coexistence, non-violence, and empathy. The heritage walks are a powerful pedagogical tool, enabling participants to perceive their cultures through a lens highlighting a history of coexistence. This learning is crucial since if young South Asians view their diverse cultures as connectors rather than dividers, the prospects for inter-state and inter-religious understanding would increase manifold.

Deeba Nazir, a poetess, schoolteacher, and researcher, is associated with the organization and has curated independent work, such as a Jhelum River heritage trail in Srinagar, as a peacebuilding tool in the conflict zone. Titled 'Water, Women, and Sacred Spaces,' the heritage experience was part of a school initiative for fifteen schoolteachers from different regions of Kashmir. The schoolteachers mainly taught languages and history and were employed in government and private schools. During the experience, they travelled by boat on the river Jhelum and partly on foot, covering the Hindu temple of Ropa Bhawani and then walking to the Sufi shrines of Bulbul Shah and Shah Hamdan.[2]

An exciting part of the experience was the history of waterways in Srinagar, described as the City of Canals or the 'Venice of the East'. However, the city lost this title due to human greed, as waterways were sealed to make way for roads. In the 1970s, the state government filled a fourteenth-century canal, Nallah Mar.

Deeba described the *Yaarbals*—–ghats—landing steps along the river as public spaces for friends to meet and create human bonds. The women came here to wash clothes, perhaps also for other chores, share gossip, solve their petty home matters, or even engage in matchmaking. They called themselves *Yaar Kaakin* or sisters of *Yaarbal.*

Srinagar had a history of water transport, and the *Yaarbals* played a vital role in connecting people and were essential for trade. The owners of small shops along the *Yaarbals*/ghats are known as ghat-munshis. The *Yaarbals* are spaces, metaphors of bonding that counter the wider frame where conflict reigns and is an everyday reality! Including a traditional *hanji*—boatman—enhanced the river's history in the city. Together, the walk leader and the boatman intermittently recited verses by Kashmiri poets. The presenter shared the myth and reality of the river in her narration: 'Water brings *sukoon* (relief) to mind and body, and although Kashmir has innumerable springs and lakes, the Jhelum River is the backbone of our water system.' Some *buzurg*—old wise men—hold community beliefs that the word Jhelum comes from two words: '*Jal* (water) and *Hum* (cool). Ancient seers of Kashmir called the river "Vitasta," the daughter of a powerful King in the Himalayas.' Meanwhile, continued the presenter: 'The twelfth-century scholar Kalhana, in his masterpiece, *Rajatarangini* (Chronicle of Kings), writes that this is the river "Vitasta" where inhabitants find the purest, coolest water created from the mountain snow.'

In the historical journey, Deeba, the walk leader, invited the *Hanji* or boatman to tell his story. He shared that the *Hanji* community is a Master of Water and has skills linked with water.

Traditionally, the community included fishermen and agriculturists who grew crops like lotus stems (*Nadru*), a delicacy in the heritage of Kashmiri cuisine. The *Hanjis* traditionally lived along the waterbodies, but now many live elsewhere and have adopted occupations such as formal employment in the fisheries department. The conflict in Kashmir has affected tourism and waterway transport systems. The most famous in the community is the revered Rehman Daar Hanji, who took Jawaharlal Nehru in his *kishti* (boat) for his election rallies. There was a time when election rallies happened on the lakes of Srinagar. Rehman Dar Hanji was a poet who would take girls to a missionary school daily, concluded the boatman.

Communicating the idea of history in various curated public outreach programmes creates the potential of lively experiences of history that often involve visits to workshops, homes, and shops to witness demonstrations, a culinary presentation, a musical or narrative performance or a lively conversation. Such inclusive exercises of self-representation are vitally essential for recounting family histories, comprehending the continuity of intangible cultural heritage and ensuring the inclusion of tradition-bearers to provide local people with the benefit of the cultural economy of tourism. Moreover, the recreation of the heritagescape results in value addition and increases the understanding of these communities who breathe life into the heritage tableau: 'This involvement strategy represents what was or has been the apotheosis of the World Heritage Convention, the Intangible Cultural Heritage Convention, as it currently evolves from its passage in 2003.'[3]

However, amidst the burgeoning popularity of heritage walks and other activities involving engagement with local and other histories, an insidious crisis looms—the hijacking and distortion of history. History, once the purview of erudite discourse, now finds itself relegated to the arena of truncated narratives propagated through social media channels, often serving partisan agendas. The advent of using history to promote political propaganda has exacerbated the trend of historical misinformation.[4] In response to this erosion of historical veracity, a clarion call emerges for historians to reclaim public spaces and disseminate rigorously researched accounts in the vernaculars in different regions. Heritage walks and other public outreach activities centred around history are a powerful way to combat the spread of misinformation, whether in the physical world or the virtual realm.

For the young and unemployed trained historian, there is primarily an economic sustainability risk in opting for such a career to use their knowledge. On the other hand, investing in a business model of 'start-ups' to create innovative history-oriented public outreach activities has provided exciting ways to generate income.[5]

At the same time, some corporations have supported these activities under their corporate social responsibility charters. An example is the Heritage Walk project in Vadodara by the Gujarat Alkalies and Chemical Limited, whose website shows that:

> The Company has contributed some amount towards organizing a Heritage Walk and Support for website development of Vadodara by Foot. To promote the government initiative of Tourism and Digital India, efforts to uphold the cultural legacy were also embarked upon to promote Art, Culture and Heritage. A Mobile Application and website called 'Vadodarabyfoot' has been launched. This has enabled heritage enthusiasts to experience Vadodara's rich culture and heritage via self-guided tours.[6]

Another initiative, like the role played by the Conservation Society of Delhi in the 1980s, is the more recent effort by the Citizens' Heritage Society in Hyderabad.[7] The successful citizen-led coalition relies mainly on crowdfunding to preserve the city's geological heritage embedded in its ancient rock formations. These rocks are part of the more significant geological history of the Deccan. They are among the oldest rocks on the planet, coming in various formations such as the whaleback, the domed, and the castellated Inselberg Island rocks.[8]

Over time, humans have given these rocks both mythical and modern names. Historically, cities like Hampi, capital of the Vijayanagar Empire, a world heritage site in Karnataka, emerged from these rocks. However, modern urban development has subverted this progress, and many rocks have disappeared due to rapid urban growth.[9] Hyderabad has transformed into a hi-tech hub and now juxtaposes towering modern edifices with the silent antiquity of imposing granite outcrops. These monoliths testify to a continuum of human efforts spanning centuries and constitute integral components of the Hyderabad Granitic Region (HGR), composed of granites and volcanic igneous rocks dating back to the Hellenic Achaean Epoch.[10]

These rocks also function as biotopes that nurture various indigenous flora and fauna while facilitating groundwater replenishment and serving as natural aquifer reservoirs. To preserve these heritage rocks, the Hyderabad Metropolitan Development Authority (HMDA) initiated a campaign to raise awareness.

Approximately twenty-four to twenty-five rocks have been granted heritage status by the organization, with governmental bodies like the Metropolitan Development Authority endorsing citizen-led initiatives such as the non-governmental Society to Save Rocks (STSR) in their conservation efforts. The Society orchestrates a range of engaging programs, including Rock Heritage Walks, art competitions, photographic exhibitions, and the production of apparel adorned with rock motifs, such as t-shirts and caps emblazoned with catchy slogans, which are distributed across various community gatherings and public venues. The Society's efforts have enticed numerous heritage enthusiasts to support the 'Save the Rock' crusade and actively participate in preserving the city's natural heritage. These rocks have been given names that reflect their distinctive morphological attributes, granting them a semblance of civic personhood. Examples of these names include Mushroom Rock, situated at the University of Hyderabad, alongside other venerable formations christened Bear Nose, Cliff Rock, Tortoise, and Obelisk. The Society aspires to inspire property owners and landscape architects to integrate historical boulders into residential designs, gardens, architectural blueprints, and communal spaces, thereby perpetuating their legacy for posterity.

Heritage Education: A Multidisciplinary Approach

In 2020, schools in India witnessed sweeping overhauls in social science textbooks for Grades 6 through 12. These changes were made in the name of 'syllabus rationalizing' and were ostensibly aimed at easing students' study load. Yet, the new textbooks do not provide a complete view of history. References to several contentious but essential events, eras and people from India's political and social history were removed from the books, including the 2002 Gujarat riots. A report by India's National Human Rights Commission on the violence, which contained a searing indictment of Gujarat's government at the time was similarly omitted. Vital chapters on Mughal courts, a poem on the Dalit Movement (of the so-called untouchables caste) and a chapter on the Cold War were also among the materials deleted. Verses by the revolutionary Urdu poet Faiz Ahmad Faiz and references to various important Dalit writers who spoke up about the indignity of the caste system were also withdrawn. Equally significant was the elimination of stories about protests and demonstrations, such as those led by activists like Medha Patkar of the Narmada Bachao Andolan (a social movement against large dam projects across the Narmada River, spearheaded by adivasis [tribals], farmers, environmentalists, and human rights activists). Writings about the massive protests during India's first so-called Emergency period between 1975 and 1977, when fundamental political rights were suspended, have also been nixed. Another book asserts that the Mughal Emperor Akbar, who was the monarch when the Mughal Empire was at its zenith, 'did not win the Haldighati battle against Maharana Pratap in 1576'. The book maintains that the 'victory of the Mughal forces was not certified'.[11]

Responding to the article quoted above, it is evident that recent textbooks often contain false or missing historical information, which can be problematic for students' understanding of the past. Historians and social scientists can intervene in established 'Heritage Clubs' in government and private schools to address this issue. One example of this approach is Salwan Public School's Heritage Club called 'Dharohar', which adopted the monument Bhuli Bhatiyari ka Mahal, a fourteenth century hunting lodge located in Karol Bagh, in central Delhi, as part of the Central Ridge Forest Reserve. This monument is currently managed by the Archaeological Survey of India and the Delhi Forest Department.

Salwan Public School's teachers collaborated with a historian for one academic year and conducted multidisciplinary activities culminating in a heritage mela. During this time, the children planted trees and staged various cultural activities that connected different themes and histories of the heritagescape. For instance, while the history class performed a small theatre on the monument's story, the sociology teacher developed an exhibition on the indigenous community of the Warlis and their engagement with forests. The biology teacher also conducted tree mapping alongside the histories and stories of various trees. This approach provides students with accurate and comprehensive knowledge of history and encourages them to engage with their cultural heritage.[12]

Urban landscapes are often marred by heedless and illicit human interventions that take a toll on diverse historical vistas in the region. Recognizing the significance of these historical sites among the populace residing in and around such areas is crucial to instil a heightened sense of citizenry. One such prominent example is the ancient reservoir Shamsi Talab, located in Mehrauli, New Delhi, dating back to the thirteenth century. It is a testament to hydraulic ingenuity and the city's intricate water management systems. However, the encroachments through unauthorized construction, untreated sewage discharge, accumulation of refuse, and proliferation of water hyacinths threaten the integrity of this historical site.[13]

In 2018, a non-profit organization named Society for Protection of Culture, Heritage, Environment, Traditions and Promotion of National Awareness (CHETNA), orchestrated a heritage walk and a street performance protest.[14] This engaging theatrical enactment aimed to highlight the gradual erosion of the region's water heritage and propose feasible remedies and actions that citizens could undertake to spur authorities into addressing the deterioration of the historic precinct. During the event, one *bahurupiya*, a traditional impersonator, transformed into a djinn and destroyed the lake. At the same time, the street snake charmers played tunes inspired by the sounds of wind and water to drive away the djinn. Another *bahurupiya*, a traditional impersonator, narrated Mehrauli's history with the help of a street magician. The event predominantly drew residents from the vicinity, including small shopkeepers and itinerant vendors. The amalgamation of these two activities recounted the narrative tapestry of Mehrauli's past, facilitating a platform for citizens to voice their concerns and implore the representatives of their local welfare associations to ally with the NGO, thereby exerting pressure on authorities to redress the issues spotlighted during the performance and heritage walk. Such initiatives serve as pedagogical tools, galvanizing citizens towards proactive engagement in tackling environmental challenges, safeguarding historical landscapes, and conserving age-old living heritage practices and traditions. These initiatives go beyond the mere dissemination of environmental awareness among ordinary people and provide a way for citizens to contribute towards safeguarding their environment and heritage.

The essay underscores the vital importance of democratizing history and making it more accessible to the public through innovative outreach endeavours, serving as avenues to convey historians' research efforts. Such initiatives combat misinformation and cultivate a more profound societal reverence for history. Nevertheless, a notable gap lies in the need for more historical research available in local languages and the potential of these endeavours to bolster historians' research.

Drawing upon examples of organizations leveraging public outreach to foster civic awareness and intercultural empathy, the essay advocates for a multidisciplinary approach to heritage education. For instance, historians' involvement in school heritage clubs can give students an accurate and nuanced historical understanding. Additionally, the essay underscores the imperative of integrating broader urban concerns with historical engagement. Initiatives addressing environmental awareness and urging citizens to safeguard historical landscapes and traditions exemplify this intersection.

Ultimately, reclaiming public spaces and disseminating meticulously researched historical narratives through activities like heritage walks can counter the proliferation of historical inaccuracies while instilling a collective sense of stewardship over our shared heritage.

Notes

1. M. Gopinath and M. Sewak, eds., *Bridging the Divide: Peacebuilding for a New Generation,* New Delhi: Women in

Security, Conflict Management, and Peace Foundation for Universal Responsibility of His Holiness the Dalai Lama, 2014, see http://wiscomp.org/Publications/Bridging%20the%20Divide:%20Peacebuilding%20for%C2%A0%20a%20New%20Generation.pdf, accessed 29 July 2024.

2. Navina Jafa, *Exhibiting India: Art of Heritage Walks*, New Delhi: Publication Division, Government of India, 2024, pp. 145–51.
3. Ibid., p. 8.
4. R. Maaz, 'How BJP is Distorting Indian History for the Upcoming Generations', *Outlook*, 27 June 2022, see https://www.outlookindia.com/national/how-bjp-is-distorting-indian-history-for-the-upcoming-generations-news-204937, accessed 12 March 2024.
5. Nidhi Adlakha, 'Ever Tried a Walking Tour in India? Meet Locals Doubling as Historians and Curating Walking Tours Across India', *The Hindu*, 14 February 2023, see www.thehindu.com/life-and-style/travel/meet-locals-doubling-as-historians-and-curating-walking-tours-across-india/article66470689.ece, accessed 10 July 2024.
6. CSR Project by Gujarat Alkalies and Chemicals Limited, Project Sector: Heritage Conservation, Promoting Art, Craft and Culture, Public Libraries: Project Heritage Walk, 2017–18, see https://www.csrbox.org/India_CSR_Project_Gujarat-Alkalis-And-Chemicals-Limited-Heritage-Walk-Gujarat_9606, accessed 10 July 2024.
7. Society to Save Rocks, 2005, see https://saverocks.org/Help.html.
8. CIS Cambridge. 'Rocks From a Brush: Artistic Encounters with Deccani Rocks, Hills and Landscapes—Navina Haidar', *YouTube*, 17 May 2021, see www.youtube.com/watch?v=w5jTxtA4Vng, accessed July 2024.
9. Ibid.
10. Ragi Mallikarjuna Reddy, 'Petrography of Ferrosyenites from the Cuddapah Intrusive Province, Peninsular India', *International Journal of Earth Sciences and Engineering*, vol. 10, no. 2, April 2017, pp. 462–6, see https://doi.org/10.21276/ijee.2017.10.0250.

11. Seema Chishti, 'Rewriting India's History Through School Textbooks', *New Lines Magazine*, 9 March 2023, see https://newlinesmag.com/argument/rewriting-indias-history-through-school-textbooks/, accessed 10 July 2024.
12. 'School Notes', *Indian Express*, 19 August 2012, see indianexpress.com/article/cities/delhi/school-notes-58, accessed 10 July 2024.
13. Rashmi Verma, '13th-century Water Body in Delhi Dying for Lack of Attention, Sustained Revival Plan', *DownToEarth*, see www.downtoearth.org.in/news/water/13th-century-water-body-in-delhi-dying-for-lack-of-attention-sustained-action-58133, accessed 10 July 2024.
14. See www.spchetna.com/Aboutus.aspx.

23

Does Making (History) Textbooks Matter?

Our Pasts and Possible Futures

KUMKUM ROY

WHILE I had heard about Narayani for several years and admired her from a safe distance, our first close encounter left me suitably chastised. A colleague had asked me to deliver something to Parthoda or PSG as he was affectionately known. When I made my way to their home, quiet, warm, and admittedly a bit dark, and was about to sit down, Narayani intervened: 'Maybe you should sit somewhere else unless you are fond of sitting on cats!' Even as I was embarrassed, that was the beginning of what has turned out to be a long and fruitful friendship that I have cherished for more than three decades.

I soon discovered that unlike most of us who pursue a narrow set of interests, and are often indifferent even towards these, Narayani straddles and strides, only apparently gently, through diverse worlds with ease, empathy, and unflagging perseverance. This is often daunting, even intimidating, but over the years I have learnt to respect, cherish and admire these qualities and much else.

One of the areas where our worlds intersected, and where I had an opportunity to work closely with her was on textbooks, as part of two separate projects. The first was for the Delhi State Council of Educational Research and Training (SCERT), and the second was for the National Council of Educational Research and Training (NCERT). Each of these projects has their own complex histories, which will hopefully be documented for posterity at some point of time.

It was while working together that I discovered that Narayani could be meticulous, imaginative, demanding, and indefatigable. While both these projects are now part of history, it is perhaps time for us to try and rethink what we can do about the discipline in terms of pedagogical strategies. I will outline some broad possibilities, and offer tentative suggestions about how they might work. I will try and illustrate these by focusing on a single chapter of a classic text of ancient India, the *Arthashastra*, even as I acknowledge that our present moment demands far more creative interventions.

Our Pasts at Present: Chronology, Content, Concepts

It is a major challenge to think about the future of history in general and history books in particular at a time when the latter are being rapidly revised and rewritten, and when events around us, both within the country and outside, are moving at a breakneck pace. To step back from this frenzy, and reflect on what it is about the past that is significant, and how and why a historical sense may be relevant is by no means easy. So, these are simply some observations, not necessarily illuminating.

Recently, while interacting with a small group of young adults in their late teens and early twenties, I was struck by their unique sense of chronology. For them, everything prior to the twenty-first century was ancient. There was no sense of the divisions between ancient, early medieval, medieval, early modern, modern, the chronological categories over which professional historians have agonized for decades. Everything beyond the very recent past was remote and distant. Perhaps, those were irrelevant too.

It is likely that this chronological perception has emerged from the enormous and rapid changes that we have experienced during Covid times—including losses, personal, economic and other, and disruptions within the formal educational system as learners and teachers grappled with various combinations of online and offline modes. At another level, an imminent and unprecedented climate catastrophe hovers over us, with sharp, apparently unpredictable disasters, reminders about a possibly grim future. It is also possible that the tidal waves of changes in modes of communication that have swept through our lives, in terms of our reliance on social media, have transformed our perceptions of time and space and much more in ways that we may not be fully conscious of. For the young, who have grown up and into this world, the immediate must seem far more real and tangible than anything that preceded it. So, we need to acknowledge and understand this perception of chronology and develop ways and means of addressing it and communicating through it. It may not be fruitful, and it may even be counter-productive to ignore it and simply impose our own familiar periodization, with all its complexity and ambiguity, apart from the fact that painstakingly produced credible chronologies are being rapidly dismantled and dismissed.

In fact, we are also witnessing an obsession with creating a chronology that extends into the hoary past, claiming an unreal and unverifiable antiquity for 'everything' that is considered valuable. In this context, reminding ourselves and others of the need for a reasonably accurate, reliable chronology is crucial, even as it often seems tedious and futile. Also, it is equally important to share the uncertainties of our chronological reconstructions, the fact that some, though not all the dates we rely on, especially for ancient history, are tentative. These are liable to change with refinement in dating strategies through scientific methods, new modes of textual analysis, etc. In other words, dates must be understood as subject to analysis rather than assertion, no matter how vociferous the latter might be.

At the same time, it is necessary to communicate a sense that while chronology is important for historical understanding, it is not a substitute for it, nor is it self-explanatory. In other words, simply because an event or a process happened before another does not mean that they are connected in a causal chain. We need to ask whether they are connected, and if so how, rather than assume a neat, often linear connection. Conveying a sense of this to learners through a discussion of specific examples is probably one way forward.

We also need to figure out how to address issues of content meaningfully, creatively, and constructively. This, of course, like much else, is easier said than done. We are, more often than not, faced with a plethora of criteria on the basis of which content is selected, and striking a balance, even in the best of times, is never easy. If anything, this is likely to become more challenging in the future.

To start with, it is best to acknowledge that selection of content is inevitable, given that textbooks and timetables are finite, and while the abilities, interests and needs of learners and teachers are more elastic, they are also context-specific. At the same time, we can recognize that the potential content of historical studies is virtually infinite.

How then do we go about selecting content? Ideally, this should be through a process of constant dialogue amongst teachers and specialists in the discipline and through exploring learners' responses. This does not mean an unthinking acceptance of stated 'likes' and 'dislikes' but engaging with the why and wherefore of such opinions, and treating them as possibly subject to change rather than being fixed forever. In practice we often tend to rely on far more rough and ready methods. What we can do, and what has at least occasionally been attempted, is to be transparent about the principles of selection, so that these can be scrutinized, refined, improved on, revised.

So here is a tentative list of themes that may be significant, with brief explanations of why they are important. Let me add that these need to be visualized as intersecting spheres rather than water-tight compartments, and their interconnections would have to be highlighted through pedagogical interventions.

Given the environmental crisis engulfing us, a short history of life on earth, including all forms of life, is perhaps increasingly necessary, to provide us with a sense of perspective, of our location within this vast expanse of time and space, hopefully encouraging a sense of responsibility and humility, and acknowledging the limitations of anthropocentrism. This may enable future generations to address these issues meaningfully and respectfully.

Second, a focus on socio-economic institutions, change and diversity in human history. This would require careful selection to ensure that the content is representative of both change and diversity, even and especially if this is something that the learners may not be familiar with. As someone who has been concerned with foregrounding gender relations for some time, I think this might provide us with an opportunity to begin with issues of gender in particular and social hierarchies in general. We could focus on the everyday, on divisions of labour, on what is transacted within and between households, in terms of production, reproduction, distribution, consumption, cultural practices, relations of power. We could provide space for discussing and historicizing kinship relations, class relations, the constitution of identities in terms of caste and community amongst other things. Learners could be encouraged to explore and understand their inter-linkages as well as their unique features, continuities as well as change. Further, questions of perspective could be introduced through these discussions—what does it mean to be a father in a patriarchal family? What does it mean to be a mother or a maternal uncle in a matrilineal family? How are children perceived? Who is regarded as kin, and who is defined as an outsider? These are simply illustrative questions. Obviously, many more can be posed.

Similarly, in terms of livelihoods and economic activities, we could consider a variety of possibilities—from hunting-gathering, fishing, a whole range of agrarian relations, an immense variety of crafts and craft production, trade, and the many ways in which these have been organized, as well as their implications, moving into the bewildering range of present-day services and industries, including the media that has become so crucial. Selecting examples, and discussing how these have evolved, transformed and their significance, from the perspectives of those who control these domains, those involved in production, as well as consumers would be enriching. Needless to say, focusing on diversity would remain crucial in this area as well.

A third area would be what one could broadly designate as cultural practices, including but not be confined to institutionalized religious traditions, explorations of what is identified as knowledge, both textualized and part of everyday practice, and modes of transmission and communication, verbal as well as non-verbal. Once again, examples could be selected for detailed analysis in terms of who participates in the production of these cultural artefacts, how are they transmitted, viewed, understood, consumed, and transformed.

Even while acknowledging that power relations are intrinsic to the three domains mentioned above, a fourth theme would focus on political institutions, exploring these at different levels—from the local to the regional and imperial, rather than privileging the last-named at the expense of the others. Once again, who controls and participates in these institutions, how they are organized and sustained, who are subjected to their control, how and why, and whether and how these change, could be opened for discussion.

Instead of attempting an encyclopedic survey, one could think about salient examples for each of these themes. In other words, we can reduce the fear of an information overload by choosing examples carefully. Focusing on political institutions would allow us to find a way out of the present impasse where we are confronted with long lists of victories and defeats in wars, and are left with the virtually thankless task of refuting deadly combinations of half-baked fact and fiction.

A few more suggestions, already tried and tested, probably need to be foregrounded and used more consistently. For each of the examples that we choose, it is important to share at least some of the strategies by which we arrive at our understanding with learners. This means discussing how we analyse archaeological evidence, texts, inscriptions, coins, documents of all kinds, sculpture, painting, film, oral traditions, and any other evidence that we may rely on.

For each of these, we can discuss why they were produced. For example, if Asoka did not have twenty-first century students of history in mind when he got his message inscribed on stone, who did he have in mind? We also need to understand what our sources meant when they were produced—by whom, for whom, from whose perspective, alerting our learners to the fact that no source is transparent, and that our understanding is shaped both by the context of the source as well as our own.

Second, for all the cases that we explore, it is important to alert learners to the possibility of unintended consequences, to guard against a teleological notion of historical inevitability, even while acknowledging connections at a variety of levels.

Third, we should be willing to share with learners that much that we know is plausible rather than certain, that there are other possibilities, and that there is almost invariably more than one perspective. Coming to terms with uncertainties, and becoming wary of what is proclaimed as the one single truth is perhaps one of the most difficult yet important learnings of the discipline.

Finally, and perhaps most important, we must be far more aware about the many sites of learning in which our learners are enmeshed. These range from family and peers to an enormous variety of material accessible on social media and online. Information, attitudes, and perspectives available through these modes can be uneven—some may be valid and insightful, but as we are well aware, much that swirls around reinforces the worst stereotypes. Sadly, because these are constantly reiterated, and are often presented with considerable finesse, they are frequently accepted unquestioningly. Enabling learners to develop strategies of sifting through these is critical. Here, blanket condemnation may prove counter-productive. Instead, we need to create the space to understand these modes of communication, and explain how they can be engaged with meaningfully. As is obvious, the challenges for teachers and learners are likely to grow, adding to the excitement, and possibly the dangers of studying history.

A Small Experiment with the *Arthashastra*

Let me illustrate some of the possibilities suggested by discussing a small section (only one of 150 chapters) of the *Arthashastra.* This is a particularly exciting text for several reasons: it contains a wealth of information about a whole range of things—animals, plants, agricultural produce, crafts, articles of trade. It also enumerates a wide variety of peoples, identified not only or even primarily in terms of varna or jati, but in terms of occupation and geographical location. The sheer wealth of detail, often overwhelming, allows one to pose a range of questions, even if answers are not always available. But that allows us to explore the plausible, possible, and uncertain.

Let me begin by stating that we need not take it for granted that young learners have heard about the text, or even about Chanakya/Kautilya, who is traditionally regarded as its author. It is also unlikely that they would have watched the TV serial on Chanakya. While they may have heard about the text, they may have little or no idea about its content, language, or structure. So, it is possible to introduce them to these without having to engage in long, polemical debates. What they may find interesting and even exciting is the story of the discovery of the first manuscript, its subsequent fate, and information about the handful of other manuscripts that have been found, including fragments. Even if this may be a digression, one can create space for a discussion on the relationship between script and language—that the two are not synonymous, and the implications of this.

Sharing a discussion on how dates have been assigned to the text can also enable learners to understand how plausible inferences can be made. It can be challenging, for reasons both anticipated and otherwise. Some of the arguments about dating the text rely on issues of form and structure, which may make little sense to young learners encountering the text for the first time. But there are, fortunately, other arguments based on the contents of the text, or, in some instances, the absence of references to things that one would expect to find in it. In the case of the *Arthashastra,* one such striking absence is of gold coins. This is significant because the text reveals a familiarity with the use of coins, which were evidently used to pay salaries and demanded as fines. The goldsmith and gold-working are also mentioned. However, gold coins do not figure in the text. Given that we have the earliest numismatic evidence of gold coins in the subcontinent from the time of the Indo-Greek rulers (*c.*second century BCE onwards), it can be argued that the text belongs to an earlier period.

While this argument, which has a neat simplicity, would appeal to an older generation, it is worth remembering that many young people are not as familiar with coins as we were as children. In fact, even currency notes may seem a rarity to some. In this situation, enabling them to engage with the nitty gritty of dating can run into unanticipated rough weather. Yet, it can lend itself to a discussion on change and continuities in terms of how economic transactions take place. As far as I know, there have been no claims as yet regarding the invention of online payments in ancient India.

Once we move beyond dates, the *Arthashastra* is incredibly rich in terms of content. While this can be illustrated by a detailed discussion on virtually any chapter of the text, I will focus on the one pertaining to the superintendent of the storehouse (*koshthagaradhyaksha*, Book 2, Chapter 15).[1] This officer was expected to know about all possible sources of income, including begging and borrowing. There is mention of as many as ten different heads of revenue, more or less regular, that could be obtained from rural areas. This in itself provides an insight into the kinds of pressures that could have been exerted on rural populations if they were subjected to so many exactions.

Taxes and revenue collection may or may not seem remote to young learners; but, given that the storehouse was ideally to be replenished with all kinds of materials, these can provide an entry point into a lively discussion. The text mentions four kinds of fats, including lard, four kinds of sugars, six varieties of salt, two kinds of honey, and a wide variety of 'fermented juices':

> One of (the following, viz.) sugar-cane juice, jaggery, honey, treacle, the juice of *jambu*-fruit and the juice of *panasa*-fruit, infused with a decoction of *mesasrngi* and long pepper, kept for one month, six months or a year, (and then) mixed with *cidbhita, urvaraka,* sugar-cane stalk, mango fruit and myrobalan, or unmixed (with these) constitute the group of fermented juices.[2]

But this is not all; at least eight varieties of sour fruit are listed, as are sour liquids, and eleven varieties of spices. The list of vegetables, *shaka,* includes dried fish and dried meat, as well as roots, fruits, and vegetables. As Kangle drily observes: 'Anything with which broths are made is evidently included here.'[3]

Apart from keeping track of such diverse produce, the superintendent had to ensure that the supplies were used to support people in distress as well as for regular handouts (about which we will discuss more later). Moreover, he had to be well-versed in food processing—knowing all about which grains and vegetables expanded or shrank when soaked, boiled or fried, how much oil would different varieties of oilseeds yield, and much more.[4]

It is unlikely that the virtually encyclopedic knowledge about a wide range of food and drink expected of the superintendent was acquired from books. It could have only been consolidated through close and constant contact with those who were engaged in procuring a whole range of plant and animal produce and converting these into consumables. In other words, what we have is possibly a codification of a vast realm of knowledge, painstakingly accumulated by ordinary women and men over several generations.

There is more. The superintendent was expected to provide regular rations to animals and people. The allotments were evidently based on a combination of perceived need and social status or importance, and, almost invariably, the two criteria did not coincide. Elephants, especially young elephants, received priority, followed by the infantry, the chief (of the army), the queen, and princes, with the king at the end of this list.[5] This is followed by a more general list, which laid down rations for the Arya man (possibly belonging to the first three varnas), and others. Women and children were to receive less than them.[6] There are also detailed provisions for a whole range of domesticated and wild animals, the latter, including deer and birds, probably kept for the pleasure of the king and his entourage. In case there were others who did not figure in the list, their requirements had to be assessed: 'He should cause an estimate to be made from one meal (consumed by them).'[7] This was by no means an easy task—imagine having to observe what a cat or a dog, or a rare bird ate and drank, and then having to provide for it.

The text goes on to list a few more chores—recycling waste, where charcoal and husks were to be sent to metal workshops and/or used for plastering walls. Broken grain was also to be passed on to slaves, labourers, and cooks. Apart from this, equipment for food processing, including those for weighing and measuring, as well as grinding stones, pestles, mortars, equipment for pounding and crushing, winnowing baskets, sieves, boxes and brooms had to be acquired.[8] Storage was also a matter of concern—we find mention of bags, earthen jars, and wooden casks.[9] There is a list of those who are involved in the work:[10] 'Sweeper, watchman, weigher, measurer, supervisor of measuring, giver, supervisor of deliveries, receiver of tallies, and the group of slaves and labourers—these are the workmen.'

Let us return to the four intersecting themes that we had suggested as focal points for a historical enquiry. Even a cursory glance at the chapter provides information about a whole range of plants, primarily domesticated, and animals and birds, both domesticated and wild. It allows us a glimpse into attitudes towards the non-human world, and can perhaps be used, fruitfully, to initiate a discussion into what may seem to be identical to our present-day perspectives, and what appears different. This can lead to a discussion on trying to understand and explain these similarities and differences.

At a different level, the lists of fruits, vegetables, spices, oils, etc., can be examined to discuss presences and absences. The banana is missing. Possibly because storing it (unless it could be processed into banana chips!) would have been difficult. There is no mention of coconut oil. These are just some examples. Detailed comparisons can obviously yield far more information, and once more, provide the basis for fruitful and stimulating comparisons.

Turning to the socio-economic content and context, this section gives us an idea about the attitude of the author(s) of the text towards rural producers—they were clearly expected to generate a wide range of resources, and provide a considerable portion of these to the state. Here one can enter into a discussion on the feasibility or otherwise of these demands and their implications. Once more, there is scope for comparison with the present.

In terms of social categories, it is evident that the author(s) did not invent these, even as he made little or no attempt to alter social hierarchies. As we have seen, while the varna order was acknowledged, it appears that other identities based on occupation were more immediately relevant for administrative purposes. Again, the implications of foregrounding these identities can be thought through. It is also interesting to see that while the queen was supposed to receive a more substantial ration than the king, ordinary women, and children received substantially less than men. These and other provisions can be used for discussion and comparison.

Turning to cultural practices, this section is replete with references to an enormous variety of edible substances, and given that most of these lists end with the term *adi* (etc.), it seems that other foods could be added on if necessary, allowing for a discussion on the presence or absence of taboos on food and drink. Acknowledging the existence of such a wide range of foods in what is, after all, acknowledged as a 'high' shastra can provide possibilities for comparison with our present-day worlds, where we often encounter a sharp polarization and a definition of identities, including religious and caste identities, in terms of rather narrowly defined food practices.

At another level, as mentioned earlier, the enormous, encyclopedic information about varieties of food and drink and food processing would indicate that there was a complex web of social networks, allowing for communication and conversations between those who produced and processed food and drink and those in charge of the administration. It is unlikely that these conversations were conducted in lofty shastric Sanskrit. Implicit in the information codified in the text then are glimpses of subterranean social relations.

Finally, let us imagine what life may have been like for the *adhyaksha* if he had to actually do everything laid down in the text—supervising boiling, drying, frying various foods, measuring, and weighing them before and after, ensuring that routine rations were disbursed to a wide range of animals and humans, ensuring that things were stored in appropriate containers. Not particularly enviable, even if he may have had the trappings of power. We can ask whether there could have been alternatives—if so, what would they imply? In other words, once we create the space for viewing situations from more than one perspective, almost endless possibilities emerge.

Let me add that similar experiments can be envisaged not only with other texts, but also with a range of visual material. While there is a commonsensical perception that visual material—whether painting, sculpture or even elements of material culture like tools, pottery and other artefacts—is more easily legible, even a cursory examination would indicate the importance of contextualizing such artefacts. Once again, this can provide a range of insights.

What Lies Ahead?

Given our present location, it would be hazardous to predict the future of either the discipline of history or of textbooks. For the present, I will not even venture to speculate on the former. Turning to the latter, will textbooks, as we have known them, become redundant? Will learning take place through audio-visual modules? Will these become more interactive? While these possibilities may appear catastrophic to diehard bibliophiles, it is perhaps necessary to acknowledge that we cannot expect young learners to unscroll or unbrowse. What we can do is to try and ensure that they are able to scroll and browse more meaningfully and critically. This is by no means easy, because it would require careful scrutiny of existing and emerging content, devising and sharing modes of analysing these, and making these accessible. At the same time, generating and disseminating material through these new modes of communication is crucial. While there have been some attempts along these lines, imaginative, creative, and accurate, these are often lost in the flood of more partisan material that is churned out in bulk. The latter range from the hysterical to the suave and smooth, obviously targeting diverse audiences and viewers. Engaging with these is not easy, to say the least.

It is in this context we have much to learn from Narayani—her doggedness, her insistence on accuracy, her ability to pore over each page, sentence, phrase and improve on it, her obsession with detail combined with a vision encompassing everything from the narrow lanes of Shahjahanabad to the vast oceans crisscrossed by seafarers through the millennia. She has inspired and will continue to inspire many—what is also likely is that we will see more of her, and continue to hear her voice of sanity as we navigate the choppy waters that lie ahead.

Notes

1. All references to the *Arthashastra* are from R.P. Kangle, *The Kautiliya Arthasastra,* part II, Translation with Critical and Explanatory Notes, Delhi: Motilal Banarsidass Publishers, 1972; 7th repr., 2nd edn, 2010.

2. Ibid., p. 123.
3. Ibid., p. 124.
4. Ibid., pp. 124–5.
5. Ibid., p. 125.
6. Ibid., pp. 125–6.
7. Ibid., p. 126.
8. Ibid.
9. Ibid., p. 127.
10. Ibid.

Editors and Contributors

PARTHO DATTA taught undergraduate history and now teaches music studies at the School of Arts and Aesthetics, Jawaharlal Nehru University. He has been a Fellow at the Nehru Memorial Museum & Library and has published on the history of town planning.

MUKUL KESAVAN is a writer based in Delhi. He taught history at Jamia Millia Islamia, along with Narayani Gupta, for many years.

KUMKUM ROY taught for several years in colleges and universities in Delhi, and retired from the Centre for Historical Studies, Jawaharlal Nehru University, in 2021. Her interests lie in gender history, textual traditions, and pedagogical processes.

INDU BANGA is Professor Emerita in History, Panjab University, Chandigarh, and formerly Professor of History, Guru Nanak Dev University, Amritsar. She has authored/edited several books on the agrarian, urban, institutional, social, and cultural history of medieval and modern India and the Punjab. Some of her works include *Five Punjabi Centuries* (2000); *The City in Indian History* (2005); *Early Nineteenth Century Panjab* (2016); *A Political Biography of Maharaja Ripudaman Singh of Nabha* (2018); *Agrarian System of the Sikhs* (2019); *Ports and their Hinterlands, 1700–1950* (2019); and *Punjab in Prosperity and Violence* (2024).

PRABHAT KUMAR BASANT taught at the Department of History and Culture, Jamia Millia Islamia. The Indian History Congress awarded his work, *The City and The Country in Early India: A Study of Malwa,* the Braj Dev Prasad Memorial prize for the best book on ancient India, 2012–15.

MEENA BHARGAVA is former Associate Professor, Department of History, Indraprastha College for Women, University of Delhi. She specializes in medieval and early modern Indian history. Her research interests are diverse, focusing on the social and economic history of India in the sixteenth to the eighteenth centuries. She has authored and edited several books and published research articles in peer-reviewed national and international journals and collected works.

RAMU DAMODARAN is Permanent Observer of the University for Peace to the United Nations. He earlier served the international organization for thirty years, including as the first Director of the United Nations Academic Impact initiative. As a member of the Indian Foreign Service, he has served in assignments in Moscow, New York and New Delhi, including as Executive Assistant to the Prime Minister of India.

GEETA WAHI DUA is the Co-Founder and Co-Editor of *LA, Journal of Landscape Architecture,* a quarterly publication she launched with Brijender Singh Dua in 2001. Her passion for exploring the interrelationship of nature and culture within spatial design has led to studies and documentations that culminated in publications and nature-culture maps of Indian historic cities.

RANJEETA DUTTA teaches at the Centre for Historical Studies, Jawaharlal Nehru University, New Delhi. Her research interests include the history of religion, urbanization, and regions in medieval and early modern India. Her publications include several essays, a monograph titled *From Hagiographies to Biographies: Ramanuja in Tradition and History* (2014) and a co-edited book, *Negotiating Religion: Perspectives from Indian History* (2004).

AMAR FAROOQUI is former Professor of History, University of Delhi. He taught history for many years at Hans Raj College, Delhi. His publications include *Zafar and The Raj: Anglo–Mughal Delhi, c.1800–1850* (2013) and *The Colonial Subjugation of India* (2022).

SOHAIL HASHMI studied at Delhi University and Jawaharlal Nehru University. He has worked full-time with the Communist Party of India (Marxist) among youth and trade unions as well as worked with the National Literacy Mission, made documentaries, and ran a Creative Activity Centre for Children.

NAVINA JAFA, a historian and an accomplished Kathak classical dancer, shares India's rich cultural mosaic with a diverse audience through her heritage walks and insightful academic tours. Dedicated to fostering sustainable and responsible cultural tourism, her work emphasises heritage and cultural skill mapping. She develops innovative strategies to offer immersive cultural experiences encapsulated in the unique concept of 'Performing Heritage'. Additionally, Dr Jafa leads capacity-building workshops, focusing on integrating grassroots heritage-skilled communities into the wider domain of heritage tourism.

SHAILAJA KATHURIA works on the sustainability of traditional knowledge and skills with marginalized communities and on the relevance of history and heritage. Her research, under the supervision of Dr Narayani Gupta, has focused on nineteenth-century Agra.

ATIYA HABEEB KIDWAI is a geographer and a professionally trained Urban and Regional Planner from IIT Kharagpur. She has been a Senior Fulbright Fellow at the Universities of Chicago and Illinois. A teacher for almost half a century, she has taught at IIT Kharagpur, Jawaharlal Nehru University, and the School of Planning and Architecture, New Delhi. Her research interests and major publications have focused on historical and maritime geography, colonial urbanization, ports and port cities, and theoretical issues in urban research.

KRISHNA KUMAR taught educational theory for most of his career at Delhi University. He was Director of National Council of Educational Research and Training from 2004 to 2010. He is a bilingual author. His books in English include *What is Worth Teaching; Politics of Education in Colonial India; Education, Conflict and Peace; Prejudice and Pride; Battle for Peace; A Pedagogue's Romance;* and *Thank You, Gandhi.*

SWAPNA LIDDLE is the author of several books on the history of Delhi. For many years she has also been closely involved in the movement to preserve historic sites and monuments. She works to popularize history and the cause of heritage protection through talks, heritage walks, and social and mainstream media.

JIM MASSELOS has lectured and researched on Indian history at the University of Sydney. He is the author of *Indian Nationalism: A History,* and his essays on Bombay have been collected in *City in Action: Bombay Struggles for Power.* He has co-authored, with Narayani Gupta, *Beato's Delhi: 1857 and Beyond.*

RAHUL MEHROTRA is the founder principal of RMA Architects and teaches at the Graduate School of Design at Harvard University where he is Professor of Urban Design and Planning and the John T. Dunlop Professor in Housing and Urbanization. Mehrotra has written, co-authored and edited a vast repertoire of books on Mumbai, its urban history, its historic buildings, public spaces and planning processes.

HELEN MELLER is Professor Emerita of urban history at the University of Nottingham. She has published widely on social, urban, and planning history, with a focus on the work of Patrick Geddes. She is on the founding board of *Planning Perspectives* and served as Editor from 2006 to 2012. She is also the Editor of the 27-volume *Studies in International Planning History.*

A.G. KRISHNA MENON is an architect, urban planner, teacher and conservation consultant practicing in Delhi for over five decades. In 1990 he co-founded the Tulsi Vidhya Bharatiya (TVB) School of Habitat Studies in New Delhi, which became the University School of Architecture and Planning of the Guru Gobind Singh Indraprastha University, Delhi, in 2007. He is actively involved in urban conservation and in 2004 drafted the *INTACH Charter for the Conservation of Unprotected Architectural Heritage and Sites in India* for the Indian National Trust for Art and Cultural Heritage.

SNEHANSHU MUKHERJEE is an architect with over forty years of professional experience and thirty-six years of teaching experience. His major works include the New Wing of the National Gallery of Modern Art, New Delhi; Chancery Building Embassy of Spain; and the Apeejay School, Bhubaneswar. He currently teaches interior architecture and design at th Indian Institute of Art and Design, and has previously taught at the School of Planning and Architecture, New Delhi and Centre for Environmental Planning and Technology University.

ANISHA SHEKHAR MUKHERJI is an architect with a specialization in conservation. She has been a consultant on conservation projects including the Delhi Jantar Mantar and the Red Fort. She is currently Visiting Faculty at the School of Planning and Architecture, Delhi, and is a Founding Director at Ambi Knowledge Resources, a publishing house focusing on the heritage of the subcontinent. She has authored books on the architecture, astronomy, and craft traditions of India.

Ratish Nanda is CEO of the Aga Khan Trust for Culture (AKTC) and a Conservation Architect by training. He heads the multi-disciplinary AKTC teams presently undertaking two major urban conservation projects in India: the Nizamuddin Urban Renewal Initiative, Delhi and the Qutb Shahi Heritage Park Conservation, Hyderabad.

T.C.A. Raghavan is a former diplomat and a former Director General of the Indian Council of World Affairs (2018–21). His first book, *Attendant Lords,* was awarded the Mohammad Habib Memorial Prize for Medieval India by the Indian History Congress in 2017. His latest book is *Circles of Freedom: Friendship, Love and Loyalty in the Indian National Struggle* (2024). He was awarded the Sir Jadunath Sarkar Gold Medal in 2023 by the Asiatic Society, Kolkata.

Srimanjari is Associate Professor at the Department of History, Miranda House, University of Delhi. She is the author of *Through War and Famine* (2009). Her doctoral work at the University of Delhi was based on the social and political history of Bengal during World War II.

Select Bibliography of Narayani Gupta's Writings

Monographs and Edited Volumes

ed., *Urban Spaces in Modern India* (with Partho Datta), Shimla: Indian Institute of Advanced Study, 2018.

ed., *A Work of Beauty: The Architecture and Landscape of Rashtrapati Bhavan*, New Delhi: Publications Division, Government of India, 2016.

Delhi Then and Now (with Dilip Bobb), New Delhi: Lustre Press, Roli Books, 2007.

Beato's Delhi: 1857 and Beyond (with Jim Masselos), New Delhi: Ravi Dayal Publishers, 2000; repr., New Delhi: Penguin/Viking, 2011.

Delhi, The Built Heritage: A Listing (with Ratish Nanda), vols. 1 & 2, New Delhi: Indian National Trust for Art and Cultural Heritage, 1999.

Delhi: Its Monuments and History, by Percival Spear, 1943; updated and annotated with Laura Sykes, 1995; 3rd edn., New Delhi: Oxford University Press, 2009.

ed., *India's Colonial Encounter: Essays in Memory of Eric Stokes* (with Mushirul Hasan), Delhi: Manohar Books, 1993.

ed., *Craftsmen and Merchants: Essays in South Indian Urbanism*, Chandigarh: Urban History Association of India, 1993.

The Painter's Eye: Egron Lundgren and India (with Sten Nilsson), Stockholm, National Museum, 1992.

Delhi between Two Empires 1803–1931: Society, Government and Urban Growth, 1981; repr., Delhi: Oxford University Press, 1998.

Children's Books and Textbooks

Qutb Minar: Head in the Clouds, Ahmedabad: Mapin Publishing Pvt. Ltd., 2018.

Let's Explore Humayun's Tomb, New Delhi: Archaeological Survey of India in collaboration with Aga Khan Trust for Culture, 2011.

ed., *Aspects of World History* (history textbook for Class 11), New Delhi: National Council of Educational Research and Training, 2006.

Discover India (textbooks for Classes 6, 7 & 8), author, vols. 2 & 3, and co-author, vol. 1, New Delhi: Orient Blackswan, 2004.

Modern India (history textbook for Class 8), New Delhi: State Council of Educational Research and Training, 2004.

'Die Herausforderungen bluehenden Reichtums: Bengalen zwischen Mogulreich and Raj' ('Bengal, 17th to 19th century: The Challenges of Abundance'), *Sekunderstufe 1/II*, pp. 26–9 [high school textbook for German students].

Delhi, A Diary for Children (with Meenakshi Banerjee and Deepa Nag), New Delhi: Tej Publishers, 1991.

Our City, Delhi, New Delhi: Oxford University Press, 1987.

India: The Land and the People, New Delhi: National Council of Educational Research and Training, 1969.

Articles in Books, Periodicals and for Symposia

'The Idea of Delhi', in *The Indians: Histories of a Civilization*, ed. G.N. Devy, Tony Joseph and Ravi Korisettar, New Delhi: Aleph Book Company, 2023, pp. 413–6.

'Urbanism in India', in *The Indians: Histories of a Civilization*, ed. G.N. Devy, Tony Joseph and Ravi Korisettar, New Delhi: Aleph Book Company, 2023, pp. 509–14.

'Practitioners, Academicians, Thinkers: Discourse on Central Vista', *LA, Journal of Landscape Architecture*, vol. 62, 2022, pp. 70–3.

'Introduction' (with Partho Datta), to *Urban Spaces in Modern* India, co-edited with Partho Datta, Shimla: Indian Institute of Advanced Study, 2018.

'Every Day is the Start of Another' (tribute to Mohammad Shaheer), Notes, *LA, Journal of Landscape Architecture*, 2016, pp. 3–5.

'They made a Difference: Of Papiya Ghosh and Patrick Geddes' (text of the Papiya Ghosh Memorial Lecture delivered at Patna, 3 December 2009), *Mainstream*, vol. 49, no. 31, 23 July 2011, pp. 19–24.

'Delhi's History as Reflected in its Toponymy', in *Celebrating Delhi*, ed. Mala Dayal, New Delhi: Ravi Dayal Publisher and Penguin/ Viking, 2010, pp. 95–109.

'Taj Mahal', in *Great Monuments of India*, New Delhi: Dorling Kindersley, 2009, pp. 236–55.

'A "Notified" Future for Delhi's Past', *South Asia: Journal of South Asian Studies*, vol. 29, no. 1, April 2006, pp. 101–15.

'Imagining Delhi', *LA, Journal of Landscape Architecture*, vol. 14, 2006, pp. 21–37.

'The Indian City', in *The Oxford India Companion to Sociology and Social Anthropology*, ed. Veena Das, vol. 1, Delhi: Oxford University Press, 2004, pp. 458–76.

'A Letter from India', in *Think Global, Act Local: The Life and Legacy of Patrick Geddes*, ed. Walter Stephen, 2004; revd. edn., Edinburgh: Luath Press Ltd., 2018, pp. 118–20.

'Pictorializing the "Mutiny" of 1857', in *Traces of India: Photography, Architecture, and the Politics of Representation, 1850–1900*, ed. Antonia Pelizzari, Montreal: Canadian Centre for Architecture; New Haven, CT: Yale Center for British Art 2003, pp. 216–39.

'Concern, Indifference, Controversy: Reflections on Fifty Years of "Conservation" in Delhi', in *Delhi: Urban Space and Human Destinies*, ed. Veronique Dupont and Denis Vidal, New Delhi: Manohar/Centre De Sciences Humaines/IRD, 2000.

'Chronology of Significant Events in Delhi', in *Delhi: Urban Space and Human Destinies*, ed. Veronique Dupont and Denis Vidal, New Delhi: Manohar/Centre De Sciences Humaines/IRD, 2000.

'From Architecture to Archaeology: The "Monumentalising" of Delhi's History in the Nineteenth Century', in *Perspectives of Mutual Encounters in South Asian History 1760–1860*, ed. Jamal Malik, Leiden: Brill, 2000, pp. 49–64.

'Urbanism in India' in *History of Indian Science, Technology, and Culture, A.D. 1000–1800*, ed. A. Rahman, New Delhi: Oxford University Press, 2000, pp. 359–79.

'The Present and the Cultural Heritage of India: A View from Delhi', paper for the symposium, 'The Present and the Cultural Heritage of India', *Indian History Congress*, 59th Session, Patiala, December 1998.

'Visible Cities', *The Eye*, vol. 4, no. 4, July–September 1997, pp. 43–6.

'India and the Victorian Cultural Inheritance: The Victoria Memorial Hall', in *The Victoria Memorial Hall, Calcutta: Conception, Collections, Conservation*, ed. Philippa Vaughan, *Marg Magazine*, vol. 49, no. 2, 1997, pp. 37–48.

'Anderun-e-Fasil-Shahar', *Seminar* no. 445, September 1996, pp. 14–16.

Chapters in *Delhi, Jaipur, Agra: India's Golden Triangle*, ed. Manjulika Dubey, Hong Kong: APA Publications, 1995, 'The Golden Triangle', 'A Tale of Three Cities', 'The Forever Capital', 'The Cities of the South', 'Hauz Khas Village', 'Jaipur: The Rajput City', and 'Agra: City of the Mughals'.

'Kingsway to Rajpath: The Democratisation of Lutyens' Central Vista', in *Perceptions of South Asia's Visual Past*, ed. Catherine Asher, New Delhi: American Institute of Indian Studies, 1994, pp. 257–69.

'Urbanism in South India: Eighteenth and Nineteenth Centuries', in *The City in Indian History: Urban Demography, Society and Politics*, ed. Indu Banga, New Delhi: Manohar Publishers and Distributors, 1994, pp. 121–47.

'Public Places in Modern Indian Towns', *Trialog* 43, 1994, pp. 19–23.

'The British Town-Planners and India: A Postscript to Eric Stokes' *The English Utilitarians and India*', in *India's Colonial Encounter: Essays in Memory of Eric Stokes* (with Mushirul Hasan), Delhi: Manohar Books, 1993, pp. 237–47.

'Urban Form and Meaning in South Asia: Perspectives from the Modern Era', in *Urban Form and Meaning in South Asia: The Shaping of Cities from Prehistoric to Precolonial Times*, eds. D. Sreenivasan and Howard Spodek, Washington: Washington University Press, 1993, pp. 243–52.

'Walking Tall', (guest editor for special issue on walking), *The Eye*, vol. 2, no. 3, 1993, pp. 6–9.

'A People's Movement: Conservation Society, Delhi', *The Eye*, vol. 1, no. 3, May–June 1992, pp. 39–40.

'Pondicherry in the Nineteenth Century: A Port without a Hinterland', in *Ports and Their Hinterlands in India (1700–1950)*, ed. Indu Banga, New Delhi: Manohar Publications, 1992, pp. 89–101.

'Calcutta: Form and Function (1690–1990)', in *Calcutta: Foundation and Development of a Colonial Metropolis*, ed. J.S. Grewal, Chandigarh: Urban History Association, 1990.

'History for the Subalterns', *Economic and Political Weekly*, vol. 25, no. 13, 31 March–6 April 1990, p. 663.

'The Useful and the Ornamental: Architecture in India in the Last Two Centuries', *Indian Economic and Social History Review*, vol. 25, no. 1, 1988, pp. 61–77.

'Indian City in History', report annexed to the *Report of the National Commission on Urbanisation*, ed. Charles Correa, in three volumes, Delhi: National Commission on Urbanisation, 1987–88.

'Introduction', *Indian Art at Delhi 1903: Being the Official Catalogue of the Delhi Exhibition 1902–1903*, by George Watt; repr., Delhi: Motilal Banarsidass, 1987, pp. xi–xvi.

'Delhi and its Hinterland: the Nineteenth and Early Twentieth Centuries', in *Delhi Through the Ages: Selected Essays in Urban History, Culture and Society*, ed. Robert E. Frykenberg, New Delhi: Oxford University Press, 1986, pp. 250–69; revd. edn., 1994.

'City Profile: Delhi', *Urban India*, March 1982, pp. 47–52.

'The Hunt for that Elusive Hero: The Indian Craftsman-Builder', *Design Magazine of Arts and Ideas*, October–December 1982, pp. 23–30.

'Shahjahanabad to Delhi: Continuity or Change?', in *Studies in Urban History*, ed. J.S. Grewal and Indu Banga, Amritsar: Department of History, Guru Nanak Dev University, 1981, pp. 150–64.

'Twelve Years on: Urban History in India', *Urban History Yearbook*, vol. 8, 1981, pp. 76–9.

'Military Security and Urban Development: A Case Study of Delhi 1857–1912', *Modern Asian Studies*, vol. 5, no. 1, 1971, pp. 61–77.

Prefaces, Forewords, Afterwords, and Interviews

'Afterword', *In Search of Delhi: A Translation of Brij Krishan Chandiwala's* 'Dilli ki Khoj', by Brij Kishan Candivala, translated and edited by Jitender Gill and Namita Sethi, New Delhi: Routledge, Taylor & Francis, 2023, pp. 267–78.

'Foreword', *Conserving the Spirit of a Historic Garden: The Florence Charter on Historic Gardens, Interpreted, Expanded, Adapted and Illustrated in the Indian Context,* by Priyaleen Singh, New Delhi: INTACH, 2022.

'Foreword', *Princely Palaces in New Delhi,* by Sumanta K. Bhowmick, New Delhi: Niyogi Books, 2016.

'Preface', *A Fighting Spirit: Selected Writings of Ashoka Gupta* (with Sarmistha Dutta Gupta), New Delhi: Niyogi Books, 2012.

'A Conversation with A.K. Damodaran', *India International Centre Quarterly,* vol. 34, no. 3/4, 2007–8, pp. 184–95.

'A Conversation with Ebba Koch', *India International Centre Quarterly,* vol. 34, no. 2, 2007, pp. 138–50.

'Foreword', *Delhi: Lights, Shades, Shadows,* by D.N. Chaudhuri, New Delhi: Niyogi Books, 2005.

'Foreword', *Interesting Times in India,* by Dan O'Connor, New Delhi: Niyogi Books, 2004.

'Foreword', *The British Raj and Its Indian Armed Forces, 1857–1939,* ed. Partha Sarathi Gupta and Anirudh Deshpande. Delhi: Oxford University Press, 2002.

Articles/Reports in Newspapers/Newsletters

'Our City Planning must preserve Built-Heritage', *Hindustan Times,* 9 August 2024, see https://www.hindustantimes.com/opinion/our-city-planning-must-preserve-builtheritage-101723217827310.html.

'Learning from Delhi-uge: Cosmetic Plans won't Do' (with Narayan Moorthy), *Hindustan Times,* 13 July 2024, see https://www.hindustantimes.com/opinion/learning-from-delhi-uge-cosmetic-plans-won-t-do-101720885445058.html.

'Akhoondji Mosque: Finding a Better Way to protect Heritage', *Indian Express,* 18 February 2024, see https://indianexpress.com/article/opinion/columns/akhoondji-mosque-is-gone-it-need-not-have-9164114/.

'NCERT Deletions Discourage Debate', *Indian Express,* 26 June 2023, see https://indianexpress.com/article/opinion/columns/ncert-textbooks-syllabus-asi-historical-monuments-8685884/.

'Mughal Gardens to Amrit Udyan: Lost in the Renaming is a Sense of Delhi's History', *Indian Express,* 29 January 2023, see https://indianexpress.com/article/opinion/columns/mughal-gardens-to-amrit-udyan-lost-in-the-renaming-is-a-sense-of-delhis-history-8411455/.

'The Problem with Cherry-picking Facts from History', *Indian Express,* 1 April 2022, see https://indianexpress.com/article/opinion/columns/s-y-quraishis-on-hate-speech-and-indian-political-culture-of-cherry-picking-facts-from-history-7885481/.

'When two Backbenchers taught their Teachers the "Why" and "How" of Learning History?', *Indian Express,* 14 November 2021, see https://indianexpress.com/article/express-sunday-eye/when-two-backbenchers-taught-their-teacher-the-why-and-how-of-learning-history-7621431/.

'What would a Republic Day Jhanki of Delhi look like?', *Indian Express,* 24 January 2021, see https://indianexpress.com/article/express-sunday-eye/republic-day-parade-jhanki-delhi-india-7158452/.

'Time and Again, Delhi has opened its Gates to the Helpless and Hopeful', *Indian Express,* 15 August 2020, see https://indianexpress.com/article/express-sunday-eye/time-and-again-delhi-has-opened-its-gates-to-the-helpless-and-hopeful-6546443/.

'Disaster Foretold: The Proposed Central Vista will Destroy Delhi's Cultural Landscape', *Indian Express,* 19 February 2020, see https://indianexpress.com/article/opinion/columns/delhi-central-vista-redevelopment-project-6274751/.

'Not Le Corbusier, Chandigarh's Original Designer was a Polish Architect who loved the Gita', *The Print,* 19 January 2020, see https://theprint.in/opinion/sahapedia/not-le-corbusierchandigarhs-original-designer-was-a-polish-architect-who-loved-the-gita/349527/.

'The Delhi Prof who said Tombs & Mosques were not just "Muslim", but "Indian Muslim"', *The Print*, 12 January 2020, see https://theprint.in/opinion/sahapedia/the-delhi-prof-who-said-tombs-mosques-were-not-just-muslim-but-indian-muslim/348390/.

'Mirza Ismail, the "serial Diwan" who made Industrial Bangalore Beautiful, painted Jaipur', *The Print*, 5 January 2020, see https://theprint.in/opinion/sahapedia/mirza-ismail-serial-diwan-who-made-industrial-bangalore-beautiful-painted-jaipur/344807/.

'Why Delhi's grand monuments will always remember young archaeologist Gordon Sanderson', *The Print*, 29 December 2019, see https://theprint.in/opinion/sahapedia/why-delhis-grand-monuments-will-always-remember-young-archaeologist-gordon-sanderson/342158/.

'Edwin Lutyens' Delhi is Unique: India's Political Class must not Tamper with It', *The Print*, 22 December 2019, see https://theprint.in/opinion/sahapedia/edwin-lutyens-delhi-is-unique-indias-political-class-must-not-tamper-with-it/339065/.

'How Scotsman Patrick Geddes may have started India's Obsession with Vastu', *The Print*, 15 December 2019, https://theprint.in/opinion/sahapedia/scotsman-patrick-geddes-started-india-obsession-with-vastu/332888/.

'Lucknow isn't just Chikan and Kebabs, these 100-year-old essays by "Sharar" reveal its Spirit', *The Print*, 8 December 2019, see https://theprint.in/opinion/sahapedia/lucknow-isnt-just-chikan-kebabs-these-100-year-old-essays-by-sharar-reveal-its-spirit/329242/.

'Syed Ahmad Khan's book on Delhi and its ruins would "numb" other writers, said Mirza Ghalib', *The Print*, 1 December 2019, https://theprint.in/opinion/syed-ahmad-khans-book-on-delhi-and-its-ruins-would-numb-other-writers-said-mirza-ghalib/328660/.

'How Cities have been Interpreted over Time', Sahapedia, 12 December 2019, see https://www.sahapedia.org/how-cities-have-been-interpreted-over-time.

'The Age of Replacement: Proposed Reinvention of Delhi, ironically, bears Affinity to Colonial Thinking', *Indian Express,* 19 September 2019, https://indianexpress.com/article/opinion/columns/chandni-chowk-development-delhi-6007795/.

'The Litchis of Wrath', *Indian Express,* 22 June 2019, see https://indianexpress.com/article/opinion/columns/muzaffarpur-tragedy-acute-encephalitis-syndrome-aes-deaths-nitish-kumar-bihar-5793865/.

'From Refugee Market to Elitist Outpost: The Curious Journey of Khan Market in the national capital', *Indian Express,* 3 June 2019, see https://indianexpress.com/article/opinion/columns/a-refugee-market-an-elitist-outpost-khan-market-new-delhi-5761562/.

'Remembering Archana' [on architect Archana Gupta], *Indian Express,* 10 January 2019, see https://indianexpress.com/article/opinion/columns/delhi-celebratory-firing-archana-gupta-dead-mla-raju-singh-5530946/.

'What's in a Name', *Indian Express,* 9 December 2018, see https://indianexpress.com/article/express-sunday-eye/renaming-places-replacing-history-india-5483417/.

'Time to Rescue "Pandrah Agast" from the Drab Ritual of Independence Day', *The Wire,* 15 August 2018, see https://thewire.in/society/independence-day-celebrations.

'Every City Deserves a Vocal Art Commission to Ensure the Aesthetic of Public Spaces', *The Wire,* 15 July 2018, see https://thewire.in/urban/every-city-deserves-a-vocal-art-commission-to-ensure-the-aesthetic-of-public-spaces.

'Dalmiafication of the Qila-e-Mubarak Will Lead us Nowhere', *The Wire,* 8 May 2018, see https://thewire.in/history/dalmiafication-of-the-qila-e-mubarak-will-lead-us-nowhere.

'Invitation to a Jugalbandi', *Indian Express,* 6 December 2017, see https://indianexpress.com/article/opinion/columns/heritage-sites-democracy-unesco-invitation-to-a-jugalbandi-4969726/.

'Joining the Dots, Gathering Traces' [tribute to Lotika Varadarajan], *Indian Express,* 19 October 2017, https://indianexpress.com/article/opinion/columns/joining-dots-gathering-traces-lotika-varadarajan-4897131/.

'The Citizens' Corner', *Indian Express*, 11 October 2017, see https://indianexpress.com/article/opinion/columns/jantar-mantar-jantar-mantar-protest-ban-ngt-the-citizens-corner-4884179/.

'With Custodians like These', *Indian Express*, 22 February 2017, see https://indianexpress.com/article/opinion/columns/agencies-charged-with-the-upkeep-and-protection-of-delhis-historic-buildings-find-little-thrill-in-their-job-heritage-4536883/.

'Delhi bids Adieu to renowned Persian Scholar Yunus Jaffrey', *The Hindu*, 18 October 2016, see https://www.thehindu.com/news/cities/Delhi/Delhi-bids-adieu-to-renowned-Persian-scholar-Yunus-Jaffrey/article14598193.ece.

'Name Games' [on the re-naming of Akbar Road], *Indian Express*, 28 May 2016, see https://indianexpress.com/article/opinion/columns/akbar-road-renamed-history-is-victim-2822492/.

'History Needs Informed Debate, Not the Erasure of Aurangzeb to Install Kalam', *The Wire*, 29 August 2015, see https://thewire.in/history/history-needs-informed-debate-not-the-erasure-of-aurangzeb-to-install-kalam.

'If Delhi's Trees Could Speak, They Would Say, "Do You Know Who I Am?", *The Wire*, 29 August 2015, see https://thewire.in/urban/if-delhis-trees-could-speak-they-would-say-do-youknow-who-i-am.

'When Delhi was only about Villages', *Hindustan Times*, 16 November 2006.

'Libraries Galore, but for Whom?', *Hindustan Times*, 12 October 2006.

'Spare Chandni Chowk Please', *Hindustan Times*, 27 September 2006.

'Let us Bring Back the City's Nahars', *Hindustan Times*, 13 September 2006.

'Is Delhi's Heritage a Link to its Past?', *Hindustan Times*, 10 September 2006.

'Stop Colonising the Capital', *Hindustan Times*, 30 August 2006.

'Get Better Ideas for "Walled City"', *Hindustan Times*, 16 August 2006.

'Of Rubbish and Rules', *Hindustan Times*, 1 August 2006.

'"Human Furniture" makes a City Special', *Hindustan Times*, 18 July 2006.

'City's Past Perfect but Future Tense', *Hindustan Times*, 4 July 2006.

'Of Pattanams and Rajdhanis', *Namasté: The Welcomgroup Magazine*, January–March 2005, pp. 6–10.

'Unlearning Histrionics: A New NCERT Advisory for Teachers could Change the Way History is Taught in our Schools', *Hindustan Times*, 30 September 2004.

'Educated Illiteracy' (with Kumkum Roy), *The Asian Age*, 13 March 2001, p. 13.

'Give Us our Daily Read', *Indian Express*, 10 March 1999, p. 5.

'Inconvenience Regretted', *Indian Express*, 20 January 1999, p. 5.

'Where People Live for the Present: India 50', *The Asian Age*, 11 August 1997, p. 9.

'Let's Run Delhi: Not Run Away from It', *The Sunday Times of India*, 3 November 1996, p. 18.

'The Game of the Name', *The Sunday Times of India*, 27 August 1995, p. 17.

'Reshaping our Heritage', report on round table discussion remembering Gandhiji organised by the Conservation Society Delhi, 15 July 1995, *IIC Diary*, vol. 9, no. 4, August 1995, p. 1.

'Fearing for the Next Generation: Ramnavami once Celebrated what the Young Prince stood for', *The Pioneer*, 12 April 1993, p. 9.

Report on lecture, 'Design for Conservation: Fatehpur and Hampi', by Kulbhushan Jain and Ashoke Chatterjee (on the Satish Davar and the study, *Fatehpur Sikri Integrated Development Plans*), *IIC Diary*, December 1991, p. 3.

'Delhi's Master Plan: The Site and the City', *Indian Express Weekend*, 18 August 1990.

'Calcutta, 1790', *India Week*, 16–22 March 1990.

'The Paris that Hausmann Built', *India Week*, 6–12 April 1990.

'Two Cheers for DTC', *Indian Express Delhi*, 16 January 1988.

'India's Architectural Heritage: An Endangered Species', *Indian Express: Sunday Edition*, 24 April 1988.

Report on seminar, 'Conservation of Monuments in Delhi' convened by the India International Centre Delhi in collaboration with the Conservation Society Delhi (18 April 1987), *IIC Diary*, vol. 1, no. 3 June 1987, p. 1.

Book Reviews

Review of *Empire Building: The Construction of British India 1690–1860,* by Rosie Llewellyn-Jones (New Delhi: Penguin Random House India, 2023), *The Wire,* 28 August 2023, see https://thewire.in/books/book-review-empire-building-rosie-llewellyn-jones.

Review of *Gandhi and Architecture: A Time for Low-cost Housing* by Venugopal Maddipati (Oxford and New York: Routledge, 2021), *Indian Express,* 12 September 2021, see https://indianexpress.com/article/books-and-literature/book-review-venugopal-maddipati-recalls-gandhi-to-meditate-on-low-cost-housing-7502788/.

Review of *Indian Cultures as Heritage: Contemporary Pasts,* by Romila Thapar (New Delhi: Aleph Book Company, 2018), *Indian Express,* 7 July 2018, see https://indianexpress.com/article/lifestyle/books/when-the-twain-shall-meet-romila-thapar-5249088/.

Review of *From Quetta to Delhi: A Partition Story,* by Reena Nanda (New Delhi: Bloomsbury India, 2018), *The Wire,* 1 March 2018, see https://thewire.in/228790/a-one-way-ticket-from-quetta-to-delhi/.

Review of *Dastan-e-Ghadar: The Tale of the Mutiny,* Zahir Dehlvi's memoir translated from the Urdu by Rana Safvi (New Delhi: Penguin Random House, 2017), *The Hindu,* 22 July 2017, see https://www.thehindu.com/books/books-reviews/the-great-revolt/article19325477.ece.

Review of *Monuments Matter: India's Archaeological Heritage Since Independence,* by Nayanjot Lahiri (Mumbai: Marg Foundation, 2017), *LA, Journal of Landscape Architecture,* vol. 53, 2017, pp. 104–6.

Review of *New Delhi: The Last Imperial City,* by David A. Johnson (Basingstoke: Palgrave Macmillan, 2015), in *Journal of British Studies,* vol. 55, no. 1, 2016, pp. 218–20.

Review of *Delhi: Adventures in a Megacity,* by Sam Miller (New Delhi: Penguin, 2009), *Daily News and Analysis,* updated 19 November 2013, see https://www.dnaindia.com/lifestyle/review-expat-sday-out-1235106.

Review of *Islamic Gardens and Landscapes,* by D. Fairchild Ruggles (Philadelphia: University of Pennsylvania Press, 2011), *LA, Journal of Landscape Architecture,* vol. 34, 2012, pp. 945.

Review of *History in the Making: The Visual Archives of Kulwant Roy*, by Aditya Arya and Indivar Kamtekar (New Delhi: HarperCollins, 2010), *Outlook*, 24 May 2010, p. 66.

Reviews of *Invisible City: The Hidden Monuments of Delhi*, by Rakshanda Jalil (New Delhi: Niyogi Books, 2008) and *Delhi Metropolitan: The Making of an Unlikely City* by Ranjana Sengupta (New Delhi: Penguin India, 2008), *Outlook*, 10 March 2008, p. 98.

Review of *The Complete Taj Mahal and the Riverfront Gardens of Agra*, by Ebba Koch (New York: Thames and Hudson, 2006), *LA, Journal of Landscape Architecture*, vol. 17, 2007, pp. 40–1.

Review of *Bhuj*, by Azhar Tyabji (Ahmedabad: Mapin Publishing in association with Environmental Collective, 2006), *The Book Review*, vol. 31, no. 3, March 2007, p. 50.

Review of *Senji (Gingee): A Fortified City in the Tamil Country*, by Jean Deloche (Pondicherry: Institut Français de Pondichéry and Ecole française d'Extrême-Orient, 2005), *The Book Review*, vol. 30, no. 8, August 2006, p. 24.

Review of *Lucknow: City of Illusion*, ed. Rosie Llewellyn-Jones (Munich, Berlin, London, New York: Prestel Verlag–The Alkazi Collection of Photography, 2006), *Biblio*, May–June 2006, p. 54.

Review of *The Last Mughal: The Fall of a Dynasty, Delhi, 1857*, by William Dalrymple (New Delhi: Penguin India, 2006), *Swagat*, December 2006, p. 192.

Review of *A Moral Reckoning: Muslim Intellectuals in Nineteenth-Century Delhi*, by Mushirul Hasan (New Delhi: Oxford University Press, 2005), *Biblio*, July–August 2005, p. 27.

Review of *Splendours of Imperial India: British Architecture in the 18th and 19th Centuries*, by Andreas Volwahsen (Munich and New Delhi: Prestel and Timeless Books, 2005), *Biblio*, March–April 2005, pp. 26–7.

Review of *Historical Thinking in South Asia: A Handbook of Sources from Colonial Times to the Present*, ed. Michael Gottlob (Delhi: Oxford University Press, 2003), *The Book Review*, vol. 28, no. 5 & 6, May–June 2004, pp. 9–10.

Review of *The Ganga Trial: Foreign Accounts and Sketches of the River Scene*, by Jagmohan Mahajan (Varanasi: Indica Books [2nd. edn.], 2004), *Biblio*, March–April 2004, p. 30.

Review of *White Mughals: Love and Betrayal in Eighteenth-Century India*, by William Dalrymple (New Delhi, Viking Penguin Books, 2002), *Biblio*, March–April 2003, pp. 4–5.

Review of *Travel and Ethnology in the Renaissance: South India through European Eyes, 1250–1625*, by Joan-Pau Rubiés (Cambridge: Cambridge University Press, 2000), *The Book Review*, vol. 26, no. 1, January 2002, p. 46.

Review of *Chitra: Cities and Monuments of Eighteenth-Century India from French Archives*, by Jean-Marie Lafont (New Delhi: Oxford University Press, 2001), *Biblio*, July–August 2001, p. 19.

Review of *India: The Social Anthropology of a Civilization*, by Bernard S. Cohn (New Delhi: Oxford University Press, 2000), *The Book Review*, vol. 25, no. 3, March 2001, p. 38.

Review of *A History of India for Children*, by Roshen Dalal (New Delhi: Penguin Books India, 1997), *The Book Review*, vol. 24, no. 11, November 2000, p. 15.

Review of *Mapping an Empire: The Geographical Construction of British India, 1765–1843* (Delhi: Oxford University Press, 1999), *The Book Review*, vol. 24, nos. 1 & 2, January–February 2000, p. 23.

Review of *Representing the Other? Sanskrit Sources and the Muslims (Eighth to Fourteenth Century)* by B.D. Chattopadhyaya (New Delhi: Manohar Books and Publishers), *India International Centre Quarterly*, vol. 26, no. 2, 1999, pp. 168–71.

Review of *The City in Time and Space*, by Aidan Southall (Cambridge: Cambridge University Press, 1998), *The Book Review*, vol. 23, no. 3, March 1999, p. 23.

Review of *Indian Mansions: A Social History of the Haveli*, by Sarah Tillotson (New Delhi: Orient Longman, 1998), *India Today*, 27 July 1998, p. 72.

Review of *Architecture and Independence: The Search for Identity–India 1880 to 1990*, by Jon Lang, Madhavi Desai and Miki Desai (Delhi: Oxford University Press, 1997), *The Book Review*, vol. 22, nos. 1 & 2, January–February 1998, pp. 57–8.

Review of *Popular Religion, Elites and Social Reform: Hook-swinging and its Prohibition in Colonial India, 1800–1894* (New Delhi: Manohar Publications, 1995), *The Book Review*, vol. 20, no. 1, January 1996, p. 16.

Review of *The Grand Indian Tour: Travels and Sketches of Emily Eden*, by Jagmohan Mahajan (Delhi: Manohar Books, 1996), *The Book Review*, vol. 21, no. 5, May 1997, pp. 7–8.

Review of *Patrons and Philistines: Arts and the State in British India* (Delhi: Oxford University Press, 1995), *The Book Review*, vol. 20, nos. 2 & 3, February–March 1996, p. 37.

Review of *Popular Religion, Elites and Social Reform: Hook-swinging and its Prohibition in Colonial India, 1800–1894* (New Delhi: Manohar Publications, 1995), *The Book Review*, vol. 20, no. 1, January 1996, p. 16.

Review of *Bombay: The Cities Within*, ed. Sharada Dwivedi and Rahul Mehrotra (Bombay: India Book House, 1995), *Indian Economic and Social History Review*, vol. 33, no. 4, 1996, pp. 483–4.

Review of *Bhubaneswar: From a Temple Town to a Capital City*, by Ravi Kalia (Delhi: Oxford University Press, 1994), *Indian Economic and Social History Review*, vol. 33, no. 3, 1996, pp. 353–5.

Review of *A History of Sindh*, by Suhail Zaheer Lari (Karachi: Oxford University Press, 1994), *The Book Review*, vol. 19, no. 9, September 1995, p. 18.

Review of *Art and Nationalism in Colonial India 1850–1922: Occidental Orientations* (Cambridge: Cambridge University Press, 1994), *The Book Review*, vol. 19, no. 8, August 1995, pp. 9–10.

Review of *Saving Delhi's Green Areas: A Citizens' Action Guide*, by Gitanjali Singhal (New Delhi: Kalpavriksh 1994), *The Eye*, vol. 2, no. 5, 1995, p. 54.

Review of *Shahjahanabad: The Sovereign City in Mughal India, 1639–1739*, by Stephen Blake (Cambridge: Cambridge University Press, 1991), *Journal of the Economic and Social History of the Orient*, vol. 37, no. 2, 1994, p. 194.

Review of *The New Cambridge History of India 1:4: Architecture of Mughal India*, by Catherine B. Asher (Cambridge: Cambridge University Press, 1992), *The Book Review*, vol. 18, nos. 2 & 3, February–March 1994.

Review of *City of Djinns: A Year in Delhi*, by William Dalrymple (New Delhi: HarperCollins, 1992), *Indian Express*, 7 November 1993.

Review of *A Very Ingenious Man: Claude Martin in Early Colonial India*, by Rosie Llewellyn-Jones (Delhi: Oxford University Press, 1992), *The Book Review*, vol. 17, no. 4, April 1993.

Reviews of *Chronicles of the Mutiny and Other Historical Sketches* (New Delhi: HarperCollins, 1992) and *A Star Shall Fall: India 1857* (New Delhi: HarperCollins, 1995), *Economic Times*, 6 February 1993.

Review of *Cities in the 1990s: The Challenge for Developing Countries*, ed. Nigel Harris (London: UCL Press, 1992), *Financial Express*, 20 December 1992.

Review of *The Politics of Urban Redevelopment: A Study of Old Delhi*, by Ajay K. Mehra (New Delhi: Sage Publications, 1991), *The Journal of Asian Studies*, vol. 51, no. 4, November 1992, pp. 963–4.

Review of *Imperial Simla: The Political Culture of the Raj*, by Pamela Kanwar (Delhi: Oxford University Press, 1990), *Planning Perspectives*, vol. 7, no. 1, 1992, pp. 121–2.

Review of *Old Cities, New Predicaments: A Study of Hyderabad*, by Ratna Naidu (New Delhi: Sage Publications, 1990), *Financial Express*, 11 August 1991.

Review of *Haveli: Wooden Houses and Mansions of Gujarat* by V.S. Pramar (Seattle: University of Washington Press, 1990), *The Journal of Asian Studies*, vol. 50, no. 3, 1991, pp. 722–3.

Review of *Delhi: Stones and Streets*, by C.S.H. Jhabvala (Delhi: Ravi Dayal Publisher), *Architecture + Design*, vol. 8, no. 2, March–April 1991, p. 107.

Review of *Patrick Geddes: Social Evolutionist and City Planner*, by Helen Meller (London: Routledge, 1990), *The Book Review*, vol. 15, no. 2, March–April 1991.

Review of *Chandigarh: The Making of an Indian City*, by Ravi Kalia (Delhi: Oxford University Press, 1987), *Indian Historical Review*, vol. 18, nos. 1 & 2, January 1991, pp. 280–2.

Review of *The Making of a Metropolis: The Planning and Growth of New Delhi*, by A.K. Jain (Delhi: National Book Organisation, 1990), *Planning Perspectives*, vol. 6, no. 3, 1991, pp. 352–3.

Review of two books by Susan Gole, *Maps of Mughal India* (New Delhi: Manohar Publications, 1988) and *Indian Maps and Plans from Earliest Times to the Advent of European Surveys* (New Delhi:

Manohar Publications, 1989), *The Book Review*, vol. 14, nos. 7 & 8, July 1990, pp. 12–4.

Reviews of *The Indian Metropolis: A View Towards the West*, by Norma Evenson (Delhi: Oxford University Press, 1989), and *Imperial Vision: Indian Architecture and the Raj*, by Thomas R. Metcalf (London: Faber and Faber, 1989), *The Book Review*, vol. 14, nos. 1 & 2, January–February 1990, pp. 25–6.

Review of *The Asiatic Society of Bengal and the Discovery of India's Past*, by O.P. Kejariwal (Delhi: Oxford University Press, 1988), *The Book Review*, vol. 13, nos. 3 & 4, March–April 1989, pp. 7–8.

Review of *The Raj Landscape: British Views of Indian Cities*, by Jagmohan Mahajan (Delhi: Spantech, 1988), *The Times of India*, 29 April 1988.

Review of *Delhi and its Monuments*, photographs by D.N. Dube, text by Promodini Varma (Delhi: Spantech, 1987), *The Book Review*, vol. 12, nos. 5 & 6, May–June 1988.

Review of *An Anthropologist among the Historians and Other Essays*, by Bernard S. Cohn (Delhi: Oxford University Press, 1987), *The Book Review*, vol. 12, nos. 1 & 2, January–February 1988, pp. 33–6.

Review (with Partha Sarathi Gupta) of *Indian Diary: Sidney and Beatrice Webb*, ed. Niraja Gopal Jayal (Delhi: Oxford University Press, 1988), *Express Magazine*, 2 August 1987.

Review of *Awadh in Revolt 1857–1858: A Study of Popular Resistance*, by Rudrangshu Mukherjee (New Delhi: Oxford University Press, 1984), *Indian Historical Review*, 1987, pp. 1–2.

Review of *Stones of Empire: The Buildings of the Raj*, by Jan Morris and Simon Winchester (Oxford: Oxford University Press, 1983), *Indian Book Chronicle*, 16 July 1984, pp. 250–1.

Reviews of *Taj Mahal and the Glory of Mughal Agra*, by John Lall (Varanasi: Lustre Press, 1982); *City of Gold: The Biography of Bombay*, by Gillian Tindall (London: Temple Smith, 1982); *Indian Summer: Lutyens, Baker and Imperial Delhi*, by Robert Grant Irving (New Haven and Oxford: Yale University Press and Oxford University Press, 1981), *Urban History Yearbook*, vol. 11, 1984, pp. 214–5.

Review of *Towards a Political Economy of Urbanization in Third World Countries*, ed. Helen I. Safa, *India International Centre Quarterly*, vol. 10, no. 4, December 1983, pp. 553–6.

Review of *Delhi in 1857*, vol. 1, 'The Trial of Bahadur Shah', by K.C. Yadav (Gurgaon: The Academic Press, 1980), *Indian Historical Review*, vol. 7, nos. 1 & 2, 1980–1, p. 305.

Review of *The Outlook Tower: Essays on Urbanisation in Memory of Patrick Geddes*, by J.V. Ferreira and S.S. Jha (Bombay: Popular Prakashan, 1986), *Indian Historical Review*, vol. 5, nos. 1 & 2, 1980, pp. 345–7.

Reviews of *Calcutta and its Hinterland 1833–1900*, by Prajnananda Banerjee (Calcutta: Progressive Publishers, 1975), and of *Rediscovering Delhi: The Story of Shahjahanabad* by Maheshwar Dayal (New Delhi: S. Chand and Co., 1975), *Urban History Yearbook*, vol. 5, 1978, pp. 142–3.

Review of *The Siege of Delhi*, by Alexander Llewellyn (London: Macdonald and Jane's, 1977), *Indian Book Chronicle*, 16 December 1977, p. 395.

Review of *Colonial Urban Development: Culture, Social Power and Environment*, by Anthony S. King (London: Routledge and Kegan Paul, 1976), *Hindustan Times Weekly*, 20 February 1977, p. 14.

Reviews of *Urban Politics in India: Area, Power, and Policy in a Penetrated System*, by Rodney W. Jones (Berkeley: University of California Press, 1974); *Traditional Neighbourhood in a Modern City*, by H. Doshi (New Delhi: Abhinav Publications, 1974); *Economic Development of Bhopal: A Socio-Economic Survey, 1901–1973*, by Syed Ashfaq Ali (Bhopal: Jai Bharat Publishers, 1974); *Benares in Transition, 1738–1795: A Socio-Economic Survey*, by K.P. Mishra (Delhi: Munshiram Manoharlal, 1975); *History of Bombay, 1661–1708*, by M.D. David (University of Bombay, 1973); *The City in Early Historical India*, by A. Ghosh (Simla: Indian Institute of Advanced Study, 1973), *Urban History Yearbook*, vol. 3, 1976, pp. 57–9.

Reviews of *Studies in India's Urbanization 1901–1971*, by Ashish Bose (Bombay and New Delhi: Tata McGraw-Hill Publishing Co. Ltd, 1973); *Morphology of Indian Cities*, by Kusum Lata Taneja (Varanasi: National Geographical Society of India, 1971); *Calcutta: A Study in Urban Growth Dynamics*, by M. Ghosh, A.K. Dutta and B. Ray (Calcutta: Firma K.L. Mukhopadhyay, 1972); *Calcutta: Story of its Government*, by Keshab Choudhuri

(New Delhi: Orient Longman, 1973); *Visakhapatnam: A Study in the Geography of a Port Town*, by B.P. Rao (Varanasi: National Geographical Society of India, 1971); *Towns in the Tribal Setting*, by B.R. Chauhan (Delhi: National Publishing House, 1970), *Urban History Yearbook*, vol. 2, 1975, pp. 73–76.

Reviews of *Urbanisation and Urban Centres under the Great Mughals*, by H.K. Naqvi (Simla: Indian Institute of Advanced Study, 1971); *Ahmedabad: A Study in Indian Urban History*, by Kenneth L. Gillion (Berkeley and Los Angeles: University of California Press, 1968); *Urban Leadership in Western India: Politics and Communities in Bombay City 1840–1885*, by Christine Dobbin (Oxford: Oxford University Press, 1972); *Essays in Gandhian Politics: The Rowlatt Satyagraha of 1919*, by R. Kumar (Oxford: Clarendon Press, 1971); *Delhi: Capital City*, by Asok Mitra (New Delhi: Thomson Press [India] Limited, Publication Division, 1970.), *Urban History Yearbook*, vol. 1, 1974, pp. 67–70.

Review of *Freedom Movement in Delhi (1858–1919)*, by Sangat Singh (New Delhi: Associated Publishing House, 1972), *Indian Historical Review*, vol. 1, no. 2, 1974, pp. 431–4.

Reviews of *Chhatrapatis of Kolhapur*, by Manohar Malgonkar (Bombay: Popular Prakashan, 1971) and *Bombay and the Marathas up to 1774*, by W.S. Desai (Delhi: Munshiram Manoharlal, 1971), in *Sunday World*, 3 September 1972.

Series Edited

Chief Editor, Roshni Series on UNESCO World Heritage Sites of India in collaboration with Mapin, 2018 (five books on the Qutb Minar, Mahabalipuram, Sanchi, Chhatrapati Shivaji Maharaj Terminus and Keoladeo Bird Sanctuary, published in English, Hindi, Gujarati, Marathi and Tamil).

Series Editor, *Discover India* (textbooks for Classes 6, 7 & 8), New Delhi: Orient Blackswan, 2004.

Chief Editor, Social Science Textbooks for the State Council for Educational Research and Training, Delhi, 2003, included *Meri Dilli* ('My Delhi') for Class 3.

Interviews

'Changing Landscapes and Preservation of Delhi's Spaces: An Interview with Prof. Narayani Gupta' Dhaara magazine, March 2021, see https://dhaaramagazine.in/2021/03/31/changing-landscapes-and-preservation-of-delhis-spaces-an-interview-with-prof-narayani-gupta/.

'Conversations with the Past: Narayani Gupta' TEDx NIIT University, June 2018, see TEDxNIITUniversity https://www.youtube.com/watch?v=yc8-XT-awzY.

'Shahjahanabad and its Havelis: In Conversation with Narayani Gupta', Sahapedia, June 2018, see https://www.sahapedia.org/shahjahanabad-and-its-havelis-conversation-narayani-gupta.

'Looking Back is to Look Forward', *LA, Journal of Landscape Architecture*, vol. 45, 2015, pp. 34–9.

Index